FITZ LEE

FITZ LEE

A Military Biography
of Major General Fitzhugh Lee, C.S.A.

Edward G. Longacre

Da Capo Press
A Member of the Perseus Books Group

For
Sister Ann Cecelia, O.P.,
my first fan

Cataloging-in-Publication data for this book is
available from the Library of Congress.

ISBN 0-306-81384-X
First Da Capo Press edition 2005

Maps by Paul Dangel
The map on page 186 is based on a map by Chris Calkins.

Published by Da Capo Press
A Member of the Perseus Books Group
http://www.dacapopress.com

Da Capo Press books are available at special discounts for
bulk purchases in the United States by corporations, institutions, and other
organizations. For more information, please contact
the Special Markets Department at the Perseus Books Group,
11 Cambridge Center, Cambridge, MA 02142,
or call (800) 255-1514 or (617) 252-5298,
or email special.markets@perseusbooks.com

1 2 3 4 5 6 7 8 9 – 09 08 07 06 05

Contents

Contents

Acknowledgments

This book originated as a suggestion by Ken Gallagher, then editor of Combined Books, Conshohocken, Pennsylvania. It was nurtured through years of research and writing by Bob Pigeon, president of Combined Books, and brought to fruition by the staff of Da Capo Press of New York. I am indebted not only to these persons but also to many librarians, archivists, research assistants, and other individuals who helped locate pertinent sources—many of them obscure, some of them quite rare—on Fitzhugh Lee and his military, political, and diplomatic associates.

Those who provided the greatest assistance include Rich Baker and Steve Bye, U.S. Army Military History Institute, Carlisle Barracks, Pennsylvania; Donna Barber and Greg Johnson, Alderman Library, University of Virginia, Charlottesville; Margaret Cook, Earl Gregg Swem Library, College of William and Mary, Williamsburg, Virginia; Susan Cornett and Cheryl Nabati, Bateman Library, Langley Air Force Base, Hampton, Virginia; John and Ruth Ann Coski, Museum of the Confederacy, Richmond, Virginia; Lauren Eisenberg and Sandra Trenholm, Gilder Lehrman Collection, New York, New York; Lisa Hazarian, William R. Perkins Library, Duke University, Durham, North Carolina; Bruce Kirby, Library of Congress, Washington, D.C.; Clayton McGahee, Virginia Heritage Project, Virginia Polytechnic Institute and State University, Blacksburg; Debby Pogue, United States Military Academy Library, West Point, New York; Gregory Stoner, Virginia Historical Society, Richmond; and Peggy Vogtsberger, Hampton, Virginia. The maps were prepared by Paul Dangel, Berwyn, Pennsylvania. Illustrations were furnished by Bill Godfrey, Hampton, Virginia; Jeff Reggles of the Virginia Historical Society; and Nancy Sherbert of the Kansas State Historical Society, Topeka. As always, my wife, Ann, assisted in all phases of the book's preparation.

Preface

Douglas Southall Freeman called him "The Laughing Cavalier." The appellation is deserved: throughout his life, Fitzhugh Lee (1835–1905) was unfailingly jovial, convivial, and outgoing. During the Civil War, he often would slip away from the fighting front to attend balls and collations in Richmond and Petersburg, where he acted in skits, supervised minstrel shows, and sang duets with his immediate superior and bosom companion, James Ewell Brown Stuart, commander of the cavalry, Army of Northern Virginia (ANV). And yet Fitz Lee was also a dedicated and conscientious soldier whose steady rise through the Confederate ranks was due more to his martial abilities than to his family connections (his father, Sidney Smith Lee, was a highly regarded officer in the Confederate Navy, while his uncle, Robert E. Lee, won international renown as commander of the ANV).

A graduate of the West Point Class of 1856, where his fondness for off-grounds recreation helped lower his standing to forty-fifth out of forty-nine cadets, Fitz Lee began the Civil War as a lowly staff officer but quickly rose—by all indications, upon his own merit—to commander of the 1st Virginia Cavalry, the hard-fighting regiment that Stuart had led to war in 1861. After effective and sometimes distinguished service throughout the first half of 1862, especially during Stuart's famous Chickahominy Raid, Fitz won the wreathed stars of brigadier general and command of a brigade under Stuart. His always competent and often exceptional service at Second Manassas (Bull Run), Fredericksburg, Chancellorsville, Hartwood Church, Kelly's Ford, and Gettysburg not only befit his status as scion of one of Virginia's most distinguished families but also brought him career advancement. In the fall of 1863, he became a division leader; the following summer he took charge of Confederate mounted operations in the Shenandoah Valley; and in late March 1865, on the eve of the war's final campaign, he assumed command of the cavalry in his uncle's army. The proud Virginian refused to surrender his exhausted, depleted command at Appomattox Court House. Only days later, however, he harnessed his emotions, gave himself up to Union authorities, and accepted parole in the hope of helping his state and region rise from the ashes of defeat.

Fitz Lee's postwar years were crammed with activity. He married and raised a large family, including two sons who became officers in the U.S. Army. He lived the life of a gentleman farmer, commercial and industrial promoter, historian and biographer (author of an influential volume about his famous uncle), customs official, railroad executive, public speaker, governor of Virginia (1885–87), unsuccessful candidate for the U.S. Senate, and, in the months leading up to the Spanish-American War, U.S. consul general in Havana, Cuba. In 1898, with the outbreak of hostilities against Spain, he helped solidify sectional reunion by donning a blue uniform for the first time in almost forty years and serving as a major general of U.S. volunteers. His brief wartime service was followed by a productive and sometimes controversial stint as an occupation commander in war-torn Cuba. Returning to civilian life in late 1899, he closed out his colorful life as a private businessman and civic organizer. At the time of his death, he was serving tirelessly—too much so for his own health, relatives and friends feared—as chairman of the Jamestown Commission, formed to supervise the three hundredth anniversary of the founding of the first permanent English settlement in the New World.

Although neglected by biographers for several decades after his death, since 1981 Fitz Lee has been the subject of three book-length studies, two of which have been published: James L. Nichols's *General Fitzhugh Lee: A Biography* (Lynchburg, Va., 1989), and Ardyce Kinsley, comp., *The Fitzhugh Lee Sampler* (Lively, Va., 1992). The third, and most detailed, source is a master's thesis: Harry W. Readnor, "General Fitzhugh Lee, 1835–1905: A Biographical Study" (University of Virginia, 1971). While these works have their strengths, each is marred by an overuse of artistic license or a skewed perspective. Although occasionally useful, Kinsley's work is a pastiche of contemporary correspondence, memoirs, newspaper accounts, verse, and miscellaneous material loosely arranged, inadequately identified, and often fictionalized. A disproportionate amount of Nichols's book and Readnor's thesis are concerned with Lee's postwar commercial, political, and diplomatic activities. To some extent, each neglects its subject's Civil War career, by any standard the most significant and productive period of his life. The present work attempts to redress this imbalance by focusing on Fitzhugh Lee, the quintessential cavalier—hurtling toward the enemy at the head of a charging column, risking all for home, state, and cause, a fierce expression on his heavily bearded face but with sparks of joy and jollity flashing in his dark blue eyes.

ONE

A Son of Old Virginia

Thus far the punitive expedition had been uneventful to the point of tedium. Two weeks earlier, on the morning of April 30, 1859, the mounted column, 430 strong, had left Camp Radziminski, in the southwest corner of the Indian Territory (present-day Oklahoma), marching northwestward through the valley of Elk Creek toward the Kansas border. The compact and fast-moving force—six companies of the 2nd U.S. Cavalry, augmented by a handful of scouts from friendly tribes, the whole led by Brevet Major Earl Van Dorn—was bound for the winter camp of a band of Comanches who had been raiding homes, farms, and ranches in northern Texas. As Edward Mortimer ("Jack") Hayes, the sixteen-year-old bugler of Company B of the 2nd, observed: "These Indians, leaving their families and villages in the far-distant Indian Territory, would form into small bands and, penetrating into the very heart of the settlements, murder men, women and children and return in comparative safety to their villages, with their spoils of scalps and horses." Future depredations had to be prevented at all costs, and the most effective means was to inflict on the hostiles the same violence and devastation they had wrought on the luckless whites in their path.[1]

Although the first several days of the march turned up no signs of warriors, Van Dorn believed that his command would see action by the time it reached the Canadian River, which bisected Indian Territory from east to west. His expectations seemed to be realized when, soon after leaving the supply depot he had established on the Sweetwater River, two hundred miles north of Camp Radziminski, he picked up the trail of a Comanche war party. The trail led the column to and across the Canadian border, but on the north side it began to peter out. The horsemen pushed on across the dun-colored desert for several days, encountering no fresh signs of their quarry. For troopers and scouts eager to chastise a hated foe, this was demoralizing news.

Early on May 13, after making camp in a grove of cottonwoods along Crooked Creek, a tributary of the Arkansas River, Van Dorn informed his subordinates that the column would strike off in a new direction. The scouts had barely been dispatched to locate a more promising route, however, when the cry of "Indians!" went up from the rear. After a few minutes' confusion it was ascertained that perhaps one hundred Comanches had left their camp to strike the horse herds that Van Dorn had turned out to graze on the buffalo grass lining Crooked Creek. The attack came as a rude surprise to the bluecoats, most of whom were afoot, preparing their midday meal. "In a moment," Jack Hayes recalled, "officers and men were rushing for their horses, some [mounting] them bareback . . . and the greatest excitement prevailed."[2]

First to challenge the attackers were the troopers who had been guarding the herds. Under First Lieutenant William B. Royall, a distinguished veteran of the Mexican War, this force not only sent several Comanches into quick retreat but pressed them so closely that they abandoned their ponies and took refuge in one of the heavily wooded gorges that abounded in that area. There the Comanches opened fire with bows and arrows that at first glance appeared no match for the rifles and pistols wielded by the soldiers.

The soldiers' superior firepower enabled Royall to isolate the Comanches from their mounts, which his men captured and spirited away. Their means of escape gone, the Indians prepared to defend their position and sell their lives as dearly as possible. Along a small, tree-fringed stream they constructed rude breastworks of logs that, according to Bugler Hayes, eventually stretched for three hundred yards. From behind this cover they showered Royall's band with stone-tipped arrows that began to take a toll on the dismounted horsemen.

Upon reaching the scene of battle with the balance of the column, Van Dorn found Royall and his men hunkered down behind trees and rocks, firing ineffective volleys at their well-protected foe. To improve the situation, the major divided his command into several parties, which went forward in hopes of surrounding the Indians. His initial dispositions complete, Van Dorn had Bugler Hayes sound the charge.

In open-skirmish order, dismounted cavalrymen swept forward against all sides of the Comanches' position. To Van Dorn's surprise and frustration, however, none reached his assigned objective. Blocked by the breastworks and the nearly impenetrable timber that lined them, every attacker reeled to the rear in defeat.

At this critical juncture, one of Van Dorn's youngest subalterns offered to lead a dismounted charge against the flank of the main breastwork, where the foliage in front appeared slightly thinner than elsewhere. After briefly considering the proposal, Van Dorn gave permission for Second Lieutenant Fitzhugh ("Fitz") Lee to make the attempt at the head of a detachment of his unit, Company B.

The twenty-three-year-old Lee, a native of Fairfax County, Virginia, gave his superior a smart salute, turned on his heel, and began to round up the men who would accompany him on the daring mission. He did so with great enthusiasm, for, although he had been serving as Van Dorn's adjutant on the expedition, he was eager for field service. As a member of the 2nd Cavalry for the past three years, Fitz Lee had established himself as one of the most affable, outgoing, and good-hearted members of his regiment. He had yet, however, to establish his combat credentials—the operation he had sought and that Van Dorn had approved would be his baptism of combat.

With the assistance of his immediate superior, Captain Edmund Kirby Smith of Company B, Lee assembled his detachment of Company B, explained his plan of attack, and, at a given signal, led it forward under a covering fire from the rest of the unit. With a yell reminiscent of a war whoop, the lieutenant led his men through the trees, across the ground in front of the nearest breastwork, and then over the barricade. Striking down the few defenders in that sector, the troopers quickly penetrated to the rear of the Comanches' position. There they found a gaggle of women and children, guarded by a couple of warriors. The attackers cut down the braves, corralled the noncombatants, and led them back to the starting point of the assault.

Flushed with success in his first experience in close-quarters fighting, Lieutenant Lee regrouped his detachment and led it back toward the breastworks, this time striking closer to its most heavily defended point. At first the assault proceeded as smoothly as its predecessor, especially after Van Dorn pressed other sectors of the works at the head of his main force. Suddenly, however, a phalanx of screaming warriors materialized across Lee's path. The result was, as Jack Hayes put it, "a desperate encounter."[3]

Although the Comanches eventually gave ground, they took a heavy toll on the attack force, including its leader. Squaring off against a husky brave, Lieutenant Lee fired his pistol at the very moment his antagonist let fly with his arrow. Both weapons struck their targets. As the Indian toppled with a fatal wound to the skull, Lee staggered backward against the trunk of a tree, gasping for breath. The arrow had struck him beneath the arm he had raised to fire; the shaft had penetrated his right lung, and the tip protruded from his back.

While the battle continued, a squad of troopers hustled the wounded officer to the rear. There, as Jack Hayes recalled, "he lay stretched on the ground in an apparently dying condition. He motioned me to him and I sat down beside him, taking his head in my lap. The blood was streaming from his mouth, but not a drop came from his wound. He was unable to speak but could, by motions, make himself understood."[4]

FITZ LEE

As the lieutenant lay prone, fighting for breath, Major Van Dorn reached him in company with the column's surgeon. The latter worked feverishly to save the wounded man. Already the arrow had been extracted by Lieutenant George B. Cosby, Fitz Lee's self-defense instructor at West Point. The arrowhead, however, was nowhere to be found, creating uncertainty as to whether it had become separated from the shaft or had lodged inside the victim.

The surgeon poured salt water down the lieutenant's throat, an expedient that eventually stanched the flow of blood from the mouth, then probed the track of the arrow. While he tended to the patient's physical needs, Van Dorn attempted to bolster Lee's morale by praising the attacks that had inflicted numerous casualties on the Comanches, eventually driving them from their neigh-impenetrable position.

Despite the surgeon's ministrations, the fallen man remained in critical condition. Making what he considered to be a thoughtful gesture, Van Dorn produced a notebook and prepared to take down any words the dying man might leave for posterity. Jack Hayes recalled that Lee, who "could only speak with great effort," gasped out a message to his parents in Virginia, including the apparent fact that "he was dying a soldier's death, the one he preferred above all others."[5]

The communication recorded, the major ordered all bystanders to disperse. At last, only Hayes remained by Lee's side, holding his head to help him breathe. Despite the difference in their ages and positions, the bugler had grown quite fond of Lieutenant Lee, as Fitz had of him. Hayes's concern for Lee's condition only worsened when the lieutenant gazed up at him and whispered, "Jack, you are going to lose your best friend."[6]

The bugler's distress was relieved only when Lieutenant Manning M. Kimmel, Lee's closest comrade among the officer corps, reached the victim's side. Kimmel had just returned from pursuing the few horseless Comanches who had made a futile attempt to flee the battlefield. Thirty-six had been overtaken and captured, making a total of eighty-five casualties for the day. Now Kimmel grasped the hand of his fellow Virginian. "Fitz, old man," he said, "we can't afford to lose you." He too had been a victim of enemy fire. Removing his tall "Jeff Davis" hat, he displayed the hole in its crown that had been made by a ball from a captured rifle in the hands of a Comanche. The exhibition produced a gratifying response. With a faint smile and in halting words, Lee asked his friend if he expected such a story to be believed: "Acknowledge the corn, old man; didn't you go behind a tree and shoot the hole in your hat yourself?" The humor in the reply—so typical of Fitz Lee in happier situations—persuaded both Hayes and Kimmel that their friend would beat the odds and recover from his wound.[7]

And recover he did, although the process was long and difficult, marked by numerous setbacks as well as by further physical and mental distress. When the last of the Indians had been run to earth, Van Dorn ordered a withdrawal to

Camp Radziminski. Along with several other wounded soldiers, Fitz Lee accompanied the return march on an improvised litter—no more than a length of canvas stretched between twenty-foot-long poles. The poles were strapped to the flanks of two pack mules, one in front of the patient and the other behind, led by a dismounted trooper.

Via this serviceable but uncomfortable contrivance, Lee was conveyed across 350 miles of desert. By itself the journey was a grueling, bone-wracking experience, but the lieutenant's discomfort increased geometrically when, during the first day of the trip, his litter came loose as the mules stumbled down a steep hill. Both poles, and the wounded man in between, thudded to the ground. The jolt so frightened the mule in front that it broke free of its drover and took off across the prairie at a shambling gait. Lieutenant Lee, "clinging to the poles for dear life," was pulled across hard, stony ground for several hundred yards before the mule could be caught and halted. Jack Hayes and several comrades rushed to Lee's side, expecting to find him in extremis, "but to the relief of all, except [for] a little shaking up, he was found all right." In fact, the jarring ride had reopened the wound in his lung. A complete recovery would require months of bed rest.[8]

When the column finally reached its old camp among the Wichita Mountains, Fitz Lee was placed in the regimental infirmary, where surgeons and attendants worked long and hard to return him to stable health and active duty. They did their job well; by the first week in June, the patient could prop himself up on his cot and write a letter to his family, which began: "I have been as near to death's door, as it falls to the lot of a mortal to be, & still not enter."[9]

In time, the wound healed without apparent damage to lung function. By the narrowest of margins, Lieutenant Lee had been spared to fight again—and again. In the years remaining to him, he would fight scores of battles against opponents clad in breechcloths and war paint, as well as those wearing the same uniform he himself had proudly donned upon graduating from West Point.

*   *   *

Fitzhugh Lee was born on November 19, 1835, at Clermont, an expansive estate five miles west of Alexandria, Virginia. His was a distinguished pedigree, his paternal grandfather being "Light-Horse Harry" Lee, George Washington's cavalry commander, delegate to the Continental Congress, three-term governor of his state, and one-term U.S. congressman. Fitz's maternal great-great-grandfather was George Mason, author of the 1776 Virginia Declaration of Rights, the basis of the first ten amendments to the U.S. Constitution. The child's father was Sidney Smith Lee, an accomplished and well-regarded officer in the U.S. Navy, while his uncle—five years his father's junior—was Captain Robert Edward Lee, a distinguished engineer officer in the U.S. Army.[10]

Of perhaps greater advantage to the child and his family, his widowed godmother, Anna Maria Goldsborough Fitzhugh of Ravensworth, Fairfax County, bestowed on Smith Lee's firstborn not only her married name but also her life-long solicitation and patronage, which included the kind of financial support that a naval officer's salary could not provide. Member of a distinguished Maryland family (her father, Charles Goldsborough, had been governor of the state), Aunt Maria added to the social status of the Lee family just as, through her devotion to Episcopalianism, she enhanced its religious influence. Through her strong personality, constant solicitude, and physical proximity to Clermont, for almost four decades Aunt Maria would play a major role in the life of the child she called Fitzhugh in contrast to the more informal appellation favored by other family members, friends, and acquaintances.[11]

From the day he entered the world, Fitz Lee was his mother's pride and joy. In a letter to a cousin in Philadelphia a few months after the boy's birth, Ann Maria Mason Lee called her son "a prodigy, the eighth wonder of the world . . . handsome, but no one can decide who he is like—very fair & very dark blue eyes (which seems to be a great mystery) a quantity of soft brown hair curly all over his head. . . . [N]ow is not this a great inducement to come and see us[?]"[12]

In addition to a pleasing appearance, the youngster grew up full of energy and devilment. According to a family friend, these attributes were a legacy not of the pious Lees, most of whose scions were models of rectitude, but of the Mason family, which, despite its many sober contributions to American politics, had a reputation for "figetting, fiddling and fun." With his father absent from home on extended sea voyages or shore duty at distant locations, Fitz came under the early and sustained influence of his mother, his godmother, and other leading females of the Lee clan. Still, he grew up all boy, as reflected in the attitudes he adopted toward amusements, hobbies, education, and the choice of a future career.[13]

Even in early youth, he took great interest in outdoor recreations including fishing, hunting, and especially riding. He happily took part in the few organized field sports of the day. He delighted in roughhousing with his five younger brothers: Sidney Smith Jr., John, Henry, Daniel, and Robert. (A sister, Elizabeth Mason Lee, was born into the family in 1853, but she died before her first birthday.) And when his Uncle Robert and Aunt Mary paid a visit or received Fitz's family at their baronial estate, Arlington, Fitz enjoyed playing with his cousins, George Washington Custis and William Henry Fitzhugh "Rooney" Lee.[14]

Fitz's rambunctious spirit and early interest in sports—especially wrestling, at which he became adept in his teen years despite his short stature and slight build—followed him onto the school grounds. First when attending a private school in Alexandria and later when boarding at a secondary school at Catonsville, Maryland, he cut a conspicuous figure, but more often at play than at study. As an elementary school student, he would arrive almost every day clad in a shirt of scarlet, "a color so striking that it completely cut off all attention from any other article of apparel he may have worn." He also drew attention to himself by riding, not walking, to school "on the back of a burly coal-black negro, screaming and struggling" and pulling at the servant's hair.[15]

As the anecdote suggests, young Fitz was something less than a model scholar. One classmate recalled him as "a bright, manly boy, full of life and fun; preferring the pleasures and exercises of the playground to the dull routine of the school-room." He also indulged a fondness for mischief-making. One day while at the school in Alexandria, he poked fun at the headmaster of an adjacent Episcopalian preparatory academy known as the Virginia Seminary. The careless administrator had driven his buggy so close to a farmer's field that he had run down a duck. Fitz, who witnessed the incident from his school grounds, began to quack loudly in imitation of the victim's dying cries. His antics merely embarrassed the headmaster, but they incited some of his students to physical retaliation. Angry seminarians rushed onto the grounds of Fitz's school and began to pummel the younger boy and some of his equally annoying classmates. Although felled, bruised, and battered, the irrepressible Fitz kept quacking away until his instructors broke up the melee.[16]

He may have spent more time playing pranks than poring over textbooks, but he was not a below-average student. When sufficiently motivated, he could excel in the classroom, at least for a time. Soon after entering the Catonsville school, St. Timothy's Hall, he wrote his godmother that he was settling comfortably into the local routine (well "fixed up," as he put it) and that he enjoyed his new surroundings. Although he preferred fiction and light verse to classical literature and the theatrics of visiting thespians to his professors' lectures, he passed enough examinations to have a realistic hope of making a career in the profession he had chosen for himself years before.[17]

*   *   *

Since early youth Fitz Lee had been inspired by his family's military achievements, especially the attainments of his father and uncle. Smith Lee had gone to sea at fifteen, been appointed a midshipman at eighteen, and made lieutenant in his early twenties. His active duty career included distinguished service in the Pacific, Mediterranean, and West India Squadrons, and in 1846–47 he had won distinction during some of the few naval engagements in the war with Mexico. His exemplary record in junior command led to his appointment as acting captain of the USS *Mississippi,* flagship of Commodore Matthew C. Perry's fleet. In 1852, Fitz Lee's senior year at St. Timothy's Hall, his father commanded the *Mississippi* during Perry's celebrated expedition to the Orient, a journey that opened Japan to the economic, diplomatic, and social influences of the Western world.[18]

In some ways the career of Smith's brother had eclipsed his own. During and after the fighting in Mexico, Robert E. Lee had parlayed engineering skill and tactical acumen into a brilliant stint on the staff of Commanding General Winfield Scott. Robert's calculated daring and coolheadedness under fire, especially when reconnoitering behind Mexican lines, had earned him no fewer than three brevets (honorary promotions) for gallantry. An even more prestigious honor was bestowed on him in the spring of 1852: the superintendence of the United States Military Academy (USMA) at West Point, New York. The plum assignment served notice that no officer in the army, whether of staff or line, had a more enviable reputation or a brighter future than Brevet Colonel Robert Edward Lee of Arlington, Virginia.[19]

Captivated by a desire to further the family tradition, Fitz Lee had decided to pursue a career in arms. He seemed ably fitted for the soldier's life, given his love of competitive sports, his early acquaintance with hunting rifles and knives, and his riding ability. He was not an imposing physical specimen—by his late teens he had reached his full height of five feet, six inches, and his face was smooth enough and his frame spare enough to make him look younger than he was. Even so, he was sufficiently hardy to withstand the rigors of military duty, and his heart was with the army. His proficiency at horsemanship suggested an aptitude for a position in one of the two dragoon outfits of the regular service or the single Regiment of Mounted Riflemen.

Anxious to give his career the best possible start, he desired an appointment to his uncle's school on the Hudson River. A West Point education was among the best available at the time, grounded as it was in those engineering-based studies that promised employment in either the military or a civilian sector. It facilitated entry into the inner circles of military society and provided a pathway to promotion and career advancement. Moreover, a USMA education was tuition-free, a consideration of no small importance to the son of a socially secure but far-from-wealthy family.

Yet a distinguished pedigree could not be measured in dollars alone. Fitz must have suspected that, as a member of one of the oldest and most notable families in the South, any application he submitted would receive serious consideration, especially if Brevet Colonel Lee personally sponsored his candidacy. The celebrated officer was prevailed upon to do so, the local congressman duly recommended him, and in the spring of 1852 Fitz was notified that he had been granted an at-large appointment to the academy. On July 1 of that year, after being tutored in some of the courses to which he had devoted less than adequate attention at St. Timothy's, especially higher mathematics, the sixteen-year-old, accompanied by a retinue of relatives and family friends, traveled north by stagecoach, train, and steamboat to his future alma mater.[20]

The next four years were among the most memorable of Fitz Lee's life. From the start, his outgoing nature and determined pursuit of pleasure and amusement won him many friends, not only among the other plebes but among upperclassmen as well. He even impressed those few instructors who saw beneath his brash personality and sometimes-shallow interests and discerned that he was promising officer material. To be sure, he could be serious and studious when it suited him. During his fourth-class year (July 1852–June 1853) he attained relatively high grades in his language-based courses, ranking thirteenth and eighteenth, respectively, in French and English studies out of a class of seventy-seven. Mathematics, however, continued to give him trouble; at year's end, he stood no higher than forty-sixth in that discipline.

His difficulties with math not only continued into his third-class year but worsened; by June 1854 he ranked fifty-second in the subject in his pared-down class of fifty-seven cadets. His ranking in math helped lower his overall "order of general merit" to forty-ninth—the previous year, he had ranked thirty-third. His slide continued through his last two years at the academy. During the 1854–55 academic year, out of forty-nine cadets he finished forty-fourth in philosophy, fortieth in engineering drawing and chemistry, and forty-sixth in general merit. Even in his senior year, when students finally received formal instruction in military tactics—courses in which Fitz might have been expected to excel—his grades were dismal. In his class, which still comprised forty-nine cadets, he ranked thirteenth in cavalry tactics. Yet he placed no better than forty-sixth in infantry tactics and forty-seventh in artillery drill. In the textbook-bound courses, he stood fortieth in mineralogy and geology, forty-third in engineering, and forty-sixth in ethics. During those last two years, his general-merit standing rose only slightly, to forty-sixth and forty-fifth, respectively.[21]

Major factors in his inability to rise above academic mediocrity, even briefly, were his lax study habits and frequent inattention to the demands of his course work. At the academy, he continued to indulge his preference for light fiction over the less entertaining tomes that buttressed classroom study. A glance at his library-circulation records reveals a fondness for the romances of Scott and Cooper and the comic sketches of Irving, as well as a studied neglect of military texts and treatises on the campaigns of the great commanders—the reading material in which Robert E. Lee had immersed himself during his West Point days.[22]

Another reason for Fitz's continually low standing was his less-than-model deportment. Demerits that could play hob with a cadet's overall standing were meted out to those who failed to adhere to a long and detailed code of conduct. Cadets were gigged for everything from ineffective classroom recitation and neglect of duty to failure to keep shoes shined or barracks rooms policed. Some forms of misbehavior incurred especially harsh penalties. These included breaking bounds to seek prohibited pleasures such as offered by an off-limits drinking hole known as Benny Havens's Tavern.

Infractions and demerits held no terror for Fitz Lee, who throughout his West Point career behaved, as one biographer has put it, like "a wild fellow."

From the day he first set foot on the grounds of the USMA to the day he graduated, he seemed motivated by a desire to experience as much jollification as possible in such a sequestered environment. Not surprisingly, at the end of each class year he stood dangerously close to the number of demerits—200—that normally triggered instant dismissal. He acquired 118 black marks in his first year at the academy, 197 the following year, 196 in his second-class (third) year, and 169 in his final year as a cadet. Upon graduation, his rank on the institution-wide conduct roll was 177th out of 211 cadets.[23]

The ways in which Fitz flouted the conduct roll were many and varied. He was cited for unsoldierly bearing, including many instances of talking and laughing in the ranks. On numerous occasions he was careless of his attire, standing inspection in a dirt-stained jacket, dusty shoes, or nonregulation headgear. Remarks in his disciplinary log indicate that he could not resist drawing attention to himself through conspicuous (and often rhythmic) displays of merriment such as "dancing across the parade ground, dancing in front of guard tent . . . allowing boisterous noise in his tent at one a.m., etc., etc." Another common offense was his use of tobacco products in the cadet barracks as well as in the halls and latrines of the academic buildings. While representative of the conduct of many other high-spirited, risk-taking cadets, Fitz's standing on the merit roll contrasted sharply with that of his uncle. In 1829 Robert E. Lee had graduated from the academy second in his class, virtually without a blot on his behavioral record.[24]

Some of Fitz's infractions showed great skill in both planning and execution. It was said that he "used to pass the sentries whenever [he] pleased and roam about contrary to all regulations." He managed this by propping a dummy under his bedcovers to circumvent hasty bed checks and then slipping out of his room in various forms of disguise. On at least one occasion, the petite, smooth-faced cadet donned "a dress and fixings," took the arm of a fellow cadet in civilian clothes and a fake beard, and flounced past an inattentive sentry.[25]

During many, perhaps most, of these escapades, his destination was Benny Havens's, which squatted at the foot of a steep and craggy Hudson River bluff. There he and equally adventurous comrades quaffed jugs of lager, flirted with the Irish barmaids, and slurred their way through various drinking songs including that tuneful tribute to the proprietor, "Benny Havens, Oh!" Sometimes Fitz would return from a carousal in a state of severe intoxication. On these occasions, only the mantle of night or the assistance of less inebriated classmates enabled him to slip past the sentries with the same dexterity he had displayed in breaking bounds.

While some of his escapades went undiscovered and unpunished, others incurred harsh penalties. One such incident nearly forced his dismissal. Midway through his third-class year, he and four classmates, including two seniors, were charged with conduct to the prejudice of good order and military discipline.

The quintet had spent the better part of the evening of December 16, 1853, at Benny Havens's, from which they staggered home in the wee hours of the morning. By then all five had been reported missing, and the disciplinary officer was waiting to get his hands on them. Somehow they managed to sneak back unseen, but at 5 A.M. they were found drunk in a barracks latrine. The two seniors were in possession of liquor; one of them, as well as one of the underclassman (not Cadet Lee), was dressed in civilian clothes.

Fitz professed no fear of the consequences. But if he believed his uncle would intervene to save him from punishment, he was quickly disabused of the notion. In presenting the facts of the case to his superior, Colonel Joseph G. Totten, inspector of the USMA, Robert E. Lee recommended that the offenders be court-martialed and, if convicted, be dismissed. Totten agreed and set up the court, which convened the following month.

By then some of the defendants had drawn the sympathy and support of numerous fellow cadets—a tribute to their popularity and testimony to the severity of their predicament. In fact, before the court met, the entire Class of 1856 pledged to abstain from alcohol through the rest of the year if their classmates were permitted to remain at the academy. Although not specifically endorsing the gesture, Superintendent Lee forwarded word of it to Inspector Totten along with his observation that past guarantees of the sort had "shown the happiest results."[26]

Totten's response went unrecorded, but he referred the matter to the secretary of war, who quickly weighed in on it. Kentucky-born Jefferson F. Davis, future president of the Confederate States of America, rejected the pledge because it applied only to Fitz Lee and the two other underclassmen; the classmates of the senior culprits had not made a similar offer. Thus, the proceedings went forward. In the end, however, only the first-year cadets suffered the ultimate penalty, being forced to resign. Fitz and his classmates were permitted to remain at the academy but were assessed extra tours of guard duty while confined "to the usual limits of cadets until July 1, 1854." This denied them the leave of absence granted to cadets during the summer encampments that preceded each class year.[27]

Almost incredibly, Cadet Lee failed to learn from his narrow escape. Resentful of the onerous duty that his transgression had earned, some weeks later he again absented himself from academy grounds on a nocturnal carouse. This time he failed to return from Benny Havens's until 2:30 the next morning. Again a court-martial was recommended, and again Fitz's classmates stepped forward to pledge their abstinence if he were let off. Apparently without troubling the secretary of war for another opinion, Colonel Totten accepted the offer, again sparing Fitz from the consequences his conduct merited.

Following this repeat offense, the young cadet refused to tempt fate a third time. In the spring of 1855 he wrote his godmother about his many assaults on the conduct code, which he claimed to regret. He had entered the academy, he confessed, "a wild, careless and inexperienced youth," but he intended to leave it "a wiser and I hope a better man." While his sincerity may be questioned, he did reform, at least to a degree. Demerits continued to come his way, sometimes in profusion, through the balance of his time at West Point. They brought him detention and confinement, extra rounds of guard duty, and other punishments. They also prevented him from rising above the grade of cadet corporal, even as many of his closest friends advanced to sergeant or lieutenant. Even so, he never flouted regulations with the careless abandon he had displayed during his third-class year.[28]

*   *   *

The alacrity with which his fellow cadets offered him their support when he needed it most indicates the depth and breadth of the friendships that Cadet Lee—by all indications, the most popular member of the Class of 1856— forged at the academy. While he counted nearly every member of that class as a friend, he was especially close to George D. Bayard of New York, Lunsford L. Lomax of Virginia, Samuel Wragg Ferguson of South Carolina, and Richard S. L. Lord of Ohio. Interestingly enough, five years after leaving West Point all four would join Fitz Lee in the ranks of the Civil War cavalry.

He also forged cordial relations with a number of upperclassmen, including William Woods Averell of New York and James Ewell Brown Stuart, the Virginian who would become the most famous cavalryman of them all. While Stuart had an open and affable nature akin to Fitz's, the latter professed to admire him for qualities he himself lacked, including "a strict attention to his military duties, [and] an erect, soldierly bearing." And although Fitz rarely had physical confrontations with other cadets, he applauded the prideful Stuart's "immediate and almost thankful acceptance of a challenge from any cadet to fight, who might in any way feel himself aggrieved."[29]

One reason Fitz retained his popularity with cadets from all parts of the Union was his unwillingness to engage in the political debates that by the mid-1850s had begun to divide the cadet corps along sectional lines. It was not that he was unaware of, or uninterested in, the great issues of the day—the proposed expansion of slavery into the western territories, the growing social and economic disparities between the sections, the rise of Southern nationalism, the looming specter of secession. Rather, he viewed these and other divisive subjects with a rare degree of detachment and objectivity. He opposed abolitionism and the sectional antagonisms he believed the movement engendered—for this reason, he refused to follow other family members into the ranks of the American ("Know-Nothing") Party, which included many antislaveryites. Moreover, he regarded the newly formed Republican Party as a nest of fanatics and agitators.

On the other hand, he objected to the increasingly strident and bellicose rhetoric of Southern "fire-eaters." Nor did he betray a fondness for the institution of chattel slavery. Before entering West Point, he had emancipated the only slave he had ever owned by inheritance (perhaps the man on whose shoulders he had ridden to his earliest school). Indeed, he appears to have refrained from any discussion on so inflammatory an issue as the Peculiar Institution. After Fitz's death, his brother Daniel recalled that "I never heard him express himself on the Question, 'Pro or Con.'" Like most native Southerners, he accepted the practice on the grounds of economic necessity, but he never considered it a social boon, much less a political entitlement.[30]

If he supported slavery less than wholeheartedly, he never doubted that the Southern way of life, with its emphasis on agrarian values, polite behavior, and the sacredness of personal and family honor, was preferable to the materialistic society of the North and the frontier culture of the Northwest. Like many another member of his region and class, he believed that the machinations of politicians, especially those above the Mason-Dixon Line, were inimical to the maintenance of national harmony. Although no political savant, by his latter days at the academy Fitz Lee foresaw a time in which, to defend their homes, institutions, and ideals, men of integrity and conscience would raise their hands against their countrymen. When that day came, he had no doubt as to the direction in which his heart and mind would lead him.

TWO

The Rough Service of the Horse

Despite his best efforts to bring a premature end to his academic career, Fitz Lee was graduated from West Point on July 1, 1856, ranking forty-fifth of forty-nine cadets. It is said that only his prowess at horsemanship—in which he ranked high in his class—prevented him from succumbing to his lax study habits and abominable conduct record. But he had survived to become a brevet second lieutenant in the U.S. Army, a provisional status in which he would remain until a vacancy opened in the regiment to which he was assigned.[1]

As it turned out, his low class standing, rather than hurting his chances for a favored position, worked to his advantage. The highest-ranking students in each class could expect postings to the elite branches of the service, the topographical and construction engineers. Those near the foot of the general merit roll were usually assigned to the infantry, cavalry, or dragoons, units that stressed leadership over scholarship. This arrangement was fine with Fitz, who desired nothing more than to become an officer of mounted troops, a preference he shared with his closest comrades, Bayard and Lomax. Recent War Department decisions would play a large role in granting the wishes of all three.

When the Mexican War ended with the defeat of the enemy's army and the capture and occupation of his capital, many of the U.S. Regular Army units serving below the Rio Grande redeployed to the stateside forts and seacoast garrisons they had left at war's outbreak. These included the three regiments of mounted troops that a parsimonious Congress allotted the army, two composed of dragoons and one of mounted riflemen.

Over the next seven years, it became clear that these horsemen were too few to patrol the Great American Desert, which stretched nearly from the Rio Grande to the Canadian border. Demographic shifts in the 1850s made it imperative that more mounted troops be recruited to safeguard the paths of westward expansion. Thus, one year before Fitz Lee left the USMA, Congress authorized the formation of two additional horse regiments. Both were designated cavalry in contrast to the existing regiments, each of which combined infantry and cavalry arms, equipment, and tactics.[2]

Some of the most gifted and talented officers in the army received commissions in the new regiments. The 2nd U.S. Cavalry attracted an unusually promising array, including several who would play major roles in a future war: Majors William J. Hardee and George H. Thomas and Captains Van Dorn, Kirby Smith, William H. Emory, George Stoneman, John Bell Hood, Innis N. Palmer, Kenner Garrard, and Richard W. Johnson. One of the most distinguished officers in the service, Albert Sidney Johnston, former infantry and staff officer and Mexican War hero, and from 1838 to 1840 secretary of war of the Republic of Texas, was commissioned colonel of the regiment. The post of lieutenant colonel went to a transferee from the engineer corps—Fitz's Uncle Robert, who in March 1855 had closed out his term as West Point's superintendent. His commissioning suggested that the mounted branch was no longer the province of the strong hand and the weak mind.[3]

At least partly because of his relative's connection with the regiment, Brevet Lieutenant Fitz Lee petitioned the War Department to assign him to the 2nd Cavalry, which since December 1855 had been serving in Texas. In that vast and arid country it had taken on the unenviable task of protecting outlying settlements, government installations, mail routes, and railroad lines from marauding Comanches and Kiowas. Thanks to its able leaders and the patronage of Secretary of War Davis—which assured the regiment of the best available horses, equipment, and weaponry—the 2nd quickly proved itself equal to its mission. A few weeks after Fitz's graduation, an Indian agent in south Texas observed that "our frontier has, for the last three months, enjoyed a quiet never heretofore known. This state of things is mainly attributable to the energetic action of the 2d Cavalry, under the command of Colonel A. S. Johnston."[4]

One month before completing their studies at the academy, Cadets Lee, Bayard, and Lomax had traveled to Washington in hopes of personally lobbying Secretary Davis for commissions in Johnston's outfit or, failing that, a posting to the equally new 1st U.S. Cavalry. Whether through design or coincidence, their hopes were realized. Early in August, Bayard, whose studious ways had earned him higher grades than his companions, was assigned to the 1st Cavalry and dispatched to the regiment's latest duty station, the Kansas Territory. Sometime afterward, Lee and Lomax were posted to the 2nd Cavalry. Fitz and his friend were ecstatic; they celebrated their good fortune at a series of parties in

15

Washington and Alexandria, where, presumably, alcoholic spirits flowed as freely as they had at Benny Havens's.[5]

Their ebullience somewhat dissipated when, in future weeks, they learned that they were not going to follow George Bayard to an active duty station. Their initial assignment was not to the Indian-infested frontier but to a peaceful settlement in the bucolic Northeast—the Cavalry School of Practice at Carlisle Barracks, Pennsylvania. There the newly minted officers would train recruits while they themselves learned the basic elements of their profession and sampled garrison life for the first time.

In the early autumn of 1856, at the end of the three-month leave granted to all recent graduates of West Point, Lee and Lomax arrived at their first duty station, one of the oldest permanently occupied installations of the U.S. Army. They reported to the post commander, Colonel Charles May of the 2nd Dragoons, one of the true heroes of the fighting in Mexico. Along with a small contingent of instructors, May had only recently reoccupied Carlisle Barracks, which had been run by a caretaker detachment since the previous October when its garrison had been ordered to the frontier.

In a matter of days, the newcomers made the acquaintance of fellow officers and began to forge close ties with more than a few of them. One of these, William Averell, USMA Class of 1855, now a junior officer in the Regiment of Mounted Riflemen, described the life they were about to embark on, so different from that they had experienced in their secluded sanctuary on the Hudson: "With all the elements of science and rudiments of art with which we had been loaded during the past four years, we were, most of us, now to be used simply and solely to supervise the living and disciplining of soldiers and to train them in the art of killing Indians and other enemies."[6]

That work proved to be arduous and sometimes exasperating but also rewarding. Under Colonel May's direction, Lee and Lomax began to train the small contingent of recruits who had reported to the post. The workload was light, and they had the satisfaction of imparting what they had learned on the West Point drill field to awkward and inexperienced but eager and enthusiastic rookies. Fitz particularly enjoyed instilling in the trainees his abiding love of horses and showing off his skill at equitation. He also enjoyed connecting with enlisted men who might later serve under him in the field, including the teen-aged musician Jack Hayes.

Training these would-be troopers was one thing—disciplining them was quite another. As a local historian observed, discipline among the recruits of 1856 "was extremely poor and they spent many of their hours, when off duty, annoying nearby farmers, robbing the orchards and gardens and making themselves generally obnoxious. . . . These events were the beginning of a long period of unpleasant relations between the garrison and the citizens of Carlisle, minor outbreaks of fighting occurring frequently." In addition to "minor outbreaks," the recruits precipitated "near riots," including one in which a farmer suffered a fractured skull.[7]

The locals responded by calling citizens' meetings, during which grievances over the "outrages of the soldiers of our Garrison" were freely aired, as well as by protesting directly and frequently to Colonel May. When these measures brought no relief, some townspeople appear to have taken the law into their own hands. Over the next several months, a series of fires, many of suspicious origin, struck the enlisted barracks, the officers' quarters, and other sections of the garrison. Most were extinguished before serious damage could occur, but a fire on May 18, 1857, destroyed a large stable at the north end of the post.[8]

These unhappy events aside, Fitz enjoyed his tour at the School of Practice, which extended until the spring of 1858. In addition to taking satisfaction from his instructorship, the handsome, outgoing subaltern found himself an object of interest—including romantic interest—to the distaff portion of the local community. He often accepted invitations to the homes and dinner tables of residents who did not hold him responsible for the excesses of his recruits. His relative proximity to Virginia and Washington, D.C., and the general availability of leaves of absence enabled him several times to visit his family in Alexandria and Lomax's family in the capital. In the Lomax home he was greeted as warmly as he was by the good people of Carlisle. On one occasion, his friend's mother wrote joyfully in her diary of having "dear Fitz with us, he is so light hearted and gay—he will never grow up."[9]

Fitz's stint at Carlisle also afforded him recreational opportunities while providing adventures he would remember the rest of his life. In the summer of 1857 a singing troupe made up of college students and a voice coach calling themselves "The Continentals" performed at a local venue before an enthusiastic audience. Some months earlier, Fitz, who had loved music since early youth and had a fine singing voice, had formed a trio with Averell and another West Point compatriot, Virginia-born George Jackson of the 2nd Dragoons. As Averell noted, he and his fellow musicians "were captivated by the singers and had them out to the garrison, learned some of their songs, and listened with unspeakable delight to some of their best selections as they rendered them in the quiet summer moonlight before Colonel May's house and other married officers' quarters." Averell never forgot the sight of "Fitz Lee lying on the grass and quietly clutching it and pulling it up by the roots in the ecstasy of his enjoyment."[10]

Fitz had at least one other notable off-duty experience at Carlisle—not surprisingly, it involved his passion for horses. While at the post he had acquired a personal steed, named "Whalebone" probably for his physical features. Lieutenant Averell described the beast as "a high bay horse" whose "plan and elevation were attractive but his cross section showed a great lack of breadth, or thickness. . . . [H]e had high action and a tremendous stride. It was impossible to say what he was made for but Fitz imagined for a buggy and so equipped him."[11]

Fitz was mistaken; as soon as harnessed to the rig, the horse began to protest: "He pranced and curveted like a gigantic English greyhound for a while about the drives on the garrison while the friends of Lee trembled, and then he started for the town" at something close to full speed just as a locomotive came chugging into the midtown depot. The screeching of the engine drove the bay to greater speed and fractiousness, and the driver, for all his experience with horseflesh, could not maintain control.[12]

Before disaster could overtake him in the center of town, Fitz bailed out. An English-born employee of a nearby hotel, who witnessed the sight, enjoyed recounting the denouement: "the Leftenant just rolls over the seat backward and lets him go. Then the Leftenant picks himself up and walks into the barroom and asks for a cigar and has the dirt brushed off his coat. In two minutes that horse comes a tearin' down the street agin with two pieces of the shafts and runs right into the barroom not hurt a bit, and one of the tires off a wheel of the buggy comes a rollin' in after him." Fitz and the other patrons dove for cover, where they huddled until the beast ran so short of nervous energy he could be subdued. The unsettling experience—which provided the local folk with years of memorable storytelling—appears to have been Fitz Lee's last attempt to hitch an unbroken animal to a conveyance.[13]

For Fitz, life at Carlisle became less exciting and enjoyable with the departure of friends for active duty stations in the West. Lomax and Averell joined this group in April and August 1857, respectively. Afterward, Fitz felt pangs of loneliness as well as frustration over his extended instructorship, which had lost much of its early charm. His status appears to have been a result of his low grades at West Point, for he was the last member of his graduating class to win promotion to the full rank of second lieutenant. He finally achieved this distinction on the first day of 1858, when, shortly after returning to Carlisle from a brief leave in Philadelphia, he received orders to report to the headquarters of the 2nd Cavalry at Fort Inge, Texas. Within days he was traveling by rail, stage, boat, and horseback halfway across the country to the site of some of the bloodiest encounters ever recorded between red men and white.[14]

*　　*　　*

Fort Inge straddled the left bank of the Leon River about eighty miles southwest of San Antonio. Situated at the junction of the road to Eagle Pass with the lower road from San Antonio to El Paso, for nine years the post had guarded a once-flourishing inland commercial route. That route had since dwindled in importance to the point that Inge had been abandoned as an active duty installation in May 1855. The place maintained a small administrative detachment, however, and there Fitz Lee reported in the spring of 1858 for a period of orientation. Following a few weeks given to making professional acquaintances and studying the history and mission of his regiment, he left that "bleak post" for Fort Mason, more than one hundred miles to the north, which defended settlements of German immigrants along the upper San Antonio–El Paso Road.[15]

It was at Fort Mason that Lieutenant Lee began what he later called "nine months of frontier tedium." Life at that isolated post was replete with hardships and privations, while lacking in the kind of drama and excitement he had expected in such a hostile environment. His most frequent duty at Mason was to patrol outlying reaches of his regiment's area of operations—lengthy, bone-numbing treks across semiarid territory under a scorching sun. As he informed his godmother in a letter, he considered these missions typical of the "rough service of the horse. I put on a blue flannel shirt, top boots & soldier pants & I am equipped. Carry along a pack mule for provision and wander over the prairies, having no fixed direction, except to try & get on a trail and then follow it, until we come up with the Indians. They have been very bad this season, killing the citizens and drawing off horses, etc."[16]

The Comanches were also furtive and fast-moving. Rarely if ever did the 2nd Cavalry experience tedium-breaking encounters with the enemy. On one mission Fitz accompanied a detachment of his outfit from the Rio Grande to Fort Smith, Arkansas, then back to Fort Mason, a journey of more than twelve hundred miles during which he saw only friendly Indians. He survived the ordeal thanks to his youth, his hardy constitution, and his "splendid horse." In a letter home, he admitted that he had nothing to show for his exertions "except [that] my face [is] a little more tanned perhaps, and my beard more of a mahogany color."[17]

Life in southwest Texas was not all boredom and hardship. There Fitz could indulge his love of outdoor activities including fishing; "fine hunting" especially "buffalo, deer, turkeys, & grouse"; and riding his two thoroughbreds, "Bumble-Bee" and "Minnehaha." In off-duty hours, he played poker with fellow officers, shot billiards on the single table in the makeshift officers' mess, and lost himself in the same dramatic fiction he had preferred to his West Point textbooks. He was in intermittent contact with Uncle Robert and through him was introduced to the leading officers of the 2nd, including Colonel Johnston and Major Thomas, the latter a fellow Virginian who had been a well-regarded artillery and cavalry instructor at West Point.[18]

Fitz's natural conviviality enabled him to make many friends among the junior officers. More than a few of these associations would endure for years, some for a lifetime. His outgoing personality, native wit, and musical talent made him a leading participant in garrison songfests, theatricals, and the other homemade entertainments of the frontier garrison. Post routine failed, however, to prevent intermittent bouts of homesickness. Writing to his godmother in September 1858, he noted that visiting newspapermen often praised the local scenery, "but I have been now nearly over the whole of this large state, on horseback too . . . and I have never yet seen such scenery as I have in old Virginia—I am very lonely now indeed."[19]

The boredom endured no matter how dangerous the missions in which he took part. By the fall of 1858, the lieutenant had acquired enough leadership experience to command parties that roamed far from Fort Mason. On one such mission, he guided a small detachment, lightly armed and supplied, on a wide-area search for hostiles who had attacked one of the German settlements. Somewhere along his roundabout route he must have expected to experience his introduction to combat, but he was disappointed. The expeditionary force was gone for almost two months and covered hundreds of miles of sun-baked prairie but failed to locate, much less chastise, a single hostile.[20]

His appetite for combat was not satisfied until after November 1858, when his unit, Company B of the 2nd, moved into Indian Territory and occupied newly established Camp Radziminski, named for a recently deceased Polish-born subaltern of the regiment. Sprawling at the foot of the Wichita Mountains in the territory's southwestern corner, Radziminski was a major base of operations against marauding bands of Kiowas and Comanches. Here Fitz could expect the kind of action he had sought unsuccessfully in southwest Texas.

Life at that tent city on Otter Creek, which lacked permanent facilities of any kind, was spartan at best, but it offered an opportunity for the officers and men of the 2nd to earn their pay in close-quarters action with the enemies of white civilization. Two months before Fitz's arrival, Major Van Dorn had led four companies of the regiment on a ninety-mile expedition to confront a Comanche village consisting of 120 lodges, home to between four hundred and five hundred warriors under Chief Buffalo Hump. Van Dorn, whom Fitz would come to admire for his fearlessness as well as for his unique blend of audacity and coolheadedness, attacked at once despite the odds. In a "most desperate struggle" lasting ninety minutes, his troops overran the village, scattered its inhabitants, killed almost sixty of them, took dozens of captives along with more than three hundred animals, and confiscated or destroyed a large stock of provisions. The few survivors of the savage assault were said to have "dispersed among the mountains in a destitute condition."[21]

Along with several of his officers and men, Van Dorn, who commanded through the fight despite a dangerous wound in his side, came in for high praise from his departmental commander, Brigadier General David E. Twiggs. Being as ambitious and career-oriented as any other junior officer in the army, Fitz Lee hungered for the same sort of official recognition.

In the aftermath of the victory over Buffalo Hump, Fitz got his chance for glory and official notice. Although badly beaten, the displaced warriors of the Comanche village fight reconstituted themselves, joined with other lodges, and resumed their depredations against settlements on both sides of the Texas border.

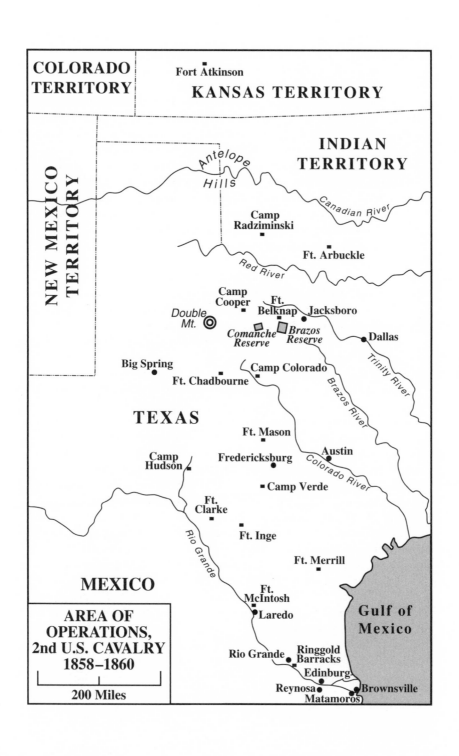

COLORADO
TERRITORY

Fort Atkinson

KANSAS TERRITORY

NEW MEXICO TERRITORY

INDIAN
TERRITORY

Antelope Hills

Canadian River

Camp
Radziminski

Ft. Arbuckle

Red River

Camp
Cooper

Ft.
Belknap   Jacksboro

*Double
Mt.*

*Comanche
Reserve*   *Brazos
Reserve*

Dallas

Trinity River

Big Spring

Ft. Chadbourne

Camp Colorado

Brazos River

TEXAS

Ft. Mason

Camp
Hudson

Fredericksburg

Austin

Colorado River

■ Camp Verde

Ft.
Clarke

Ft. Inge

Ft. Merrill

MEXICO

Rio Grande

Ft.
McIntosh

Laredo

Gulf of
Mexico

Rio Grande

Ringgold
Barracks

Edinburg

Reynosa   Brownsville
Matamoros

AREA OF
OPERATIONS,
2nd U.S. CAVALRY
1858–1860

200 Miles

Studying the situation, the officials in Washington decreed an all-out effort to overawe the hostiles and selected Van Dorn to carry it out. The major spent several months making meticulous preparations for his new campaign. He was closely assisted by Lieutenant Lee, who was gratified to be selected as Van Dorn's adjutant—chief administrative officer—for the upcoming expedition.[22]

Van Dorn did not consider his command ready to start out until the last day of April 1859. On that bright, clear morning he led six companies north from Camp Radziminski toward the new haunts of his enemy. At the head of the serpentine column that slithered northward across the arid wastes, Fitz Lee rode happily by Van Dorn's side, confident that before the mission was over he would have emerged from his crucible of battle. In this belief he was correct, but he could not imagine that the road ahead led to pain, suffering, and near-death as well as to honor, commendation, and promotion.

*　　*　　*

The return march from the battlefield of Crooked Creek to Camp Radziminski covered two hundred miles and consumed almost three weeks. Given the severity of his wound, and especially after his ordeal with the runaway mule, Fitz Lee might have expected to end the trip more dead than alive. In fact, throughout the journey he remained in tolerable health and good spirits, even joking to Captain Cosby that he wished to have the mule at the rear of his litter replaced because "every step he takes his muzzle comes within a few inches of my face," and his breath was less than refreshing.[23]

At journey's end, understandably, he was weak and hurting, but as soon as he reached the camp infirmary and received regular care from his regiment's surgeons, James Simons and W. H. Babcock, he commenced a remarkable recovery. By early June he was writing to his parents of his rapid progress, which he called "contrary to the expectations of the doctors, and a good many other persons including even myself. . . . I have been as near to death's door, as it falls to the lot of a mortal to be, and still not enter." Yet not until late summer could he report himself "entirely recovered, minus a little, very little strength, which however is coming to me daily—I experience no inconvenient effects at all, [and] I can now scarcely realize that I have passed through such a severe ordeal."[24]

That ordeal was worth it, Fitz thought, because the battle at the heart of it had earned him favorable mention in Major Van Dorn's official report of the Wichita Expedition. He also won the commendation of his immediate superior, Captain Kirby Smith, who soon after the column's return had written Fitz's parents of the wound their son had sustained while "gallantly leading in the thickest of the fight." Van Dorn's report had circulated around the country in the newspapers, to the delight of Fitz's friends and relatives. One who read it, Lieutenant George Bayard of the 1st Cavalry, wrote to his family from Fort Riley, Kansas Territory: "We have just read of Van Dorn's fight in Texas [sic].

Fitz Lee was wounded! Of course he would be, if being foremost in the fight were any warrant." The news left Fitz's classmate, whose duty station lay miles from the scene of active operations, jealous and discontented: "While the 2nd Cavalry are having these fights, we literally do nothing, unless it is to aid and feed the infernal [friendly] Indians."[25]

Fitz's health was sufficiently restored by late summer that he took part in the most famous horse race ever held at Camp Radziminski. "Amid great hurrahs and flag waving," he rode his spirited Glencoe colt, Bumble-Bee ("as he alone knew how to ride," a spectator recalled) to a narrow victory over the famously fast steed of Lieutenant Royall. The triumph solidified Fitz's reputation as the most accomplished horseman in his regiment.[26]

A few weeks after besting Royall, Fitz accompanied his unit on a 150-mile trek south to Camp Cooper, Texas. At that outpost on the Clear Fork of the Brazos River, which guarded the El Paso–Red River Trail and the route of the overland post, Company B of the 2nd Cavalry came under the command of Major Thomas. During his stint of duty here, Fitz developed a close relationship with his superior, a dignified gentleman with a twenty-year record of distinction and a deliberate gait that had earned him the nickname "Old Slow Trot."[27]

Because he considered the native Southerner a kindred spirit, Fitz was shocked when, two years later, at the height of the secession crisis, Thomas chose to ally himself with his nation and his army, not his state and his region. Late in life Fitz would add fuel to a public controversy over Thomas's 1861 conduct by claiming in print that the major had declared his intent to accept a command in the state forces of Virginia, only to renege on his pledge at the eleventh hour and go on to high command in the Union forces. By the time Fitz lodged his accusation (which he failed to buttress with hard evidence), Thomas was dead and could not defend himself against the charge of wavering allegiances. The controversy appears to have been a vindictive attempt by ex-Confederates to sully Thomas's reputation, and Fitz Lee was a willing party to it.[28]

At Camp Cooper, Fitz completed his recuperation while easing himself back into the routine of daily operations, including the same long-distance patrols that had taxed his endurance and patience. He remained there, however, for only a few months. By December his company was again on the move, this time to Camp Colorado, about two hundred miles northwest of San Antonio. Soon after arriving at this, his fifth duty station in less than two years, Fitz felt well enough to secure a furlough during which he and Jack Hayes played tourist in San Antonio and Austin. At the former place, they visited the Alamo; at the latter, they observed another icon of southwestern culture, Sam Houston, take the oath of office as governor of Texas.[29]

The winter of 1859–60 was a memorably cold one in south Texas, and Fitz and his companion returned to Camp Colorado in a blinding snowstorm. On

January 15, 1860, days after resuming his ordained duties, Lieutenant Lee was sent at the head of a twenty-two-man detachment to overawe a band of Comanches who had raided a nearby ranch and made off with two dozen horses and cattle. Despite weather so severe that stiff-legged riders had to be helped into their saddles, the soldiers tracked the marauders for twenty-four hours. Near Pecan Bayou, several miles north of Camp Colorado, they finally caught up with two of them, who were driving numerous captured animals before them. Unworried that other hostiles might be lingering nearby, Fitz immediately attacked the two. One they quickly dispatched, but the other, mounted on a swift pony, took off at a rapid gait, pursued by Fitz, Jack Hayes, and two other enlisted men.

Given the warrior's head start, the chase went on for several miles, the pursuers slowly gaining on the pursued. When the latter discovered he could not shake the troopers, he dismounted on the run and raced through a brushy ravine. Lee and Hayes continued the chase afoot, overtaking the warrior only to duck a stream of arrows from his bow, one of which broke the butt of the carbine Fitz had been carrying. Recovering from the jolt he reached for his pistol, but the Comanche closed with him, reaching for the firearm while also slashing at him with a knife. Fitz grabbed his opponent's wrists, and they began to grapple for control of both weapons. As they gyrated from side to side, Jack Hayes attempted to fell the Indian with his own revolver but could not get a clear shot.

The fight went on, neither antagonist giving ground, until Fitz recalled a wrestling trick—the "Virginia Heel"—he had learned as a schoolboy. Hooking his heel behind the Indian's, he jerked the warrior's other leg forward, causing him to topple over. Fitz fell with him, landing on his chest and knocking the air from his lungs. The pistol fell free; snatching it from the ground, Fitz sent a bullet through the warrior's left cheek. An instant later, Jack Hayes put a second, fatal shot into the victim's body.[30]

The following day, Fitz and his men returned to Camp Colorado, the dead Indians and the recovered livestock in tow. Once back at the garrison, the victor penned a straightforward report of the operation. More dramatic, vocal accounts by other members of the expedition convinced the lieutenant's superiors that he had comported himself coolly, bravely, and with commendable dash and energy. Despite the one-sidedness of the fight on Pecan Bayou, in later days praise poured in from many quarters—not only from Captain Smith but also from Robert E. Lee, who had succeeded Twiggs in command of the Department of Texas, as well as from Commanding General Winfield Scott. The seventy-four-year-old Scott, another native Virginian and a veteran of the War of 1812 and the Mexican conflict, proclaimed that the recent expedition "served to exhibit qualities, on his [Fitz's] part, which cannot fail to lead to like distinction in operations against an enemy at the head of a much larger force."[31]

This implied recommendation for promotion was echoed by the editors of several newspapers, both regional and national, who chronicled the incident and commended Lieutenant Lee's role in it. After two years of suffering under the weight of his West Point record, Fitz now seemed assured of a successful career in his chosen profession.

*   *   *

The much-heralded subaltern spent the next five months on routine duty, including more of the desultory patrols, bereft of enemy encounter, that typified his duty in Texas. By early June, as he informed one of his female cousins in Virginia, "your Fitzhugh is going home on a leave of absence," his first since embarking on field service. He did not know it, but his Indian-fighting days were over.[32]

He reached Virginia in late summer or early autumn of 1860, where he spent the first part of his furlough visiting family and friends. By early October he was staying with Lunsford Lomax's people in Washington, much to the delight of his friend's mother, who found Fitz "as light hearted and gay as ever." In quick time, however, her guest experienced a mood swing. Only five weeks after portraying him as happy and talkative, Elizabeth Lomax noted that the lieutenant, during a return visit, was "not at all his usual light hearted, gay self. I have never known Fitz to have so little to say."[33]

A couple of events, one personal and the other affecting the entire country, appear to have been at the heart of the personality change Mrs. Lomax described. One was the recently received news that Fitz was going to be assigned to his alma mater as an assistant instructor in cavalry tactics. While a return to his old haunts on the Hudson had some allure, and although he had enjoyed his prior stint as a tutor, he preferred to remain in field service where he could take advantage of any career benefits accruing from his exploits against the Comanches.

The other likely source of his sudden gloom was another piece of recent news. On November 6, the voting population of the country had gone to the polls to elect America's sixteenth president. Months before, the national Democracy, long the party of the Lee family and most other Southerners, had fractured internally by nominating two candidates for the presidency. Former Vice President John C. Breckinridge of Kentucky was a vocal supporter of states' rights, slavery, and secession as a counter to Northern coercion. Senator Stephen A. Douglas of Illinois, a moderate conservative, favored less sweeping measures to determine the future of slavery and the validity of secession, while hoping to avert the shooting war that so many Americans, in and out of political circles, were currently predicting. A third-party candidate, John Bell of Kentucky, had sought the presidency on a platform of compromise, conciliation, and mediation.

Since all three candidates had some appeal to Southerners, it was expected— and rightly so—that they would split the Democratic vote. The true beneficiary of this political tug-of-war was the so-called abolition candidate of the fledgling Republican Party, the former congressman Abraham Lincoln of Illinois. By November 7, most of the country had learned that Lincoln's rivals had canceled each other out, giving Lincoln enough electoral votes to gain the White House although pulling two million fewer popular votes than his combined opposition.[34]

To citizens in many quarters of the nation, Lincoln's election made the sundering of the Union a fait accompli. For years, Southern spokesmen had made it known that they would not submit to the rule of any Republican who would circumscribe slavery's existence or, worse, seek to expunge it. Even those not disposed to inflammatory rhetoric or precipitate action—including Fitz Lee, his relatives, and many of his friends in and outside the army—believed a sectional crisis to be at hand. On the very day she spoke of Fitz's moodiness, Elizabeth Lomax was visited by family friends visibly troubled by "the state of our country" and "the fate of the South." She added, unnecessarily: "Things look very ominous politically."[35]

Although fast running out, time remained in which to avert a national calamity. This thought may have buoyed up Fitz Lee as he left his family's home, for the second time in his short life, for the picturesque vistas of the Hudson River valley. Immediately upon his return to West Point, which was currently experimenting with a five-year course of instruction, Fitz entered upon his duties in the department of tactics. One biographer notes that the new instructor enjoyed almost carte blanche to shape his course because his immediate superior, Brevet Major John Fulton Reynolds, who taught artillery tactics and also served as commandant of cadets, "had neither the training nor the time to do more than approve Lee's ideas, methods, and decisions. Lee's position on the staff thus proved to be stimulating but laden with responsibility." One consolation was that he could share that responsibility with a close friend, George Bayard, who early in 1861 was also assigned to West Point as assistant instructor of cavalry tactics.[36]

Despite the demands upon him, Fitz adapted quickly and wholeheartedly to his new duties. Not only was he a skillful and inspiring teacher, but he also managed to win and maintain the good opinion of virtually all of his students. It was not long, in fact, before the most popular member of the Class of 1856 became the most popular faculty member of his era—in the words of one of his students, "liked by the officers, cadets, ladies, and in fact by everyone that knew him." One historian of West Point notes that Fitz's popularity among the cadet corps was "probably attributable to his relaxed attitude toward regulations." The record indicates, however, that, unlike his earlier stint at the institution, Fitz took his academic responsibilities as an assistant instructor quite seriously, an attitude in keeping with his suddenly sober frame of mind.[37]

That sobriety grew as the country moved ever nearer to civil strife. The first true spark in the powder keg had been lit a week before Fitz entered upon his instructional duties. On December 20, 1860, South Carolina, home of the most rabid of Southern fire-eaters, declared itself out of the Union. For some weeks it appeared that the Palmetto State would stand alone in secession, but soon after the new year came in her action was duplicated by Mississippi, Florida, Alabama, Georgia, and Louisiana. Between February and April, the Southwest—Texas and Arkansas—joined the Deep South in rebellion.

Each of the seceded governments began to arm itself against the prospect of invasion by the North. They raised troops, commissioned officers, and procured weapons, largely by seizing those federal armories and arsenals on their soil. By early February the states that had voted for secession had taken steps to form a centralized government at Montgomery, Alabama, and later in the month they appointed Jefferson Davis, the former secretary of war and more recently U.S. senator from Mississippi, to serve as president of the fledgling Confederate States of America.[38]

The upper South had a more difficult time adopting the secessionist mind-set. North Carolina and Tennessee would not declare for secession until May, and in Tennessee's case a ratification vote would not occur until early June. Although a secession convention sitting in Richmond voted on April 17, 1861, to take Virginia out of the Union, the action had to be ratified by a statewide referendum in late May. The delay left Fitz Lee—recently promoted to first lieutenant in his regiment—in limbo. Little more than a week before the Richmond convention met, he revealed in a letter to his mother his conservative views on secession while declaring his loyalty to his state and noting his growing discontent with serving in a blue uniform: "You need be under no apprehension about my injuring myself talking secession—'Tis only occasionally, when I hear something exceedingly hard and unjust about the South that I am unable to hold [it] in—I wrote Papa a letter not long ago, telling him I wanted to resign—That I was tired of serving a Black Republican administration etc. . . . The Army, while it rather likes occasionally a little brush with a foreign foe, equally loathes the idea of civil war—and our only wish is to be allowed to stand aside and let the politicians who have got us into all this trouble, fight it out—were that the case . . . the speck of war now visible upon the horizon would soon disappear." In closing, he reiterated, in block letters, "I WANT TO RESIGN."[39]

By the time he wrote to his mother, some Northern newspapers, strictly on the basis of Fitz's Virginia roots, were reporting that he had already resigned his commission. In fact, he did not take that decisive, unalterable step for another six weeks. By then he had been offered—apparently through the efforts of relatives or friends—a commission as first lieutenant in the Confederate artillery. He did not accept the proffer, even writing the Adjutant General's Office in Washington "to relieve myself from any suspicion of having accepted an appointment in one army, before my resignation has been tendered in the other." As his disavowal suggested, however, he rejected the idea neither of resigning nor of accepting a position in defense of his state.[40]

For six weeks he marked time, as if uncertain of his course. He threw himself into his teaching duties, tutoring in the nuances of horsemanship cadets whom he was fated to meet in battle months and years hence, including George Armstrong Custer of Ohio and H. Judson Kilpatrick of New Jersey. Aware of the struggle he was waging between loyalty to his family and region and allegiance to the army and its institutions, academy officials made efforts to persuade him to remain indefinitely at West Point, "where good pay and easy duty would be his portion." While grateful for the effort in his behalf, he rejected this offer, too.[41]

Toward the close of this term of trial, the pressure to act overtly, to make a final determination of his status, became almost unbearable. It was especially so after April 12, when South Carolina cannons and mortars bombarded the U.S. Army garrison inside Fort Sumter at Charleston Harbor. Three days after the guns opened, and barely a month after his own inaugural, Abraham Lincoln issued a call for seventy-five thousand volunteers to repress "combinations too powerful to be resisted" by lesser means. These were the opening acts in a national tragedy of unimaginable proportions.[42]

On April 27—by which time almost fifty Southern-born cadets had left West Point for their home states—Fitz joined the exodus, the first step toward severing his ties with the army he had served for almost a decade. It was an emotion-laden parting, made all the more so by the well wishes he received from cadets and officers from all parts of the country. The night before his departure, he made the rounds of the cadet barracks and faculty quarters, bidding farewell to everyone he met. A Northern-born cadet, Tully McCrea, described the poignant scene: "He went to every room and shook hands with every one of us, with tears in his eyes, and hoped, he said, that our recollections of him would be as happy as those that he had of us. When he shook hands with me, I expressed my regrets that he was going away. He said that he was sorry to leave, but as he belonged to the other side of the line, it was time that he was going."[43]

The leave-taking extended into the following morning, when McCrea and his classmates gathered in front of their barracks to see Fitz off. McCrea later wrote to his sweetheart in Ohio: "As he passed in the omnibus we took off our hats and waved them as he passed. This may appear very natural and matter of fact to you, for you do not know enough about military usage to recognize the great difference that there is between an officer and a subaltern. I believe that it is the second time I ever shook hands with an officer, although it is three years that I have been here."[44]

After stopping off at Carlisle, Pennsylvania, to explain his course to Old Army friends and bid them farewell, Fitz entrained for Washington, D.C., where he submitted his resignation at the Adjutant General's Office. Then, with a heart full of both regret and resolve, he returned to Virginia. At Arlington he met with his Uncle Robert, and in Alexandria he was reunited with his father. The Lee brothers had already severed their own ties with the U.S. Army and Navy, respectively—in Robert E. Lee's case, only days after General Scott had offered him command of all U.S. Army forces during the coming crisis.[45]

Throughout the volatile weeks preceding and following the Fort Sumter crisis, Fitz Lee had looked to the example of his father and uncle as a guide to his own actions. Their decisions and the reasons behind them had greatly influenced his own. The day he rejected General Scott's offer, R. E. Lee had written Fitz's father of his action, declaring that he could not bear the thought of waging war against his kinsmen and fellow Southerners. He had closed by observing that "I am now a private citizen, and have no other ambition than to remain at home. Save in defense of my native State, I have no desire ever again to draw my sword." Within weeks, however, he would assume command of the troops answering Virginia's call to arms, while brother Sidney, on the basis of his long and exemplary career as a seaman, would become a lieutenant commander in the fledgling Confederate States Navy. Fitz Lee would not be long in joining them on the front lines of the tragic conflict that lay ahead.[46]

THREE

An Officer of Rare Merit

The War Office accepted Fitz Lee's resignation on May 21, 1861. That day the erstwhile lieutenant was abed at his godmother's home in Fairfax County, recovering from a minor medical procedure. From Ravensworth he wrote to an army friend, Charles W. Field, a native Kentuckian who had recently tendered his resignation as well. In his letter Fitz infused his recent actions with a firmness of resolve that had long been lacking. He had not learned of the government's response to his decision, "nor do I care. I have severed my connection with the North forever and I sorrow to think that I did not do it months ago, since I hear the talk concerning invasion."[1]

That talk gave him pause, but he was confident that when the moment of trial came, his state would successfully defend its honor:

> As far as I am able to see there are no Union men in Va. They are all anxious to fight and seem determined to act, as well as fight. They say they have never had any idea of [attacking] Washington unless Maryland seceded, and intend to act entirely on the defensive. . . . Should the [Lincoln] Administration ever get up to the sticking point—Viz.—invading Virginia our hope and prayer to God is that no one of Southern sentiment or birth will cross the Potomac. The reception of the invading force is going to be very warm, (if the summer hasn't fairly set in yet) and I regret extremely having to meet officers of the Army in this test, whom I know enter in it unwillingly and with whom I used to associate upon friendly terms.[2]

Fitz's recovery from the operation was rapid—fortunately so. On the twenty-third, Virginia held her statewide referendum; by a three-to-one margin, she ratified the secession ordinance adopted the previous month. The result had been so widely expected that the Provisional Confederate Congress sitting in Montgomery had already voted to move the seat of government to Richmond. Only hours after ratification was announced, however, the incursion Fitz had anticipated began with boatloads of Union Regulars and volunteers crossing the Potomac and debarking on the wharves of Alexandria. By midday on the twenty-fourth, the city and its environs, including the Lee mansion at Arlington, were securely in the possession of U.S. forces.[3]

By then Fitz, able to ride once again, had left his godmother's estate for more secure territory farther south. At some point he visited the offices of the embryonic War Department in Richmond to seek a field position to which his military experience and family ties recommended him. His quest was successful: sometime in late spring or early summer the lieutenancy he had been tendered in the Provisional Army of the Confederacy was converted into a commission as first lieutenant of cavalry in the Confederate Regular Army. The latter organization, a bit of wishful thinking on the part of the new nation, would not be fully staffed until the Confederacy was granted her independence or, as seemed more likely, won it on the battlefield.[4]

In his May 22 letter to Charles Field, Fitz had mentioned three high-ranking officers who were expected to command the troops assembling in Virginia and elsewhere in the South. One, unsurprisingly, was Fitz's uncle; the others were Brigadier General Pierre G. T. Beauregard, the Louisiana Creole who, by forcing the surrender of Fort Sumter, had become one of the Confederacy's first heroes; and General Joseph E. Johnston of Virginia, one of the most distinguished U.S. Army officers to tender their services to the government at Richmond.

By mid-June 1861, all three men were furiously busy mobilizing the would-be defenders of Southern soil and honor. Robert E. Lee, now a brigadier in the Confederate regular service, was in overall charge of the resources that had recently passed from the control of Virginia governor John Letcher into the hands of the Confederate government. Beauregard had already left Charleston to assume command of the mob of raw recruits occupying Centreville and Fairfax Court House, Virginia, less than twenty-five miles southwest of Alexandria. This makeshift defensive line stretched as far south as a stream called Bull Run and a depot on the Orange & Alexandria Railroad known as Manassas Junction.

Seventy-some miles farther west, Joe Johnston had taken charge of twelve thousand equally green troops who had rendezvoused at Harpers Ferry, in the lower Shenandoah Valley. While Beauregard attempted to defend his position against an expected advance by twice as many troops, Johnston was working against time to develop a credible deterrent to forces organizing in the Military Departments of Pennsylvania, Delaware, and Maryland. The last-named state, contrary to Fitz Lee's hopes, had been prevented from seceding through a combination of military and political maneuvering; it had become a staging area for an advance into the Shenandoah.[5]

By early July it had become apparent that an invasion of Virginia on at least two fronts was imminent. Fitz Lee was desirous of participating in the defense of his state, but because the regiment in which he had been commissioned had not yet been organized, he had no formal opportunity to do so. Fearful he would be left out of the pending fight, he offered his services in any capacity to the Confederate War Department. After a few days' wait, he was told to report to the Centreville-Fairfax line. He would serve, in a provisional capacity, as adjutant general to Brigadier General Richard S. Ewell, commanding a brigade of infantry under Beauregard.

If Fitz's assignment did not place him in the service branch he desired, it did unite him with a well-known officer of horse. Richard Stoddert Ewell (West Point, 1840) had commanded mounted units in Mexico, where he won a brevet for gallantry, and later in several actions against the Plains Indians, where he had won plaudits for his leadership at the company and squadron level. At the outbreak of the present conflict, he had commanded the cavalry camp of instruction at Ashland, Virginia, just above Richmond, before winning promotion and command of the 2nd Brigade in Beauregard's Army of the Potomac.[6]

Probably attired in the same blue uniform he had worn since West Point, Fitz joined the bald-headed, beak-nosed ex-dragoon near Sangster's Station on the Orange & Alexandria, five miles south of Fairfax Court House. Ewell's troops—three infantry regiments from Alabama and Louisiana, four guns of the Washington Artillery of New Orleans, and a Virginia cavalry battalion—manned a series of outposts well in advance of the Bull Run line. In his bailiwick the first fighting of the coming campaign would occur.

The new arrival had barely begun to reacquaint himself with duties he had not performed since serving in Kansas when the invasion of Virginia truly began. On July 16, some thirty-five thousand raw levies under Brigadier General Irvin McDowell left Washington and Alexandria, heading for Richmond via Bull Run. McDowell—General Scott's fallback choice to lead the armies of the North to victory over the forces of disloyalty and disunion—hoped to occupy Virginia's capital before the Confederate Congress convened there on the twentieth of the month. Before descending on the Rebel capital, he expected to brush aside the rabble at Beauregard's disposal, then sever the railroads via which Richmond got much of its manpower and supplies.

Upon McDowell's approach, Ewell's troops fell back—slowly, grudgingly, disputing every acre of Virginia soil—to Bull Run. There Beauregard used them to form his right flank at Union Mills Ford. Initially, that sector was McDowell's primary objective, but when reconnaissance persuaded him that the area between Sangster's Station and Union Mills featured poor roads and rough terrain, he revamped his strategy. He decided, instead, to feint against his enemy's center near Stone Bridge on Bull Run, then assail Beauregard's left via Sudley Springs Ford.[7]

The fight-and-fall-back tactics of the Confederates in advance of Bull Run gave Beauregard time to make final preparations to meet McDowell; it also enabled him to telegraph Richmond for reinforcements. By the seventeenth, a plea for help had gone to Johnston's new headquarters at Winchester, where his Valley forces were under pressure from the advancing Army of Pennsylvania, under Major General Robert Patterson. The following day, when the enemy in Johnston's front suddenly pulled back—testimony to the timidity and vacillation of their sixty-nine-year-old commander—Johnston prepared to send most of his army, by foot and troop train, to Beauregard's assistance. The transfer operation, though sizable and complex, proceeded with relative smoothness, and by midafternoon of July 20—twelve hours before McDowell could strike—Johnston's advance echelon reached Manassas Junction. The additions deprived the Union commander of his heavy numerical advantage.[8]

His first battle in a year and a half—and his first ever against white opponents—was a frustrating experience for Lieutenant Fitzhugh Lee. Not content to permit his enemy to open the action, Beauregard planned to attack him soon after sunrise on the twenty-first. He intended to smite the Union left—a mirror image of McDowell's strategy. Given its position, Ewell's brigade was the logical choice to spearhead the operation, curling around the Yankees opposite it via the road to Centreville. For unknown reasons, however, an attack order never reached Ewell, although two other brigades prepared to support him were sent across Bull Run as planned.

After 9 A.M., when the slow-moving Yankees finally splashed across the run and struck Beauregard's left, the battle began to rage at white heat. Ewell, his staff, and his regimental officers reacted to the sounds of combat with concern and then anxiety. Having heard nothing from army headquarters, Ewell, some time before ten o'clock, sent his assistant adjutant general to the field headquarters of Brigadier General David R. Jones, whose brigade was stationed near McLean's Ford, about two and a half miles northwest of Union Mills. Fitz would recall that "I found General Jones making preparations to cross Bull Run, and was told by him that, in the order he had received to do so, it was stated that General Ewell had been sent similar instructions." Aboard his sprightly mare, "Nellie Gray," Fitz galloped back to Union Mills and gasped out the news. His superior "at once issued the order for his command to cross the Run and move out on the road to Centreville."[9]

No sooner did his vanguard set foot on the north side of the stream than Ewell received a courier-borne dispatch from Beauregard's headquarters ordering him not to advance but to fall back to his original position. Fitz helped guide the confused and frustrated troops back to Union Mills, only to find Ewell in animated conversation with one of Beauregard's aides-de-camp. As Ewell later wrote, the officer had delivered an order "to cross again, proceed up the run, regulating my movements upon the brigades of Generals Jones and [James] Longstreet." With the assistance of his adjutant general, Ewell crossed the stream a second time. On the north bank Fitz guided the men onto the road to Centreville. They had progressed about a mile and a half when yet another courier from Beauregard redirected the brigade toward Stone Bridge.[10]

By the time Ewell's command countermarched to Stone Bridge, it was late in the afternoon and the principal fighting was over. Reinforcements that had been rushed into action on the left at a critical time—including Brigadier General Thomas J. Jackson's Virginia brigade of Johnston's army, which had stood "like a stone wall" against the Federal advance—had turned the tide of the several-hour battle. Checked in front, menaced on their flanks, the Union forces had given way to the combined effects of inexperience, poor leadership, heat, fatigue, and thirst. By late afternoon they were retiring from the field in increasing numbers. When Confederate sharpshooters and cannoneers laced their rear, a once-orderly retreat became a chaotic and demoralizing rout.[11]

Worn out by excessive marching and countermarching under the summer sun, Ewell's brigade followed its commander back to Union Mills, reaching there at nightfall. While comrades farther to the west exulted in their army's success, by day's end Fitzhugh Lee was too frustrated and fatigued to be jubilant. There was no denying that the Confederates had emerged victorious from this first major clash of arms and wills. Beauregard and Johnston had turned back the first wave of enemy invasion, perhaps winning (as the most optimistic participants dared predict) independence for their fledgling nation. Yet events had conspired to deny Fitz Lee and many other soldiers the chance to make a meaningful contribution to the outcome. Although for hours fighting had raged not far from his position, the temporary staff officer could hardly consider himself a veteran. All in all, it was a most unsatisfying way to begin one's war service.

*   *   *

Johnston, who had assumed command of the combined armies on Bull Run, made only the most cautious effort at pursuit. As a result, McDowell's fugitives were permitted to seek refuge inside the defenses of their capital, where they regrouped and made preparations to carry on the fight under a new chieftain, Major General George B. McClellan. It seemed obvious that a war that both armies had expected to be brief and virtually bloodless was going to be a long and sanguinary affair.

Studying the results of the fight, Fitz Lee decided that the failure to follow up the victory of Manassas (as the Confederates called this first large-scale land battle of the war) was an immense blunder. For this he blamed not only Johnston but also President Davis, who visited the battlefield shortly after the fight to congratulate the victors and confer with them as to their future course. Fitz came to believe that the Confederates should have advanced at once on Washington, to capture the city by attack or siege. Instead, Johnston contented himself with establishing outposts within sight of the U.S. Capitol and clamping a partial blockade on Potomac River shipping. These half measures hardly warranted the title that many Southern and a few Northern editors gave to the operation: "The Siege of Washington."[12]

In truth, Johnston could not have hoped to accomplish much more than this. Whether or not Fitz admitted it, the still-raw Confederates had been as disorganized by victory as their opponents had been by defeat. Although they had learned something of fighting on the defensive, a large-scale offensive was beyond their ability, especially when the objective was a heavily fortified seat of government. It would be months before the Confederacy could develop a well-disciplined, well-trained force capable of a sustained offensive. The same was true of the demoralized mob that had fled to Abraham Lincoln's city. Even the "Young Napoleon," McClellan, with his organizational and tutorial gifts, would not produce an army ready to retake the field until early the next spring.

Until then the war would go on, but mostly at the small-unit level. Realizing this, Fitz left the Bull Run line within days of the battle in hopes of securing in Richmond a new assignment—preferably in the cavalry, and at a higher rank. He trusted that his military background, his skill at horsemanship, and the strong recommendation of General Ewell would gain him a commission in the mounted arm of his state.

Perhaps because his family was so well connected militarily and socially, by the end of July he was being carried on the rolls of Virginia state troops as a lieutenant colonel. It was a heady advancement over his lieutenancy in the prewar army, but his parallel rank in the Confederate Provisional Army remained that of captain. In fact, either title seemed like a hollow honor, for he had yet to be assigned to a field unit.

His limbolike status must have weighed on his mind, for he appeared pensive and distracted during subsequent visits to his family's temporary home in the Confederate capital. His younger brothers may also have experienced difficulty securing the military positions and rank they believed themselves entitled to. A few weeks after Manassas, their mother accompanied her sister, the wife of Adjutant and Inspector General Samuel Cooper, to a soiree at the home of Confederate congressman James Chesnut Jr. of South Carolina and his wife, Mary Boykin Chesnut. Their hostess, one of the most acerbic chroniclers of the Confederate social scene, described Mrs. Lee as complaining to anyone who would listen: "What good does it do my sons to be Light Horse Harry Lee's grandsons, and George Mason's? I do not see that it helps them at all." Mrs.

Chesnut added that once Fitz's mother and the Coopers departed, "what a rolling of eyes and uplifting of hands!" With an indignant flourish, she declared that both Fitz Lee and his cousin Rooney "are being promoted hand over fist."[13]

Although Mrs. Chesnut exaggerated the pace of Fitz's advancement, on the last day of September he received orders to report to Camp Cooper, northeast of Annandale, to assume the duties of executive officer of the 1st Virginia Cavalry. He had been recommended for the position by no less a personage than Joseph E. Johnston. In a dispatch to the Confederate War Department, the commanding general had referred to the erstwhile adjutant as "an officer of rare merit, capacity, and courage," adding that he "belongs to a family in which military genius seems an heirloom."[14]

As far as plum assignments went, the 1st Virginia was one of the plummiest, a tribute both to Fitz's military potential and his coveted pedigree. The regiment, which had been formed by incorporating several well-known militia units, was populated by scions of the state's most distinguished families. Upon their rendezvous at Harpers Ferry, these promising but disparate elements had been welded into a cohesive force by Fitz's West Point comrade, Lieutenant Colonel (later Colonel) J. E. B. Stuart.

Through the caliber of his leadership, Stuart had also made the outfit famous. After leading Johnston's column from the Valley to Bull Run and Manassas Junction, the tall, heavily bearded twenty-eight-year-old Stuart had committed his outfit—at the time, no larger than a battalion—to battle on at a critical point on July 21. Spying a phalanx of Yankee infantry advancing toward the left and rear of General Jackson's recently deployed brigade, Stuart promptly attacked at the head of two companies comprising some 150 officers and men. Striking with a power out of proportion to their numbers, the Virginians absorbed a raking fire from a New York Zouave regiment before slamming into the head of the enemy force.

With saber swipes and pistol blasts, Stuart and his men felled Yankees right and left, breaking up their formation, spreading panic through their ranks, and sending dozens into headlong flight. Lieutenant William M. Blackford of the 1st Virginia described the Zouaves as "completely paralyzed by this charge, and though their actual loss in killed and wounded was not very great, their demoralization was complete." Had Stuart not led his men into the fray when he did, the enemy might have swept over Jackson's "stone wall" and turned the tide of combat: "The arrest of their dangerous move upon the exposed flank of our main line of battle . . . saved the day." Pride of accomplishment may have led Blackford to overestimate, at least slightly, the effectiveness of Stuart's assault, but it was one of a small number of events on which the battle turned. The success of the maneuver suggested the quality of the material at Stuart's—and now Fitz Lee's—disposal.[15]

However, the 1st Virginia was no longer Stuart's. On September 24, the dashing cavalier had been elevated to brigadier general. He now commanded the several mounted units that patrolled the Alexandria Line, a cordon of out-posts that stretched for thirty miles from Annandale, on the Little River Turnpike within hailing distance of Washington, to Leesburg, on the upper Potomac. Four days after taking over his enlarged command, Stuart had been succeeded as commander of the 1st Virginia by William Edmondson Jones—West Pointer, former subaltern in the Regiment of Mounted Rifles, and more recently a gentle-man farmer from Washington County.[16]

Founder of a militia company that had served capably under Stuart at Man-assas, Jones was known for his tactical adroitness and no-nonsense approach to discipline, as well as for an irascible, argumentative personality that would gain him the nickname "Grumble." To many observers, he was the antithesis of the colorful Stuart, who reveled in ornate trappings such as ostrich-plumed hats and golden spurs, sought the company of dashing young officers, courted the attentions of pretty women, and favored banjo music, dancing, and amateur theatricals. For his part, Jones dressed plainly, spoke gruffly, cared little for mil-itary pomp, had no discernible sense of humor, and enjoyed pointing out the shortcomings of his fellow officers. He spared no effort to promote the well-being of his troopers, thereby winning their approval as well as their grudging respect. Yet he never inspired those feelings of admiration and affection that Stuart evoked so effortlessly.

Had Fitz Lee had his druthers, he would not have begun field service under such a dour, contentious officer. Much more to his liking was Stuart, whose company he had not shared since Stuart's last, and Fitz's second, year at the U.S. Military Academy. In the prewar army, Stuart, a member of the Mounted Rifles and later the 1st U.S. Cavalry, had served far apart from Lieutenant Lee. He had made a solid if not spectacular record in the Old Army, but in the weeks and months following Fort Sumter, when organizing the 1st Virginia for field service, the native of Patrick County had established himself not only as a gifted administrator but as an adept gatherer of military intelligence. In the days lead-ing up to Manassas, his reconnaissance and counterreconnaissance skills had enabled Johnston to slip away from Patterson's Federals outside Winchester and depart for points east. This invaluable service, added to his dramatic feat on the twenty-first, had made Stuart the most celebrated cavalryman in Virginia.[17]

Yet his laurels had not gone to his head. When Fitz Lee, upon joining his new regiment, visited the newly minted brigadier at his headquarters on the road from Centreville to Fairfax Court House, he found Stuart essentially the same man he had known at West Point. Open and aboveboard in his dealings with everyone, he exuded honesty and integrity as well as a spirit of goodwill that put others at ease. Fitz would come to consider him a model Virginian, dignified without being haughty, authoritative without being overbearing, a man to obey but not to bow to. Fitz noticed one change in Stuart since his cadet

years: he no longer seemed so sensitive to perceived attacks on his honor, so willing to take offense at slights, real or imagined. A twinkle in his eye hinted at a
sense of humor, which matched that of his new subordinate and found expression in the practical jokes he played on those closest to him. In brief time, this
group would include Lieutenant Colonel Lee.

*　　*　　*

Perhaps predictably, Fitz's relations with his immediate superior were, from
the outset, less than intimate. One reason was Fitz's early and strong identifi-
cation as a Stuart partisan. It was obvious that Colonel Jones neither liked nor
approved of Stuart, whom he considered a foppish publicity hound. Fitz got
the distinct impression that Jones was jealous of Stuart's popularity with the
rank and file and even of his physical gifts. It was true that when in the company of the tall, robust, neatly bearded, and nattily attired Stuart, the stooped
and grizzled Jones seemed to shrink away before observers' eyes. Being constantly overshadowed in this way was a perhaps understandable source of
Grumble's grumbling.

Early on, Fitz Lee perceived that the 1st Virginia Cavalry was divided into
cliques personally and philosophically at odds—a large class of Stuart devotees,
a much smaller group of Jones loyalists. If an officer made a comment that could
be construed as a compliment to Stuart, he usually suffered some form of
punishment at Jones's hand. Since Fitz often made such comments, innocently
enough at first and later more provocatively, his official relations with Jones
came under strain at an early date.[18]

By contrast, Fitz developed close relationships with the line officers of the
regiment. These included Captains James H. Drake of Company A, William A.
Morgan of Company F, Richard Welby Carter of Company H, and William
Thompson Martin of Company N (the 1st Virginia was initially composed of
fourteen companies rather than the standard ten). More junior officers including
Lieutenants William Blackford (the First Manassas chronicler), Frank Augustus Bond, and Gustavus W. Dorsey won not only Fitz's friendship but also his
patronage, which helped them gain higher rank.

Among the few officers with whom Fitz did not establish cordial relations
was his immediate junior, Major Robert Swan. A principal reason was Swan's
early departure from the muster rolls, an event directly attributable to his conduct at First Manassas. While Stuart was leading his 150 men in that hell-
for-leather charge on the gaily attired New Yorkers, Swan had marked time in
the rear with the rest of the battalion, purportedly defending some cannons
already guarded by infantry. One of those with Swan, Trooper John Singleton
Mosby, observed that by refusing to reinforce Stuart the major ensured that his
squadron would emerge from the battle unscathed: "He did a life insurance
business that day. Instead of Swan supporting the battery, the battery supported

Swan." Swan's conduct had cost him the confidence of Stuart and that of the enlisted men. It also cost him the position that opened up when the battalion expanded to regimental size—the lieutenant colonelcy that had gone instead to Fitz Lee.[19]

Because he never lost the common touch, Fitz got along well with the rank and file. One of the few exceptions was Mosby, a young lawyer from Bristol, Virginia, whose frequently unkempt appearance and unmilitary bearing offended his lieutenant colonel. Lieutenant Bond recalled that from his earliest days with the 1st Virginia, Fitz attempted to set a standard of decorum by acting the part of "the precise and punctilious soldier, with great regard for all the etiquette of the profession." In contrast, Mosby "was absolutely careless of all this, and seemed to take a pride in violating every rule that it was safe to do."[20]

Such behavior was bad enough in an enlisted man, but after Jones elevated Mosby to regimental adjutant, his informal ways were too much on display to satisfy Fitz. Even minor infractions of military decorum brought a sharp response. One evening in camp, Mosby sauntered up to Lieutenant Colonel Lee, offered a lackadaisical salute, and announced with a pronounced drawl, "Colonel, the horn has blowed for dress parade." Fitz glared at the offender and growled: "Sir, if I ever again hear you call that bugle a horn, I will put you under arrest." Although it cannot be determined if this admonition had the desired effect, there is no record of subsequent confrontations between the two.[21]

Animosity, however, continued to define their relationship. By the spring of 1863, Mosby would leave the 1st Virginia to form a band of irregulars at the head of which he would gain a reputation as the war's premier partisan leader. In this capacity he would benefit from the patronage of J. E. B. Stuart, whom he often served as scout and guide. He would receive no such support from Fitz Lee, who viewed partisans as freebooters and marauders motivated more by personal gain than allegiance to cause. On several occasions Fitz would try to persuade Stuart not only to withdraw sponsorship of Mosby's Rangers but to disband the unit and reassign its members to the regular service. For his part, Mosby professed to regard Fitz as a hidebound idealist as well as a malevolent influence on his benefactor. In his voluminous postwar writings, Mosby would take his revenge by ignoring Fitz's contributions to Stuart's cavalry. In his personal correspondence, he would characterize Fitz as dim-witted, incompetent, even cowardly.[22]

The latter charge would have been all but impossible to sustain, even during the lieutenant colonel's earliest days in the field. Through the early autumn of 1861, he personally led numerous patrols across the enemy-infested environs of Washington and Alexandria, exchanging pistol shots and saber blows with the few Yankees who dared cross his path. For the most part, the Union cavalry clung to its capital's defensive works. Those stationed on the fringes of the Alexandria Line rarely strayed from supporting infantry and artillery units.

Unlike their counterparts in gray, few Northerners had been born to the saddle; they had to learn the intricate tactics of their arm at a slow and deliberate pace. In fact, almost two years would pass before the Union horse soldier would be considered capable of standing boot to boot with his opponent. Until then, Fitz Lee and his men would enjoy an almost unbroken series of victories in the field.[23]

When not leading in active operations, Fitz performed yeoman service instructing the recruits of the 1st Virginia, a responsibility that Colonel Jones was happy to leave in his hands. Fitz's teaching experience at Carlisle Barracks and West Point served him so well that he quickly became known throughout the regiment as a master tutor. He was so knowledgeable and so adept at communicating that knowledge that under his guidance William Blackford, for one, "learned more about it [drill] than I had ever done before."[24]

One of Fitz's gifts was a seemingly infinite fund of patience. He refrained from criticizing even the greenest recruit, and he never felt the need to embarrass or bully. This attitude, coupled with his willingness to risk his neck alongside those he led on patrol and in skirmishes with the enemy, made him immensely popular among both officers and men. The result was detrimental to the public standing of his superior. As Captain Blackford observed, "Colonel Jones was not popular with his regiment, and the contrast between our ugly, surly Colonel and our handsome, dashing Lieutenant Colonel Lee, made him appear in a still more unfavorable light."[25]

Because of his allegiance to Stuart and Lee, Blackford himself fell afoul of Jones on a regular basis. In the late fall of 1861, Jones went so far as to court-martial him on trumped-up charges. When the court convened he was quickly acquitted, but during the six weeks Blackford had been held in arrest pending his trial, Jones "disorganized and demoralized" his company "to such an extent that my influence was undermined and destroyed. After resuming command any attempt at restoring discipline was resented as a tyrannical assumption of power, and the men would go over to pay the Colonel a visit and receive his condolences."[26]

The Jones-Lee relationship never experienced such a serious rift, but it was always productive of tension and friction. Fitz's sincere commitment to making the 1st Virginia the most effective regiment in Stuart's command, in addition to his unassailable popularity with officers and men, spared him from the kind of treatment meted out to Blackford.

*   *   *

That popularity grew with every encounter with the Yankees. By early November Fitz was leading scouting missions ever closer to the Yankee-held end of the Alexandria Line. On the eighteenth, cavalry headquarters directed that a reconnaissance be made as far as Falls Church, a village permanently held by neither side but frequented by both. As was his wont, Colonel Jones delegated the mission to his second-in-command, who accepted it enthusiastically. The next morning Fitz set out from camp at the head of a large detachment of the 1st Virginia, including now-Captain Bond's Company A.

En route to his objective, Fitz learned that the main road was occupied by several picket posts manned by members of a New York Zouave regiment—not the Manhattan-based outfit that Stuart had assailed at Manassas, but another brightly clothed unit nicknamed "The Red-Legged Devils from Brooklyn." Contemptuous of such a gaudy opponent, Fitz resolved to capture every picket. After a quick confab with Bond and other subordinates, he led his command in a series of attacks that broke up each outpost in succession, killing or wounding several occupants and driving the rest into roadside woods about a mile south of Falls Church.[27]

Cutting between this place of temporary refuge and the camp of his enemy's picket reserve, Fitz surrounded the fugitives, making their capture a matter of time. Despite their predicament, the Yankees resisted manfully, demonstrating, as Fitz wrote, "much more bravery than the Federal troops usually exhibit." In the face of this opposition, the Virginians and Marylanders, many of them afoot, pressed forward over ground made muddy by recent rains.[28]

At this early stage of the war, dismounted fighting was not a major ingredient of Confederate cavalry tactics. In the prewar service, J. E. B. Stuart had learned the effectiveness of a mounted charge, with saber and pistol, even when directed against such a highly mobile opponent as the American Indian. This lesson he impressed upon his lieutenants in the 1st Virginia, and they upon their men. Fitz Lee was himself a devotee of classical cavalry warfare, which featured the shock tactics of Napoleon. Yet in the present instance, when opposed by infantry, fighting on foot appeared the best response.[29]

His men did so effectively, methodically decimating the enemy but not without taking casualties in return—one being their lieutenant colonel. While most of his force operated against the front of the Union position, Fitz led two columns of horsemen toward a swamp-bordered patch of woods on the enemy's flank. His conspicuous position, added to certain Stuart-like elements of his attire including a "heavy black ostrich plume in a broad-brim slouch hat," made him an inviting target.[30]

Captain Bond was riding behind Fitz in one of the attack columns. He lost sight of his superior as the latter bounded among the trees. A few minutes later, as Bond's column prepared to follow, a dismounted man by the edge of the woods called out to him, ordering him to abort the attack and withdraw. Bond failed to recognize the speaker as either friend or foe, for the fellow was covered from boot to hat with mud. Deciding he must be a Confederate enlisted man— an annoyingly loud one—Bond told him to shut up before he attracted a hail of rifle balls. Instead of obeying, the man loosed a torrent of commands, punctuated with some choice expletives. Bond had "never heard such peremptory orders given in so loud a voice and accompanied by some very bad language. Something about the speaker caused me to look again, more carefully, and to my horror I saw it was Col. Lee."[31]

Minutes before, Fitz's horse (borrowed for this occasion) had stopped a Union bullet and in falling had deposited his rider into the middle of the roadside swamp. Slightly dazed but otherwise unhurt and still anxious to fight, Fitz had joined his dismounted men in pressing the attack. Now he directed an apologetic Bond to lead his company against a different portion of the woods, there to outflank the infantry "and put an end to the fight at once." Bond did as ordered, and the tempo of fighting slackened noticeably.[32]

Eventually the enemy, who had lost eight men killed and three wounded, saw the hopelessness of their situation. Firing ceased, and ten Red Legs, including a lieutenant, came out of the trees, weapons down and hands up. They were promptly corralled and marched back to their camp, which the Virginians combed for weapons, ammunition, and anything else worth appropriating.

Having rid his person of as much mud as possible, Fitz interrogated the enemy officer and his first sergeant. From them he gleaned the intelligence he had been sent to Falls Church to gather. In the meantime, Stuart's chief surgeon, who had accompanied Fitz's detachment, ministered to the wounded on both sides. One member of the 1st Virginia had been killed, as had a civilian guide who had been escorting the detachment. Two enlisted men had been slightly wounded.

Factoring in the drag that his prisoners would exert on his column and concerned by the reported presence of larger bodies of the enemy closer to Falls Church, Fitz decided to proceed no farther. After burying the dead and burning the captured camp, he returned with his spoils to home base. There, two days later, he wrote an official account of the operation—the first of a limited number of after-action reports he would compose over the next three and a half years.[33]

The following day, the recipient of the report, J. E. B. Stuart, sent it on to army headquarters with an endorsement that might have caused Fitz's chest to swell: "The gallant and successful affair of Lieutenant-Colonel Lee and his detachment of 1st Virginia Cavalry against the enemy's best troops in chosen position receives my unqualified praise and commendation." Fitz's conduct also received favorable notice from General Johnston, who, when relaying it to the authorities in Richmond, emphasized the fighting ability and "good conduct" of Fitz Lee.[34]

The most popular officer in the 1st Virginia was fast becoming equally popular with the leading lights of his army.

FOUR

Raiding and
Reconnoitering

The 1st Virginia saw action several times more during the first autumn of the war, mostly at small-unit strength and on routine patrol duty. In every instance the outfit acquitted itself honorably—so much so that it became the centerpiece of Stuart's brigade, which also consisted of the 2nd, 4th, and 6th Virginia Cavalry, the 1st North Carolina, and the Jeff Davis Legion. The latter was a nine-company outfit to which Captain (now Lieutenant Colonel) Martin and two companies of the 1st Virginia had transferred and also consisted of units raised in Mississippi, Alabama, and Georgia. Supporting the cavalry of the brigade was the recently organized Stuart Horse Artillery, comprising four 12-pounder howitzers, one Blakely rifle, one 6-pound rifle, and two highly maneuverable "mountain howitzers," the whole under command of a dashing young Alabamian, Captain John Pelham.[1]

Throughout the fall and well into the winter, Fitz Lee's field leadership and tactics instruction continued to win the approbation of Johnston and Stuart and even the grudging approval of Colonel Jones. The executive officer was a major factor in keeping the regiment's morale high even as other units wallowed in gloom over a minor debacle. On the morning of December 20, 1861, Stuart, who had been assigned command of the advanced forces of Johnston's army, led a sixteen hundred-man force of all arms in covering a foraging party along the Alexandria-Leesburg Turnpike. Encountering near Dranesville a Union force on the same mission, Stuart's mounted contingent (which did not include the

1st Virginia) fought well enough, but his attached infantry performed poorly, botching an attack and being forced into retreat.[2]

Confederate spirits, which had soared following Manassas, took further blows when 1862 came in and reports circulated of major setbacks in other theaters. These included the loss of the garrison on Roanoke Island, North Carolina, and the surrender to Major General Ulysses S. Grant of Forts Henry and Donelson in Tennessee. The series of reverses shook the belief—until then prevalent in many quarters—that the field forces of the Confederacy were invincible. The unhappy events merely reaffirmed the conviction of more realistic observers such as Fitz Lee that the war was far from over.

During the Christmas holidays, Fitz appears to have taken leave of his outfit to visit his relocated family. Presumably his travels included Norfolk, where his father, then on the verge of being promoted to captain in the Confederate Navy, had been appointed second-in-command of the local naval yard (the following March he would become its commander).[3]

After the first of the year, it is doubtful that Fitz could have gone on furlough anywhere. Every officer was needed at the front in response to mounting indications that McClellan's army was about to leave its defenses and occupy Virginia in full force. A harbinger of the coming movement was a notable increase in the number of Union patrols on the roads out of Alexandria. By mid-February, the 1st Virginia and its comrades under Stuart found themselves skirmishing virtually every day.

The enemy's stirrings influenced Joe Johnston to plot the withdrawal of his forces from their positions almost within cannon-shot of Washington. By the first days of March, Jefferson Davis and his cabinet had given their reluctant approval to the plan, and on the morning of the sixth Johnston began to implement it. Over the next three days the army marched south to Fredericksburg on the Rappahannock River, approximately equidistant between Washington and Richmond.

The 1st Virginia Cavalry's role in the operation consisted of guarding the rear of one or more of the several retreat columns as well as helping dispose of equipment and supplies that could not be carried off but must not fall into Yankee hands. When the withdrawal reached Gainesville Station on the Manassas Gap Railroad, the regiment was ordered to destroy eight hundred barrels of flour stored at the depot. A private in the 1st Virginia recalled that the job was accomplished by "knocking in the tops of the barrels and scattering the flour over the ground. I thought that this was a terrible waste and many of the men remarked that we would see the day when we would regret it."[4]

Moving south to Warrenton Junction, Fitz's outfit destroyed bridges and culverts to stymie the progress of pursuers. For several days, however, none appeared, suggesting that Johnston's withdrawal had been premature. While the main army continued south, the cavalry remained on the railroad. Stuart had no intention of offering battle but merely wanted to observe the enemy—when he finally showed himself—and threaten him "with demonstrations toward his flanks and in front, and by every possible means delay his progress and secure accurate information of his strength and, if possible, his designs."[5]

In pursuance of these objectives, for a full week the 1st Virginia marked time at and near Warrenton Junction before sighting a sizable column of infantry and cavalry coming down the railroad. The Yankees halted along Cedar Run, just above the junction, where Colonel Jones and Lieutenant Colonel Lee determined to hold them. While William Blackford's company fought a delaying action in front, a larger body of the 1st Virginia struck the enemy's right, coming away with two dozen prisoners.

The combined opposition did indeed delay the invaders, who appeared bound for Fredericksburg and, ultimately, for Richmond. It also enabled supplies not marked for destruction to be spirited out of their path while permitting infantry that had been supporting Stuart, including Ewell's brigade, to disengage from perilous positions. The accomplishments of the 1st Virginia did not go unnoticed. In his report of the withdrawal to the Rappahannock, Stuart commended the regiment warmly for its effective fight-and-fall-back tactics. He also praised the other elements of his command, including the Stuart Horse Artillery. Although he cited by name only the senior officers, a proportionate share of the credit for slowing McClellan's advance perforce went to Fitz Lee.[6]

Because the Confederates had gotten such a head start, McClellan cut short his pursuit and recalled most of his troops to the Alexandria area. There he put into motion a plan of campaign he had developed weeks earlier and had revised several times since to conform to shifting circumstances. By the end of the month, Stuart's northernmost scouts were reporting that McClellan's command (now styled the Army of the Potomac, the same title Beauregard had bestowed on his army before Manassas) was boarding transports in its namesake river. The operation appeared to be the start of a mass movement south.

On April 2, Stuart informed James Longstreet, his immediate superior, that the embarkation was continuing. Within a few days he could report that the first wave of troops had come ashore at Union-held Fort Monroe, about seventy miles below Richmond. Evidently, George ("Little Mac") McClellan intended to march on the Confederate capital via the Virginia Peninsula rather than from the north. He was not about to repeat the miscues of his luckless predecessor, McDowell.[7]

*   *   *

There were few resources on the peninsula capable of stopping the 120,000 Federals at and en route to Fort Monroe. For a time the ironclad warship *Virginia* (a Confederate incarnation of a dredged-up Union steamer, *Merrimack*), had terrorized Union shipping in Hampton Roads. Had she maintained her local dominance, McClellan could not have reached Fort Monroe in safety, but on March 9 an equally ungainly Union ironclad, the *Monitor,* had battled *Virginia* to a draw after an all-day battle. Effectively neutralized, the Confederate warship retreated to Norfolk, where, early in May, Fitz Lee's father scuttled her to prevent her capture.[8]

The only remaining obstacle to McClellan's ascent on Richmond was the 13,500-man army of Major General John Bankhead Magruder in and about Yorktown. Magruder had stretched his lines so thinly across the peninsula that the 60,000 Federals who had embarked at Fort Monroe by the first week of April should have shredded them without effort. Instead, as befit his cautious bent and his engineering training, McClellan gave thought to besieging the city where the Revolutionary War had ended.

Little Mac's slow and methodical advance gave Joe Johnston the time he needed to reinforce Magruder. By April 4 Johnston was moving to Yorktown at the head of his 60,000-man army. For several days, however, Stuart's cavalry remained on the south side of the Rappahannock, where, it was feared, the Yankees were establishing a second front. When that prospect faded and Stuart turned south, he made a loping, roundabout march, as if Johnston and Magruder had all the horsemen they required. Not until April 8 did the cavalry chieftain move below Richmond, and not until the eighteenth did he reach Yorktown at the head of his command.[9]

The 1st Virginia arrived to find a siege well under way. Magruder had made dramatic use of his limited resources, marching his men across fields in full view of the enemy until sheltered by woods, whereupon they doubled back across the same ground. The impressionable McClellan feared he was facing an equal or greater number of troops. By the time he realized he had been cozened, Johnston's advance echelon was taking its place beside Magruder's people. Giving in to his initial instincts, Little Mac determined to lay siege to the port city.

Digging and occupying siege lines took time, and thus for the first two weeks of its service on the Peninsula the 1st Virginia, in common with the rest of Stuart's command, saw little action except at long range. Unwilling to dismount his horsemen and put them in the trenches, Johnston, who had assumed overall command at Yorktown, used them to picket his rear and right. Occasionally he had them patrol the area between the armies, studying McClellan's ever-expanding works and taking prisoners who could be gainfully interrogated.[10]

When not serving at the front, the cavalry, along with the rest of Johnston's army, devoted itself to politicking. The Confederate Congress had decreed that all regiments in the field—including those whose men had signed up for one- or two-year hitches—would be held in service for the duration of the conflict. To soften the blow thus dealt, each outfit was permitted to elect or reelect its field and line officers. The legislation gave Stuart an opportunity to divest himself of subordinates he considered incompetent, troublesome, or obstructive.

While Stuart had commended Grumble Jones for the recent achievements of his regiment, the colonel remained a baleful influence that had to be neutralized. Whenever possible, Stuart discreetly encouraged the officers of the 1st Virginia to vote Jones out of office. The logical alternative was Lieutenant Colonel Lee, whose popularity remained high throughout the regiment. Even without Stuart's behind-the-scenes influence, Fitz would have fared well in any competition. And so it came as no great surprise that on April 23, when the regiment-wide vote was held, Fitz displaced Jones as colonel of the 1st Virginia. The lieutenant colonelcy that Fitz vacated went to L. Tiernan Brien, a multitalented officer and a trusted member of J. E. B. Stuart's staff.

A majority of the rank and file rejoiced at the outcome. Even those who had not voted for Fitz expressed a cheerful willingness to serve under him. One of the few who decried the result was Jones himself, who left the regiment for Richmond a few days later vowing revenge against Stuart and exuding confidence that he would win reinstatement or promotion. He succeeded in the latter effort, although it took six months to gain the wreathed stars of a brigadier. In the interim, Jones was appointed to command another Virginia regiment, which he led in the Shenandoah Valley and later in the main theater of operations, again under Stuart.[11]

Another who regretted the outcome of the election was John Mosby. Aware that Fitz considered him too unmilitary to be a proper adjutant, the young lawyer immediately tendered his resignation, and Fitz just as promptly accepted it. Soon afterward Mosby was invited to join Stuart's headquarters, an offer he readily accepted. Apparently he expected a commission as a staff officer, but instead he served as a courier with no increase in rank. He seems to have blamed Fitz, not Stuart, for his "ambiguous condition," which lasted until year's end when he finally embarked on the career that won him success, fame, and the appellation "Gray Ghost."[12]

*   *   *

By the start of May, McClellan's siege works were nearly complete, and all but a few gun positions had been mounted and stocked with ammunition. He designated May 5 as the opening round of a tremendous, all-along-the-line barrage that would lay waste to Yorktown and send its occupants fleeing for their lives. Joe Johnston got wind of his opponent's timetable, however, and decided to play spoilsport. On the rainy afternoon of May 3, he began to evacuate his lines west of the city and head for the multilayered defenses of Richmond. There he could make a more effective stand against a numerical superior enemy.

In advance of the pullout, Stuart's troopers went into position to cover the rear and flanks of the retreat column. On May 3 the 1st Virginia had quit its most recent duty station, King's Landing on the James River, and had withdrawn to the other side of the peninsula. The movement marked the outfit's first operation in full strength under its new commander. Colonel Lee rode proudly at the head of the regimental column as it moved north and east toward Richeson's Landing on the York River, six miles below the village of West Point. From that vantage point, the 1st Virginia could report any waterborne attempt by McClellan to cut off his enemy's retreat—once he finally realized that a retreat was in progress.[13]

By midday of May 4, thousands of Union troops had poured into Yorktown, occupying Magruder's works and attempting to mount a pursuit. When finally launched, it was led by cavalry under George Stoneman, one of Fitz Lee's colleagues in the 2nd Cavalry, now a brigadier general of U.S. volunteers. Late in the afternoon Stoneman overtook the Confederate rear guard, which included Stuart's main body, on the outskirts of Williamsburg. The fighting this day was spirited, but it paled in comparison to that on the fifth, when McClellan's infantry came up to grapple in the rain with the divisions of Longstreet and Major General D. H. Hill. The day's combat, which cost McClellan twenty-two hundred casualties and his adversary sixteen hundred, failed to curtail Johnston's withdrawal to Richmond.[14]

The end run that McClellan made on the seventh via the York River in hopes of cutting off the Confederate rear guard near Barhamsville also failed. From their newly assigned position along the river near West Point, Fitz Lee's scouts warned Major General Gustavus W. Smith, whose command protected the right flank of the retreat column, of the approach of transports loaded with soldiers and protected by gunboats. Thus prepared, Smith sent an infantry division to Eltham's Landing, at the head of the York, to oppose the embarkation. The show of resistance cowed the invaders, who after feeble efforts to move inland pulled back to the safety of their gunboats. There they remained until Smith's troops fell in with the retreat column.[15]

The 1st Virginia had taken no part in the fighting at Williamsburg. It had provided only remote support to the foot soldiers engaged at Eltham's Landing before falling back to Slatersville, about thirty-five miles south of Richmond, late on the seventh. Two days later, however, the regiment, which had begun to cover the rear of Johnston's army, fought its first major engagement under its new colonel. That morning Stoneman's column, which had been dogging Stuart's heels since early the previous day, interposed between the Confederate horsemen and their infantry friends. For a time the attackers threatened to cut off a portion of the 1st Virginia from the rest of the regiment, but a wild ride cross-country saved most of its men.

Seeking revenge, Colonel Lee positioned his main body across the road from Slatersville and, when the head of the pursuit force came into view, had his bugler sound the charge. The attack so surprised the Federals—elements of the newly organized 6th U.S. Cavalry, portions of two infantry regiments, and a battery of light artillery—that they fled the scene, leaving behind seven men dead or wounded. An unknown number of survivors fell into the hands of Fitz's outfit, which reported a small loss of its own.

From the scene of its small but welcome victory, the 1st Virginia marched north to Saint Peter's Church, near Tunstall's Station on the Richmond & York River Railroad. Evidently, the check its advance had received at Slatersville had a cautionary effect on McClellan's entire army, which thereafter moved so slowly up the peninsula that Fitz's troopers remained at their new station for a full week. On May 16 they finally withdrew up the railroad to the defenses of their capital.[16]

Soon after it reached Richmond, Stuart sent the 1st Virginia north toward the Chickahominy River to patrol the countryside in the direction of Mechan- icsville and Brook Church. Once ensconced on the south bank of the stream, the regiment patiently awaited the arrival of the Army of the Potomac. By the seventeenth, Stoneman's advance guard was within spitting distance of the Chickahominy, but its main army did not complete its ponderous advance for another three days. As of the twenty-fourth, however, Union horsemen were probing upriver toward Mechanicsville, which told Fitz Lee that major fighting was imminent.

Preliminary actions took center stage during the next several days as detach- ments of the 1st Virginia clashed with Union cavalry and infantry engaged in the destruction of bridges on the Chickahominy and trackage on the Virginia Central Railroad. Some of the railroad demolition was conducted by Fitz's old Regular Army outfit, which had been redesignated the 5th U.S. Cavalry. Dur- ing these early actions, the 1st Virginia did not directly encounter the regiment whose ranks continued to include Jack Hayes, William Royall, and many other Northern-born troopers whom Fitz continued to regard as friends. Yet the colonel with the old-school attitude toward friendship must have wondered if they were fated to meet in combat in the not-too-distant future.[17]

*   *   *

At six-foot-four and more than 250 pounds, Johann Augustus Heinrich Heros von Borcke made a lasting impression wherever his huge, booted feet car- ried him. On the rainy evening of May 30, 1862, they carried him to the camp of the 1st Virginia Cavalry, where he hoped to meet his hero, J. E. B. Stuart. The Prussian-born soldier of fortune, member of an aristocratic family, son of a career army officer, had crossed the Atlantic by running the Union's shipping blockade. He had come to offer his services to the Confederacy, whose struggle for independence had struck a chord in his libertarian heart. An avid horseman and a veteran of his country's dragoon service, he desired a position on the staff of Stuart, whose exploits he had eagerly followed in the foreign press. His quest would be spectacularly successful. Of the dozens of foreign-born officers who migrated to America to join the Confederate forces, none would win more renown than Heros von Borcke.[18]

He may not have found Stuart on his first night in Virginia, but he did encounter Fitz Lee and his subordinates, who greeted their visitor warmly and made him an honorary member of the headquarters mess of the 1st Virginia. In his memoirs, von Borcke recalled that the colonel "received me with great kindness and hospitality and invited me to spend the night in his roomy tent. . . . A number of the regimental officers were gathered there, about to enjoy an excellent supper of turtle eggs. Spirits flowed freely. Later, one of the younger officers played jolly tunes on the banjo, and rollicking Soldier's songs resounded above the noise of the incessant thunder and rain rattling against the walls of the tent."[19]

Given a perfect opportunity to study his host, von Borcke was as impressed by Fitz's appearance as he was by his hospitality. He described him as "a short, thick-set man, with a tendency toward stoutness, but still a first-rate horseman. He had [a] fresh, intelligent face with an extraordinary full, flowing beard. He was characterized by an especially jolly temperament and an irrepressible sense of humor."[20]

Perhaps because he wrote long after the war, von Borcke appears to have erred in characterizing Fitz's physique, which at this stage of his life did not approach the corpulence it attained in later years. However, the Prussian did accurately depict other features of the colonel's appearance, including the luxurious beard that flowed more than halfway down his chest in contrast to the less hirsute look he had favored in the prewar army. Von Borcke was also on the mark when describing the outgoing personality and the great capacity for mirth that had accompanied Fitz from youth into adulthood.

Von Borcke enjoyed his first night as guest of the 1st Virginia, but he was absolutely delighted the following morning when, at Fitz's suggestion, he accompanied the eight hundred-man regiment as it marched through Richmond to the front. His Germanic heart "beat with joy when I caught sight of the magnificent troops ready to march. . . . The troopers, mostly fresh, tough young fellows, sat easily and elegantly in the saddle. One could see immediately that they had been dedicated to the sport of riding since their earliest years. . . . They owned their horses which were, without exception, noble, splendidly groomed animals, the likes of which I had never seen in my life. . . . With such material as this, one certainly ought to be able to perform outstanding achievements."[21]

When the 1st Virginia had passed through the city where cheering crowds bade it Godspeed, von Borcke left his new friends and rode off to find the general who would become his superior, patron, and friend. As per his orders, Fitz turned his men eastward and led them out one of the major thoroughfares toward its junction with the road to Williamsburg. Waiting up ahead was the main body of Stuart's command, which the 1st Virginia would join. The horsemen had instructions to guard the flanks and rear of their army's right wing, commanded by James Longstreet. The three-division column would play the pivotal role in a multipronged offensive devised by Joe Johnston, aimed at driving McClellan's army from the gates of Richmond before it could attack or lay siege to the capital. Longstreet's advance would be supported not only by Stuart's horsemen but also by the army's left wing, led by G. W. Smith, as well as by reserve forces under Magruder.[22]

The preponderance of strength opposite the Union left did not alter the overall numerical inferiority of the attackers. Thus Johnston's plan appeared not only a desperate gamble but an exercise in futility. But Johnston had perceived an opportunity in McClellan's faulty dispositions, the most glaring feature of which was the isolation of two of his five corps south of the rain-swollen river.

Johnston's strategic vision may have been sharp, but his battle plan was overly complicated and he failed to communicate it clearly to Longstreet. One result on the appointed morning was a near-fatal delay caused by Longstreet's moving out on the Williamsburg Road—which had been reserved for Hill's division—instead of his assigned route farther to the north. The error created crowding and confusion, causing an attack scheduled for dawn to be withheld until after 1 P.M. When finally launched, the assault routed many units on McClellan's left, but reinforcements shored up the break and prevented the flank from giving way. Throughout the afternoon fighting raged near Seven Pines on the Williamsburg Road, farther north at Fair Oaks Station on the York River Railroad, and at numerous points in between. It claimed thousands of casualties, including Johnston who was badly wounded, but it left neither army with a decisive advantage.[23]

While the opposing infantry clawed at each other, the cavalry waited restlessly in the rear and on the flanks of Longstreet's column, seeking but not finding a clear path to the front. Along with other regimental commanders and their common superior, Fitz Lee was frustrated and chagrined to find the ground in his area too rough and heavily wooded to permit large-scale mounted operations. Thus the 1st Virginia remained largely unemployed throughout May 31 as well as during the greater part of June 1, when the close-quarters combat that had died down at Seven Pines and Fair Oaks resumed in full fury. Early on the second day, when Longstreet failed to sustain an attack ordered by General Smith, Johnston's temporary successor, the battle tapered off without a clear victor.

Thus ended a frustrating experience for Stuart's command, and especially for the leader of his old regiment. At the outset, Fitz Lee had anticipated leading a regiment into battle for the first time. Instead only the infantry and artillery had seen action, of which there was much, and had reaped the glory, of which there was little.[24]

Soon after the dejected cavalry accompanied Longstreet's wing back inside the Richmond defenses, Fitz learned of a personnel change at the top of the army. Early on June 1, his uncle, who had spent the past three months at a desk job—military advisor to President Davis—had been appointed to succeed Smith in command of what would soon be widely known as the Army of Northern Virginia. While the botched, indecisive battle of the past two days was a cause of lingering disappointment to Fitz, as indeed to everyone else under Johnston, he took comfort in the knowledge that henceforth the army would be led by one who could develop a coherent battle plan and convey it clearly to his subordinates.[25]

But it would take the army time to get to know the new man at the top. About all it knew was that Lee had yet to achieve success either as a field leader or as a departmental commander. Late the previous year he had been at the center of a failed campaign in western Virginia, although the tactical situation had been a losing proposition from the outset and had revealed no tactical or strategic shortcomings on his part. A subsequent assignment to improve South Carolina's coastal defenses had failed to burnish the reputation that had faded in the Kanawha Valley—but he had been expected to accomplish too much with too few resources. Things would be different now. Fitz was confident that Robert E. Lee's considerable talents would assert themselves in his new position and that his efforts would be crowned not only with success but also with glory.[26]

*   *   *

Although Colonel Lee had been with his outfit for less than six weeks and had yet to direct it under fire, a few days after the army's return to Richmond J. E. B. Stuart recommended him for brigadier general. In a letter to Adjutant General Cooper, the cavalry leader cited his subordinate's "distinguished services, skill and ability" and called his promotion "important to the service." This last phrase was an indirect reference to the recent buildup of Stuart's brigade, which now consisted of seven regiments and legions with more units expected to be added quite soon. The manpower was sufficient to warrant organizing the command into a two-brigade division, each brigade to be led by a general officer. If Robert E. Lee approved the action, Stuart did not know whom he would appoint to the second vacancy, but he was certain that Fitz Lee was the man for the first.[27]

Stuart counted on his new superior to support any reasonable request he made. The two men had a long and close history dating to Stuart's West Point days, when Lee was superintendent of the Academy. They had teamed up in October 1859, when Lieutenant Stuart served as a volunteer aide to Colonel Lee, leader of the U.S. forces opposing John Brown's raid on the government arsenal and armory at Harpers Ferry, Virginia.[28]

Presumably, it was this long association that gave Stuart the courage to offer Lee the unsolicited advice he sent to army headquarters on June 4, 1862. Apparently he was afraid that the new commander would be influenced by past events to adopt defensive tactics, with disastrous results. Because "we have an army far better adapted to attack than defense," Stuart encouraged him instead to go on the offensive as soon as possible and offered some suggestions on how Lee might do so.[29]

Some recipients would have considered Stuart's letter the height of presumptuousness. Lee, however, took no offense and, instead, devised a mission for his cavalry leader. Upon reporting to him on the tenth, Stuart was gratified to learn that Lee had determined to "make a diversion to bring McClellan out" of his siege lines. Since the fight at Seven Pines and Fair Oaks, Little Mac had repositioned his army astride the Chickahominy, but the result left one of his flanks just as vulnerable as before—perhaps more so. Now it was McClellan's right wing—the V Corps of Major General Fitz-John Porter, holding the north bank of the river—that was isolated from its comrades across the stream. Lee, like Johnston, proposed to exploit this gaffe by throwing most of his troops against Porter while feinting toward the Union right and center with the few brigades stationed on the south bank.[30]

The Confederate leader required one piece of information before being able to strike. He had to know everything worth knowing about McClellan's upper flank—specifically, how many troops held the heavily forested strip of land between the Chickahominy and, farther north, the Pamunkey River, and where they were posted. He wanted Stuart, at the head of a body of fast-moving horsemen, to find out and report back to him as soon as possible.

The assignment, which would launch the first large-scale independent operation by the army's cavalry, so pleased Stuart that he offered to ride across the rear of the entire Army of the Potomac, fixing the location of each of its elements. Lee politely but firmly demurred, but he did give Stuart a couple of additional objectives: securing as much grain and livestock as he could find and capturing or destroying the supply trains that passed continually from McClellan's supply depots on the Pamunkey to the camps of his army. Lee cautioned Stuart, however, to move carefully. Unconfirmed reports suggested that the troops on McClellan's right—however many that was—had recently been reinforced.[31]

As soon as Stuart returned to his own headquarters, he set to work building an expeditionary force. At Lee's suggestion, he kept it small in order to facilitate speed and maneuverability. Because the object of the mission was intelligence, not battle laurels, he was expected to outrace, not outfight, the opposition. Stuart finally settled on four units, two of which were commanded by relatives of his superior—Fitz Lee's 1st Virginia and Colonel Rooney Lee's 9th Virginia Cavalry. The third component consisted of 250 members of the Jeff Davis

Legion under Colonel Martin. Stuart also decided to take six companies of the 4th Virginia, formerly commanded by Rooney Lee's brother-in-law, Colonel Williams Wickham, who was recuperating from a wound received at Williamsburg. Fearing to leave the detachment in the hands of junior officers, Stuart assigned four of the companies to Fitz Lee and the rest to his cousin. Accompanying the horsemen would be a Blakely rifle and a 12-pounder howitzer under Lieutenant James Breathed.[32]

In the predawn murk of June 12, the twelve hundred-man force rode north along the Richmond, Fredericksburg & Potomac Railroad, crossed the Chickahominy, and headed for enemy territory. Colonel Lee rode ramrod-straight in the vanguard side by side with his friend and commander, Stuart. Fitz did not know the specifics of the assignment—an unusual degree of secrecy kept Stuart's subordinates in the dark as to their objectives until the expedition was well under way. Even so, he was in high spirits, reflecting that Stuart had twice honored him—not merely by including the 1st Virginia in his plans but by enlarging it with Wickham's troopers. The inheritor of Stuart's old regiment vowed to comport himself throughout the operation in a manner that validated the confidence thus placed in him.

He had no opportunity to do so on the first day out, during which the raiding column covered twenty miles in a northward and then eastward direction without encountering any bluecoats. That night, Stuart bivouacked his units so close to Williams Wickham's plantation home that Rooney Lee and he spent some hours visiting the patient. Fitz Lee—now privy to Stuart's orders and intentions—remained with the troops in the role of acting expeditionary commander, a position that could be construed as yet another honor.

Early on the thirteenth, everyone was back in the saddle as the column angled southeastward in the direction of Hanover Court House and Old Church. By now even the least perceptive trooper understood that he had passed McClellan's right flank and was trotting along in the Union rear. Approaching unknown territory, every rider moved warily but with a degree of confidence and aplomb that validated J. E. B. Stuart's efforts to maintain esprit de corps.[33]

Fighting flared as the column approached its first objective, historic Hanover Court House, where Patrick Henry had begun his career as a revolutionary. Scouts from Rooney Lee's regiment, riding in the advance, sent back word that a body of blue-clad horsemen—which turned out to be part of the newly formed 6th U.S. Cavalry—occupied the village and its environs. Unable to determine the size of the force and unwilling to hit it head-on, Stuart turned to Fitz and ordered him to detour around and into the enemy's rear. Once he had, Stuart would charge the Yankees with the 9th Virginia, driving them into Fitz's arms and opening the road to Old Church.

Fitz saluted smartly, quickly briefed Lieutenant Colonel Brien and other subordinates, and led the 1st Virginia south. The regiment's outriders located a

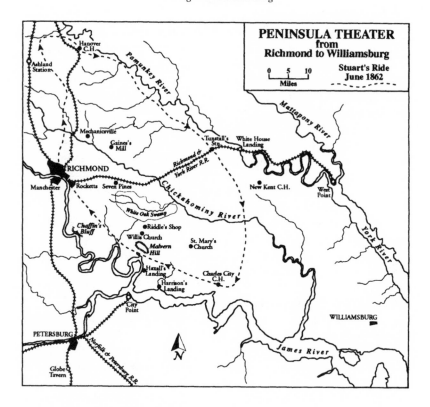

byroad that led in the proper direction, and this the regiment took. Unfortunately, the road also led through a thick marsh, which so slowed the outfit's
progress that it failed to reach its objective before Stuart's attack hit home. Dislodged from their position, some 150 members of the 6th Cavalry raced past
the 1st Virginia down the southward-leading road to Mechanicsville.[34]

Fitz was mortified by his failure to bag the quarry, but there was no help for
it. He ordered a pursuit, but the enemy's retreat was so rapid and roundabout
that Stuart called off the effort. The column resumed its journey toward Old
Church, first by the main road, then by a side road through Taliaferro's Mill and
Enon Church to Haw's Shop. At the latter site—which many of Stuart's men
would revisit two years hence, an experience few of them would ever forget—
Rooney Lee's regiment gobbled up mounted pickets from a company of Regulars who had been patrolling the local area for the past several weeks. Spying a
larger contingent of that regiment a short distance farther east, the main body
of the 9th Virginia, Stuart at its head, charged the Federals, mixed with them
briefly, and drove them as a body toward Totopotomoy Creek. A dogged pursuit enabled the 9th to overtake the runaways and secure additional captives.

Minutes later, the 1st Virginia caught up with the charging troopers of the 9th. When the latter's prisoners were escorted to the rear, Fitz Lee was delighted to discover they were members of his old regiment. Dismounting, he mingled freely with the captives, several of whom—once they peered beneath the gray uniform and the thicket of facial hair—greeted him like the old comrade he was. Lieutenant John Esten Cooke of Stuart's staff recorded the improbable reunion: "I could not refrain from laughter at the pleasure which 'Colonel Fitz' . . . seemed to take in inquiring after his old cronies. 'Was Brown alive? Where was Jones? And was Robinson sergeant still?' Colonel Fitz never stopped until he found out everything. The prisoners laughed as they recognized him. It was difficult to believe that the Union prisoners and the dashing young colonel represented opposing armies mustered to slaughter each other."[35]

While the friendly enemies swapped tales of times past, other raiders drove the fugitives of the 5th U.S. Cavalry across Totopotomoy Creek and, on the other side, down the road to Old Church. At a crossroads two miles in advance of the latter village, the Regulars were joined by the main body of their regiment and made a stand. The combined force barely had time to form, however, before being struck by the charging, shouting troopers of Rooney Lee. The fierce saber and pistol duel astride the crossroads resulted in the death of one of Rooney Lee's captains, the severe wounding of the senior Union officer, and the resumption of the 5th Cavalry's retreat. A few hundred yards down the road the Regulars attempted to rally once again, but when the more numerous Virginians caught up to them, they fled all the way to Old Church.[36]

Before Stuart could resume his pursuit, Fitz rode up and asked permission to forge on ahead to Old Church, site of the 5th Cavalry's camp—he wished to pay a personal call on his old outfit. Undoubtedly he also saw an opportunity to amend for his failure at Hanover Court House, but he sincerely wished to mingle with other members of the old 2nd Regulars.

So many of those he had campaigned with on the frontier had accompanied him into the Confederate ranks. Major Earl Van Dorn was now Major General Van Dorn, an army and departmental leader stationed in Mississippi. Fitz's old company commander, Edmund Kirby Smith, was currently serving in east Tennessee; he too had risen to major general and departmental command. George Cosby, who had extracted the arrow from Fitz's chest at Crooked Creek, was a colonel of cavalry in the western theater and six months away from promotion to brigadier general. Fitz's close friend Manning Kimmel was serving on the staff of General Braxton Bragg, one of the ranking Confederate leaders in the West. But other ex-comrades including Jack Hayes and William B. Royall remained with the outfit. Hayes was still a bugler, although seven months hence he would accept a commission in a volunteer cavalry regiment from Ohio. He had not been involved in today's fighting, but Fitz was saddened to learn that Royall was the officer who had been wounded by the 9th Virginia.[37]

Permitted by Stuart to act on his impulse, Colonel Lee led the 1st Virginia toward Old Church at a pace both brisk and cautious. Finding the better part of the 5th Cavalry drawn up to defend its camp, Fitz's leading ranks spurred into a charge that for speed and verve equaled anything the 9th Virginia had accomplished this day. Their eyes agog at the sight, the undermanned Federals evacuated the area with all possible haste. Though determinedly pursued, they managed to ford Matadequen Creek to safety.

In the wake of their departure, Fitz rode through the camp the Regulars had abandoned, which teemed with tack, weaponry, and edibles including the fixings of a midday meal they had lacked the time to consume. After several minutes given over to taking spoils, the 1st Virginia was joined by Stuart, Rooney Lee, Martin, and Breathed. It was also joined by residents whose village had been occupied for weeks by Yankees on patrol. They greeted Stuart's people as deliverers, shouting out their gratitude and joy. Some of the ladies presented Stuart, Fitz, and many of the other officers with bouquets of spring flowers. Fitz Lee felt like a conquering hero—which, perhaps, he was.[38]

*　　*　　*

Already the raiders had ascertained what Robert E. Lee had sent them to find out. The fact that a single understrength cavalry regiment patrolled the country between Hanover Court House and Old Church told Stuart that McClellan's right flank was unanchored. Bodies of all arms, some small, some heftier, were reported to be elsewhere in the general vicinity, but much closer to the river. By all indications, they could be turned out of their positions by such an offensive as the commander of the Army of Northern Virginia was contemplating.

All that remained was for Stuart to return to Richmond. If he acted prudently, he could do so without incurring more losses than he already had—one officer killed, perhaps twenty men wounded. The logical choice was to go by the way he had come. But as if R. E. Lee's injunction against such a move had never registered with him, Stuart determined to continue across the enemy's rear and slip around McClellan's left. He was persuaded to do so not only because of the pleasurable risk the proposition entailed but also because en route he could sack the Army of the Potomac's bustling supply base at Tunstall's Station on the York River Railroad, thereby meeting another objective Lee had given him.

When Stuart revealed his decision to his subordinates, each of them, including the usually adventurous Fitz, voiced his disapproval. No one could foresee the dangers that lurked along Stuart's proposed route, although rumor had various pursuit forces hot on his trail. In fact, elements of several cavalry regiments, supported by units of infantry and artillery, had mobilized to run the raiders to earth. Ironically, most were commanded by George Stoneman's senior subordinate, Brigadier General Philip St. George Cooke, the father of Stuart's wife,

Flora. If the forces moved fast enough and cooperated with each other, they would give Stuart's people a large helping of trouble.[39]

But the potential hazards they represented never materialized. Several factors combined to defeat Cooke and his men, including logistical deficiencies, faulty intelligence, poor communication, and a laggardly pace—the result, perhaps, of the general's fear that if he pressed his son-in-law too closely he might be captured by him. Therefore, in a sense, what followed the fighting near Old Church smacked of anticlimax. By midday on June 13, Stuart was already home free on his circuitous route to Richmond.

He made the most of the ride that remained. En route to Tunstall's Station, he captured several supply wagons bound for McClellan's army, which he relieved of weapons and rations. Late on the thirteenth, one of Fitz's squadrons, assisted by an equal number of the 9th Virginia, plundered and burned the small supply base at Garlick's Landing, on the Pamunkey. While fires still raged at Garlick's, Stuart, with Fitz and the main body, swept down on Tunstall's Station, stunning and capturing its feckless garrison, downing telegraph lines to prevent an alarm from being spread, and felling trees across the railroad to stop incoming and outgoing trains. As soon as the last defender had surrendered, Stuart's men were hard at work torching, axing, or otherwise destroying a vast array of military stores.

By early evening, with the demolition nearly complete, Stuart pondered his next move. Eventually, reluctantly, he rejected an idea he had hatched hours earlier—to continue up the tracks to McClellan's supply hub at White House on the Pamunkey. Even larger than Tunstall's Station—and consequently better guarded—its capture would have been a coup for any raiding leader. But such an undertaking might overburden his command; it would certainly delay Robert E. Lee's receipt of critical intelligence. Thus, late in the day, Stuart put his column on a southeastward-running road and led it toward Sycamore Springs, where he planned to recross the Chickahominy.[40]

The next leg of the journey was an especially debilitating one. Benumbed by near-constant travel and with the attention-riveting excitement of battle behind them, the men of the 1st Virginia began to doze in their saddles, coming awake only when prodded by comrades or struck in the face by low-hanging branches. It appears that their commander fell asleep as well, for at some point that evening Fitz and his men briefly lost contact with the rest of the column and almost wandered off on a shadowy byroad. The error was discovered before it could cause trouble, but other problems prevented the vanguard from reaching Sycamore Springs until well after sunrise on the fourteenth.[41]

A shocking sight greeted the raiders at the river. The water level at the ford where Stuart had been advised to cross was running so high from recent rains that it was impassable. Surveying the freshet from the soggy riverbank, Fitz Lee shook his head in dismay. Even Stuart appeared to give in to gloom, telling Esten Cooke, "Well, Lieutenant, I think we are caught." He huddled with his ranking subordinates, but no one came up with a viable solution. Perhaps Stuart's father-in-law would yet bag them all.[42]

At the suggestion of some of his enlisted men, Stuart rode a mile downstream to study the ruins of a bridge recently destroyed by the Yankees. There the water level was low enough that expert swimmers and their horses might straggle across, but no one else. After lengthy deliberation, Stuart ordered Fitz's men to strip the lumber from a warehouse and other nearby buildings. Under the direction of Stuart's engineers, squads of troopers-turned-pioneers fashioned these materials into a temporary bridge and laid it on the intact abutments of the original span.

In something under three hours, the makeshift bridge was sufficiently in place to permit dismounted men to cross and deposit their equipment on the south side of the river. Additional hours were consumed by the main body crossing afoot while their horses swam the river alongside them. More timbers were then added to permit the temporary span to bear the weight of Lieutenant Breathed's cannons and teams. By 1 P.M., the main force had gotten across, whereupon Stuart's rear guard, a large detachment of the 1st Virginia, crossed to the south side, Fitz being the last man over. Minutes later, Rooney Lee's men burned the bridge to prevent the nearest pursuers—just now coming into view in the distance—from using it.[43]

Via Charles City Court House and New Market, Stuart's raiders made it safely through the last miles of Yankee-infested country, capturing pickets and bypassing larger outposts. After another night of slumber on the edge of no-man's-land, they passed inside Confederate lines early on June 15. While Stuart rode on ahead to bring the information he had gleaned to the man who would make the best use of it, Fitz Lee conducted the column through the streets of Richmond where, for the second time in three days, he received a rousing welcome from a throng of well-wishers. By midday Fitz had divested himself of the baggage collected on the hundred-mile circuit of McClellan's army: 164 prisoners; 250 horses, beef cattle, and other animals that would help meet the transportation and nutritional needs of Lee's army; hundreds of stands of arms taken at Garlick's Landing and Tunstall's Station; and enough ammunition to supply those weapons during a month's worth of service.[44]

The operation that had just ended—the first large-scale cavalry raid of the war in the eastern theater—would gain for the participants, and especially their ranking officers, a huge measure of acclaim. Newspapers North and South— even those whose editors were ignorant of the true value of the expedition— would laud all involved for their pluck, daring, endurance, and courage.

A certain amount of this praise, especially that served up by the Richmond-area journals, attached itself to the commander of the 1st Virginia, who accepted it with becoming modesty. At the same time, Fitz did not fail to remind himself of the recent sins of omission and commission of which he had been guilty, especially his failure to bag the 6th Regulars at Hanover Court House and the inattention that nearly permitted his outfit to wander off on the homeward leg. J. E. B. Stuart had proven himself a veteran raider throughout the operation. Fitz could not say the same of himself—he had much to learn about the business. He may not have had a reputation for diligent study, but this was one subject he intended to master.

If he found it easy to accept praise for himself, he was just as adept at awarding it to others. In his June 17 summary of his regiment's part in the expedition, he cited by name only one member of his outfit, an enlisted man who, although badly wounded, had cut down a Yankee officer in a dramatic close-quarters confrontation. Still, he could not conclude his report "without certifying to the highly creditable manner in which both officers and men bore the danger and fatigue of a trip which has yet to be excelled—a noble band of circuit-riders."[45]

FIVE

Brigade Command

If Fitz Lee was guilty of missteps on the recent expedition, they had not cost him Stuart's confidence or regard. In an appendix to his own report of the raid, the cavalry leader sought promotions for those subordinates he considered deserving of them. Number one on the list was Fitz, of whom Stuart wrote: "In my estimation no one in the Confederacy possesses more of the elements of what a brigadier of cavalry ought to be than he." The endorsement warmed the recipient's heart, solidified his already close relationship with his superior, and made him vow to strive even harder to become worthy of such praise.[1]

He would have the chance to do so soon enough. On learning from Stuart about the unanchored Union right, Robert E. Lee recalled Thomas J. Jackson to his side for support in the offensive he was about to launch. Early in March he had dispatched the officer now known as Stonewall to the Shenandoah Valley to oppose a Union force that had captured Winchester. Jackson's presence there was intended to prevent further losses as well as to keep the Yankees from augmenting McClellan. He had accomplished his mission so spectacularly that late in May a full corps of reinforcements earmarked for the Army of the Potomac had been shunted westward to oppose Jackson. The last-minute shift of resources sent McClellan into a towering rage and slowed his once-confident advance on Richmond.[2]

When Jackson fell back in the face of the new arrivals and appeared suddenly quiescent, President Lincoln agreed to recall the corps and send it to McClellan by overland march from Washington. Porter's infantry, supported by most of Stoneman's cavalry, had been sent to the north side of the Chickahominy to facilitate the expected linkup. In his isolated position, however, Porter furnished

Robert E. Lee with an objective whose overthrow might drive the Federals from the gates of Richmond. Lee's plan called for throwing at Porter more than sixty-five thousand troops of all arms—the divisions of Longstreet, D. H. Hill, and Major General Ambrose P. Hill, supported closely by Jackson's fifteen thousand foot soldiers and the majority of Stuart's horsemen. Meanwhile, General Magruder, with the rest of the army—fewer than twenty-five thousand men—would make a bold diversion south of the river. Since Magruder's troops would be opposed by twice their number, Lee's strategy rested on an immense gamble, but one he felt compelled to take. The probable alternative was the slow, agonizing death of his army by siege and starvation.[3]

Lee put his plan in motion on June 25, the same day that McClellan launched a sharp but indecisive strike against the Confederate right near Oak Grove, the first of the so-called Seven Days' Battles outside Richmond. The next morning it was Lee's turn to attack. Given the careful preparation that had gone into the effort, the result should have been much more satisfying than it turned out to be. In fact, the offensive, directed against Porter's men at Mechanicsville, fared just as poorly as McClellan's drive toward Oak Grove. Ironically, the outcome was largely the fault of Jackson, whose success in the Shenandoah against three Union armies had made him the most famous Rebel east of the Mississippi.

Stuart, on the other hand, could not be blamed for any miscues this day. Adhering precisely to his orders, late on the twenty-fifth the cavalry, "without baggage, equipped in light marching order and three days' rations in haversacks," marched through Richmond, heading north toward Ashland Station on the Richmond, Fredericksburg & Potomac. Stuart moved at the head of a two thousand-man column consisting of the regiments of Fitz and Rooney Lee; the Cobb Legion, named for its commander Colonel Thomas R. R. Cobb; and Pelham's horse artillery. Two other components of Stuart's command—the 4th Virginia and the Jeff Davis Legion, currently on reconnaissance along the South Anna River, above Richmond—would join the main body at Ashland.[4]

The Cobb Legion was a recent addition to Stuart's growing command, as were some of the outfits he had left behind to support Magruder: the 3rd, 5th, and 10th Virginia and the cavalry squadron of the Hampton Legion. The latter unit—which would soon be recruited to regimental size—was the mounted contingent of a South Carolina force of all arms that had been bankrolled, recruited, and led to war by a nonprofessional soldier, Wade Hampton III. Hampton, reputedly the richest planter in all the South and one of its largest slaveholders, had proved to be such a talented field leader that he had risen to brigadier general of infantry. The cavalry squadron that formerly reported to him was commanded by another citizen-soldier of inherent military ability, Major Matthew Calbraith Butler (although this day the unit was led by one of Butler's company commanders).[5]

With Fitz's 1st Virginia leading the way, Stuart's column struck the Brook

Turnpike north of Richmond, crossed the meandering Chickahominy via Upper Bridge, then moved on to Ashland. There, as planned, it met the advance of Jackson's "foot cavalry," which had left the Valley a week earlier—just in time to participate in the most critical offensive in the early history of the Army of Northern Virginia. The infantry had gone into bivouac by the time Stuart reached the railroad. The cavalry leader placed his regiments in Jackson's left rear and then went to confer with the colleague with whom he had been cordial since their pre-Manassas service together in the Valley. Jackson's march down the north side of the Chickahominy had placed his men in near-perfect position to strike Porter's exposed flank, and Stuart, based on his scouts' observations, assured him that no major obstacle lay across his proposed path of attack.

At dawn on the twenty-sixth, as other elements of the Army of Northern Virginia farther south waited to go forward, Stuart's column passed along the length of Jackson's left flank, screening it from enemy view and probing the Yankee lines up ahead. The 1st Virginia again held the post of honor at the forefront of the column, Fitz Lee at its head with the newest member of Stuart's staff, Lieutenant Heros von Borcke, riding beside him. Also in the vanguard was a second trooper on loan from cavalry headquarters, John Mosby. Although Fitz continued to look askance at the man's deportment, he had to admit that Mosby was one of the ablest scouts in Stuart's employ. The lawyer from Bristol had proven as much on the recent excursion inside McClellan's lines, where his tracking skills and intimacy with the Chickahominy River country had aided Stuart immensely.[6]

Not far beyond Ashland, Fitz's outfit began to clear roadblocks, human and inanimate, from Stuart's path. These included a picket post near Taliaferro's Mill whose occupants fled after spraying an ineffectual volley at the head of the regiment. From this point to as far as a crossroads in front of Jackson's column where Stuart halted to wait for the infantry, the 1st Virginia experienced constant skirmishing. In his postaction report, Stuart lauded the regiment for displaying "the same courage . . . which has already distinguished it on so many occasions, killing and wounding several of the enemy without suffering any loss."[7]

From the crossroads Stuart sent a squadron of the 1st Virginia, under Captain Charles Irving, ahead of the rest of the regiment to seize a partially dismantled bridge on which Jackson intended to cross Totopotomoy Creek. A dismounted attack in front by the 1st Virginia and in flank by Rooney Lee and Pelham drove off its defenders. The success permitted Captain Blackford, now Stuart's chief engineer, to supervise fatigue parties of the 1st Virginia in repairing the bridge. The work consumed barely thirty minutes, whereupon Jackson crossed and moved out on the road to Cold Harbor, well beyond Porter's exposed flank. Stuart's men took the lead, heading for a familiar site—Old Church.[8]

By midafternoon Jackson's men were in position to strike, unhinge, and roll up Porter's line, making McClellan's position astride the Chickahominy extremely perilous if not untenable. Instead, while fighting raged to the south, Jackson did nothing. When his scouts reported that Porter's position had been reinforced and that A. P. Hill, who was supposed to have attacked on the right, was nowhere to be found (tired of waiting for Jackson, he had struck other sectors of Porter's line), Stonewall remained immobile, then pulled back and went into bivouac. It is true that Jackson was not his usual self this day, benumbed by days of overwork and nights without sufficient sleep. Still, his conduct was inexcusable as well as potentially disastrous to his army.[9]

Even without his help, the fighting ended in the Confederates' favor. Although Porter held his ground throughout the day, he was so badly battered that after nightfall, when he finally learned of Jackson's proximity, he fell back three miles to Gaines's Mill, an old granary along a Chickahominy tributary known as Powhite Creek, where he dug in for another stand.

If Stuart had been surprised or dismayed by Jackson's physical fitness or mental condition, he made no mention of it in his report of the day's action. On the morning of the twenty-seventh, as on the previous day, he prepared to support Jackson in battle. At least today Stonewall was moving to the sound of the guns, crossing Beaver Dam Creek and trudging toward Porter's new position. Diverging somewhat from that route, Stuart made a sweeping circuit to the east via the Old Church Road and then southeastward toward the Union right rear. "All day long," he remarked, "we were skirmishing with, killing and capturing, small detachments of the enemy's cavalry," including members of the only lancer regiment in Union service, the 6th Pennsylvania.[10]

At Old Cold Harbor, a mile and a half east of Gaines's Mill, Stuart returned to Jackson's flank only to be told to remain there, in a reserve position, when the fighting commenced. Jackson's order must have disappointed Stuart, but the cavalryman had to admit that the ground stretching toward Porter's position was unsuited to the free movement of horsemen. As a result, Fitz Lee and his comrades spent the balance of the day listening to Jackson's infantry and artillery grapple with their counterparts in blue. The only segment of Stuart's command to see action was Pelham's battery, which late in the afternoon advanced to counter an artillery movement against the cavalry's right flank. With what Stuart called "a coolness and intrepidity only equaled by his previous brilliant career," Pelham silenced two batteries through the incessant and well-directed fire of a single 12-pounder Napoleon, later augmented by some of Jackson's guns.[11]

The fighting at Gaines's Mill, like that of the twenty-sixth, was, for the better part of the day, bloody but indecisive. Toward evening, however, the Confederates opposite Porter's left breached the defenses in their front, opening the entire position to overthrow. In gathering darkness, Porter's harassed and exhausted soldiers fled to the north bank of the James River. Support troops tried to stem the rout, but to no avail. Later Fitz Lee was shocked and saddened to learn that a forlorn-hope counterattack by the former 2nd Cavalry cost it sixty casualties without strategic recompense. The debacle would end the field career of the officer who had engineered it, Stuart's father-in-law, Brigadier General Cooke. Fitz probably reflected that a cavalryman of Cooke's experience ought to have foreseen the futility of throwing 250 mounted men against thousands of well-armed foot soldiers.[12]

Soon not only the V Corps but virtually all of McClellan's troops were retreating below the Chickahominy. After burning the bridges they had crossed, they continued their multicolumn withdrawal, via White Oak Swamp, to the James. There they could huddle under the protective fire of their gunboat fleet.

Because many Federals south of the Chickahominy held their positions following Porter's retreat, and because it did not seem logical that McClellan would end his offensive after one or two defeats, Robert E. Lee remained uncertain of his enemy's intentions for more than twenty-four hours after Gaines's Mill. He believed that his opponent, if truly withdrawing from the Chickahominy, would move not south but up the Richmond & York River Railroad, his line of communications, to White House, his base of supply. Thus, early on the twenty-eighth, Lee called J. E. B. Stuart to his field headquarters and instructed him to move down the river and then out along the railroad, destroying that supply line as he marched. Based as it was on an erroneous assumption, Lee's decision would effectively remove his mounted arm from the scene of action for the balance of the campaign.[13]

In company with Dick Ewell's division, Stuart dutifully started for the railroad. At Dispatch Station, nine miles from White House, units of Fitz Lee's regiment and others tore up track and cut the telegraph wires by which, presumably, McClellan was directing the movements of his scattered army. Then the cavalry forged onward to the familiar site of Tunstall's Station, which they occupied—this time without resistance—for the second time in two weeks.

Learning that elements of Stoneman's command were near White House, Stuart anticipated a brisk confrontation when he reached that bustling depot. He would have to face it alone, for he had forged on ahead of Ewell's slow-moving infantry. He had no inkling that as he rode, quartermaster's and commissary personnel were putting final touches to the evacuation of White House and the transfer of its supplies to the James. Stuart began to grasp the true state of affairs only after he overtook well-stocked forage wagons, escorted by a handful of cavalry, trundling south from White House. The wagons were duly captured and their guards scattered; so too were the occupants of picket posts along the roads to the depot.[14]

From the sights visible up ahead—especially the smoke clouds climbing above distant trees—Fitz Lee must have suspected what he and his comrades would find at the river. His cousin, who for years had lived nearby and whose comfortable, white-washed home had given the landing its name, must have had the same suspicions—to his dread. The smoke continued well into the afternoon, by which time the dismantled bridge over Black Creek had been captured and was under repair by pioneers from Fitz's regiment. While the bridge work went on, the rest of Stuart's column bivouacked. Throughout the night his men's slumber was challenged by crashing explosions from White House, where the flames had reached ammunition stockpiles.

When Stuart's men pulled up at the depot on the morning of June 29, they found a vast expanse of charred debris. The fires had consumed not only supplies and equipment that the Federals could not carry off but also Rooney Lee's house, which his wife and children had fled before McClellan's coming.[15]

Some Union stragglers were found at the base appropriating whatever they could salvage from the flames. Their only source of protection was a gunboat, USS *Marbelhead,* anchored offshore. For a time the vessel threatened Stuart's ability to assess the local situation, but steps were quickly taken to neutralize her. At his superior's order, Fitz dismounted one of his companies, which he led, in unison with sharpshooter units from the other regiments, down to the river. There his men began peppering the gunboat with rifle fire. The volleys drove crew members from her deck, but *Marblehead* did not weigh anchor and churn downriver until one of Pelham's cannon began to throw shells in her direction.[16]

Their three days' rations having been consumed, Stuart's men gratefully partook of the few provisions they recovered from the ruins. While the main body ate or slept, some of Fitz's scouts scoured the riverbank for signs of enemy troops, however distant. Other elements of the 1st Virginia set to work destroying those stores that the Confederates, for whatever reason, could not take with them and that the flames had failed to consume.

From the captive stragglers as well as from local residents, Stuart learned what he already suspected—that McClellan had moved his base of supply to the James. He communicated the information—rather belatedly, as it would turn out—to General Lee's headquarters. Then, having completed his work on the Pamunkey, he wheeled his column back toward the Chickahominy. Reaching that stream on the afternoon of June 30, the 1st Virginia pulled up at Long Bridge, while the rest of the column scattered along the river in the direction of Forge Bridge. Fitz's scouts reported enemy pickets on the far side, while comrades near Forge Bridge discovered both infantry and artillery opposite them. To counter these forces, Stuart divvied up Pelham's battery, parceling out pieces to his regiments. To the 1st Virginia he assigned a single Napoleon. Fitz trained it on the pickets, but with the first shot the gun's trail broke, rendering the piece unusable. Even so, the Yankees eventually disappeared from his front, while Pelham, by an accurate fire from some of his other guns, drove off the foot soldiers and horsemen at Forge Bridge.[17]

The next morning Stuart received a communiqué from army headquarters fixing McClellan's position near Malvern Hill, a lofty eminence close to the north bank of the James, and directing the cavalry to cross the Chickahominy and fall in on the flank of the main army. Even as he moved to comply, the sounds of a distant battle reminded Stuart just how far from the scene of decisive fighting he had ridden in pursuance of his June 28 orders. Over the past three days, while his brigade operated well to the north and east, the armies had grappled fiercely on the road to the James—at Savage's Station and Allen's Farm on the twenty-eighth and along White Oak Swamp the following day.

Nor was the bloodletting done. On the morning of July 1, a substantial portion of McClellan's army was fighting a rear-guard action atop Malvern Hill. The high ground, the hundreds of sharpshooters positioned along its slopes, and especially the one hundred cannons that crowned its summit, made the position impregnable. Yet even as Stuart rode south to the sound of musketry and cannon fire, Lee was attacking the crest in waves—with disastrous results. By day's end, the Army of Northern Virginia would have suffered almost fifty-five hundred casualties, compared to thirty-two hundred for its opponent, and McClellan's army would be safe at home at Harrison's Landing on the James. George McClellan had been driven from the suburbs of Richmond, but he maintained a foothold within striking distance of the city.[18]

*   *   *

By July 2 Stuart was within sight of the James, and his troopers were in contact with Jackson's infantry for the first time in five days. On the third, Stuart probed McClellan's new position on the river. Approaching an outlying encampment without being detected, on a whim he had Pelham shell the position from atop a plateau known as Evelington Heights. The cannonade caused havoc until Union artillery got Pelham's range and sent his gunners scurrying. The affair did not put Stuart in good odor with his infantry colleagues, who considered it a foolish stunt. If nothing else, it made him look like he was seeking revenge on an enemy that had made him look foolish by eluding him for almost a week.[19]

Over the next several days, the cavalry—including Fitz Lee's regiment, now stationed near Charles City Court House—continued to keep watch on McClellan's riverside base, but at a more respectful distance. For several days in a row, Fitz's report to Stuart was the same: nothing of importance appeared to be going on there. By July 9 Robert E. Lee had persuaded himself that his adversary would not retake the road to Richmond anytime soon. That day he led the better part of his army toward the capital, leaving a couple of infantry brigades, supported by some of Stuart's battalions, to keep tabs on the fugitives at Harrison's Landing.[20]

By July 12, after pitching and then striking a series of camps in Charles City

County, the 1st Virginia accompanied Stuart's main body north of Richmond, putting down roots near Atlee's Station on the Virginia Central Railroad. En route, Fitz stopped in the capital to visit his refugee family. He also took the time to look up old acquaintances incarcerated in the city's military prisons. The conditions he found at Libby Prison appalled him, and the sufferings of its inmates moved him greatly.

Fitz was particularly distressed by the plight of one of his West Point instructors, Major Henry B. Clitz of the 12th U.S. Infantry, who had been wounded and captured at Gaines's Mill. After Fitz rejoined his regiment at Atlee's, he wrote to Robert E. Lee about the deplorable situation facing Clitz and numerous fellow officers. Aroused by his nephew's humanitarianism, the army leader expressed a desire to help but explained that the solution lay with George B. McClellan. Lee had written his counterpart proposing to "parole and send to him all his wounded if he would receive them." After some delay, arrangements to that end appeared to have been settled; moreover, the Federals had tentatively agreed to a formal prisoner of war exchange: "I hope in this way much relief will be afforded." The elder Lee added, however, that "Friend Clitz ought to recollect that this is a matter of his own making, and he has only to blame himself. I will still be happy to do for him all I can, and will refer your letter to the director of the [Libby Prison] hospital if I can find him."[21]

By the fourteenth, the 1st Virginia Cavalry had returned to the daily routine of drill and dress parades, which it had not experienced since the outset of the Seven Days' Battles. The predictable regimen lasted barely a week before Stuart had his command pull up stakes yet again and follow him five miles up the railroad to Hanover Court House. There, at last, Fitz's regiment went into fixed camp.

While at the courthouse, Stuart received authorization from Richmond to organize his growing command into a division, which he would command with the rank of major general. Enough units were available to support two brigades, each led by a brigadier general. Acting on his long-held inclination, he put forward Fitz Lee's name, and on July 25 his choice was promoted to the rank in order to assume command of Stuart's first brigade. When Stuart sent Fitz his appointment, he attached a cover note: "Please accept Gen R. E. Lee's and my own congratulations on the within but . . . I reserve the 'main body' of my congratulations for myself and the Country in having such a Brigadier."[22]

Given his superior's high regard for him, Fitz naturally supposed that his informal status as Stuart's ranking subordinate would be officially recognized. Stuart thought so, too, for when he sent army headquarters a proposed table of organization for his new command he identified Brigadier General Lee as commander of his 1st Brigade. Robert E. Lee, however, did not approve of the arrangement, for it implied that Fitz was senior to another of Stuart's subordinates—one who had worn the wreathed stars of a brigadier for more than two months.[23]

This was Wade Hampton III, the newest member of the cavalry, Army of Northern Virginia. His arrival had been arranged by Jefferson Davis as a means of rectifying an unusual and, by all indications, unjust personnel action. Following exemplary service at Seven Pines/Fair Oaks, where he had received his second wound (the first had come at Manassas), Hampton had gone to his home in South Carolina to recuperate. Upon returning to the army, he had found his infantry brigade broken up and parceled out to four others. During the Seven Days' Battles he had temporarily led one of Jackson's brigades, but when its original commander returned Hampton was again out of a job. He had switched arms of the service strictly to retain the rank he had worked so hard to earn.[24]

In the minds of many of Stuart's officers, Hampton was not a fit candidate for a high position in the cavalry. It was true that he was an accomplished administrator, a strict disciplinarian, and an unflappable combat commander as well as an expert horseman, a master swordsman, and a dead shot with a pistol. But he was forty-four, twenty years older than many of the dashing roughnecks he would lead in the mounted arm; moreover, he lacked a military education and, prior to 1861, military experience of any kind. Finally, it was common knowledge that Hampton disdained the cavalier mind-set of Stuart, Fitz Lee, and others who could view war as both a disgusting bloodbath and a glorious pageant. He would be as much out of place in his new branch of service as a gunboat in a desert.

But not everyone felt this way. Hampton made a formidable first impression on many open-minded observers, including John Esten Cooke. The staff officer was equally struck by the man's physique ("straight, vigorous, and stalwart, but not too broad for grace") and his demeanor and behavior (he possessed "a certain grave and simple courtesy which indicated the highest breeding. He was evidently an honest gentleman who disdained all pretense and artifice"). In turn, Hampton—despite his preconceived impressions and his settled intent to leave the cavalry the moment a vacancy opened up in his former arm—developed a favorable opinion of many of his new colleagues. He found that he could work closely and comfortably with Stuart, whom he came to regard, for all his foppish inclinations, as an honorable gentleman as well as a gifted tactician, an inspiring leader, and an expert intelligence gatherer.[25]

Within days or weeks of his arrival at Hanover Court House, Hampton had allayed the concern of many that he was too old, too rigid, and too much the foot soldier to find his niche in the cavalry. One exception was Fitz Lee, who neither initially nor later approved of the newcomer. Although the source or sources of this attitude remained unknown, they may be surmised. First of all, Fitz regarded the South Carolinian as an interloper, a Johnny-come-lately whose only qualification for his new position was his friendship with Jeff Davis. Moreover, instead of coming up through the ranks of his adopted profession, Hampton had bought his way into Confederate service. Without formal training in either arm, he had succeeded to high rank first in the infantry service and now in the cavalry—higher rank than Fitzhugh Lee, who had earned his position through rigorous training and years of exemplary service in two armies. Quite possibly, Fitz was also jealous of the seniority that had been handed to Hampton as if on a silver platter—seniority that would give him close and regular access to Stuart. That access might someday enable him to unseat Fitz Lee as Stuart's closest advisor and confidante.

Other possible reasons for Fitz's early and continuous dislike of Hampton had a social context. As the proud member of an old and distinguished, albeit somewhat impoverished, Virginia family, Fitz, either consciously or unconsciously, may have looked down on a Cotton Belt pedigree that appeared to be built more on wealth and possessions than on breeding, culture, and public service. Finally, given his ambiguous attitude toward slavery, he may have tended to disdain one who owned many thousands of chattels. If Fitz betrayed even a hint of these attitudes, his new colleague would certainly have taken offense, and his resentment would have had a long life.

*   *   *

After Robert E. Lee prodded Stuart to change the numerical order of his brigades, Hampton took over the 1st Brigade. As befit his roots, he was given command of every non-Virginia regiment in the division, including the 1st North Carolina, the newly created 2nd South Carolina (an expanded version of the cavalry arm of Hampton's old legion), the Cobb Legion Cavalry, and the horsemen of the Jeff Davis Legion. A Virginia regiment, the 10th, was temporarily added to Hampton's command, apparently to balance out the five regiments that were assigned to Fitz Lee.[26]

Those five were among the oldest and most notable units of horse in Confederate service: Fitz's old 1st Virginia, now led by the recently promoted Colonel Brien and Lieutenant Colonel Drake; Colonel Thomas F. Goode's 3rd Virginia; the 4th Virginia, nominally commanded by the still-recuperating Williams Wickham and in his absence by South Carolina-born Colonel Stephen Dill Lee (no relation to the Virginia Lees); the 5th Virginia, under a recent transferee from the mounted artillery, Colonel Thomas L. Rosser; and Rooney Lee's 9th Virginia. With the regiments came a brace of staff officers, many of whom would serve Fitz for months and years to come. They included Surgeon John B. Fontaine, the brigade medical director, as well as Major Robert F. Mason, Captains Thomas S. Bowie and J. D. Ferguson, and Lieutenants Garland M. Ryals and Charles Minnegerode. An additional aide-de-camp joined the staff on July 30—twenty-year-old Lieutenant Henry C. Lee, who would continue to serve as aide-de-camp to his older brother Fitz until May 1864.

From the start, Fitz enjoyed the close cooperation of each of his regimental and legion commanders, and the comradeship of most. If his subordinates ever thought to resent their general's promotion—they would have been forgiven for ascribing it to Fitz's friendship with his immediate superior, or to his blood ties to the army's commander—they were careful not to express their views in the company of the less discreet. In truth, such attitudes would have done Fitz an injustice. If anyone suspected that family or professional ties explained his rise to brigade leadership after only three months in regimental command, he had only to look at the new general's résumé, which included a credential that none of his subordinates possessed—a West Point diploma. Furthermore, only one of those lieutenants, Rooney Lee, had frontier military experience, brief as it was, to match Fitz's—and Rooney would have been the last person to criticize someone for tapping his family connections.

Each of these subordinates and their outfits would accompany Fitz into the field in the next imminent campaign of the Army of Northern Virginia. George B. McClellan might have been neutralized—it seemed doubtful that in his present position he would again menace Richmond—but a new danger to the continued existence of the Confederacy had recently materialized one hundred miles to the west. This was an army of fifty-one thousand, created from the three corps-size armies that had failed to bring Stonewall Jackson to heel in the Shenandoah. Designated, rather presumptuously, as the Army of Virginia, on June 26 it had been assigned to Major General John Pope, a West Pointer and an experienced engineer and explorer. Although the new man was wont to consider himself a military genius and enjoyed saying so to anyone who would listen, he was a mediocre strategist and tactician whose only claim to high rank was a series of minor victories on the Mississippi, credit for which should have gone to his subordinates. In time his arrogance and boastfulness would alienate not only many of his own troops but also the soft-spoken Robert E. Lee, who would brand Pope a "miscreant" whose hard-war attitude toward Southern civilians "must be suppressed."[27]

The primary mission of Pope's new command was to help capture Richmond, either through its own efforts or by supporting a renewed drive on the capital by McClellan. The Army of Virginia was also enjoined to cover both the Shenandoah Valley and Washington, D.C. Its initial objective was the Virginia Central Railroad, via which Lee's army tapped the abundant resources of the Shenandoah, the "Breadbasket of the Confederacy." Pope was expected to threaten the railroad by moving against Gordonsville and Charlottesville, a plan he began to implement within two weeks of assuming command.[28]

Robert E. Lee reacted to Pope's advance exactly as the Washington officials had anticipated. By mid-July, as the Army of Virginia marched on Gordonsville, the Confederate leader detached Jackson and prepared to send him west to counter the new threat. Lee felt that he could do so because McClellan's army remained largely quiescent on the James, as scouts from Hampton's new brigade continually reported. (Hampton's and Fitz Lee's regiments had been alternating service on two fronts: at Hanover Court House, where they drilled at the camp of instruction, and in Charles City County, where they continually scouted and skirmished with the enemy.)[29]

In mid-July, Jackson's troops entrained for the Gordonsville–Orange Court House vicinity, reaching there on the nineteenth. On August 9, after days of long-range sparring aimed at keeping the Federals away from the Virginia Central, they gave battle to a portion of Pope's army near Cedar Mountain (also known as Slaughter Mountain). The latter name seemed more appropriate given the heavy casualties that accrued from the all-day clash, during most of which Jackson's opponent enjoyed the tactical advantage. A last-minute counterattack by the Light Division of A. P. Hill salvaged a draw, but it had been a near thing. Even from his distant vantage point, R. E. Lee appreciated that Jackson would be in hot danger should Pope concentrate against him.[30]

A sudden movement by McClellan helped Lee manage the difficult situation. By the first week in August, Hampton's scouts were reporting the evacuation of the Army of the Potomac, by land and water, from Harrison's Landing to points north—a prelude, undoubtedly, to reinforcing Pope. Lee saw an opportunity to hasten west and strike the Army of Virginia before Pope joined with Little Mac to create a blue-clad juggernaut.

By the middle of August, plans were afoot to send the rest of Lee's army—Longstreet's command—to join Jackson in Pope's front. Lee would leave behind two and a half divisions of infantry, with artillery attached. This force, under overall command of Gustavus Smith, would monitor McClellan's departure and counter any last-minute movement against Richmond. McClellan's timidity and diffidence were well known, but Lee felt that he had to take into account any contingency.

Lee's mounted arm—much of it, that is—would accompany Longstreet west. Before it did, however, there was a mission closer to home that Stuart felt compelled to take on. Army headquarters, as well as refugees from Stafford County, had long complained about enemy strikes from Fredericksburg against the Virginia Central. Always troublesome, those raids now threatened to be calamitous, the railroad being the single transportation link between Jackson's command near Orange Court House and the army around Richmond. On an earlier occasion, Stuart had set out to punish the raiders but had been defeated by high water and bridgeless streams. Since then a strategic bridge had been restored to operation, rendering the operation feasible. "I soon saw," he wrote, "that there was no repose for my command at Hanover Court-House" until he tried again.[31]

On the morning of August 4, Stuart set out for the railroad via Bowling Green and Port Royal on the Rappahannock. He was accompanied by the 2nd Brigade, plus Pelham and the horse artillery. Fitz was gratified to have been selected for the assignment—the latest of many indications of Stuart's high regard for his services. He was also quietly pleased that Hampton had been relegated to the less glamorous mission of monitoring McClellan.

At Port Royal on the fifth, Stuart's outriders snatched up a dozen cavalry pickets. Turning toward Fredericksburg, the column gained the historic Telegraph Road the next morning. Near Massaponax Church, south of the town, they spied the rear guard and supply wagons of a sizable column—two infantry brigades and some cavalry, evidently bound for the Virginia Central. Stuart gave Fitz free rein, and the new brigadier spurred his men forward in an all-out charge. They struck, Stuart wrote, "like a thunderbolt upon the enemy." Within minutes they were attacking the Union rear "in both directions, capturing baggage wagons and prisoners, who are thronging already my presence."[32]

While his other regiments secured spoils on wheels, Fitz hurled elements of the 3rd and 4th Virginia at the rear guard of the six thousand-man expedition. Flailing about with swords and pistols, they broke up that force and sent its fragments scrambling up the road to Fredericksburg. Many were overtaken and compelled to surrender; the rest were permitted to escape after a brief but productive pursuit. In the end, Stuart took eighty-six prisoners plus "11 fine wagons and teams complete, besides about 15 cavalry horses, arms, and equipments." An unknown but substantial number of Yankees had become casualties, while Stuart had lost two men mortally wounded. After securing their spoils, Stuart and Fitz returned to Bowling Green, where they spent the night. The next day, they were on their way back to Hanover Court House.[33]

Throughout the return trip everyone was in good spirits, the result of a mission well and faithfully performed. Yet few—perhaps none—experienced as much self-satisfaction as Fitz Lee, who on his maiden outing as a general officer had proven himself worthy of his current station in the army. He doubted that Wade Hampton could say the same.

SIX

"I Cannot Spare
Genl Fitz Lee"

On August 8, one day after his return from chastising the railroad marauders, Stuart traveled alone to Jackson's headquarters near Orange Court House. He returned one week later, having inspected Jackson's cavalry at the behest of Robert E. Lee. He found that in his absence Lee, with Longstreet's infantry, had headed west. Lee had hoped to meet with his cavalry leader before leaving Richmond, but he feared that the window of opportunity against Pope was closing too quickly to defer his departure.

Stuart spent barely twenty-four hours at Hanover Court House before orders called him west once again, this time in the company of his staff. Before he left, he briefed his subordinates on their short-term responsibilities. The 2nd Brigade and the horse artillery were to join him as soon as possible. Fitz should outfit and provision the two commands for a several-day campaign, then lead them by overland march to the army's new theater of operations. He was to meet Stuart at Raccoon Ford on the Rapidan River, twelve miles northeast of Orange Court House, on the afternoon of the seventeenth.

To Fitz's delight, Hampton's brigade would be left behind, remaining on station between Richmond and Charles City Court House and keeping watch over the still-withdrawing Army of the Potomac. It would turn west only after the defeated enemy had disappeared from its front.[1]

Fitz probably viewed Stuart's dispositions as another sign of his superior's reliance on him over his senior colleague from South Carolina. And yet it was

74

perfectly understandable that a subordinate new not only to Stuart but also to cavalry service should be spared from combat duty. By placing Hampton in a relatively quiet sector, Stuart was giving him the time he needed to assimilate the basics—and perhaps learn some of the nuances—of the technically complex arm he had joined.

Stuart claimed to have impressed upon Fitz the necessity for speed in moving to the Rapidan, but for some as yet unknown reason, his favorite subordinate failed to get the message. After Stuart had entrained a second time for Jackson's bailiwick, Fitz moved off to an unconscionably slow start. The delay was not due to the demands of supplying his troops, for it appears they started out with half-full haversacks and cartridge boxes. When finally under way, the column moved at a deliberate pace; moreover, it deviated from the direct route to Raccoon Ford in order to stop over at Louisa Court House, more than twenty miles from the rendezvous with Stuart. There Fitz caught up with his supply wagons, which had been sent ahead of his column. It appears he took his time distributing the rations and ammunition they carried.

On this occasion, as on others when he moved slowly or erratically when celerity and precision were required, Fitz Lee made no effort to account for his behavior. In later years he made a single published reference to the stopover at Louisa, claiming that he had not understood "from any directions received that it was necessary to be at this point [Raccoon Ford] on that particular afternoon [the seventeenth], and had marched a little out of his direct road in order to reach his wagons." This was hardly an explanation, although by writing in the third person he invested the account with a sense of detachment, as if he had been caught up in events beyond his control.[2]

The wayward march had near-dire consequences. On the afternoon of the seventeenth, Stuart left Lee's new headquarters at Orange Court House and, accompanied by John Mosby, Heros von Borcke, and other officers, set out to meet Fitz. The party halted at New Verdiersville, on the Orange Plank Road within hailing distance of Raccoon Ford. There Stuart and his party waited—and waited. Fitz and his men did not appear that day or the following morning, but a Union cavalry patrol did. Early on the eighteenth, a band of Michigan troopers—members of the brigade of John Buford, one of the war's finest cavalry officers—splashed across the Rapidan and swept through Verdiersville. Learning that Stuart was in town, they came within minutes of nabbing the general and his retinue. He escaped on foot but so precipitately that he left behind his crimson-lined cape, plumed hat, and other items of clothing easily identifiable as belonging to the "Beau Sabreur of the Confederacy."

The Yankees crowed over these prizes, but they were astonished and elated over another capture: Stuart's slow-footed adjutant, Major Norman FitzHugh, whom they found in possession of confidential papers, including a recent letter from Robert E. Lee to Stuart describing the imminent junction of Longstreet and Jackson. The document also mentioned a plan Lee was about to put in motion, aimed at turning the left flank of the Army of Virginia near its headquarters at Culpeper Court House. Lee's idea was to thrash Pope's troops before they withdrew north of the Rappahannock River to unite with McClellan's army. The letter was so eye-popping that Buford's men returned at once to their side of the Rapidan, Major FitzHugh in tow. Placed in Pope's hands, the document alerted him to the looming threat and persuaded him to turn toward the Rappahannock fords.[3]

His near-capture left Stuart not only embarrassed but livid with rage, emotions that deepened once he learned of Pope's fallback and the subsequent cancellation of Lee's turning movement. Quick to praise those whose performance reflected positively on his command, Stuart could be just as quick to condemn those who brought upon it censure and ridicule. When Fitz's brigade finally reached the Rapidan late on the eighteenth, Stuart treated him to some of the most caustic criticism ever unleashed against a subordinate. He repeated it, albeit in less vituperative language, in his report of the campaign, effectively blaming Fitz for costing the Confederacy a chance to win the war in one stroke of strategic genius.[4]

Fitz's reaction to Stuart's tirade can only be imagined, for he failed to record it either then or later. He would have felt mortified, condemned, even stigmatized. For a time, he must have believed himself under a cloud of official disapprobation, which he could escape only through some feat of extraordinary skill or daring. His only hope was that he could make amends to the satisfaction of Stuart, Robert E. Lee, and everyone else privy to the details of his unconscionable blunder.

*　　*　　*

As it happened, Robert E. Lee merely postponed and redirected his movement against Pope's flank. Although his enemy was now in full flight to the Rappahannock, Lee intended to beat him there—or, failing that, to cut off Pope's rear guard and force it to stand and fight south of the river. The Army of Northern Virginia would cross the Rapidan in full force, Longstreet's wing on the right, Jackson's farther west. The cavalry would precede both columns, angling toward Stevensburg—Pope's current location—and, beyond, Rappahannock Station on the Orange & Alexandria Railroad.

Before dawn on the twentieth, as ordered, Stuart moved his troopers from their most recent bivouac, near Mitchell's Ford, to the north bank of the lower river. Fitz Lee's troopers and Pelham's gunners crossed at Raccoon Ford, while a second brigade that had been furnished Stuart for this campaign splashed across at a more westerly point. The latter command, which for some months had been serving with Jackson, was the focus of Stuart's recent inspection tour. Jackson, who had been unhappy with the support he had received from the brigade, had initiated Stuart's mission by communicating his displeasure to Robert E. Lee.[5]

As he informed Lee, Stuart had come away impressed with the fighting quality of Jackson's mounted arm, which consisted of four regiments and one battalion of Virginia cavalry and a battery of horse artillery—with one exception. He recommended the replacement of its commander, whom he considered not only incompetent but also incapable of gaining the confidence of his troops. This opinion tallied with that of Jackson, who had already called for ousting the officer in favor of a more inspiring horseman—Fitzhugh Lee. It had taken a personal letter from Fitz's uncle to persuade Jefferson Davis to refuse Jackson's request. As the army leader told his president, "I cannot spare Genl Fitz Lee, as by so doing it will defeat the object of his promotion. Viz his services here" in Stuart's command. But the army leader offered no alternative to his nephew.[6]

The officer at the center of the continuing controversy was Brigadier General Beverly Holcombe Robertson, a West Pointer, a prewar dragoon, and Williams Wickham's predecessor as colonel of the 4th Virginia. Robertson had lost that position after falling afoul of Stuart, who early on had formed the opinion that the man was temperamental, erratic, and obtuse. Their relationship was reminiscent of another personality clash involving Stuart and a disgruntled subordinate—Colonel William E. Jones, commander of the 7th Virginia Cavalry, ironically now serving under Robertson.

Wishing to keep an eye on both of his troublesome lieutenants, Stuart accompanied Robertson's brigade while allowing Brigadier General Lee free rein in his sector. The arrangement hinted that Stuart had put his recent outburst, and the incident that had provoked it, behind him. He was willing once again to place his trust in the leadership abilities and tactical judgment of his favorite lieutenant.

It was well that Stuart was so inclined, for Fitz's mission was a difficult and delicate one. His assigned route placed his brigade in early and continual contact with the rear of Pope's main column—forces of all arms, including the veteran cavalry of Buford. To permit their army to reach the Rappahannock in one piece, the blue troopers engineered a skillful delaying action. Their fight and fall back tactics prevented Fitz from having a clear shot at them until they reached the riverbank, where they drew up in line, dismounted, to cover the crossing of their comrades. Finally presented with an immobile target, the 2nd Brigade, covered by Pelham's cannons, attacked Buford's position. With swords, pistols, carbines, and other shoulder arms they felled several defenders, captured almost as many others, and seized a trophy especially prized by cavalrymen, a regimental guidon.[7]

Fitz's troopers might have accomplished even more, but at the height of the melee Stuart summoned a major portion of the brigade to his side. Midway between the O & A depot of Brandy Station and the Rappahannock, Robertson's brigade had encountered a feisty, well-led, and apparently larger body of Union cavalry in line of battle atop a ridge. Then, and later after falling back to Rappahannock Station, the Yankees put up a stiff fight. Robertson's column having outdistanced its artillery, the horse battery of Major R. Preston Chew, Stuart was at a decided disadvantage. As he later wrote, the ground between the opposing forces "was such that cavalry alone could not have attacked the enemy under such protection [as the Federals enjoyed] without sacrifice inadequate to the risk."[8]

Thanks to the pluck and determination of Robertson's forward units—including Grumble Jones's regiment, as Stuart was forced to admit—the brigade held its position until Fitz's people reached the scene, Pelham close on their heels. The Federals, their numerical advantage suddenly gone, turned and galloped to the river. Before Fitz's sharpshooters and Pelham's gunners could get their range, they splashed through the water under a covering fire from infantry on the north bank. By now it was late afternoon, and darkness was approaching. The enemy gone, the race lost, Stuart could do nothing but concentrate his force and await the coming of Jackson and Longstreet: "The remainder of the day," he noted succinctly, "was devoted to rest."[9]

But not everyone in gray enjoyed a respite. From the north side of the river, Yankee pickets kept up a long-range fire, forcing Fitz to answer in kind. While the indecisive duel went on, Fitz interrogated some of the prisoners his command had taken. From them he learned to his surprise that for the past couple of hours Robertson's men, then his own, had been grappling with a brigade of New York, Pennsylvania, and New Jersey cavalry commanded by his dear friend from West Point days, now-Brigadier General George Dashiell Bayard.

*   *   *

The next day, with Jackson's infantry within supporting distance, Stuart tried to turn the enemy's right flank by forcing a crossing at Beverly Ford, two and a half miles north of Rappahannock Station. This was not a good idea, principally because Stuart lacked an appreciation of how well that sector was defended—which was quite strongly. Not surprisingly, the effort failed. Robertson's brigade handled most of the work and suffered accordingly; only one of Fitz's regiments—the 5th Virginia, under Colonel Rosser—was involved, and it managed to scramble back across the stream on the approach of two brigades of Union infantry and a light battery.[10]

The following day, Robert E. Lee made an attempt similar to Stuart's but with Dick Ewell's division of Jackson's wing as the primary force. Although Ewell crossed well upstream from Rosser's ford and enjoyed cavalry support, the mission failed when that sector, too, proved to be well defended. Frustrated, anxious, desperate to find some way to smite Pope before thousands of reinforcements reached him from the Potomac, Lee decided that his next move would be a wide thrust into the Union rear, punctuated by a strike at Pope's main supply line, the O & A. An unexpected blow at his communications might force the braggart in blue to evacuate the high ground and accept battle on more level and open terrain.

Since Stuart had proposed the wide-area envelopment, it was fitting that he should spearhead it. On the morning of the twenty-third, he set out with seven of the nine regiments at his disposal, backed by a two-gun section of Chew's battery. This time he moved far enough upstream to circumvent Pope's right. Crossing the river at Waterloo Bridge and Hart's Ford, he directed his fifteen hundred troopers and horse artillerymen toward Warrenton, ten miles inside Pope's lines. As he had done when encircling McClellan's army on the Chickahominy, he moved gingerly, warily, alert to the possibility of being blocked, cut off, or even surrounded, but for all that confident in the power and maneuverability of his command.[11]

His column may have been stealthy, but it was not invisible. Detecting its approach, the Federals who had been occupying Warrenton for the past several weeks fled before forced to fight for their survival. As at Old Church two months earlier, upon entering the town the raiders were hailed as deliverers by a local populace that offered them many comforts while alerting them to outposts, camps, and supply depots in their path. Armed with this information, Stuart decided to advance on Pope's rear headquarters at Catlett's Station, seven miles to the east, where hundreds of supply wagons were parked, ripe for plundering. In addition to despoiling that lightly guarded depot, he intended to destroy a railroad bridge over Cedar Creek.

Leaving Warrenton late in the afternoon under a steady rain, the column reached Auburn, within easy reach of its destination, after dark. The advance guard alertly captured a picket post, preventing an alarm from reaching Catlett's Station. Then it was on to the depot, which Stuart's vanguard reached on the drizzly morning of August 23. By now Stuart had divided his command to strike several targets. At his signal, the columns charged the depot as well as the trackside village adjacent to it.

The 2nd Brigade had been assigned to hit the camp of the local garrison. Shouting and shooing, Fitz's men thundered through the streets of the tent city, collapsing canvas dwellings and scattering their sleep-befogged occupants. Most surrendered on the spot, but several took refuge in nearby woods. Meanwhile, other elements of the brigade made for the Cedar Run bridge only to find it impervious to damage. The continuing rain, which intensified as the morning went on, prevented efforts to burn its planking, while axes and hatches made little impression on its iron superstructure.[12]

Forced to concede failure in this effort, Stuart contented himself by reviewing the magnitude of his spoils, which included not only a vast amount of rations, forage, weaponry, ammunition, and equipment but also John Pope's personal baggage wagon, containing among other items one of the most splendid dress uniforms Stuart had ever seen. At Fitz's request, Stuart allowed him to appropriate the gilt-encrusted ensemble, which he enjoyed modeling. A few days later, when his brigade was supporting a detachment of Jackson's command, Fitz hailed a passing friend, Major General Charles Field, and told him he had something to show him. One of Field's officers recalled that as the general dismounted, Fitz "slipped behind a big oak-tree, and, in a moment or two, emerged dressed in the long blue cloak of a Federal general that reached nearly down to his feet, and wearing a Federal general's hat with its big plume. This masquerade was accompanied by a burst of jolly laughter from him that might have been heard for a hundred yards."[13]

Other spoils inspired not laughter but expressions of wonderment, including a safe containing hundreds of thousands of dollars in Yankee greenbacks and ledger books crammed with official papers. One volume held documents at least as important as those Stuart's adjutant had been relieved of at Verdiersville. They not only revealed the location of various elements of the Army of Virginia but also gave details of McClellan's pending reinforcement of Pope's army.[14]

Stuart's unexpected and destructive raid had long-term benefits for his army. Although it did not force Pope to quit his station on the Rappahannock, it did make him overly sensitive to the safety of his communications. It also prompted Robert E. Lee to dispatch Jackson's wing on the same roundabout route into Pope's rear. Once Jackson gained a lodgment in that quarter, Lee would accompany Longstreet and the rest of the army to a junction with him.

Stuart's horsemen would make the journey as well, in support of Jackson. By the morning of the twenty-fifth, the Catlett's Station raiders, towing a gigantic cache of booty and dozens of prisoners, had returned to Lee's side. That night Stuart conferred with the army commander, who issued orders governing the cavalry's role in the coming operation.

Shortly after 2 A.M. on the twenty-sixth, Stuart's command was again in motion—this time at full strength, including Pelham's battalion. At first in the rear of Jackson's column, then on its right flank, they supported the infantry as it crossed the river at Henson's Mill, passed the villages of Orlean and Salem, debouched through the Bull Run Mountains to Haymarket and Gainesville, forded Broad Run, and swept down on enemy-held Bristoe Station. Part of Robertson's brigade captured the depot via an old-fashioned saber charge.[15]

En route from Gainesville to Bristoe, Stuart detached Fitz Lee's brigade to run down a forage train bound for Pope's army, an assignment accomplished without incident. Jackson took note of this minor feat and determined to enlarge upon it. Soon after dusk, he ordered Stuart to proceed up the railroad to Manassas Junction. At that landmark of the war's first battle, Pope's army maintained a major supply depot that Jackson wished seized in order to provision his underfed and poorly clothed command.

Stuart saluted and started off on the mission, accompanied mostly by Robertson's troopers; the only component of Fitz's command that went along was the 4th Virginia. Led this day by Williams Wickham, finally recovered from his Peninsula wound, the regiment moved by a circuitous route at the rear of the depot while Stuart and Robertson approached it frontally, followed at a distance by one of Jackson's brigades.

Soon after dawn on the twenty-seventh, with Wickham in his assigned position, Stuart attacked the junction from three sides. As at Catlett's Station, the assault took the local garrison by such surprise that at least three hundred of them surrendered on the spot or soon thereafter. Within minutes, the depot and its vast riches ("millions of stores of every kind," as Stuart described them) were in the hands of the attackers. While infantrymen and troopers helped themselves to whatever they could eat, drink, wear, or use, comrades rounded up would-be escapees, a pastime Stuart termed "great sport."[16]

Sometime in the late morning or early afternoon, Pope's troops crashed the party. Advancing along the north side of the river, a brigade of New Jersey infantry challenged Stuart and Jackson to a rifle and artillery duel. The fight quickly went against the Jerseymen, especially after their commander, Brigadier General George W. Taylor, fell mortally wounded. In the end, they retreated in wild haste up the railroad.

Early in the fracas, Stuart sent Fitz, with the 4th and 9th Virginia, backed by a portion of Robertson's command, on a detour to the north and west in the direction of Fairfax Court House. Stuart hoped Fitz would cut off and capture the retreating enemy and also descend on the railroad, damaging it enough to make supplying Pope's army from Washington a Herculean task.[17]

Fitz's mission proved to be almost as difficult. The trip to Fairfax, much of it made in evening darkness, carried his regiments across Bull Run and, once on the north side, "over fences, across ravines and through swamps." Reaching the courthouse at sunrise on the twenty-eighth, Fitz's advance gobbled up some pickets, apparently the only Yankees in the area. Beyond the town, however, the little column thudded into a larger force of blue-jacketed cavalry, part of Pope's rear guard. Fitz learned that the Army of Virginia was falling back from the Rappahannock toward even more defensible ground in the vicinity of Centreville. At his command, Rooney Lee charged the Yankees, eventually driving them back on an infantry force that had been supporting them at a distance. The fight quickly degenerated into a standoff. The long-range skirmishing accomplished nothing, and so Fitz recalled his cousin's regiment and withdrew it beyond rifle-shot.[18]

The enemy presence around Fairfax Court House prevented Fitz's main body from accomplishing anything of substance. Two side expeditions also came up empty. A company of Wickham's regiment, which Fitz had sent to destroy the O & A bridge over Cub Run, chased off a fifty-man guard but was itself shooed away by a roving body composed of units of all arms. Yet another Union column forced the retreat of a detachment Fitz had sent to tear up the railroad near Burke's Station, ten miles west of Alexandria, his hometown.[19]

After bivouacking for the night, the frustrated brigadier wheeled about to rejoin Stuart and Jackson. During his absence, the latter had moved north from Manassas to a point above the Warrenton Turnpike. The previous afternoon and evening, Jackson had grappled fiercely with one of Pope's divisions west of the village of Groveton, leading the withdrawal to Centreville. Losses had been heavy on both sides, and although the Federals had drawn off near midnight, they would return in greater force thanks to John Pope's erroneous assumption that he had Lee's entire army cornered above Groveton. Pope was unaware that Lee and Longstreet were marching rapidly toward a linkup along Jackson's right flank.[20]

On the twenty-ninth, the 2nd Cavalry Brigade recrossed Bull Run and made a long, roundabout march to Groveton. Some time during the afternoon, Fitz took up his assigned position near Sudley Mill on Jackson's left flank. There he was reunited with the regiments he had left at Manassas, the only exception being Rosser's, then on detached service farther south.

Fitz and his men remained in position throughout the next day, August 30, when Pope, having concentrated opposite Groveton, launched a series of uncoordinated frontal assaults against Jackson's line. Although inflicting heavy casualties, the effort failed to drive Stonewall from his breastworks north of the turnpike.

The ground Fitz occupied on the thirtieth—like his position at Seven Pines/Fair Oaks—was insufficiently open and flat to offer cavalry an opportunity to earn its pay. He was held relatively idle throughout the first day of the battle and again on the thirty-first when Longstreet, having slipped into position, undetected, on Jackson's right, dealt the Federals a staggering blow. On the other side of Jackson's line, however, less wooded terrain near Lewis Ford enabled Stuart, on the second day of the fight, to hurl a portion of Robertson's brigade at Buford's cavalry. Under Stuart's close supervision, Robertson routed Buford's brigade and wounded its leader.[21]

Longstreet's attack unhinged the Union left and rolled it up toward the center of Pope's line. Unable to stanch the tide of defeat, a dazed Pope ordered a withdrawal. By late afternoon, his army was streaming across Bull Run, a somewhat more orderly reprise of McDowell's retreat over much the same ground little more than a year ago.

Robert E. Lee proposed to cap his smashing victory with a dogged pursuit. At first, however, only his infantry took up the chase. Finding the roads in front of him blocked by foot soldiers, batteries, and wagons, Stuart bivouacked his troopers for the rest of the day. At midday on the thirty-first, his way clear at last, he started for Fairfax Court House, Centreville, and Chantilly—brief stopovers on the enemy's flight to the Washington defenses. En route he was joined by Wade Hampton, whose brigade, having certified McClellan's withdrawal from the Peninsula, had been released from guarding Richmond.[22]

Despite their late start, Fitz's troopers, now united with Robertson, moved so quickly up the Little River Turnpike that they outpaced Pope's rear guard on a parallel road. Coming in behind it, the brigades teamed to strike a Union outpost about three miles from Fairfax Court House. Supported closely by Robertson, Fitz's command surrounded a squadron of the 2nd U.S. Cavalry—the erstwhile 2nd Dragoons—and captured it intact.

One of those forced to surrender, Captain Thomas Hight, was an Old Army comrade of his captor. Fitz had the man ride beside him as the pursuit continued; they chatted animatedly throughout the ride, telling jokes, swapping memories, inquiring after mutual friends. This was war as Fitz Lee knew it—deadly, destructive, and cruel, to be sure, but also finite. Sooner or later, all wars ended. True friendships never did.[23]

*   *   *

On September 3, two days after his advance echelon botched an effort to cut off Pope's rear guard at Chantilly, the commander of the Army of Northern Virginia put in motion a plan he had been contemplating for some time. With Pope resting and regrouping around Washington, Lee began to shift his forces toward the upper Potomac near Leesburg. By early on the fifth, infantry, cavalry, and artillery were fording the river and setting foot in southern Maryland.

Lee hoped to winter his army in the Old Line State, which, having been spared the rod of war, abounded in fertile fields, well-stocked barns, and silos bursting with grain. He also hoped to recruit from among the Southern sympathizers residing in lower Maryland who were believed to be eager to enter his ranks. There was even a possibility that a Rebel presence next door would force Lincoln to husband his troops for the defense of Washington, thus relieving Virginia of their destructive presence.[24]

As soon as the movement toward Leesburg began, Stuart supported it energetically. At his command, the brigades of Lee, Hampton, and Robertson (the latter temporarily led by Colonel Thomas T. Munford of the 2nd Virginia) demonstrated loudly and often across a several-mile front in hopes of keeping any pursuers at bay. They must have believed they had accomplished this purpose, for the only troops to press them were a few cavalrymen under George Bayard. Stuart surmised that Pope's army had been so demoralized and disorganized by its defeat that it would not leave its works for days, if not weeks.

When it did, however, it would leave its commander behind. Relieved of duty at his own request pending a court of inquiry into his conduct at Manassas, Pope had been superseded by George McClellan. For lack of a viable alternative, Lincoln and his secretary of war, Edwin McMasters Stanton, permitted Little Mac not only to regain field command of his own army but to merge it with what remained of Pope's. On September 7 the Young Napoleon—as he continued to be known in a dwindling number of circles—led the combined force out of the capital on a slow and cautious course toward the Potomac.[25]

Upon entering Maryland, Stuart passed through Poolesville en route to Urbana. Near the latter village, Fitz Lee, who had the advance, attacked a phalanx of Union cavalry, "capturing," Stuart reported, "the greater portion." Moving north, Fitz and his troopers were greeted by residents weary of Union occupation who lined the sides of the road to cheer, clap, and wish them Godspeed. The objects of this outpouring of emotion were greatly impressed by it, and many were deeply moved by the plight of the local populace. In his campaign report Stuart declared, in his trademark prose, that "The hope of enabling the inhabitants to throw off the tyrant's yoke stirred every Southern heart with renewed vigor and enthusiasm."[26]

While the main army moved west toward Frederick and the Catoctin Mountains, the cavalry settled down outside Urbana to await McClellan's appearance. Little Mac being a slow mover, they remained there for nearly a week, sampling the local hospitality and on at least one occasion returning the favor. On the evening of September 8, Fitz Lee bathed, combed and pomaded his hair and beard, donned his best uniform, and departed his headquarters at Liberty, a hamlet on the Baltimore & Ohio Railroad where his brigade anchored Stuart's left flank, and rode to Urbana. There he joined dozens of other officers, prominent local civilians, and ladies fair for a night of dancing, eating, drinking, and conversing.

Stuart expected the Maryland Ball, which he and his staff were hosting, to be the social event of the season in that part of the state, and it was—for perhaps an hour. Like everyone else, Fitz was vastly disappointed when, after only a few waltzes, a noisy attack on Stuart's picket lines emptied the dance floor of officers and brought the festivities to a premature end.[27]

The clash indicated that pursuers were finally drawing near. By the eleventh, Union cavalry, moving in advance of McClellan's army, was pressing all sectors of Stuart's far-flung perimeter. That morning, Stuart called in his outposts and departed the Urbana vicinity for a new station within a few miles of Frederick, the recent location of the main army.

On the twelfth, Stuart followed Longstreet's infantry through the Catoctin gaps west of Frederick. He left Hampton's brigade and part of Munford's, later augmented by foot soldiers, to hold the defiles until Longstreet had passed into the Catoctin Valley and Jackson recrossed the Potomac to force the surrender of two garrisons—at Harpers Ferry and Martinsburg—on the flank of the invasion column.

Lee's brigade was ordered off on another assignment, one equally as important as Hampton's and Munford's. Uncertain of the size, composition, and heading of the force at his heels, Stuart sent Fitz on a wide arc to the north in hopes of getting in among the enemy and discerning his intentions. Fitz departed confident of accomplishing his mission, but Stuart was disappointed by the results. As he noted in his report, by the afternoon of the thirteenth "I confidently hoped . . . to have received the information which was expected from Brig. Gen. Fitz. Lee." As yet, however, he had heard nothing.

Because Fitz never penned—at least, never submitted—a report of his operations in Maryland, details of his foray into McClellan's midst remain lacking. All that is known is what Stuart stated, matter-of-factly, in his own report: that Fitz rejoined him at Boonsboro, beyond South Mountain, late in the afternoon of the fourteenth, "having been unable to accomplish the object of his mission." Neither officer ever revealed the basis of the failure.[28]

When Fitz reached Boonsboro, he found D. H. Hill's division of Jackson's wing in contact with the advance of one of McClellan's columns, comprising the I and IX Army Corps. Stuart assigned his subordinate to assist the infantry in holding Turner's Gap, thus facilitating the army's westward movement toward Sharpsburg. Then the cavalry commander galloped off to Harpers Ferry, whose garrison had recently surrendered, for a quick conference with Jackson.

In his absence, Fitz placed his men at the western end of the gap through which Yankee infantry, backed by the cavalry of Brigadier General Alfred Pleasonton, were passing in large numbers. Mounted and dismounted skirmishers kept Pleasonton's troopers back with carbine and rifle fire, while Pelham's batteries, which Stuart had attached to Fitz's brigade, showered them with shell and canister. When, despite the opposition, the Union infantry pressed forward, Fitz counterattacked with the charging 3rd Virginia, a tactic that stunned the enemy into temporary immobility.

He used the respite to turn west with his main body. He made it to the outskirts of Boonsboro before Pleasonton again struck his rear, covered by Rooney Lee's regiment. In street-to-street fighting, Fitz's cousin held his ground stubbornly until his horse went down with a wound and fell on him, knocking him senseless. Rooney escaped capture but was hors de combat for weeks afterward.[29]

Upon reaching the far side of the town, Fitz found that he had outdistanced his pursuers. He pointed the command, which the 3rd and 9th Virginia had rejoined, toward Sharpsburg, about five miles beyond Boonsboro. Here, with Antietam Creek in his front and the broad, swift-moving Potomac at his back, his uncle planned to group his widely separated forces. It was yet another gamble by an officer who had rolled the dice time and again since taking command of the ANV.

R. E. Lee had some cause for optimism. After entering Maryland, McClellan had been moving toward a showdown with unexpected dispatch, but Little Mac's habitual conservatism would surely resurface, giving his opponent time to secure a position outside Sharpsburg. Lee was also counting on Jackson to join him before he had to accept battle. Yet even with Stonewall's entire force on hand, Lee would have only about sixty thousand troops, half as many as his enemy.

Lee's belief notwithstanding, McClellan confronted him along the Antietam and moved against him on the sixteenth. That day's fighting reached a high pitch on several occasions, but it guttered out without decisive advantage to either army. Throughout the engagement, Fitz Lee's brigade guarded the Confederate left, Jackson's position, between river and creek. Farther south, Stuart, just returned from his conference at Harpers Ferry, placed Munford's brigade in support of Longstreet's command. Hampton's cavalry remained near Harpers Ferry, where, after being forced out of the South Mountain passes, it had gone to support Jackson's attack. Also at Harpers Ferry was A. P. Hill's division, currently engaged in corralling and paroling the 12,500 Yankees who had surrendered to Jackson. Thus, on the morning of the seventeenth, when the fighting at Sharpsburg truly began, Robert E. Lee could pit only three-quarters of his army against McClellan's multitude.[30]

Badly outnumbered it may have been, but Lee's force was powerful enough to contribute its fair share to the bloodbath that followed. It was, for the most part, an infantry and artillery battle. Munford saw little action on the right, and Hampton's men, who reached the field late in the afternoon, were used mostly as scouts, skirmishers, and couriers.

At first, it appeared that the 2nd Brigade would see more action—and suffer for the opportunity. It spent the first several hours of the battle supporting fourteen pieces of artillery that had been entrusted to Stuart's supervision. Stuart placed the guns on a rise known as Nicodemus Heights that commanded the ground in front of the Union right, and it was here that the day's first attack was launched. This effort was beaten back but only after hard fighting and heavy losses on both sides. Later in the morning, the tempo of battle shifted southward as McClellan struck the center of his enemy's line and then, late in the afternoon, its right.

When the fight moved away from him, Stuart accepted an assignment from Jackson to launch a counterattack with a force consisting of twenty-one cannons, an infantry regiment, and seven cavalry regiments, the majority drawn from Fitz's brigade. According to one of Jackson's subordinates, Stuart's offensive, aimed at curling around the upper flank of the Army of the Potomac and threatening its rear, was supposed to have begun shortly after noon but did not get under way until nearly 3 P.M. Whatever the cause of the delay, once in motion the combined-arms column did not get far before running into well-manned breastworks protected by more artillery than Stuart enjoyed.

After the war, one of Fitz's officers recalled the reason for the sudden halt: "From our position we could see on the sloping hills beyond the Antietam, the thickly frowning batteries of the enemy, while the smoke of battle rose from the infantry lines contending desperately in the vale between. The percussion shells from one of the batteries began to fall near us, and one of them striking a ledge of rocks close by, was exploded, much to our peril."[31]

At once Stuart hauled his cavalry and infantry units to the rear. He put all his energy into an artillery duel, the outcome of which was not long in doubt. The Federals got his range and silenced several of his guns, whereupon Stuart gave up the effort as a lost cause and withdrew to Nicodemus Heights. His troopers spent the balance of the day, which ended in a blood-stained stalemate, corralling infantry comrades fleeing from the front.

Fitz Lee recorded no opinion as to the denouement, but it can be surmised that with so many "frowning batteries" in his path, he was happy to have escaped more extensive participation in this, the bloodiest day in American history.[32]

SEVEN

A Sack of Coffee Beans

Punished but not beaten, the Army of Northern Virginia held its position between the river and the creek throughout September 18, as if daring McClellan to renew the battle. Had Little Mac picked up the gauntlet, Lee might have had cause to repent his rashness. But, as Captain Henry B. McClellan (a cousin of the Union commander) of Fitz's 3rd Virginia later wrote, a "bold front and an over-cautious enemy saved the Confederates from such an unequal contest."[1]

George B. McClellan's refusal to advance left his opponent no choice but to cross the Potomac into the Shenandoah Valley. Stuart, who claimed to have spent the eighteenth trying but failing to find new ways to uproot the Union right flank, was charged with supporting the river crossing, a difficult and delicate undertaking given the enemy's proximity. Significantly, he assigned the lion's share of the work to Fitz Lee.

Late on the eighteenth, Stuart, with Hampton's and Munford's troopers, led out, crossing the Potomac at "an obscure ford" and then heading upstream to Williamsport, where they could guard the upper flank of the army as it pulled out. Fitz, meanwhile, spread his regiments across the approaches to Shepherdstown Ford, where the major portion of the army crossed that evening. While the infantry, artillery, supply wagons, and army ambulances splashed across the shallow ford, Fitz skirmished with the spasmodically advancing enemy, at times quite sharply, until well after dark.

He did his job almost too well. After the last soldier and wagon had gotten safely across, Robert E. Lee sent couriers to recall his nephew, but Fitz could not be found. After an inordinate amount of searching, couriers located him in the streets of Sharpsburg at the head of his rear guard, personally exchanging pistol shots with McClellan's cavalry. Minutes before he could be cut off, Fitz led the guard through the town to the river. He arrived at Shepherdstown Ford, Captain McClellan observed, just in time to cross "in the presence of the enemy, and under the cover of the friendly guns on the southern bank." In his report of the campaign, Stuart commended his subordinate in a brief but meaningful phrase: "The duty assigned to Brig. Gen. Fitz. Lee was accomplished with entire success."[2]

Once back in Virginia, Lee decided to stay a spell. McClellan appeared to have no objection, for he remained on the Maryland side of the river for the next six weeks. The respite gave Lee time to refit, replenish his supply coffers, repair—as much as possible—the rents torn in his ranks, and assess the results of his sojourn in Maryland, which appeared depressingly meager. He had gained little of strategic value by invading that border state. He had not been able to stay long enough to succor his army or give Virginia a meaningful respite from the war. Nor had the anticipated influx of recruits, which many soldiers and politicians had predicted, come to pass. He had been forced to leave Maryland as quickly as he entered it, which could not be a spur to morale. At least he had left with head held high.

*   *   *

While the army's infantry and artillery lolled in their fixed camps farther to the rear, Stuart's cavalry spent the autumn picketing and reconnoitering along a ten-mile front from Martinsburg south to Charles Town. Stuart made his headquarters at the Bower, an opulent plantation near the lower end of this line, where, when not on duty, he and his officers enjoyed a seemingly endless round of balls, parties, and other entertainments served up by his gracious hosts, the Dandridge family.[3]

Never one to pass up off-duty recreation, Fitz Lee joined in the merriment at the Bower, but after September 23 he was incapable of taking the dance floor. That day, apparently while inspecting the supply wagons of his brigade near Martinsburg, he was kicked by a mule. The injury almost totally incapacitated him. For a time he apparently convalesced in a hospital in Winchester. When his injuries began to heal, he returned to cavalry headquarters on crutches. Even when able to walk without assistance, he moved about stiffly and with lingering pain for several weeks while the war went on without him. In his absence, Colonel Wickham, as its senior colonel, directed the 2nd Brigade. Fitz was pleased that the citizen-soldier did well in the temporary position.[4]

During the nearly two months he was sidelined, Fitz missed out on several occasions he would have enjoyed taking part in. In October, horsemen under

Pleasonton and Bayard crossed the Potomac at several points, beginning a fight that Stuart's people—still masters of their opponents on most occasions— usually finished. Then, from the ninth to the thirteenth of that month, Stuart led eighteen hundred troopers and horse artillerymen deep inside enemy lines. He penetrated as far north as Chambersburg, Pennsylvania, on the way confiscating foodstuffs and livestock, burning supply houses, wrecking railroad track, and attacking bridges over which McClellan got his supplies. After the column's return, Fitz never tired of hearing the details of the daring expedition, especially Stuart's hairbreadth escapes from various pursuit forces. While short on strategic benefits, the expedition helped persuade Abraham Lincoln to fire the lethargic McClellan early in November and replace him with a corps commander who seemed to have more energy—Major General Ambrose E. Burnside.

A few days before McClellan's dismissal, he finally stirred himself to lead his army back into Virginia, concentrating in the vicinity of Warrenton. It was there that Burnside took the reins and put in motion a plan he had devised, and Lincoln had approved, calling for a rapid descent on Richmond via Fredericksburg. By mid-November the movement was under way. Stuart reacted with unusual slowness, but as soon as he realized what his opponent was up to, his troopers spearheaded a pursuit that carried Longstreet's command rapidly eastward.[5]

At last restored to physical health, Fitz Lee was in the forefront of the movement to the lower Rappahannock. Once there, he guarded the army's flanks and picketed the bridgeless river. His brigade, now headquartered at Guiney's Station on the Richmond, Fredericksburg & Potomac Railroad, was a model of continuity compared to the other components of Stuart's command, which had undergone radical change over the past several months. Fitz still commanded the 1st, 3rd, 4th, and 5th Virginia. The 9th Virginia, however, was gone, having been transferred to a new brigade under Rooney Lee, recently recovered from his own disabling injury and now also a brigadier general. Taking its place was the 2nd Virginia of Tom Munford, who for want of seniority had returned to regimental command.[6]

Having stolen a march on his enemy, Burnside was furious to find his army stymied at Falmouth opposite Fredericksburg, the result of an errant pontoon train en route from Washington. He was still at Falmouth, and still fuming over his ill luck, when in early December Jackson, who had lingered in the Valley after the rest of the army moved to Fredericksburg, joined Lee and Longstreet in blocking Burnside's path south of the river—should the man ever get there.

Burnside did cross the river, but not until the second week of the month. By then the Army of Northern Virginia manned a well-fortified line, studded with artillery and running for almost seven miles south of Fredericksburg. Open ground stretched for several hundred yards in front of strong, well-defended works at the foot of Marye's Heights, but the pathologically stubborn Burnside determined to attack anyway, hoping to bull his way through to Richmond. It was one of the worst decisions any army commander ever made. When he attempted it on the frigid, fog-shrouded morning of the thirteenth, Confederate musketry and cannon fire mowed down wave after wave of attackers. Despite the fatal result, Burnside continued to throw regiments and brigades into the firestorm. After dark, when his subordinates finally persuaded him to call off the massacre, the Army of the Potomac had almost thirteen thousand fewer able-bodied soldiers. By fighting on the defensive throughout, Lee held his losses to below fifty-five hundred.[7]

As on several earlier fields, the Confederate cavalry saw little or no action during the one-sided battle. Stuart's single contribution was the deadly work of Pelham's horse artillery, which early in the fight unlimbered in a concealed position along the Union left and blasted unsuspecting infantrymen as they charged past. Given the carnage, Fitz Lee was probably thankful that he and his men spent the better part of the day sheltered behind strong works on the far Rebel right.

If the sights and sounds of December 13 were not enough to make him shudder in revulsion, Fitz must have reacted that way when daylight on the fourteenth revealed the dozens of corpses that dotted the frozen earth in front of his position. But he may not have appreciated fully the human dimension of the tragedy until he learned, some days later, that Burnside's casualty list included the name of Brigadier General George D. Bayard, mortally wounded by a shell fragment at the height of the battle.[8]

*   *   *

Stuart seems to have chafed at his command's inactivity throughout the thirteenth, as beneficial as it may have been in the long run. Hoping to find something useful and dramatic to do before active campaigning ceased for the winter, within days of Burnside's slow and painful retreat to Falmouth the cavalry chieftain devised a plan to raid into the rear of the demoralized enemy. Wade Hampton had shown him the way, having recently conducted three small-scale forays behind Federal lines in the vicinity of Occoquan and Dumfries. The South Carolinian, although not known as a raiding leader, had returned with a tremendous haul, including hundreds of prisoners and enough well-stocked wagons to supply an army for weeks.[9]

If Stuart coveted Hampton's success, Fitz Lee disdained it. He continued to regard Hampton as an infantry retread who had no right to compete with their common superior for laurels in independent mounted operations. Thus he warmly endorsed Stuart's plan to operate against outposts and supply depots along the historic Telegraph Road, Burnside's principal overland supply link to Washington, D.C. Robert E. Lee liked the idea as well, and a few days before Christmas he gave his cavalry leader the go-ahead.

To implement the plan, Stuart formed an eighteen hundred-man, four-gun force, comprising a portion of each of his three brigades (his fourth, recently Munford's and now led by Grumble Jones, had returned to its old station in the lower Shenandoah). The combined-arms force started from Kelly's Ford on the upper Rappahannock on the morning of the twenty-sixth. Crossing the stream, the elongated column wended its way east by northeast toward Morrisville and Bristersburg. Despite the raw weather and the stop-start pace, Fitz Lee rode gaily at the forefront of his brigade, happy to be part of an important and highly mobile operation following weeks of painful incapacitation and desultory service in the rear.

On the morning of the twenty-seventh, Stuart advanced on his objectives in three columns. Hampton's brigade—which now comprised the 1st North Carolina, 1st and 2nd South Carolina, and the Jeff Davis and Cobb Legions—took the most northerly route, toward Occoquan on the river of the same name, scene of one of his earlier expeditions. By divergent routes, Fitz's and Rooney Lee's brigades, Stuart accompanying the latter, headed for Dumfries, nine miles farther south, in the valley of Quantico Creek. The cousins Lee were to cooperate on an attack on local storehouses—Fitz from the south, Rooney from the west.[10]

At first the expedition appeared an exercise in futility. En route to Dumfries, Fitz's advance overtook, and his main body helped itself to, nine well-stocked wagons owned by sutlers—private merchants licensed to sell to the army. Rooney Lee's troopers also captured some wagons as well as a few inattentive pickets. But shortly after their columns converged on Dumfries, Stuart's scouts learned that the local commander had removed all quartermaster's and commissary stores. The forewarned Federals also gave Fitz and Rooney a rousing welcome, keeping them at bay on the outskirts of town with rifle and cannon fire that mortally wounded one of Fitz's most dependable subordinates, Captain J. N. Bullock of the 5th Virginia.

Fitz feared that if he pressed the attack Bullock would not be his only casualty. As he explained in his report of the engagement, "the probable loss of life would not compensate for the capture" of the town and whatever supplies remained there. Thus, he "continued skirmishing with the enemy until dark, my dismounted sharpshooters occupying the enemy's infantry with considerable effect, enabling the major general commanding to swing around the rest of the command on the Brentsville road, and move off in that direction."[11]

Stuart was upset by the standoff, especially as two of Pelham's guns had used up their ammunition in a meaningless duel with a Union battery. After sending the cannons back to the Rappahannock in charge of Captain Breathed, Stuart collected his forces and pushed on for Occoquan. Short of the town, he was met by Wade Hampton and more bad news. Due to the muddy roads as well as to the presence along them of numerous pickets, it had been close to dark before Hampton had reached the town, where wagons filled with military provisions were known to be parked.

As he approached, the brigadier discovered an even more tempting prize: a pea-green regiment of Yankee cavalry holding the town. Hampton teamed with his favorite subordinate, M. C. Butler, to trap the rookies via an attack in front and an ambush in the rear, but in the darkness the plan miscarried. Reminiscent of Fitz Lee's blunder at Hanover Court House eighteen months before, Butler flushed the game, but the Yankees and many of the supply vehicles they had been guarding fled the area before Hampton's main force got into position to bag them. All the South Carolinian had to show for his efforts were a dozen prisoners and very few of the wagons they had come to Occoquan to seize.[12]

At this point, Stuart strongly considered calling off the raid and returning home. Apparently he issued preliminary orders to do so, for Fitz had turned his brigade, the vanguard of the reunited column, southward before learning that his superior had changed his mind. Without even bivouacking for the night, Stuart's men would continue north with a Micawber-like purpose—waiting for something to turn up.

In fact, something had already turned up. When Fitz started south, he learned that detachments of two regiments of Union cavalry were in his rear, tailing him at a cautious distance. Now Stuart's entire column faced in that direction and advanced on the would-be pursuers. Stuart looked forward to a confrontation, for one of his ancillary objectives was to force either Burnside or the Washington authorities to detach troops to run him down.

Five miles covered at a brisk trot brought the 2nd Brigade within striking distance of the enemy troopers, who had taken refuge in a snow-covered woods. While supports went into position opposite the Yankees' flanks, Stuart directed Fitz to charge them head-on. The attack, spearheaded by Fitz's old regiment, now under James H. Drake, cleared the woods in a matter of minutes, killing and wounding several and making prisoners of one hundred more. The rest galloped madly across an Occoquan River ford, pursued by Tom Rosser's 5th Virginia and Pelham's two remaining horse artillery pieces. Upon reaching the far bank, Rosser and Pelham discovered that their quarry had disappeared in the distance. They compensated themselves by appropriating rations, extra clothing, and horse equipment found in the camps the Yankees had abandoned.[13]

Stuart soon learned that other enemy forces had picked up his trail. A 150-man detachment of Butler's 2nd South Carolina, one of the units sent to flank the Federals, had failed in its purpose because when moving into position it spied a body of Union troops—infantry as well as cavalry and artillery, probably outlying members of the defense forces of Washington—advancing toward them on a parallel road. By good luck and bold maneuvering Butler had avoided harm and extricated his detachment, but Stuart now knew he was in the sights of a force quite possibly larger than his own.[14]

Again, Stuart considered turning homeward before vowing to forge on. While Hampton's main body feinted northeastward to throw off the pursuers, Stuart led the balance of his force directly north. His heading led him, by early evening of the twenty-eighth, to Burke's Station on the Orange & Alexandria twelve miles below Washington, one of Fitz's own objectives during the Second Manassas campaign.

Though deep in enemy territory, pursued by unknown numbers of blue-coats eager to make a name for themselves by nabbing the war's most celebrated raider, Stuart was his old self again, his enthusiasm and confidence restored. He proved as much by sending scouts to capture the telegrapher at Burke's Station before he could tap out an alarm. Upon reaching the depot, Stuart had Fitz, at the head of a twelve-man party, burn a nearby bridge. The party included Fitz's twenty-three-year-old brother, Lieutenant John Mason Lee, a recent addition to Rooney Lee's staff.[15]

In addition to torching the bridge, Fitz's band ransacked freight cars and downed telegraph wire, but not before Stuart played a joke on a ranking enemy officer. At his direction, the local telegrapher addressed a cable to Major General Montgomery C. Meigs, quartermaster general of the Union Armies, complaining of the poor quality of the mules now pulling the army wagons Stuart's men had captured.[16]

Following this outlandish piece of theatricality—of which another flamboyant showman, Fitz Lee, must have heartily approved—Stuart at last turned back toward the Rappahannock. Unable to resist one final challenge, he moved by way of well-defended Fairfax Court House. This was a mistake, for its occupants, who had been alerted to his approach, blasted his column into retreat. By some miracle no casualties resulted, but Stuart vowed to push his luck no further.

The rest of the journey was made in leisurely fashion, though not in joy-ride weather. On New Year's Day the column hauled inside its army's lines an immense cache of prizes, including two complete supply trains, two hundred horses and mules, and several hundred prisoners—holiday presents to round out a season of good cheer for the Army of Northern Virginia.[17]

*   *   *

As 1863 dawned, the military situation in Virginia was encouraging, although the enemy, for all his ineptitude on the field of battle, showed no inclination to sue for peace. Yet as Fitz Lee and most of his comrades realized, it was a different story in the western theater. Early that autumn, two Confederate armies had failed to cooperate in an effort to relieve Kentucky of Union occupation; on October 8 the larger of the two, Braxton Bragg's Army of the Mississippi, suffered a major defeat at Perryville. Two months later, back in its home state, Bragg's command, now known as the Army of Tennessee, was whipped by Major General William S. Rosecrans's Army of the Cumberland during a two-day battle along Stones River. The outcome forced Bragg to withdraw below the Duck River, his hold on middle Tennessee suddenly quite tenuous.[18]

Also in December, Ulysses S. Grant's initial attempt to take Vicksburg and open the length of the Mississippi River to Union shipping had been thwarted at Chickasaw Bluffs and Holly Springs. The latter failure was engineered by Fitz's old battalion commander, Earl Van Dorn, who, on a daring raid in the Stuart tradition, cut Grant's overland supply line and forced his withdrawal to Memphis. Despite this setback, few of Vicksburg's occupants doubted that the Union commander—captor of Forts Henry and Donelson and victor at Shiloh and Iuka—would try again.[19]

If the strategic implications of these events weighed on Fitz Lee's mind, he kept his concerns to himself. Winter having greatly reduced the tempo of active operations, he spent most of his time inspecting his picket lines, sending out and receiving reports from scouting parties, questioning Federals captured during quick stabs across the river, and conducting morale-raising exercises— inspections, parades, and reviews. One of the most ambitious of these took place on January 10 when J. E. B. Stuart reviewed the 2nd Brigade near Culpeper Court House.

Stuart, who had a passion for such events, planned the occasion as a majestic pageant whose audience would include Robert E. Lee, other members of the army's hierarchy, and carefully chosen civilians including political officials and their ladies fair. But his elaborate preparations went for naught. A driving rain fell throughout the affair, washing out most of the drill-plain maneuvers and keeping most of the invited guests at home. Those evolutions that were performed did not impress a member of Longstreet's staff, who had "little patience with such vanity, and I think Fitz Lee and his command agree with me."[20]

Fitz may have missed this chance to perform before a female audience, but another opportunity soon arose. A few weeks after the soggy review, nineteen-year-old Constance Cary, a member of one of Alexandria's finest families and a close friend of the Lees, sought Fitz's help in passing through enemy lines to Washington. Accompanied by her maiden aunt, the young woman carried legal papers relating to an inheritance that they had to sign in the presence of an attorney in the federal capital.

While waiting for a means of conveyance through the lines, the ladies stayed in a comfortable manor house, Belpré, near Fitz's headquarters. There they enjoyed being waited on by "a dozen gallant knights ready to do one's lightest bidding. . . . There were visits to and from camp; rides, shooting-matches— 'General Fitz' presenting me with a tiny Smith and Wesson revolver captured by himself, which he taught me to wear and use—and, at evenings, gatherings around the big wood fire at Belpré, where we laughed and talked and sang." Recalling the happy times years later, Miss Cary (by then Mrs. Burton Harrison, wife of Jefferson Davis's former secretary) recalled that Fitz was "the leader of fun in those evenings. . . . One was as sure of jollity and good-fellowship in 'General Fitz' off duty as of soldierly dash tempered by the wisdom of a born leader when in action."[21]

When the Misses Cary proved unable to procure a horse and buggy, the general provided his guests with one of his headquarters ambulances as well as a detail to escort them as far as Warrenton, the outer limit of his lines. Following many adventures, some of them quite harrowing, the ladies accomplished their mission. On their return through the lines to Richmond they had the pleasure of again sampling the hospitality of the courtly and charming "General Fitz."

*   *   *

By late February, snow clung to the shore of the Rappahannock and icy winds buffeted the pickets on both banks. Despite the conditions, the forces on the Falmouth side were not only astir but apparently building up. At army headquarters' bidding, Fitz sent Wickham's 4th Virginia over the river at United States Mine Ford to learn what lay behind the sudden activity. Within five miles of his crossing point, Wickham encountered so many blue-clad troopers that he had to leave posthaste. When subsequent small-scale efforts failed to gain the required information, Robert E. Lee asked Stuart to send Fitz, with a much larger force, "to break through their outposts & ascertain what was occurring."[22]

The appointee was happy to comply. For one thing, Fitz, like many another cavalryman, had grown weary of the dull and burdensome routine of winter camp and was looking forward to more active employment. For another, the pickets opposite his lines were members of the cavalry division of William Averell, his West Point compatriot and fellow tactics instructor at Carlisle Barracks. Paying an unexpected visit on Averell—especially if he could take his friend's troopers by surprise, capturing men, mounts, and equipment—tickled Fitz's sense of adventure.

Suspecting that the Yankees across from him were not as vigilant as they ought to be, he was confident of striking a wide stretch of Averell's lines, creating much havoc. Events would bear him out. On the morning of the twenty-fourth he led four hundred picked men of the 1st, 2nd, and 3rd Virginia over the river at Kelly's Ford. A force of that size should have been detected as soon as it set foot on the left bank, but Fitz and his men passed unseen through the first picket lines they encountered.[23]

Early the next day, after encamping for the night at Morrisville, staging area for the Dumfries Raid, Fitz followed his scouts through the woods to Harwood Church, astride the Fredericksburg-Warrenton Road, where Averell's picket reserve was encamped. With the kind of stealth known only to Comanches and Confederates, dismounted Virginians crept up on the most distant pickets and captured them before they could alert the reserve. Then Fitz led his widely dispersed body through the trees until the reserve post was nearly surrounded. At about 2 P.M., his bugler sounded the charge and hundreds of troopers, keening the Rebel Yell, attacked from several directions.

Sensing impending doom, dismounted Yankees left the campfires around which they had been huddling and ran for their horses—and their lives. A few stood their ground and returned fire, but most of them were cut down by pistol or saber. Those who managed to mount were pursued by screaming Rebels. Relatively few reached safety; to do so some had to ride all the way to their army's infantry camps, within five miles of Falmouth. The foot soldiers mobilized to challenge the raiders, but it was a futile gesture considering how long it would take them to reach Hartwood Church.

Within a half-hour, if not less, the fighting at the church was over and 150 Yankees, including 5 officers, had been taken prisoner. Many others, as Fitz reported, had been killed or wounded, as against 14 Confederate casualties. Fitz spent some time tending to the fallen, interrogating his captives, and sending parties to probe other picket posts in the vicinity. Then he recalled all detachments and led his column northeastward to Morrisville, where everyone spent the night in bivouac. Falling asleep must have been difficult, for it is unlikely that Fitz permitted his men to light fires. Even without giving away his position in this way, camping in such close proximity to the Yankee infantry was a bold and risky move—the kind Stuart would have approved of.[24]

It would have been a reckless move, had Fitz not been correct in his prediction that Averell would not or could not mount a speedy and effective pursuit. Averell, with a sizable body of his own command, supported by detachments of Pleasonton's division, started for Hartwood Church on the afternoon of the twenty-fifth. Failing to find the Rebels at the scene of their assault, Averell subsequently teamed with his slower-moving colleague. On the twenty-sixth, Pleasonton and Averell attempted to cooperate in cutting Fitz's men off from the river, but they reached Kelly's Ford a few hours after the raiders had recrossed. All that Averell found at the ford—probably nailed to a tree trunk—was a note in Fitz's handwriting, crowing about how easily he had penetrated the Union lines and suggesting that his old colleague "put up your sword, leave my state and go home. . . . If you won't go home, return my visit and bring me a sack of coffee."[25]

Fitz may have intended the note as a playful jab, but Averell viewed it as a taunting insult and a challenge to be met. So did his army commander, Major General Joseph ("Fighting Joe") Hooker, who late in January had succeeded the inept and luckless Burnside. Since taking the helm, Hooker had gone to great lengths to upgrade the quality and quantity of his army, and especially its mounted arm. His most inspired reform was to organize the cavalry as a separate corps under General Stoneman, thus removing it from the inept hands of infantry commanders. If Averell was embarrassed by Fitz's foray, Hooker was livid. In the plainest terms, he made Averell understand that the burden of avenging Hartwood Church rested on his shoulders. Hooker expected him to do something about it, and soon.[26]

*   *   *

The Hartwood Church affair made Fitz Lee's name well known throughout the army and secured his reputation as a fast-moving, hard-fighting horseman in the mold of his ostrich-plumed superior. His new-won fame opened doors to higher command, some of which he wished kept shut.

On the day Fitz returned from Hartwood Church, Grumble Jones, now commanding the Valley District near New Market, messaged Robert E. Lee about recent attacks on his lines by the infantry and cavalry of Brigadier General Robert H. Milroy, headquartered at Winchester. Although Jones had repulsed every strike, Milroy's harassment had not abated. With active operations virtually suspended on his front, Robert E. Lee, apparently at the behest of President Davis, directed J. E. B. Stuart to accompany Fitz and as many men and horses of his brigade as could make the trip to the Valley via Middleburg and Snickersville, there to help Jones "limit the operations of Genl Milroy."[27]

For one reason or another—perhaps only to avoid serving again with the cantankerous Jones—Stuart begged off the assignment. No reinforcements went to Jones, who continued to fend off Milroy's blows. Grumble, however, appeared unable to prevent Milroy from terrorizing Confederate sympathizers within his realm. By early March, Jefferson Davis was seriously considering removing him in favor of a senior cavalry officer in Lee's army—if not Stuart himself, then a subordinate of proven ability.

Robert E. Lee responded by suggesting a swap-out of officers, Jones to rejoin the ANV and Fitz Lee to replace him in the Valley—a solution that, as the army leader must have known, would please his nephew not at all. But even as the elder Lee advanced the proposal, he deftly withdrew it. Milroy's actions notwithstanding, Jones retained his confidence. As for his proposed replacement, "General Fitz. Lee is an excellent cavalry officer, and is extremely useful in his present position. I do not know how I can spare him upon the resumption of active operations, as I feel at liberty to call upon him . . . on all occasions." This graceful demurral appears to have stayed Davis's hand; nothing more was said or done about the matter.[28]

Fitz was relieved to know that he was staying put. He had no desire to leave a cold clime for an even colder one. Moreover, he could not say how many of his horses would make the trip to New Market. All were suffering from the general shortage of forage that was hampering the army in its present locale, and many if not most had fallen prey to one or more of those winter-induced equine diseases with the makeshift names—"scratches," "hoof rot," "grease heel." His raid to Hartwood Church, as brief as it had been, had taken a further toll on his animals' health. He wished to limit any extraordinary demands on them until warmer weather returned and active operations resumed.

Another possible reason for Fitz's relief at not going to the Valley was that he would have been forced to operate closely with John Mosby and his irregulars. Since forming his battalion of partisan rangers, Lieutenant Mosby had closely supported Stuart on many occasions and thus was something of a fixture at cavalry headquarters—to Fitz's displeasure, as his relations with the erstwhile adjutant had not improved. In fact, they appear to have deteriorated as the result of a couple of incidents in the first half of March. On the tenth, Mosby escorted to Culpeper yet another of Fitz's old acquaintances in Union blue— Brigadier General Edwin H. Stoughton, USMA Class of 1859. The previous night Mosby and his men, aided by darkness and stealth, had penetrated the lines of Stoughton's infantry brigade at Fairfax Court House. With almost laughable ease they had captured pickets and staff officers as well as the general himself, whom Mosby had hauled out of bed at gunpoint.[29]

By presenting Fitz with Stoughton and some of his aides, the trophies of his first major operation in partisan service, Mosby expected to hear something in the way of congratulations—if not outright praise, then a reference or two to a job well done. Instead, while Fitz was "very polite to his old classmate and to the officers, when I introduced them . . . he treated me with indifference, did not ask me to take a seat by the fire, nor seem impressed by what I had done."[30]

In Mosby's eyes, such rude indifference was bad enough, but a few days afterward Fitz drove a larger wedge between them by ordering Mosby to return to the 2nd Brigade every member who had transferred—either officially or informally— to his organization. Mosby heatedly informed his patron, Stuart, of "this attempt to deprive me of a command." Although the cavalry leader did not rescind the order, he granted Mosby a several-week reprieve. When the army began to move in early May, Fitz's troopers were duly returned to him. By then enough recruits had joined Mosby to keep his battalion going, but he never forgave Fitz for his attitude and behavior. More than forty years after both incidents, he declared to a correspondent, "Long will my heart with this memory be filled."[31]

*   *   *

At 11 A.M. on March 16, Fitz received at his Culpeper headquarters a telegram from army headquarters alerting him to the approach of a large mounted column on the enemy's side of the river. By sending out patrols, he learned that as of 6 P.M. the Yankees—members of Averell's division—were about six miles from Kelly's Ford and coming fast. Soon afterward he knew that the column had bivouacked in the vicinity of Morrisville. Its strength could not be determined, but presumably Fitz's scouts ascertained that it included at least a couple of pieces of horse artillery. Uncertain whether Averell was building up his picket lines or had something more ominous in mind, Fitz doubled the number of sharpshooters holding the rifle pits that had been dug opposite Kelly's Ford, then turned in for the night.[32]

Through some miscommunication, not for thirty minutes or more after the event did Fitz learn that at eight o'clock the next morning, St. Patrick's Day, Averell's column had succeeded in crossing at the ford under fire. Nor did he ever learn why only a dozen of the forty carbineers at the river provided sustained resistance. As soon as he got the word, however, he led his regiments at a sustained gallop down the Orange & Alexandria toward the sounds of fighting.

Encountering the enemy about a half-mile from Kelly's, he charged them at the head of his strung-out column. Delivered in such haste, this attack by the 2nd and 3rd Virginia was not successful. As Fitz later wrote, Averell's position "was a very strong one, sheltered by woods and a long, high stone fence running perpendicular to my advance. My men, unable to cross the fence and ditch in their front, wheeled about, delivering their fire almost in the faces of the enemy, and reformed again, facing about under a heavy fire from their artillery and small arms."[33]

If Fitz's column was forced back, the left flank of Averell's column also withdrew a short distance. Perceiving an opening, Fitz hurled the 2nd Virginia, now led by Major Cary Breckinridge, at the enemy left only to see it met and repulsed by an equal number of bluecoats. The Yankee cavalry having been Stuart's playthings for so long, this was something no one in gray could have expected. It came as a rude shock to Stuart himself, who had fled a court-martial in Culpeper at which he had been testifying, to join Fitz at the front, initially in the role of tactical advisor.[34]

At Stuart's suggestion, Fitz counterattacked the enemy force that had broken the 2nd with elements of the 1st and 4th Virginia. They drove the Federals back, but it appeared to some observers that the enemy withdrew of his own will. In hopes of exploiting his advantage, Fitz called up the 3rd Virginia, which had reformed following its initial repulse. One of the regiment's captains noted that on a farmstead opposite the Union right, "we were met by Gen. Lee, who ordered Col. Owen to charge the enemy. This was done in gallant style, [the] Regiment sweeping down the fence along the road & passing through an opening between the rail fences running at right angles across the field."[35]

After passing the first barrier, the regiment ran hard aground against a second— the stone fence Fitz had referred to in his report. By the time the 3rd began its charge, many of Averell's dismounted skirmishers had abandoned the wall that had sheltered them, but when they saw the Confederates stymied, they "returned to their posts & opened a hot fire into it [the regiment] as it passed."

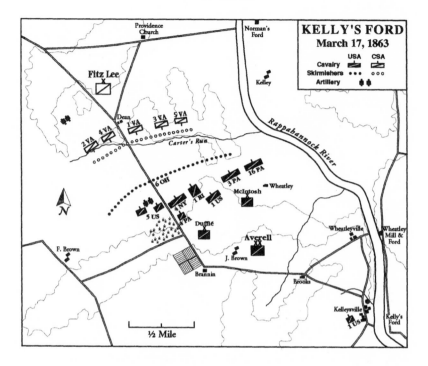

Stunned by the blast, the 3rd emulated Breckinridge's outfit, turning about with such speed and in such disorder as to cause Fitz's heart to skip a beat.[36]

Since the start of the fight, the 2nd Brigade had been at a disadvantage for lack of artillery support. In late morning, however, John Pelham galloped down from Culpeper and sent his horse batteries into action in the cavalry's rear. Barely had they started dueling with Averell's guns than the renowned artillerist received a fatal wound from a shell fragment. Regardless of the outcome of the fight, his loss would make this day a dark one indeed for the cavalry of the Army of Northern Virginia.[37]

As the afternoon wore on, the encounter seemed to degenerate into stalemate, dismounted men on both sides carrying on the fight at long range from behind good cover. In midafternoon Stuart, who had assumed command on the left, tried to recapture the offensive with a mounted attack by the 2nd Virginia, with the 1st and 4th in close support. But the charge was barely under way before well-placed shells from Averell's artillery turned it back. Those few attackers who attempted to remain on the field by fighting dismounted were finally driven off by a Union countercharge.

Stuart and Fitz soon decided that a general withdrawal was in order. At their direction, all five regiments fell back about a mile, where they were more effec-tively sheltered by the horse artillery, now under James Breathed. Averell did not at once follow, as if content to let them go, believing he had sufficiently discomfited the Beau Sabreur of the Confederacy. Late in the afternoon, he fi-nally moved in their direction but did not renew the fight.[38]

Unwilling to concede defeat, Fitz gained Stuart's permission for a final of-fensive in which he would personally lead large detachments of each of his reg-iments. The adjutant of the 3rd Virginia saw Fitz, saber raised, ride in front of the brigade, now drawn up in a single, elongated rank, and heard his "loud voice . . . commanding 'Forward gallop March'—[I] saw the gleam of his battle blade and dashed onward to the charge." Fitz himself described the movement as "a succession of gallant charges by . . . the whole brigade in line, whenever the en-emy would show their mounted men, they invariably falling back upon their artillery and sheltered dismounted skirmishers." He failed to note, however, that the attack wave lapped only briefly at Averell's battle line before receding, the result of fagged-out horses and the resolute men in blue—some mounted, some afoot—who barred Fitz's path.[39]

The unsuccessful offensive ended Fitz's attempt to throw Averell and his bat-talions across the river whence they had come. In a sense, he did not have to. The enemy remained on the right bank only until gathering darkness and a host of concerns—some valid, some the result of a queasy imagination—prompted Averell to retreat to and across Kelly's Ford. His opponents were willing to let him go. They had been fought to a standstill this day—worse, they had been forced into retreat almost too many times to count. In the process, they had suf-fered 133 casualties and the loss of 170 horses, extraordinary numbers for an all-cavalry encounter, testimony to the desperate nature of the fighting on both sides. The enemy had suffered too, but Fitz suspected rightly that Averell's losses had been fewer than his own.

The 2nd Brigade had fought well enough this day; theoretically, however, it had been overmatched from the start. Because Averell's force constituted the better part of a division while Fitz fought at brigade strength, the Confederates could take some comfort in knowing they had been outmanned and out-gunned. In his report Fitz lamented that had he been permitted to fight at full strength, "and not weakened by the absence of four squadrons on picket . . . and by the large number of horses unfit for duty by exposure to the severe winter, with a very limited supply of forage, I feel confident the defeat of the enemy would have been changed into a disorderly rout." But Fitz refused to admit a sober truth: in none of the individual encounters that defined the battle were his regiments and battalions defeated by forces that clearly outnumbered them.[40]

From a tactical if not a strategic perspective, it was Fitz's brigade that suf-fered defeat on this field, a defeat that came perilously close to the "disorderly rout" he had expected to inflict on Averell. Moreover, it had been administered by an enemy that, given its checkered history, should not have been able to compete with, let alone take the measure of, Stuart's horsemen.[41]

The taste of defeat was bitter enough, but the bile must have risen in Fitz Lee's throat when he learned, after dark, that upon withdrawing his Old Army comrade had left him a present—a sack of roasting beans, with a note attached: "Dear Fitz: Here's your coffee. Here's your visit. How did you like it?"[42]

EIGHT

What a Sight
Presented Itself!

If the Confederate cavalry had suffered a setback at Kelly's Ford, one would never know it from the congratulatory orders and addresses Stuart and his favorite subordinate published afterward. In General Orders Number 5, issued on the eighteenth, Stuart claimed that the fight had ended "in entire success to us," with an "insolent foe . . . driven, broken and discomfited, across the Rappahannock." For this outcome every officer and man in Fitz Lee's command was due great credit. In his official report of the action, submitted a week later, Stuart gave a special helping of praise to Brigadier General Lee, who throughout the battle had "exhibited . . . the sagacity of a successful general" and whose "prompt and vigorous action" was principally responsible for the victory.[1]

In his own set of general orders, dated March 21, Fitz surpassed his superior's rhetorical flight. He too pronounced the battle a clear-cut triumph, one so far-reaching that the enemy's demoralization would last for months to come: "Rebel cavalry have taught an insolent enemy that, notwithstanding they may possess advantages of chosen position, superiority in numbers and weapons, they cannot overwhelm soldiers fighting for the holiest cause that ever nerved the arm of a freeman or fired the breast of a patriot. . . . you have confirmed Abolition cavalry in their notions of running."[2]

There was a whistling-in-the-graveyard quality to these statements, set down in such overwrought prose. Assuredly, the majority of the troopers who had

104

battled Averell's people saw the addresses for what they were—unmitigated nonsense. Averell may have enjoyed numerical superiority as well as an early edge in artillery at Kelly's Ford, but Confederate cavalry had always overcome such hurdles in the past, and handily. The truth was that Fitz's men had been roughed up by an enemy whose "insolence" (i.e., self-confidence) had been evident throughout the battle. In fact, the tenor of the fight suggested that the Yankees were no longer in awe or fear of their enemy. If so, Stuart's men had lost the psychological advantage on which rested their ability to maintain mastery over their foe.

One possible reason for this change was the imminent end of the theoretical two-year training period required to turn erstwhile store clerks and day laborers into accomplished horse soldiers. Another was the Federals' ability—evident throughout the recent battle—to fight mounted and on foot with equal effect. This versatility contrasted sharply with the enemy's reliance (overreliance?) on the mounted assault, a tactic whose limitations had been thrown into high relief by the repulse of one saber charge after another.

Whatever the root cause, the Yankees' growing confidence, added to their quantum advantages in horses, weapons, and equipment, had ominous implications for the future of Stuart's command. One inference was that if a decisive turnaround in the fortunes of the opposing cavalries had not yet occurred, it was imminent. If Stuart and Fitz failed to take note of this new order of things, perhaps their ignorance was deliberate—they could not afford to admit that the Yankees were now their equals in the art and science of mounted warfare.

*   *   *

For a fortnight after the set-to at Kelly's Ford, Fitz tended to his casualties, oversaw promotions to fill new vacancies in the ranks, and tried to scare up replacement equipment and ammunition for his men and forage for their nearly famished animals. By the arrival of April, with the snow all but gone and the slushy roads having begun to solidify, his camps were abuzz with rumors of an imminent movement—somewhere. They proved true on the eleventh, when Fitz led most of his men across the Hazel and Rappahannock Rivers into Fauquier County. The command was concentrated near the town of Salem, whose fields contained the kind of provender—corn, hay, oats, and grain—that could not be obtained farther south.

Many of the enlisted men, and more than a few of their officers, supposed they had relocated only to reprovision. In fact, they had been sent to Fauquier, gateway to the Blue Ridge and the Shenandoah Valley, to provide long-distance support to a raid against one of the Union's most critical communication lines, the Baltimore & Ohio Railroad, by separate forces of cavalry and mounted infantry under Grumble Jones and Brigadier General John D. Imboden. After numerous delays, the expedition got under way on April 20. Within days, Fitz was to cross into the Shenandoah to provide reinforcements to either or both columns.[3]

As it happened, by the twentieth he and his men were gone from Fauquier, having returned expeditiously to Culpeper Court House. The reason for the recall triggered an unpleasant sense of déjà vu. Late on the thirteenth Stuart's scouts had spied another column of Union cavalry—this one trailed by supply wagons, ambulances, pack mules, and led horses—wending its way up the left bank of the Rappahannock from Falmouth. Subsequent reports identified the force as almost ten thousand horsemen under George Stoneman. Its purpose and destination could not immediately be ascertained.

Much later it was learned that Stoneman's movement was the opening act of the Army of the Potomac's spring campaign. General Hooker had determined to sweep around his enemy's left flank below Fredericksburg and hit him while his back was turned. Approximately half of his huge army would follow Stoneman upriver to make the turning movement while other forces attacked Robert E. Lee's defenses head-on. While the fighting raged, the cavalry would penetrate as far south as Richmond to cut Lee's communications as he fell back to his capital under Hooker's multidirectional pounding.[4]

Fitz's return to Culpeper—where he joined Rooney Lee, whose men had shouldered the picket duty the 2nd Brigade had relinquished—proved to be premature. On the fourteenth, before Stoneman could force a crossing at Beverly Ford, a heavy, incessant rain began to fall. The river rose so high, so quickly, that for two weeks the would-be raiders marked time on their side of the river. Fitz kept a close eye on them, regularly informing Stuart of the marching and countermarching Stoneman conducted in an apparent attempt to fool his men into believing they were still mobile.[5]

During the rain-soaked fortnight, Hooker revamped his strategy to conform to the changed situation. Now his main army would initiate the offensive—Stoneman's raid on the railroads would be an independent movement, a sideshow to the larger effort farther north. On the twenty-seventh, when the skies finally cleared, Hooker's infantry began to join Stoneman near Beverly Ford. Screened by the cavalry as well as by noisy diversions opposite Fredericksburg, Hooker's maneuver wing spent the next two days passing over the Rappahannock, then moving south to the Rapidan, which they crossed to within ten miles of Fredericksburg.

Thus far Hooker had advanced all but undetected. The scouting parties sent out by Fitz and his cousin (Hampton's brigade was wintering far to the south, beyond range of quick recall) were only partially successful in alerting Stuart and his superior to the enemy's movements. By the last day of the month, three Union corps—roughly seventy thousand infantry and artillery—had reached Chancellorsville, a strategic crossroads in the heart of a foreboding expanse of trees and brush known as the Wilderness. From there, Hooker could attack Robert E. Lee from the blind side, for the latter's attention had been arrested by the sixty thousand troops Hooker had sent to duplicate Burnside's assault on Marye's Heights.[6]

Early on the twenty-ninth Stuart's troopers made first contact with an infantry column that had crossed to the south side of the Rappahannock. By interrogating the several prisoners he took, Stuart gained a better understanding of the unfolding situation. He quickly warned his superior to watch for a movement toward his rear by way of the corridor of land below the Rapidan. Apparently it was this alarm that prompted Lee that evening to turn the division of Major General Richard H. Anderson to the rear and send it on to Chancellorsville. About twenty-four hours later, Lee dispatched to the same place the division of Major General Lafayette McLaws. Both were elements of James Longstreet's command (recently designated the First Corps, Army of Northern Virginia). They were all the troops Longstreet had left behind when, in early April, he led the rest of his command to forage among, and oppose the occupiers of, the Suffolk, Virginia region.[7]

The message delivered, Stuart accompanied Fitz and his brigade on a fast march to Raccoon Ford, upstream from Hooker's primary crossing site on the Rapidan. As they hastened along, Stuart dispatched Rooney Lee, with less than half of his brigade—all he felt he could spare—to oppose Stoneman's raiders, now advancing toward the Virginia Central. Over the next four days Fitz's cousin would do yeoman service dogging a much larger foe, striking his flanks and rear when least expected and causing him at times to veer from his intended path. Stoneman's column would inflict much damage on three railroads in the Richmond vicinity as well as on warehouses and supply depots along his roundabout route, but without Rooney Lee's intervention more critical resources might have been destroyed or put out of commission. In the end, the raid would be judged a strategic failure, contributing little or nothing to Hooker's larger offensive.[8]

Early on the evening of the twenty-ninth, Stuart and Fitz waded Raccoon Ford and on the south side turned toward Fredericksburg. While Fitz's 3rd Virginia galloped on ahead in an attempt to interpose between Hooker and Fredericksburg, Stuart led the rest of the column toward a forest landmark, Wilderness Tavern, where he could monitor the progress of the troops on Hooker's lower flank. At the tavern, early on the thirtieth, Fitz's men ran into an enemy detachment and sparred with it stubbornly. Reportedly, in so doing they held up Hooker's advance for two hours or more.[9]

During the skirmish, Stuart learned that enough Federals had gotten ahead of him on the way to Fredericksburg that his linkup with Robert E. Lee was problematic. Thus he guided the 2nd Brigade on a circuitous trek through the forest, heading southeastward.

If he hoped to avoid contact with the enemy, Stuart was disappointed. At

Todd's Tavern, a weather-beaten structure along the southern edge of the Wilderness, Fitz's vanguard was attacked by an enemy force shrouded in darkness. It proved to be a New York cavalry regiment roving well in advance of one of Hooker's corps. Temporarily stunned by the New Yorkers' plucky but foolhardy attempt to take on a full brigade of cavalry, Fitz recovered to counterattack with Rosser's 5th Virginia. Tom Rosser's regiment put the impulsive enemy to flight and killed their leader, Lieutenant Colonel Duncan McVicar.[10]

After tending to the casualties both forces had suffered, Stuart and Fitz pushed on through the night toward the not-so-distant sounds of battle. Early on May 1, they moved out the Orange Plank Road until they made contact with the army's infantry, then concentrating southeast of Chancellorsville. They found Lee, with the bulk of Jackson's Second Corps, on the scene. Finally persuaded that the main threat to his army was coming from the rear via the Rapidan, Lee had ordered Jackson to leave one division and a separate brigade, both under Major General Jubal A. Early, supported by the majority of the army's reserve artillery, south of Fredericksburg to resist the enemy's attack. With the rest of Jackson's command, Lee had left for Chancellorsville at dawn on May 1. He reached there about 8 A.M., just in time to prevent Anderson and McLaws from being overwhelmed by the heavier numbers opposing them.[11]

Stuart found Lee offensive-minded, as usual. The army leader was attempting to find a way to counter his enemy's recent pullback to an extended but apparently well-fortified position centered around the Chancellorsville crossroads. It appeared that Hooker had surrendered the initiative—the kind of mistake his opponent usually hastened to exploit. Yet Fighting Joe was dug in so deeply that neither Lee nor Jackson could find an opening for a direct assault. They had to come up with something—they could not permit the enemy to remain in force so close to Fredericksburg. One option was retreat, but Lee refused to consider withdrawing from the Rappahannock line.

During the intermittent, inconclusive fighting on May 1, Stuart's cavalry spent most of the day guarding the infantry's flanks and rear. To accomplish the mission, Fitz split his brigade, placing his 4th Virginia and a portion of the 3rd on the army's right, and guarding the more vulnerable left flank with the 1st, 2nd, and 5th Virginia, as well as with the remainder of the 3rd. His regiments remained in these positions when the day ended with Lee and Jackson still immersed in tactical calculations.[12]

By morning of the second, the commanders had settled on a westward march by Jackson in search of the far Union right. Acting on the word of Fitz Lee's scouts, Stuart had advised Lee that the flank in question, which extended beyond Wilderness Church on the Orange Turnpike, appeared to be "in the air" and therefore vulnerable to attack, especially a surprise attack. Thus, at about seven-thirty in the morning, Jackson set out for Wilderness Church at the forefront of a twenty-six hundred-man column. He left behind Lee, with fourteen thousand troops. Their job was to contain more than five times as many Yankees until Jackson could get into position to attack them.

Fitz Lee's troopers led the way through the Wilderness via a little-used wood-cutter's trail. His job was to guard the upper flank of Jackson's six-mile-long column and shield it from enemy view—a heavy task, as Jackson's route crossed almost the entire front of Hooker's army. The 1st Virginia had the post of honor at the front of the column, with the 2nd and 5th Virginia farther to the rear, and with infantry units in between. At several points, bodies of Federals advanced toward Lee's troopers, precipitating sharp fighting. Fitz's men parried their blows so deftly that the enemy appeared to remain ignorant of Jackson's movements and intentions. The counterreconnaissance skills of the 2nd Cavalry Brigade were never better displayed.[13]

At about noon the head of Jackson's column reached the Brock Road, which it took northward toward the turnpike. Sometime before 2 P.M. Fitz turned off this road at a point above its crossing of the Orange Plank Road, the byway Jackson was planning to take toward Hooker's flank. Accompanied by a single staff officer, the brigadier cut eastward through a dense woods looking for a vantage point from which to determine if he had passed the end of Hooker's line, which was held by Major General Oliver Otis Howard's XI Army Corps.

Spotting a fairly steep knoll on the property of a farmer named Burton, Fitz ascended it and peered northward. "What a sight presented itself before me!" he later wrote. "Below, and but a few hundred yards distant, ran the Federal line of battle. I was in rear of Howard's right. There were the lines of defence, with abatis in front, and long lines of stacked arms in rear. Two cannon were visible in the part of the line seen. The soldiers were in groups in the rear, laughing, chatting, smoking, probably engaged, here and there, in games of cards, and other amusements indulged in while feeling safe and comfortable, awaiting orders. In rear of them were other parties driving up and butchering beeves."[14]

Almost breathless with excitement, Fitz galloped back to Jackson's column and sought its leader. Years later he recalled having gasped, "General, if you will ride with me, halting your column here, out of sight, I will show you the enemy's right, and you will perceive the great advantage of attacking down the Old turnpike instead of the Plank road."[15]

He led the corps commander to the knoll, followed him to the top, and watched him closely as he gazed in the direction his guide was pointing. Although Jackson said not a word, "his eyes burned with a brilliant glow, lighting up a sad face. His expression was one of intense interest, his face was colored slightly with the paint of approaching battle, and radiant at the success of his flank movement."[16]

Finally breaking his silence, Jackson calmly instructed a courier who had accompanied him to the knoll to order the ranking officer at the head of the column to continue past the plank road until reaching the turnpike, where Jackson would join him. Fitz wrote of his superior that "One more look upon the Federal lines, and then he rode rapidly down the hill, his arms flapping to the motion of his horse, over whose head it seemed, good rider as he was, he would certainly go."[17]

Jackson had left without uttering another word. Years later, Fitz admitted to having "expected to be told I had made a valuable personal reconnaissance—saving the lives of many soldiers, and that Jackson was indebted to me to that amount at least. Perhaps I might have been a little chagrined at Jackson's silence, and hence commented inwardly and adversely upon his horsemanship. Alas! I had looked upon him for the last time."[18]

If Jackson overlooked Fitz's good work, Robert E. Lee did not. Days after the campaign ended, he informed his nephew that "your admirable conduct, love for the cause of your country, and devotion to duty, fill me with pleasure. I hope you will soon see her efforts for independence crowned with success, and long live to enjoy the affection and gratitude of your country."[19]

As Jackson galloped toward an encounter with Howard's troops, he developed a plan of attack. It took some hours to close up his ranks and move his divisions into proper position. Less than an hour of sunlight remained when at last all was ready, but that was more time than Jackson needed. Just after 6 P.M. his men surged forward with a wild abandon that scared the wits out of their unsuspecting enemy. The attackers quickly gathered a momentum that carried them over any breastworks they encountered and through the camps beyond, whose occupants they sent running through the trees at high speed.

By the time darkness descended and reinforcements had rushed up to stem the tide of defeat sweeping toward Chancellorsville, Hooker's line was two miles shorter than it had been an hour before. Jackson's assault so stunned Fighting Joe and so demoralized his soldiers that before dawn on May 2 the outcome of the fighting in the Wilderness had been effectively determined.[20]

*   *   *

Even after Jackson's attack struck home, Hooker enjoyed opportunities to salvage victory, especially after nine o'clock that night when Jackson rode forward with a small retinue on a personal reconnaissance. Seeking an avenue of advance for A. P. Hill's as-yet-uncommitted division, in the darkness the corps commander blundered into his own lines and was shot down by an errant volley from a North Carolina brigade. Hit three times, General Jackson was borne on a litter to the rear, where surgeons amputated his left arm. Evacuated by ambulance to Guiney's Station, he would die there on May 10, not of his wounds but of pneumonia.[21]

Events in addition to Jackson's fall seemed to favor a Union recovery. By early evening his attack had spent itself and Howard's corps had re-formed north of Chancellorsville. Moreover, reinforcements were on the way from Fredericksburg;

when they arrived to shore up the new right flank, they would give Hooker more than ninety thousand troops with which to oppose Lee's divided force of forty-eight thousand. But such an advantage counted for naught, for the Union leader's confidence had been shattered along with his right flank. When the fighting resumed on May 3, his frayed nerves led him to make tactical blunders, the worst being his withdrawal of troops from a key position, Hazel Grove, southwest of the crossroads. Jackson's successor immediately placed thirty artillery pieces on the abandoned plateau and used them to enfilade the compacted enemy line. One shell struck the Chancellor house at the crossroads, felling Hooker, who had been standing on the front porch. For hours afterward, he appeared dazed and disoriented.[22]

The exploitation of Hazel Grove, which spurred the Confederates into seizing other important points including, eventually, Chancellorsville itself, was the work of J. E. B. Stuart. Following Jackson's fall and the disabling of Hill, his ranking subordinate, Stuart was given command of the Second Corps. By all indications, throughout May 3 he performed well in the role of infantry commander, engineering assaults on and along the Wilderness Pike that forced the enemy to take up an even more circumscribed position between Chancellorsville and the Rapidan.[23]

There the Federals were effectively contained, giving Robert E. Lee an opportunity to counter the part of Hooker's army under Major General John Sedgwick that had been attacking Fredericksburg. Just before noon on May 3, Sedgwick broke through at Marye's Heights, carrying the defenses Burnside had failed to take almost five months before. Soon Sedgwick was surging westward to join Hooker. But Robert E. Lee, initially with only five brigades of Longstreet's corps, met Sedgwick at Salem Church on the turnpike and repulsed his assault. The next morning, having augmented his lines, Lee attacked Sedgwick and drove him back across the river with heavy losses. Salem Church brought a close to the major fighting at Chancellorsville.[24]

On May 3 and 4, by virtue of Stuart's temporary transfer to the infantry, Fitz Lee commanded all Confederate cavalry on the field of battle. He massed his regiments on the far left of the army, along the road to Ely's Ford on the Rapidan. He had gained access to that thoroughfare by driving from it a detachment of the single brigade of cavalry that had accompanied Hooker into the Wilderness instead of Stoneman on his raid toward Richmond. Thereafter Fitz held the position against intermittent pressure from Hooker's main body.[25]

The mission was an important one, but it was not especially taxing. On the other hand, by May 3 Fitz had already made his contribution to the battle. The personal reconnaissance that enabled him to show Jackson the most auspicious place to attack the Union right was a feat of which he could truly be proud. Judging by the many references he made to it over the years in speeches and writings, he remained proud for the rest of his life.

*   *   *

Secure in his defensive perimeter north of Chancellorsville, Hooker felt confident enough to call a war council on the evening of May 4. His self-assurance
fled, however, when a majority of his corps commanders voted to remain on
the field and renew the fight in the morning. Their superior summarily over-
ruled them. Citing the paramount need to defend Washington, he declared that
he could not afford to risk further damage to his army. Instead, he ordered a
full retreat to the north bank of the Rappahannock. By midday on the sixth the
Army of the Potomac was gone from Robert E. Lee's front.[26]

So completely demoralized was Hooker that in later weeks he avoided any
confrontation with Lee. His quiescence and immobility gave his adversary an
opening to launch an offensive of his own—in the North. Within two weeks
of Hooker's retreat, Lee was broaching a second invasion to President Davis
and his new secretary of war, James A. Seddon. Although at first reluctant to
do so, both officials approved Lee's plan, if only because it promised to draw Union
troops from Mississippi, where Grant was renewing his effort to take Vicksburg.[27]

Lee wanted his cavalry to be in the best possible condition for the coming
campaign. He directed Stuart, who had returned to command of the cavalry, to
group his recently dispersed forces, including Hampton's brigade, just up from
Southside Virginia, and Rooney Lee, returned from harassing the Richmond
raiders. "Give them breathing time," Lee advised, "so that, when you strike,
Stoneman may feel you."[28]

In fact, when the blow landed Stoneman would feel nothing. His expedition
against Lee's communications had been such a notorious failure that Hooker,
seeking to deflect criticism of his own generalship, ceremoniously fired his
cavalry commander as well as William Averell, who had performed poorly on
the same expedition. To fill their places, Hooker tabbed, respectively, Alfred
Pleasonton and Colonel (later Brigadier General) H. Judson Kilpatrick—
kindred spirits in their ability to promote themselves as bold fighters, while per-
forming erratically under pressure.[29]

Stuart took his superior's advice and collected his regiments near Culpeper
Court House. Through the remainder of May and into June, he provisioned his
troopers; supplied them with new and captured carbines, pistols, and sabers;
and assimilated into their ranks brigades and regiments assigned him for the
invasion. Fitz Lee did his part, striving to ensure that his brigade's many new
recruits received the training they needed. On June 2 a member of the 5th Virginia wrote from Culpeper that "we have a sort of a camp of instruction here,
drill every day & dress parade."[30]

While Stuart welcomed the added manpower, which swelled his command
to just under ten thousand officers and men, he could have done without some
of their commanders. These included Grumble Jones, whose Valley brigade

rejoined Stuart during the first week of June, and Beverly Robertson, who one week earlier returned from North Carolina at the head of two Tarheel regiments.[31]

To examine the materiel at his disposal while also promoting corporate morale, in early June Stuart staged a series of reviews on the plains surrounding Culpeper. On some of these occasions—which the Beau Sabreur invested with all the pomp and pageantry at his command—distinguished guests were on hand, including Robert E. Lee and former Secretary of War George W. Randolph.

Fitz Lee, who shared his superior's love of theater, greatly enjoyed these displays of martial prowess, some of which featured mock saber and pistol charges and the firing of blank rounds by the Stuart Horse Artillery under Pelham's successor, Major Robert F. Beckham. Fitz made the mistake, however, of thinking that one of his infantry colleagues might also enjoy the spectacle. At his invitation, the review of June 8 was attended by Major General John Bell Hood, formerly of the 2nd U.S. Cavalry, now a division commander under Longstreet. On a lark, Hood brought with him every foot soldier in his command. They spent the day jeering and sneering at their cavalry comrades, whom they professed to regard as comic-opera warriors.[32]

The reviews were interspersed with other social occasions at which Fitz was present either as guest or host. On May 28, one of his favorite subordinates, Tom Rosser, wed Elizabeth Winston at her family's home in Hanover County. Fitz was there to kiss the bride, pump the groom's hand, and help cut the cake. The following day many of the wedding guests attended a picnic, thrown by Fitz and his staff, at Culpeper Court House. According to one guest, "all the young ladies from the neighborhood" were on hand, as were "music and refreshments. . . . all went off very merrily."[33]

The social season ended abruptly when—perhaps as a result of overexerting himself during one of those sham battles—Fitz was laid up with what Stuart termed "inflammatory rheumatism." In all probability, this was not rheumatism as it is understood today but rather the onset of degenerative arthritis. The condition may have originated with the orthopedic trauma Fitz suffered when kicked by the mule. Whatever the origin, it laid him up for several weeks and caused him to miss action on some notable fields while Tom Munford took charge of his brigade.[34]

He was abed on June 9 when the bivouacs of Stuart's enlarged division around Brandy Station came under attack by ten thousand Federal cavalry under Pleasonton. The result was a day-long saber and pistol battle, the largest all-cavalry engagement of the war to that time. In the end, although far from soundly whipped, the Yankees withdrew to their side of the Rappahannock. They could, and did, boast of having administered a beating to the flower of the Confederate cavalry, while also disrupting an imminent raid into the North. On the other hand, Stuart and his horsemen had comported themselves well throughout the day, despite being surprised and at times virtually surrounded. Fitz was especially pleased to learn from Tom Munford that his brother, Henry, had been in the thick of the action, "rendering valuable assistance" and having a horse badly wounded beneath him.[35]

Although many of Pleasonton's claims were exaggerated—after all, more than a mere raid was in the offing—the bluecoats had taken a heavy toll of each of Stuart's brigades. The most prominent casualty was Rooney Lee, who suffered a disabling wound that required a long convalescence. During his recuperation, spent among his family in Hanover County, he would be captured and confined for several months in a Union prison.[36]

Among Stuart's claims were that he had parried a multidirectional attack, inflicted heavier casualties than he took, and held the field at day's end. These contentions, while true, did not save him in later weeks from a torrent of criticism from political officials and editors hitherto worshipful of his generalship. Another whose reputation suffered as a result of the battle was Munford, who because of a garbled order had failed to bring Fitz's brigade into the fight at a critical time, thereby contributing in some degree to the less than satisfactory outcome.[37]

Until able to assess the long-range implications of Brandy Station, R. E. Lee suspended his movement from the Rappahannock toward the Shenandoah Valley, which had begun on June 3. When the march resumed, Lee ordered most of the cavalry to remain behind until Stuart could refurbish and resupply his command, after which it would join the army in the Valley, screening its right flank from enemy view. In the meantime, the ANV would draw its mounted support from Brigadier General Albert G. Jenkins's brigade of western Virginia cavalry, yet another addition to the army for the duration of the invasion.

Chagrined to be left behind, if only temporarily, Stuart attended to the necessary repairs as quickly as possible. Early on the sixteenth, his refreshed command crossed the Rappahannock and rode hard to catch up with Lee's infantry. The Second Corps, now under Dick Ewell, led the army's march, followed by Longstreet's First Corps, with the newly created Third Army Corps of A. P. Hill bringing up the rear. The last of Hill's troops left Fredericksburg the day Stuart departed Brandy Station.[38]

There was no reason for anyone to remain on the river. On the thirteenth, Hooker, having been duped for the past ten days into believing his enemy remained at full strength across from him, finally learned of Ewell's and Longstreet's pullout. In belated haste, he yanked his army north. Fairfax Station on the O & A would be his headquarters for the next several days.[39]

When Stuart's column began its journey, Fitz Lee accompanied it in an ambulance. His joints were so inflamed and painful that he remained unfit for active duty, leaving Colonel Munford in command of the brigade. Fitz continued to believe it in good hands; he had lost no confidence in Munford's abilities despite the colonel's recent misadventure.

Fitz continued on the disabled rolls and thus saw no part in the fighting that broke out in the Loudoun Valley after Stuart overtook Longstreet and assumed a flanking position east of the Blue Ridge chain. On June 17, the troopers under Munford, while scouting near Aldie Gap in the Bull Run Mountains, clashed with the troopers of Pleasonton and Kilpatrick, who were seeking to amend for failing to alert Hooker to his enemy's pullout. The fight ended as a stalemate, although the Federals suffered three hundred casualties, three times as many as Munford.

Two days later, a division of Union horsemen, hoping to penetrate Stuart's screen, attacked Robertson's and Rooney Lee's brigades (the latter now commanded by Colonel John R. Chambliss Jr.) west of Middleburg. Stuart's response was muted by his determination to maintain the defensive, having learned that his opponents enjoyed the close support of Major General George Gordon Meade's V Army Corps. Another standoff ensued, although afterward Stuart evacuated the Middleburg area and fell back to the mountains. He had incurred fewer losses this day than at Aldie, although they included a prized aide—Heros von Borcke, whose near-fatal wound ended his passionate service in the Confederate cavalry.

The last in the series of sharp encounters in Loudoun Valley took place on the twenty-first. Stuart, having reoccupied Middleburg upon his enemy's withdrawal, was again chased toward the Blue Ridge when Pleasonton attacked him, backed by one of Meade's brigades. Despite the preponderance of Union strength, Stuart's men withdrew grudgingly. The greatest resistance came from Wade Hampton, who distinguished himself in a rear-guard action east of Upperville against the feisty Kilpatrick.[40]

At day's end, some of John Buford's Federals scaled a foothill of the Blue Ridge, peered into the valley beyond, and spied Longstreet's camps. Once informed of the sighting, Hooker had his first inkling of Robert E. Lee's location and heading. But by now Lee had moved so close to the Potomac that he could not be stopped short of his next objective, Pennsylvania.

*   *   *

Stuart, his screening mission successfully completed, presented his superior with a plan for an independent campaign north of the Potomac during which he would ride around Hooker's army. En route to Pennsylvania he would lay a heavy hand on enemy communications and secure provisions for the main army from captured supply trains as well as from the fertile countryside along his route. After outdistancing any pursuers, he would unite with Ewell's advance somewhere on the Susquehanna River below Harrisburg.

Stuart's superior approved the plan with some stipulations. In response to one of these, Stuart agreed to leave with the main army the brigades of Robertson and Jones, as well as much of Beckham's horse artillery. When added to Jenkins's brigade, then riding with Ewell, these detachments would provide Lee with the support of almost six thousand cavalrymen, more than enough, Stuart believed, to guide him through unfamiliar territory and warn of the enemy's proximity. Having thus rid himself of his least favored subordinates, Stuart then ordered the five thousand troopers of Hampton, Chambliss, and Munford to journey into the enemy's rear.[41]

Though still somewhat hobbled, Fitz fled his ambulance on the eve of Stuart's departure from Salem, west of the Blue Ridge, and was in the saddle when the expedition got under way just after midnight on June 25. The first leg of the journey went smoothly enough, even for the sore-legged commander of the 2nd Brigade. The only difficulty came when, near Glascock's Gap in the Bull Run chain, the head of the column ran into one of Hooker's infantry corps, heading northward. The meeting-engagement forced Stuart to detour farther south than he had planned. Not until the next afternoon, after passing one of his old haunts, Brentsville, did he turn north in two columns. The heading led to another familiar locale, Burke's Station on the O & A, where the 2nd Brigade, temporarily detached from Stuart's main body, wrecked track and, for the second time in six months, cut the telegraph line.

Continuing north, Fitz's column stopped at Annandale, where it plundered a cache of military provisions and sutler's supplies. Then it was on to a reunion with Hampton and Chambliss at Dranesville, scene of Stuart's December 1861 defeat. A few miles farther north, the column passed a major milestone of the expedition by crossing the Potomac River at Seneca Ford (also known as Rowsee's Mill Ford). By the wee hours of the twenty-eighth, all of Stuart's people were on dry ground in Maryland for the first time since their hurried departure the previous September.

After destroying rafts and boats on an adjacent canal and paroling their soldier passengers, Stuart pushed north to the Washington, D.C., suburb of Rockville, outside of which Chambliss's troopers, at the head of the column, pursued and overtook more than 125 supply wagons bound for Hooker's new headquarters outside Frederick, Maryland. Reaching the scene minutes after the capture, Fitz's and Hampton's troopers joined Chambliss's in helping themselves to items enumerated by an officer of the 9th Virginia: "bakers' bread, crackers, whiskey in bottles of great variety, sugar, hams, with some tin and woodware, knives and forks." The man added that "the bacon and crackers, as well as the whiskey, proved to our jaded and hungry troops most acceptable."[42]

Despite the drag it would exert, Stuart, who had left Salem without supply vehicles or pack animals, decided to add the eight-mile-long train to his column. The wagons would disrupt further his already skewed timetable, but he could not foresee the delays they would cause. To make up for time required to assimilate the train and in order to cut the Baltimore & Ohio as soon as possible, he marched his men through the night.

At Cooksville, short of the railroad, he split his column once more. Again detached from the main body, Fitz's command proceeded due north and at daylight on the twenty-ninth struck the B & O at Sykesville. While his men tore up track for several hundred yards in both directions, Hampton and Chambliss did the same a few miles farther east near Hood's Mills. More telegraph line was downed at these points, leading Stuart to exult that "communications of the enemy with Washington City [were] thus cut off at every point."[43]

The columns clasped hands at Eldersburg, nine miles below Westminster, and proceeded north, Fitz's brigade in the lead. Reaching Westminster at 5 P.M., his vanguard was charged by fewer than one hundred troopers of a Delaware cavalry regiment that had been guarding the railroad to Baltimore. Part of the advance guard was thrown into confusion, and two officers of the 4th Virginia were shot dead before Fitz pushed to the front to restore order. A trooper of the 2nd Virginia, immediately behind the 4th, reported that "Gen'l Fitz Lee came galloping up to the head of our regiment and led us in a charge entirely through the town. The enemy made no serious attempt to hold the town and fled before us." Angered by the surprise assault and the disruption it had caused, Fitz pressed the pursuit until sixty-seven of the enemy had been killed, wounded, or taken prisoner.[44]

Anxious to give his hard-riding troopers a respite, Stuart bivouacked them in the town and on the roads north of it. That night patrols probed toward the Pennsylvania line, eleven miles away. They reported no signs of Ewell's infantry, but neither did they locate the large force of Union cavalry—Judson Kilpatrick's newly acquired division—that blocked Stuart's path the next morning when he passed out of Maryland and approached the town of Hanover. Unwilling to lose more time by detouring, Stuart bulled ahead, hoping to clear the road by sheer force. He attacked the end of Kilpatrick's line, routing one regiment and menacing others, but reinforcements rushed up, counterattacked, and shoved Chambliss's men out of the town.

Noting how quickly Chambliss had fallen back, Kilpatrick determined to make a stand. He barricaded Hanover's streets, built a bulwark of cannons above the town, and extended his right flank southwestward along the turnpike to Littlestown. Soon he was opposing not only Chambliss but, farther to the west below Plum Creek, the troopers of Fitz Lee.[45]

Fitz's brigade had again been detached from Stuart's column and was marching about a half-mile west of it. While Chambliss hunkered down to battle one-half of Kilpatrick's command, the brigade of Brigadier General Elon J. Farnsworth, Fitz moved cross-country shortly before noon toward the Littlestown Pike. Several miles from Hanover, he encountered a regiment of Michigan cavalry, part of a brigade commanded by one of Fitz's West Point students, George Armstrong Custer, now a brigadier general. Fitz immediately deployed his lead regiments in line of battle, ready to charge if necessary. Then he ran to the front the two-gun section of horse artillery that had accompanied his brigade on the expedition. The show of force appeared to cow the Michiganders, who pulled back expeditiously after exchanging a few shots with Fitz's advance.

Fitz pursued the regiment up the road to Hanover. About a quarter-mile southwest of town, near the hamlet of Pennville, he ran into Custer's main force—three more regiments of the Wolverine Brigade, supported by a light battery. New to command, having been promoted from captain only days before, Custer was eager to fight. His troopers, most of whom were armed with the seven-shot Spencer repeating rifle, advanced on foot in strength. They succeeded in driving Fitz's vanguard from a long ridge, inflicting several casualties and capturing fifteen enlisted men.

Fitz countered by calling up his main body, which, after some spirited fighting, mostly dismounted, retook the high ground. With the close support of his attached artillery and some of Chambliss's men, Fitz held the position against the superior firepower of the Wolverines. Many of Custer's men, however, secured a foothold on Fitz's flank, refusing to be dislodged even by shell and canister. They clung to their position throughout the afternoon, making Stuart fret for the safety of his far left.[46]

The fighting went on until sundown. Like many cavalry versus cavalry actions, it ended as a draw, neither opponent able to advance or willing to retreat. After dark, Stuart's command carefully disengaged. Fitz recalled his brigade and, covered by Hampton, fell back to guard the wagon train, which Stuart started northeastward toward the village of Jefferson. The choice of routes, which added ten miles to the leg to the Susquehanna, was made necessary by Stuart's fear of losing his prized trophies if he passed too close to the enemy's position.

The roundabout disengagement proved unnecessary. His men having fought themselves out, Kilpatrick was in no mood to dispute Stuart's withdrawal, let alone pursue him. But even though given an open road, Stuart's journey from Jefferson north to Dover and then on a westward angle toward Carlisle was a grueling ordeal for every horse, mule, rider, and drover in his column. Days of near-constant travel and a succession of engagements from firefights to pitched battles had left the expeditionary force, as one officer put it, "broken down & in no condition to fight."[47]

The hardships of travel were exacerbated by the growing awareness that Ewell's infantry, with whom they were supposed to link somewhere north of Hanover, was nowhere to be found. Nor did Stuart, Fitz, or anyone else in the column have the faintest idea where the rest of the army might be. Stuart had sent gallopers in various directions in hopes of locating detachments, patrols, or stragglers from the Second Corps, but as yet none had reported. The comrades the messengers left behind were limping blindly through an enemy's country, not knowing what lay ahead or how they could muster the strength to oppose it if it turned out to be wearing blue.

The killing march took the column across the summit of the northernmost spur of South Mountain and into Cumberland County where, on the afternoon of July 1, it came up to the outskirts of Carlisle. Stuart had read in newspapers seized by his men that Ewell's corps recently had occupied the town. Desperately searching for his infantry comrades, Stuart sent the main body down the road to Dillsburg while dispatching Fitz to seize the town, which was now in the possession of a body of local militia under Brigadier General William Farrar Smith, formerly a corps commander in the Army of the Potomac.

Memories of service at the Cavalry School of Instruction must have flooded Fitz's mind as he led his brigade, accompanied by six horse artillery pieces, around the east side of the town to bivouac on the grounds of Carlisle Barracks. On the fringes of the now-evacuated training depot he emplaced his cannons and had their crews lob shells into the center of the town. He kept up an intermittent cannonade—to which Smith did not reply—until sundown, when he halted long enough to send a courier-borne surrender demand to the Union commander. Smith refused it, as he did a second demand that Fitz delivered around midnight.

His patience worn thin by fatigue, stress, and anger over Smith's recalcitrance, Fitz did something he once would have considered unthinkable. At his order, a squad of troopers piled combustible materials outside the post barracks, lit them, and watched the structure burn. Up in flames, too, went the adjacent commander's quarters, where Charles May had been serenaded by Fitz's vocal troupe in the palmy days of 1856. Other detachments set fire to the town's gas works and a lumber yard adjacent to it. Sparks from the conflagration leaped to private dwellings, burning them to the ground. While the vandalism continued, Fitz resumed his shelling of the town.[48]

At 2 A.M. on July 2, the barrage ceased for good. A messenger from Stuart rode up to announce that the entire column was departing Carlisle for points south. An emissary from Robert E. Lee's headquarters had met one of the messengers Stuart had sent to locate the army. The emissary disclosed that for the past twenty hours Lee's infantry and artillery had been grappling with the Army of the Potomac just outside the corporate limits of the seat of Adams County, Pennsylvania—a place called Gettysburg. That was the next destination of Fitz Lee and his comrades.[49]

NINE

Armageddon
and After

The road from Carlisle led southeastward to Papertown and Petersburg, then south to Hunterstown and, four miles farther on, to Gettysburg. "We proceeded at a trot," wrote one of Fitz's noncommissioned officers, "pushing our fatigued animals as much as we dared. For they had been constantly on the march during the last ten days. . . . We could hear the distant rumble of the cannon around Gettysburg, which reminded us of the grim business we would face upon our arrival there."[1]

The guns had been in almost constant operation since the previous morning, when the head of A. P. Hill's corps unexpectedly encountered Buford's Union cavalry on the western outskirts of the town. Buford was there in his role as the forward echelon of the Army of the Potomac, the main portion of which was strung out on the roads between its namesake river and the Maryland-Pennsylvania border. Buford and everyone else in blue now answered to George Meade. Only four days earlier the V Corps leader had assumed command of the army, replacing Joe Hooker, whose weak response to Lee's invasion had cost him the confidence of Lincoln and Stanton.

When they encountered Hill on July 1, Buford's troopers, the eyes and ears of Meade's far-flung command, had a fairly accurate idea of their enemy's position and more than an inkling of his intentions. The same could not be said of Hill or any of his colleagues. Thanks to Stuart's long and unexplained absence, the Army of Northern Virginia had been wandering in the dark since entering Pennsylvania nine days before. Through misunderstandings and a lack of communication, Robert E. Lee had failed to make use of Robertson and Jones and their forty-five hundred men. As for Jenkins's cavalry, it remained attached to Ewell's command, which did not reach Gettysburg until late in the morning of the first.

Lacking a mounted reconnaissance capability and thus uncertain of the nature of the opposition, Buford's opponents mistook his men for veteran infantry, an impression strengthened by the Federals' use of breech-loading carbines. Hill and his subordinates took so long to make sense of their situation that before they could evict Buford from his well-chosen positions, Meade's infantry advance arrived from Maryland to even the odds. Although eventually chased from the high ground north and west of Gettysburg, the Federals had hung on long enough to prevent a decisive Confederate victory. That night the greater portion of both armies reached the field. Consequently, a second day of hard fighting was in progress—its outcome very much in doubt—as Stuart's people traveled the last weary miles of the circuitous journey that had begun at Salem, Virginia, almost a week earlier.[2]

Before noon on July 2, the cavalry's vanguard moved down the road from Hunterstown to its junction with the York Turnpike, along the far left of the Army of Northern Virginia. Here Stuart left the column to report to Robert E. Lee. In his absence, the head of his column took up a position along the upper flank of Major General Edward Johnson's division of Ewell's corps. Johnson's men occupied themselves in long-range skirmishing until sometime after 6 P.M., when they joined in an attack on Culp's Hill, southeast of Gettysburg. Neither activity involved cavalry participation. This was fortunate, for the respite Stuart's men were granted was essential to restoring their energy and stamina.

The only members of Fitz Lee's and Chambliss's brigades who were kept more or less busy this day were the pickets both commands threw out northward on the Harrisburg Road and southward to a point between the York Pike and the Hanover Road. However, at the rear of Stuart's column, which took hours to close up on Gettysburg, the story was different. Shortly after 2 P.M., the roving Wolverines of Custer's brigade galloped through Hunterstown and struck the shank of Hampton's brigade, which was guarding Hooker's erstwhile supply train. In an exchange of saber charges along fenced-in farm roads, each side suffered rather heavily, to little strategic advantage. The highest-ranking casualty was Hampton, temporarily disabled by a near-fatal saber blow to the back of his head. Despite the wound, he engineered a stubborn defense that eventually persuaded Custer to withdraw to Gettysburg by a roundabout route.[3]

Early on July 3, as the mercury began a slow climb toward ninety degrees, Stuart led his several-miles-long column—to which had been added Jenkins's brigade, now led by Colonel Milton J. Ferguson, as well as a light battery from Maryland under Captain W. H. Griffin—out the northeastward-leading York

Pike. Ferguson was followed by Chambliss's brigade, then Hampton's, with Fitz Lee and his men trotting along in the rear.

Toward the south, the steadily rising racket near Culp's Hill indicated that the armies were coming awake for a third day of battle. The cavalry would take part in it, but on a front all its own. The main battlefield ran along parallel ridges south and southwest of Gettysburg, but the cavalry's sphere of operations lay three miles to the east. Robert E. Lee had suggested that Stuart pass around Meade's right flank into his army's rear. From that vantage point Stuart's division could cooperate in some way (exactly what Lee had in mind has never been determined) with an infantry offensive planned for the center of the enemy line on Cemetery Ridge.

Stuart had enthusiastically endorsed Lee's proposal, if for no other reason than because he was determined to make amends in his commander's eyes for the unconscionably long period he had spent apart from the army. If Stuart failed to burst through the Union rear at the appointed time, he could at least divert Meade's attention from the attack in front. If, on the other hand, Stuart found an unobstructed path to his objective, there was no telling how much damage, physical and psychological, he could deal the Union army.[4]

At his scouts' suggestion, at about ten o'clock Stuart turned off the York Pike and led his men southeastward along a country road. About half a mile below the turnpike, he ordered the vanguard to pass down a heavily timbered stretch of high ground known locally as Cress's Ridge. Halting on its lowermost spur, which faced the Hanover Pike a mile or so to the south, Stuart had his men halt until he could determine if an enemy force was nearby. He deployed Ferguson's troopers as skirmishers and had them take position on a farm owned by a Pennsylvania Dutchman named Rummel. Chambliss's brigade went into line on the left of Ferguson's main body, with Hampton's extending the line farther to the north. When it arrived sometime after noon, Fitz's brigade, which had been slowed by the wagons and ambulances it had been escorting (Stuart had released his captured train to officials of the quartermaster's department), moved into position along the northern extension of Cress's Ridge.[5]

Action on Stuart's front commenced minutes after he sent a large detachment of Ferguson's command to seize the Rummel farm. The move invited a countermovement by Federal cavalry sheltered in woods farther south, near the intersection of the Hanover Road and the Low Dutch (or Salem Church) Road. These were Custer's men, fresh from their tilt with Hampton outside Hunterstown. For some hours they engaged Ferguson's western Virginians, supported by elements of Chambliss's and Hampton's brigades, in long-range skirmishing. Shortly after noon, however, Custer was relieved by two brigades of Brigadier General David McMurtrie Gregg's cavalry division. When Custer subsequently decided not to abandon the road junction, Stuart found himself opposing substantial portions of both forces, supported by two horse artillery units.[6]

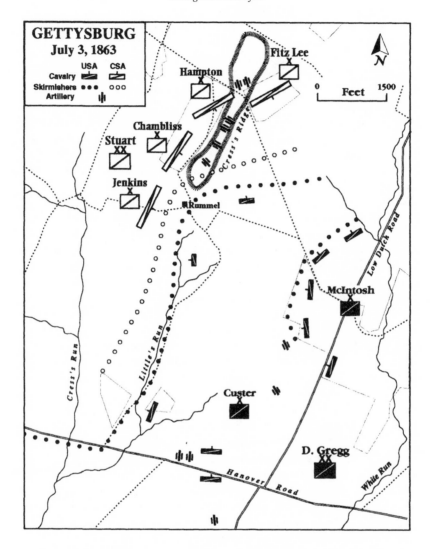

Because of their late arrival and their assigned position farthest from the fighting, Fitz Lee's people saw little action until midafternoon. By this time a series of Union advances and a devastating cannonade had chased Ferguson's men from the Rummel farm. Fitz, presumably at Stuart's order, advanced a portion of his force to cover the withdrawal. When the Union guns turned in his direction, the accurate shelling forced Fitz to recall his troopers to the cover of their heavily wooded position.

About a half-hour later, he advanced again, this time with elements of his

2nd, 3rd, 4th, and 5th Virginia. Again, the Yankee gunners concentrated against them and halted the movement. The detachment of the 3rd, which had moved to the forefront of the line, suffered most; its numerous casualties forced its commander, Colonel Thomas H. Owen, to table a plan to attack dismounted members of Custer's brigade, who had dug in along Little's Run south of the Rummel place.

Refusing to remain immobile, Fitz ordered up the 1st Virginia and advanced it toward the right center of Custer's and Gregg's adjoining positions. At Colonel Drake's word, Fitz's former regiment spurred into a charge that drove one of Custer's regiments from a post-and-rail fence that ran diagonally across the field between the cavalries. Even before it reached this barrier, however, the 1st Virginia was met head-on by another Wolverine outfit. The upshot was a desperate fight at close quarters, to which Hampton added his 1st North Carolina and the Jeff Davis Legion.[7]

Hampton had come to Fitz's support despite an earlier run-in that exuded acrimony. According to the South Carolinian, Fitz had ordered Hampton's entire brigade into action without the knowledge, let alone the consent, of its commander, who was then responding to an order to report in person to Stuart. (Fitz received the same summons but concluded that he should remain with his brigade, a decision Stuart later endorsed.) Upon his return, Hampton found his regiments in motion—he angrily recalled them to Cress's Ridge. The contretemps and its aftermath would serve to widen the already considerable rift between the brigadiers.

The hacking and shooting contest at the fence eventually forced the 1st Virginia to withdraw, although in tolerably good order. Concerned that the retrograde would jeopardize the units he had sent to Drake's aid, Hampton rode forward personally to extricate them. His action triggered the advance of every other regiment and legion under his command—this time the result of an order given in Hampton's name by his adjutant general, who misinterpreted the general's advance as the prelude to a brigade-wide attack. Quickly perceiving that he could not arrest the movement, which had already gained great momentum, Hampton joined it. Placing himself at its head, he led the massive column, at a full gallop, toward the center of the Union line.[8]

His action brought on the climactic phase of the cavalry battle. By chance, it occurred at the same hour—3 P.M.—as another critical offensive closer to Gettysburg. Even as Hampton and his horsemen galloped south, some 12,500 infantry under Major Generals George Pickett and Isaac R. Trimble and Brigadier General J. Johnston Pettigrew were advancing across a mile-wide valley toward the Federal lines on Cemetery Ridge. The attack came in the wake of a thunderous artillery barrage, clearly heard on the cavalry's front.

A segment of Fitz's brigade took part in the final action of the day but only to support Hampton's flank and rear. It incurred few additional casualties, but

Hampton's force suffered heavily when it collided in the middle of the open plain with another Michigan regiment, Custer at its head, moving at the same extended gallop. In the savage melee that followed, Hampton again suffered saber wounds that in time forced him to the rear. On his way back to Cress's Ridge he was struck in the thigh by a piece of canister. The South Carolinian's wounds would incapacitate him for many months.[9]

Seeing their commander retire, many of his troopers followed his example. Others were propelled in that direction by Custer's men, assisted by wild-charging elements of Gregg's division. By five o'clock, concurrent with the bloody repulse of what would become known as Pickett's Charge, the cavalry's field of battle had been swept clear of combatants. The ground between the lines lay littered with dead and wounded men, downed horses, discarded weapons, and scattered equipment. Stuart's attempt to reach the rear of Meade's army in time to influence the outcome of Robert E. Lee's grand offensive had failed.

*   *   *

As he had following Sharpsburg, Lee remained in position at Gettysburg for twenty-four hours after the major fighting ended. When Meade refused to oblige him by attacking as Lee had attacked the previous day, the Confederate leader turned his army southward, his second and last invasion of the North at an end.

Before his army relinquished its grip south and west of town, Lee would send forth its supply vehicles, including those Stuart had seized in Maryland, as well as a column of ambulances containing hundreds of battle casualties, Wade Hampton among them. The larger of Lee's two supply trains, hauling the rations and provender that met a key objective of his mission in the North, would be escorted by yet another body of horsemen added to the army for the invasion—a brigade of cavalry, mounted infantry, and partisan rangers led by John Imboden, Grumble Jones's partner on the recent raid against the western end of the B & O. Imboden would be supported directly by several artillery batteries and more remotely by the brigades of Fitz Lee and Colonel Laurence Baker, Hampton's replacement. Fitz would command the combined force of three thousand.[10]

Late in the afternoon of the fourth, Imboden began his ponderous journey to the Potomac in a sometimes torrential downpour. As the weather-beaten wagons and ambulances trundled west toward the South Mountain passes prior to turning south in the direction of Williamsport, Maryland, Lee dispatched a second, smaller supply train toward the same destination but via a more direct route, the gaps of Jack Mountain. The army's infantry, most of its artillery, and a large portion of its cavalry would also take the latter route. Given Imboden's head start, his column would arrive at the Potomac first, but the main body of the ANV should reach him before any Federals did.

Perhaps an hour after the larger column hit the road to Cashtown and Chambersburg, Fitz's two brigades moved off in its rear. They kept a prudent distance behind the train—not so close that they overran Imboden's escort, yet not so far off as to invite pursuers to interpose between them and their charges. Despite rain, wind, thunder, and rough roads, the only difficulty Fitz's command encountered during the first day of the march occurred when bends in the road or debris, including scattered corpses in blue and gray, caused the wagons to decelerate and the cavalry to overtake the train. At such times Fitz was forced to listen to the anguished sounds that had assailed the ears of Imboden's men ever since leaving Gettysburg—the screams, cries, and moans of the suffering wounded.[11]

The first major problem materialized early on July 5, shortly after the train crossed the mountains and turned south toward the Potomac. Despite Fitz's best efforts to prevent it, a one hundred-man detachment of the 6th Pennsylvania Cavalry under a daring young scouting leader, Captain Ulric Dahlgren, sliced between Imboden's escort and Fitz's column near Waynesboro, Pennsylvania. Armed with axes as well as more conventional weapons, the marauders spent perhaps twenty minutes hacking away at wagon wheels and shooting down mule and horse teams before being forced to desist and retreat. The damage compelled Imboden to leave several conveyances behind when he resumed his march southward.[12]

Later that same day, other pursuers, part of a cavalry regiment that Lee's army had evicted from its duty station in the Shenandoah, struck the train near Greencastle, close to the Maryland line. These members of the 1st New York cut off an isolated section of wagons and confiscated or destroyed its contents. Theoretically, at least, their success owed to the laxity of Fitz Lee's men; thus it seemed poetic justice that most of the sixty vehicles destroyed had carried their baggage, rations, and forage. An officer of the 2nd Virginia lodged a typical complaint: "Our regiment did not save a single wagon. Lost every stitch of clothing that I had but what I had on. They are nearly worn out."[13]

The forces that struck at Waynesboro and Greencastle were company-size. Early on the sixth, a larger force with the potential to inflict lasting harm—the cavalry brigade of Colonel J. Irvin Gregg, one of Stuart's opponents on July 3—struck the rear of Fitz's command near Marion, Pennsylvania. Under orders to guard the wagons, not to fight a major engagement, Fitz had his troopers form a line across the road on which Gregg had advanced. They held back the Federals, who moved to the attack somewhat lethargically, until Imboden's rear guard cleared the area. After Fitz moved on, Gregg did not follow up his attack.[14]

By the time Gregg struck, the head of Imboden's train had reached Williamsport. Imboden had expected to pass the river immediately, but the recent torrent had raised it nearly to flood stage. Having no recourse to remain in Maryland indefinitely, Imboden arranged his wagons and ambulances in as compact a formation as possible, armed their teamsters and some of the less severely wounded, removed the more serious cases to the homes of local citizens, and blocked every road leading to his position with his horsemen and the artillery assigned to them.

He had the chance to test his preparations as early as the sixth, when the main body of Buford's cavalry division approached the wagon park from the southeast. Spirited fighting broke out, but although badly outnumbered in terms of able-bodied defenders, Imboden managed to maintain his position—barely. Then, near sundown, Buford was reinforced by Kilpatrick's division, coming down from the northeast. Robert E. Lee had underestimated the ability of his enemy—the mounted portion thereof, at any rate—to pursue with speed and determination.

Just as Imboden began to fear he would never see Virginia again, "a messenger from Fitzhugh Lee arrived to urge me to 'hold my own,' as he would be up in a half hour with three thousand fresh men. The news was sent along our whole line, and was received with a wild and exultant yell. We knew then that the field was won." Fitz made good on his promise. His prompt arrival, added to an early end to daylight, prompted the Yankees to fall back and draw off. "By extraordinary good fortune," Imboden added, "we had thus saved all of General [Robert E.] Lee's trains," the loss of which would have spelled disaster for the Army of Northern Virginia, or something very near it.[15]

*   *   *

By the evening of July 7, the main body of Lee's army had reached the Potomac, guaranteeing the safety of Imboden's train. The gray line quickly expanded northeastward, its rear guard occupying the city of Hagerstown. The Confederates had begun to build a line of works stretching from Williamsport to Downsville, ten miles to the southeast, and back to the river. The cordon enclosed several crossing sites that could be used as soon as the river fell; while at Falling Waters, five miles downriver from Williamsport, Lee's engineers began laying a pontoon bridge to replace one recently destroyed by raiders out of Harpers Ferry.

Even behind its secure works, the army appeared in a precarious situation. Yet Robert E. Lee, as one of Fitz's officers recalled, "was calm and undismayed. He knew that he had a fine army with him and he was hopeful still" that Meade would attack him as he had failed to do on Independence Day. Lee's demeanor buoyed up the entire army. The only potential source of gloom was a rumor, later confirmed, that "came creeping stealthily through camp that General John C. Pemberton had surrendered Vicksburg with 25,000 men to Genl. Grant on the 4th [of] July. Yet under all these adverse influences the army was comparatively resolute and . . . not despairing and demoralized."[16]

His work at the river now done, Brigadier General Fitzhugh Lee rejoined

Stuart's command, which guarded the southern and eastern approaches to
Hagerstown. When the cavalry of Buford and Kilpatrick made threatening
gestures toward this position, Stuart pounded south early on the eighth with
five brigades, including Lee's and Baker's, the latter still under Fitz's command.
The enemy was fully prepared to meet him. After a several-hour fight, the Federals not only deflected Stuart's blow but forced him back up the Hagerstown
Pike, then across Beaver Creek to Funkstown. On the upper side of the stream,
Stuart's carbineers and horse artillerymen finally persuaded Buford and Kilpatrick to call it a day.[17]

The enemy remained quiet for the next two days. Early on July 10, with
Meade's main body at last within striking distance of Lee's defenses, Buford's
men waded Beaver Creek and attacked Stuart's main force as well as an outlying
detachment under Grumble Jones. Again Stuart withdrew, this time above a
more famous stream. Making a stand along Antietam Creek, where he enjoyed
the close support of his army's infantry, Stuart eventually shoved the Yankees
back and held them at bay.[18]

The following day, the eleventh, a general movement by Meade persuaded
any Confederates holding exposed positions to retire to their works at the river.
This day Fitz's command was stationed at Bakersville, a few miles outside the
works near Downsville. For some hours it resisted the pressure being applied
from many sides. It retired only when Stuart recalled it to Hagerstown and infantry took its place at Downsville. The next day it was Stuart whom Robert E.
Lee recalled to the river. When the evacuation of Hagerstown was all but complete, Kilpatrick's horsemen charged into the city, forcing out the Rebel rear
guard. Fitz's men were among the troops who dug in to enable the last evacuees
to reach Downsville safely.[19]

By the thirteenth, the river had receded sufficiently to be fordable at Williamsport; by then, too, the pontoons were in place at Falling Waters. Lee waited
one day longer, still hopeful that Meade would attack, confident that he would
be repulsed as signally as Pickett's Charge. When Meade reconnoitered instead,
after dark Lee began crossing his main body to the Virginia side, Ewell's corps
at Williamsport, Longstreet's and A. P. Hill's at the downstream bridge.[20]

At the latter site, Fitz's brigade, now guarding the army's right flank, aided
the pullout by taking the places of Longstreet's men behind the fieldworks and
in the trenches on the north bank. While Stuart's main body relieved foot soldiers elsewhere along the lines, Fitz spent the night guarding the bridgehead
and successfully discouraging enemy attempts to probe it.

After sunup on the fourteenth, while the rest of the cavalry forded at Williamsport, Fitz sent his advance echelon across the floating bridge in the rear of
A. P. Hill's main body. Around 8 A.M. the last trooper crossed in a drizzling rain.
He was followed by the army's rear guard, two divisions of Hill's corps. The latter crossed only minutes before Kilpatrick and Buford converged on the bridge-

head from opposite directions, ending their army's fitful, sluggish, and poorly coordinated pursuit.[21]

*   *   *

As he had following Second Manassas, Sharpsburg, and Chancellorsville, Fitz Lee failed to report his command's operations during the Gettysburg Campaign, not even documenting the losses it had sustained. From other sources, we know that his brigade suffered a total of ninety casualties during the pre-Gettysburg fighting in the Loudoun Valley, another forty-seven during the circuitous ride from Salem to Gettysburg, fifty during the fighting on July 3, and almost one hundred more on the retreat through Maryland to the Potomac. This was, by any standard of measurement, a grievous toll. The price paid by Fitz's command and the other brigades, divisions, and corps of the army during their sojourn above the Mason-Dixon Line deeply colored his later evaluation of the invasion's successes and failures.[22]

Looking back in later weeks, months, and years, Fitz judged the campaign an inherently worthwhile operation fatally compromised by poor judgment and tactical errors on the part of his uncle's subordinates. One of these was Stuart, whom Fitz believed had ample authority to go his own way into Pennsylvania but also the poor sense to utilize that authority. Although Stuart took only about forty-five hundred horsemen on his march from Salem to Gettysburg while leaving the army more than that, he had failed to ensure that the latter were properly used—in fact, used at all. The absence of the flower of the Confederate cavalry during the critical phase of the invasion was, in Fitz's eyes, the principal cause of the army's overall failure—of greater weight than the mistakes committed on July 1–3, including Ewell's inability to drive the beaten Federals from the heights below town late on the first day, and Longstreet's unconscionable delay in attacking Cemetery Ridge on the second and third.

As for Stuart's culpability, it could have been otherwise. As Fitz wrote after the war, "as soon as the Federal army began to cross the [Potomac] river, he should have marched to the west side of the Blue Ridge, crossed also, and moving rapidly to General Lee's front, have placed himself at once in direct communication with him. His bold activity would have developed the enemy's position which, General Lee being no longer in ignorance of, could then have made his plans accordingly. In that event the battle would not in all probability have taken place at Gettysburg."[23]

*   *   *

By the latter part of July, Fitz was back at his headquarters at Culpeper, writing his mother that "I am once more at my starting point. Have had many fights, and as customary some rather narrow escapes but . . . escaped without harm."[24]

He would have other chances to escape narrowly. As soon as the cavalry had taken up its old station between Martinsburg and Charles Town, the enemy crossed the river near Harpers Ferry and attacked the upper portion of that line—the part held by Fitz's brigade—in an apparent effort to gain the rear of the Army of Northern Virginia. The next morning, July 16, Fitz, the acting commander of cavalry in the temporary absence of Stuart, counterattacked with his own brigade, supported by John Chambliss's. Driven back to the river near Shepherdstown, the Yankees—Irvin Gregg and his brigade, fighting more stoutly than they had during the retreat from Gettysburg—rallied and shoved their opponents back in turn.

When a supporting force failed to menace Gregg's flank as arranged, Fitz held on at Shepherdstown by his fingertips until Stuart, back from an interview at army headquarters, arrived with reinforcements that enabled the 2nd Brigade to disengage and forced Gregg to withdraw. In the sharp fighting just ended, one of Fitz's most gifted subordinates, Colonel Drake of the 1st Virginia, had fallen mortally wounded.[25]

For eight weeks following the clash at Shepherdstown, the Yankees appeared less willing to challenge the Confederates and more intent on escorting Meade's army from the Potomac to the upper bank of the Rappahannock. The single exception was August 1, when Buford's troopers crossed at Beverly Ford on a reconnaissance-in-force and drove Baker's brigade toward Culpeper Court House. When other cavalry, assisted by foot soldiers and three horse batteries, intervened, Buford's momentum waned and he fell back, but only as far as Rappahannock Bridge. Four more days of fighting swirled along the riverbank before he conceded defeat and fell back upon his infantry supports.[26]

Upon Buford's withdrawal, a lull settled over the Rappahannock. Fitz used the respite to feed his near-starving animals. When the quiet persisted, he dispatched a substantial portion of his brigade across the river to Virginia's Northern Neck, a region where provender, especially corn and grain, was abundant. While his forage-masters gathered one thousand pounds or more of forage each day, other troopers, as one of them noted, patrolled that commercially busy strip between the Rappahannock and the Potomac "to seize Blockade-goods, arrest deserters and conscripts and do picket duty." The work was intensive as well as multifaceted: "I have never done as much riding in the same length of time since I have been in the army."[27]

The break in combat enabled Robert E. Lee and J. E. B. Stuart to attend to personnel and organizational matters. Within a fortnight of the army's return from Gettysburg, its commander notified President Davis that he considered the cavalry's table of organization unwieldy. He recommended that the mounted arm be expanded to seven brigades (reduced to six when, in late August, the Jenkins-Ferguson brigade returned to western Virginia), each brigade to consist of no more than four regiments or legions instead of the heretofore standard five or six. Davis approved the reorganization, which created vacancies for four brigadier generals. At Stuart's suggestion, promotions went to M. C. Butler, Laurence Baker, Williams C. Wickham, and a dear friend of Fitz's Lee's, Lunsford L. Lomax.[28]

The fellow West Pointer, in whose Washington, D.C., home Fitz once spent almost as much time as he had in the bosom of his own family, had spent the first two years of the war in the western armies, including a stint as an aide to his prewar superior, Earl Van Dorn. In the spring of 1863, Lomax had vacated the position of acting inspector general of the Army of West Tennessee to take command of a regiment of Shenandoah Valley cavalry under Grumble Jones. During Fitz's incapacitation at the outset of the Gettysburg Campaign, Lomax had fought splendidly at Brandy Station and later in the Loudoun Valley. Perhaps at Fitz's urging although probably because of Lomax's high qualifications, Stuart had recommended the young officer for the wreathed stars of a brigadier. Richmond approved; Lomax's appointment dated from July 23, 1863.[29]

In elevating Lomax, Stuart intended that he serve directly under Fitz. By the late summer of 1863 it had become clear that the corps organization for cavalry adopted by the Army of the Potomac had been an effective means of increasing the command's cohesiveness, cooperative spirit, and morale. With this in mind, Robert E. Lee reorganized his own cavalry into a two-division corps, Stuart to command at his present rank of major general but Hampton and Fitz Lee rising to that same rank in order to command the divisions.

Hampton's division would embrace the brigades of Butler, Baker, and Grumble Jones. (At present, only Jones was with his command, Butler having gone home, like Hampton, to convalesce from a wound—the loss of part of his leg at Brandy Station—and Baker having been hospitalized with injuries received during Buford's attack of August 1.) Fitz's division would include his former brigade, now in Wickham's hands, consisting of the same regiments as before except for the loss of Rosser's 5th Virginia. It would also embrace Lomax's newly formed brigade (the 1st Maryland Battalion as well as the 5th, 11th, and 15th Virginia) and the brigade of Rooney Lee (the 1st South Carolina and the 9th, 10th, and 13th Virginia), who was currently languishing in a northern prison. With the exception of the South Carolina regiment, which would soon transfer to another command, the unit assignments would remain in effect for the remainder of the conflict.[30]

Fitz's rise to major general and divisional command was the culmination of a career-long aspiration for recognition and advancement. It validated the confidence Stuart had long reposed in him as well as the confidence Fitz had invested in himself. Moreover, it exploded the myth that those who finished near the foot of their West Point class were destined for the bottom rung of the professional ladder, even in wartime. And it suggested that military fortune favored the man of action, determination, and spirit over the man of theoretical brilliance or textbook acumen.

As he had when Fitz was promoted to brigade command, Stuart sent him a note conveying warm congratulations. Making a pointed reference to Jones, Robertson, and other subordinates he had found difficult to manage, Stuart assured Fitz that he was "fortunate in having all pulling smoothly and together, which has not been my luck. I have never had a team without at least one nag addicted to the 'Studs.'"[31]

*   *   *

In his congratulatory letter, Stuart informed Fitz that he wished "to concert with you [on] some measures for attacking alternately Kilpatrick and Gregg with my whole force, and desire your views as well as an account of the force you would be able to bring to such an enterprise." But before the two could huddle, the enemy did the attacking. The result was a month-long series of offensives and counteroffensives that swept across the Rapidan-Rappahannock watershed, involving every branch of both armies but levying its greatest demands on the cavalry.

The period began when, in early September, Meade learned that Robert E. Lee had shipped by railroad one-third of his army, under Longstreet, to northern Georgia. There the I Corps would assist Bragg's army in its fight with the larger and better supplied army of Rosecrans. The troop transfer proved to be a masterstroke. Longstreet's timely arrival enabled Bragg, on the nineteenth and twentieth, to whip his overconfident opponent along Chickamauga Creek and force his retreat to East Tennessee.

On September 12, three days after Longstreet's column began to depart Virginia, Alfred Pleasonton sent Buford, Gregg, and Kilpatrick to probe Lee's depleted lines. Lee prudently led his army below the Rapidan River, even as the Army of the Potomac crossed to the south side of the Rappahannock. In the no-man's-land between the armies, Stuart challenged Pleasonton to fight instead of reconnoiter. The engagements that followed—including Culpeper Court House on the fourteenth and Jack's Shop (or Liberty Mills) on the twenty-second—were notable for the savage nature of the fighting and the long casualty lists that resulted. Because most of Fitz's units were still on foraging duty north and east of the theater of action, only Rooney Lee's brigade, led by Colonel Richard L. T. Beale of the 9th Virginia, took part. The spate of combat ended with Stuart escaping almost miraculously from near-encirclement at Liberty Mills and taking refuge behind the infantry lines of his army.[32]

In the last days of September, Meade, at Lincoln's behest, countered Lee's detaching of Longstreet by sending two of his corps—the XI and XII—to Tennessee. Soon after arriving, they helped Ulysses S. Grant lift the siege that

Bragg had imposed on Chattanooga, where Rosecrans's demoralized troops had holed up. When Stuart's scouts detected the transfer, it became Robert E. Lee's turn to ford one river (the Rapidan) and shove his enemy across another (the Rappahannock).

The operation began on October 10 with Stuart's crossing of the Rapidan and his advance up the turnpike toward Sperryville. Nearing the upper river, he found Meade's main body—operating under orders from Washington not to risk an engagement—falling back to the north bank, leaving its horsemen on the south side to protect the withdrawal. Stuart forged ahead in two columns, he at the head of Hampton's command, Fitz's division farther to the east and south. Near the venerable battleground of Brandy Station, Stuart hurled large numbers of Hampton's troopers at the nearest Yankees, while Fitz's command angled toward the exposed flank of the same force.

Thanks to the aggressive tactics of all three of his brigade leaders, Fitz forced Buford's division to retire to the riverbank, where it tried to cross in conjunction with Kilpatrick. Though hard-pressed, both divisions made good their escape, thanks to errors on the part of Hampton's regimental commanders as well as to the distance between Stuart's components, which made the cooperative effort he desired impossible to achieve.[33]

North of the Rappahannock, the Federals continued their army-wide withdrawal. Late on the twelfth, the ANV forded the river at several points, Stuart's now-united force via Warrenton Springs. On the north side Robert E. Lee's infantry closed up on Warrenton, but Stuart, with two-thirds of Hampton's division, forged ahead with characteristic impulsiveness toward one of his raiding landmarks, Catlett's Station on the Orange & Alexandria. Here he found himself effectively cut off from his own army by columns of Union infantry, retreating along both of his flanks. Although they had hemmed Stuart in, the Federals were ignorant of his presence in their midst and so failed to converge against him. On the morning of the fourteenth, after spending an anxious night surrounded by his enemy, Stuart led a charge that enabled him to break free of entrapment with minimal loss. He then moved on to Auburn for a linkup with Fitz's brigades. Another hairbreadth escape had saved Stuart from the effects of his own rashness.[34]

By the fourteenth, the Army of the Potomac was beyond possibility of being overtaken short of its objective, the high ground near Centreville on the old Manassas battlefield. Meade's rear guard, the II Corps, ensured its army's escape by hunkering down behind the roadbed of the O & A near Bristoe Station and decimating the nearest pursuers, the incautious foot soldiers of A. P. Hill.[35]

By the fifteenth, Meade's army was safe inside the breastworks it had erected on the heights of Centreville. That day, Stuart's scouts probed the defenses and pronounced them too formidable to be carried by assault. Two days later, after a fruitless search for weak points, Lee turned the army around and started back to the Rappahannock. He and his men would remain on the south bank of that river until Meade made them vacate the position—which would not be until early November.

Enough had gone wrong with his command during this campaign, as well as with the army as a whole, that Stuart was in a foul mood as he guarded the rear during the retreat down the Warrenton Pike. To further anger and annoy him, Judson Kilpatrick nipped at his heels every mile of the journey. The Union general continually harassed the rear of Hampton's division, which Stuart was accompanying, cutting off outriders and flankers and making prisoners of them. Whenever Hampton's men wheeled about to challenge him, Kilpatrick would back out of range with maddening dexterity.

The man's behavior became so objectionable that by midday on the nineteenth, Stuart had had enough. He sent word to Fitz, whose brigade was moving on a parallel road farther south, to watch for an opportunity to strike Kilpatrick, preferably while in the act of battering Stuart. In response, Fitz devised a sly stratagem. Through his rashness, Kilpatrick had outdistanced his infantry supports; moreover, he seemed inordinately inattentive this day. Let him come on, Fitz suggested, and we will draw him into a trap. Via courier, he explained his proposition to Stuart, who readily approved it.[36]

Kilpatrick played perfectly his role in Fitz's plan. Late that afternoon, Stuart slowed almost to a halt near Buckland Mills, where Broad Run crossed the Warrenton Pike. Unable to resist a stationary target, Kilpatrick struck again and began to round up prisoners. He was so preoccupied that he failed to detect Fitz galloping up behind him, having veered onto the turnpike just east of Buckland. As the 2nd Division fell upon Kilpatrick's flank and rear—an act of poetic justice, Fitz thought—Stuart abruptly changed front and plowed into the head of the blue column.

Many of George Custer's men, near the front of Kilpatrick's column, had halted to water their mounts at Broad Run and thus were not in line when Stuart's division struck from the front. But Hampton's division took a vicious toll on those Wolverines who had closed up with the brigade of Brigadier General Henry E. Davies, successor to Elon Farnsworth. Even worse was the fate of Davies's troopers, caught wholly unawares when Fitz's division thundered into their midst, shoving them forward at the same time that Custer's men squeezed them from the opposite direction. The Union column accordioned upon itself, bulged outward on both sides of the road leaking horses and riders, and then, under the increasing weight of charging riders on both ends, burst like a weakened dam. After a perfunctory effort at resistance, those Federals able to escape the crush took to their heels, pursued by gray troopers baying like tracking dogs. Nearly three hundred fugitives were ridden down and taken prisoner; those who resisted were dropped from their saddles with saber swipes or pistol shots.[37]

For Fitz Lee, galloping up the turnpike in the midst of his troopers, waving his saber above his head, splitting his throat with the Rebel Yell, it was the most soul-stirring experience he had known in many months. It brought back memories of the good old days when the blue horsemen fled in terror from every encounter with their more skillful, more confident enemy. Fitz had begun to doubt that he would ever again feel that sense of domination, of absolute mastery over the upstart "Abolition cavalry." Because the future was murky, he could not predict that the feeling would be his tomorrow. But it had been his today, and that was enough.

TEN

Division Command

Only two military operations of any consequence took place between Buckland Mills and year's end; Fitz saw extensive action in neither. The respite permitted him to catch up on his social life, which had suffered during the recent spate of field service. On November 1, accompanied by his brothers John and Henry, he visited his famous uncle at "Camp Rappahannock," near Orange Court House. Robert E. Lee received his nephews, whom he had not seen in many months, most cordially, inquiring of their health and the condition of the 2nd Cavalry Division. Even after they left, they remained very much in his thoughts. He informed his wife that as soon as he had a moment to himself, "I committed them in a fervent prayer to the care and guidance of our Heavenly Father."[1]

His relative was not the only one thinking warmly of Fitz these days. Later that month, or perhaps in early December, he availed himself of a furlough, during which he made the rounds of Richmond salons. At one gathering he impressed no less a personage than Mrs. Varina Howell Davis. Mary Boykin Chesnut noted in her diary that the president's wife spoke highly to her of Fitz's military abilities, which she rated above those of more celebrated officers including John Bell Hood, a hero of Chickamauga.[2]

Fitz was not in a high-society drawing room but in the field with his command during the first week in November, when Meade's army, having relinquished its defensive posture, returned to the Rappahannock and attacked Lee's defenses on both sides of the river. The forced crossing persuaded Meade's opponent to return to his old position below the Rapidan. Except for shielding their withdrawing comrades, Lee's horsemen saw little action during the proceedings.[3]

The cavalry was more actively engaged late in the month, when Meade responded to demands by his civilian superiors that he take the offensive before winter set in. The result was a flawed effort to maneuver Lee out of his breastworks and trenches below the Rapidan via envelopment of his right flank and an attack along Mine Run. Success depended heavily on surprise, but a part of Stuart's 1st Division, commanded by the fully recovered and recently returned Wade Hampton, spoiled Meade's strategy. When the Army of the Potomac crossed the Rapidan at divergent points on the morning of November 26, Hampton's Laurel Brigade, now led by Tom Rosser (Grumble Jones had been exiled following a flagrant episode of insubordination toward Stuart) saw it coming and rushed word to cavalry headquarters. Characteristically, Robert E. Lee acted swiftly to block Meade's passage with units of all arms.

Hampton's division, Stuart in personal command of it for much of the short-lived campaign, monopolized the fighting on the cavalry's front. Fitz's troopers remained on the Rapidan, guarding Morton's and Raccoon Fords against Kilpatrick's division, which several times over a period of three or four days gave the clear impression of wishing to cross at both places. Fitz considered it his duty to keep Kilpatrick out of the battle. He was proud that his former tactics student was "driven back each time" he tried to pass the fords, at minimal loss to Fitz. What Fitz did not know at the time, and refused to admit after learning the truth, was that Kilpatrick's efforts were part of a massive feint in favor of his infantry and cavalry comrades. It was Fitz Lee's troopers, not Kilpatrick's, who were prevented from adding their weight to the fighting along Mine Run.[4]

*   *   *

By the second week in December, with Meade back in his old camps where he appeared content to remain, Fitz supposed that active campaigning was done until spring. On the eleventh, after leaving Lomax's brigade to picket the army's left, he led the brigades of Wickham and Chambliss into winter camp three miles from Charlottesville. He had barely settled in at his new quarters, more than twenty miles behind the front, when he learned that the combat season was not over after all. On the fourteenth Stuart, at Robert E. Lee's behest, ordered Fitz, with Wickham and Chambliss, to head for the Shenandoah Valley. Fitz was to assist the local commander, General Imboden, in running to earth a body of Yankee cavalry, under the resurgent William Averell, that had slipped through the Blue Ridge to raid the strategic Virginia and Tennessee Railroad. In the Valley, Fitz's force—to be augmented by Rosser and the Laurel Brigade—would support a column of infantry and artillery under Major General Jubal ("Old Jube") Early that was bound for Staunton by rail.[5]

The assignment proved to be the most frustrating and physically demanding of Fitz's career. By the fifteenth, when it crossed the snow-crested mountains via Brown's Gap and forded the icy Shenandoah River at Mount Crawford, his poorly clothed force had already begun to suffer from the weather that swirled around that mountainous region. Adding to Fitz's discomfort, at Mount Crawford he learned that a report of Averell's movements northward near Strasburg, to which he had been responding, was erroneous. In mounting frustration, he turned south and hastened up the Valley Turnpike, intending to help Imboden deal with another Yankee force, this one reported to be occupying the summit of Shenandoah Mountain, near Staunton.

Fitz and his men, now including Rosser, had barely gotten under way when halted by order of General Early, who sent the troopers back to Mount Crawford. The next day, the seventeenth, Fitz, in response to yet another contradictory order, retraced his steps southward. After "marching day and night in the cold storm," early on the eighteenth he led his half-frozen troopers into Lexington. There they united with local forces under Imboden who had been trying without success to overtake Averell's fast-marching raiders.[6]

In addition to being elusive, the Federals had been extremely destructive. On the sixteenth they had descended on the rail depot at Salem, some fifty miles south of Lexington. They destroyed, as Averell reported, three separate supply caches "containing 2,000 barrels flour, 10,000 bushels wheat, 100,000 bushels shelled corn, 80,000 bushels oats, 2,000 barrels meat, several cords leather, 1,000 sacks salt, 31 boxes clothing, 20 bales cotton, a large amount of harness, shoes, and saddles, equipments, tools, oil, tar, and various other stores, and 100 wagons." Further, the Yankees downed half a mile of telegraph wire; levered up several hundred feet of track; burned three rail cars, a water station, and a turntable; dismantled five bridges; dug up several culverts; and disposed of building materials that might have helped repair some of their damage.[7]

On the night of the eighteenth, while in bivouac at the foot of North Mountain, Fitz received from Early what appeared to be a major piece of information. Based on the report of the district commander at Lynchburg, Fitz's superior informed him that Averell had recently returned to Salem to demolish further the railroad and its rolling stock. Fitz immediately guided the troopers of Wickham, Chambliss, Rosser, and Imboden across the jagged crest of the mountain, heading south toward Fincastle. By morning the long, frigid journey had brought the column as far as the hamlet of Buchanan, where Fitz learned to his disgust that the report of Averell backtracking to Salem was false.

Refusing to concede defeat, he pushed on to Fincastle, arriving on the twentieth. Learning that his Old Army colleague had pushed north to Covington, he started there despite the increasingly foul weather, arriving two days after his quarry had departed. Fitz later claimed that had it not been for geographical obstacles and the orders that sent him countermarching across North Mountain, "I should have arrived at Covington three hours ahead" of Averell.[8]

Frustrated beyond measure, he initiated as rapid a pursuit as his nearly exhausted mounts—which had traveled almost three hundred miles since breaking camp at Charlottesville—were capable of. However, when his scouts turned up no signs of Averell's column, not even a straggler, he called off the chase and proceeded north and then east to Goshen, where he could protect the Virginia Central against the kind of damage the Virginia-Tennessee line had suffered.

As Fitz saw it, the only highlight of the campaign just ended was "the cheerfulness with which both the members of General Imboden's command and my own have borne the privations and exposure of a long march in weather of uncommon severity, and the alacrity they evinced to meet the enemy." His superiors did not fault him for the lack of more tangible benefits. In endorsing his report of the operation, both Stuart and R. E. Lee noted that he had done "everything that he should have under the circumstances," which had been insurmountable.[9]

*   *   *

Believing that Fitz and his cavalry and Early and his foot soldiers could still be of value west of the Blue Ridge, Robert E. Lee held them in that snow-capped corner of the Confederacy for another three weeks. Six days after celebrating a cheerless Christmas near Mount Jackson, Fitz was sent on an expedition intended to compensate local forces for the provisions they had lost to Averell's marauders. On the thirty-first, he marched his horsemen across North Mountain and into Hardy County, in the new state of West Virginia. From there he moved to Moorefield in search of enemy supply trains and beef on the hoof. He also intended to attack and capture the well-provisioned outpost at Petersburg, ten miles southwest of Moorefield.

From the start, the going proved as difficult and exasperating as the weather. Proceeding up North Mountain and then down its back range via the Orkney Springs Road, Fitz found both ascent and descent too steep to accommodate his artillery and supply wagons (the latter lent him by the local quartermaster). Forging on without these resources, his men were assaulted by an ice storm that alternately pained and numbed them. Fitz was cheered, however, by the reports of scouts and local residents that the Petersburg garrison numbered just under a thousand troops—a force substantial enough to make its capture an achievement but small enough to pose no insurmountable obstacle.

Yet again, the information did not pan out. As Fitz approached Petersburg, patrol leaders informed him that the Federals were ensconced not only behind strong abatis but also in rifle pits from which they could be driven only by lengthy and strenuous effort. This the attackers would have to accomplish without artillery support. To make matters worse, most of the Confederates' rifle and carbine ammunition had been rendered useless by the icy rain they had recently endured.[10]

Rejecting any notion of an attack, Fitz moved, instead, against the line of communications that connected the garrison with the supply depot at New Creek, thirty miles to the north. At New Creek, he could also cut a long section of the Baltimore & Ohio. Good fortune appeared to accompany the change of plan. En route to his new objective, his outriders captured a supply train of 40 wagons—only to discover that it carried artillery ammunition, of no use on this outing. Of more value were the 250 head of cattle his men seized. That evening, however, as the beeves were being driven across the mountains, more than half the herd stampeded into the darkness and could not be recovered.

Before daylight on January 5, Fitz left his bivouac at Ridgeville, on the edge of Knobly Mountain, and headed north on the last leg of the trip to New Creek. When he started out, his spirits and those of his men were high, but by the time they neared their destination, a hailstorm had ravaged the health and lowered the endurance of both men and horses. Surveying his weather-beaten column, a disheartened Fitz decided to call off the attack "on account of the sufferings of my men and the impassability of the mountain passes to my smooth-shod horses." He solemnly countermarched his men through Romney and then, via Brock's Gap in North Mountain, to Harrisonburg in the upper Shenandoah.[11]

The only comfort Fitz could take from the return march—beyond the vision of a snug winter cabin waiting for him near Charlottesville—was the plunder that a detachment of his column under Major Harry Gilmor, a well-known scouting leader, had collected from the enemy outpost at Springfield: "about 3,000 pounds of bacon and some hard bread, horseshoes, nails, &c." Gilmor's party also "burnt the forage and other stores there and the winter quarters of the troops." Such accomplishments may have paled in comparison to Averell's, but Fitz could also boast of having gathered up twenty-seven provisions, forage, and ammunition wagons; some two hundred head of beef cattle as well as three hundred horses and mules; and no fewer than one hundred prisoners, most of them seized at Springfield and on the way to Petersburg and New Creek.

The price of these captures had been as steep as the hills Fitz's men had crossed and recrossed during the expedition. Although he had lost only two men killed and two wounded, "my whole command were more or less frost-bitten [one trooper stood to lose both feet as a result], and suffered a great deal, the weather being excessively cold during the whole trip; the ground was covered with snow and ice in going up and down the various mountains."[12]

Summing up a campaign worth forgetting but the memory of which would long endure, the raiding leader declared without fear of contradiction that "my command has marched since the 11th of last month 555 miles in weather of uncommon severity, and deserves praise for the endurance displayed and hardships undergone."[13]

*   *   *

In the wake of his recent travail, Fitz needed some playtime. He got it when in mid-January he returned to Charlottesville to find preparations nearly complete for a gala ball at division headquarters. He entered into the proceedings wholeheartedly, although his uncle, who received a courtesy invitation, expressed mild disapproval of the affair. In a letter to his youngest son, Robert Jr., a lieutenant in one of Chambliss's regiments, the army leader opined that "this is a bad time for such things. . . . We have too grave subjects on hand to engage in such trivial amusements." He would have preferred that Fitz and his officers spent their time "healing" their command, which had endured such "hardships and sufferings . . . in their late expedition." Commenting on that operation, Lee regretted his nephew's inability to bring Averell to heel: "He accomplished much under the circumstances, but would have done more in better weather. I am afraid he was anxious to get back to the ball." In closing, he declared that "I like all to be present at battles, but can excuse them at balls."[14]

His uncle's strictures notwithstanding, Fitz had his ball and enjoyed it immensely, as did his subordinates and their consorts, daughters of the leading lights of Charlottesville society. Yet the gala failed to quench his thirst for amusement. Later in the month, accompanied by Stuart, he returned to the Confederate capital. In addition to visiting family and friends, both officers attended a party for "social and official Richmond" hosted by Mrs. George Randolph, wife of the former secretary of war.[15]

Early in the evening's entertainment, the generals were pressed into service backstage during the presentation of several "charades in pantomime" authored by Constance Cary. Fitz took his responsibilities seriously, but the married Stuart spent most of his time flirting with the prettiest unattached guests. The result was that a ladder he was assigned to hold behind the scenery buckled, depositing one of the actors, Miss Cary herself, onto the stage floor. The mishap transformed the genius behind the production into "an irate stage-manager darting behind the scenes to scold an offending super. In vain General Stuart protested abject penitence. . . . General Fitz Lee, virtuously declaring that no young lady could make *him* forget his responsibility as a step-ladder, took and held General Stuart's post."[16]

Although harmless diversions such as these helped Fitz forget the war for brief periods, he always returned to it. Short days after savoring the Richmond social whirl, he was back at Charlottesville, sharing the hardships of winter quarters with the troopers and horse artillerymen of his command. For much of February, snow and ice kept officers and men confined to their makeshift cabins and stockaded tents while playing hob with the health of pickets and sentries.

Toward the end of the month, the winter war suddenly heated up. On the twenty-eighth Fitz learned that a Yankee column was moving in his direction. It was discovered to consist of the better part of Sedgwick's VI Corps, Army of the Potomac, supported by fifteen hundred cavalrymen and a section of horse artillery under George Custer. Before the day was out, Sedgwick's foot soldiers had occupied Madison Court House, between the Rappahannock and the Rapidan, about twenty miles north of Fitz's headquarters.[17]

While Fitz pounded off to oppose Sedgwick with elements of each of his brigades, Custer's horsemen split off from the Union column. They marched southwestward to Stanardsville, then almost directly south to Charlottesville. By passing around Fitz's left flank as he rushed north, Custer was free to burn a bridge over the Rivanna River and waylay warehouses, mills, and other forms of private and government property.

On the afternoon of the twenty-ninth, the Union raiders descended on the camp of the Stuart Horse Artillery outside Charlottesville, which they attacked in hopes of capturing cannons and crews. Denied the support of their cavalry comrades, the artillerymen, ably led by Captains Chew and Breathed, defended their camps with a tenacity that saved their precious guns. Much equipment, however, fell into enemy hands and was confiscated or destroyed.

Cowed by the unexpected opposition and made cautious by reports that Stuart was coming after him, Custer drew off and the next day returned to Madison Court House. His withdrawal went largely unprotested. Fitz laid a trap for Custer on his return march, but thanks to a lack of vigilance on the part of Wickham's troopers it failed to spring. On March 2, Sedgwick's corps broke contact with Fitz's men and returned to its camps near Brandy Station.[18]

Upon the retreat of Custer's column—whose mission at first baffled him— Fitz believed he had heard the last of the Yankee raiders. He learned differently when, a few days later, word reached him of a botched attack on Richmond by a cavalry force larger than Custer's, under Judson Kilpatrick. It turned out that Custer's and Sedgwick's operations, and also simultaneous movements on the Rapidan by other elements of Meade's army, had been diversions in Kilpatrick's favor. Their purpose had been to distract the attention of pickets along the Confederate left so that columns of horsemen under Kilpatrick and Ulric Dahlgren—the reckless adventurer who had attacked Imboden's train during the retreat from Gettysburg—might slip around the Rebel right on a straight line to Richmond.

Kilpatrick, at the head of thirty-six hundred picked men and six cannons, advanced on the Confederate capital from above, while now-Colonel Dahlgren, leading a support force of five hundred, came in from the west and south planning to meet his superior inside the city. Flooded streams and other unforeseeable obstacles so slowed the colonel that he reached the city too late to link with Kilpatrick's troops. Dahlgren's superior had retreated across the James River, defeated by the desperate resistance of the local defense battalion as well as by his own eleventh-hour faintheartedness. Before Kilpatrick could launch a second attack, a detachment of Wade Hampton's cavalry, having hurried down from its camps on the Fredericksburg Railroad, attacked the raiders and sent them on a demoralizing retreat down the Peninsula to occupied Yorktown.[19]

Dahlgren's band and its fiery young leader met an even more miserable end. Turned back from Richmond's gates, the column crossed the Pamunkey and Mattapony Rivers in a futile attempt to shake a growing mob of pursuers—mainly soldiers at home on furlough, including members of Fitz Lee's division, and gun-toting civilians. Ambushed near King and Queen Court House on March 2, Dahlgren was killed, as were several of his men. Almost one hundred others were captured, as were thirty-eight temporarily liberated slaves.

Dahlgren's demise ought to have written finis to the ambitious but mismanaged operation, but papers found on his body ignited a firestorm of controversy that would enjoy a long life. Placed in Fitz Lee's hands by one of the colonel's assailants, an officer in the 9th Virginia Cavalry, the pen-and-ink documents, apparently written by Dahlgren himself and perhaps read to his troops at the start of the raid, called on them to "cross the James River into Richmond, destroying the bridges after us and exhorting the released prisoners [of Libby and Belle Isle Prisons] to destroy and burn the hateful city; and do not allow the rebel leader Davis and his traitorous crew to escape." A second paper found on the body confirmed Dahlgren's mission: "once in the city it must be destroyed and Jeff. Davis and cabinet killed."[20]

On March 4, Fitz forwarded the captured documents to his kinsman, General Cooper, in Richmond with the observation that they "need no comment." Nevertheless, he commented freely, calling the expedition "ridiculous and unsoldierly" and declaring that Dahlgren "lost his life running off negroes after the failure of his insane attempt to destroy Richmond and kill Jeff. Davis." Four weeks later, Fitz sent Cooper a notebook of Dahlgren's, recently discovered, that contained a pencil draft of the address to his troops. Fitz vouched for the documents' authenticity, although how he could do so is unknown.[21]

The so-called Dahlgren Papers touched off a campaign in some circles to repay Yankee barbarity by hanging all captured raiders. Robert E. Lee, perhaps mindful of his imprisoned son, counseled moderation, especially after Meade and Kilpatrick emphatically disavowed the more incriminating statements set down in the documents. President Davis, the supposed target of Dahlgren's blood lust, came around to Lee's view and publicly rejected reprisals of any kind. In the end the controversy blew over, but not before Davis's government wrung from it as much propaganda value as possible. The true meaning of the Kilpatrick-Dahlgren Raid was its anticipation of a significant change in the tenor of the war. The genteel, chivalric mode of warfare espoused and exemplified by J. E. B. Stuart, Fitz Lee, and kindred spirits was being replaced, slowly but surely, by a ruthless, no-holds-barred mentality that would endure for the remainder of the conflict.[22]

*　　*　　*

By mid-March, Fitz had made new inroads into the Richmond social scene. He had acquired a wind-up doll painted to resemble an elegantly attired black boy. Mary Chesnut observed the toy and its owner in action: "Fitz Lee sings cornshucking tunes, and the toy boy dances. . . . He is the delight of Richmond salons, and is so much handled that his dress soon grows shabby."[23]

Fitz's opportunities to visit the capital dwindled as the winter drew to a close. By March 24, Stuart was advising him to prepare his men and horses for a resumption of active campaigning. Fitz should redouble his training efforts for the benefit of both officers and enlisted: "I want your men practiced [in] charging in columns, solid and compact so as *to shock* [the enemy]. They generally disperse too much. Also practice rear squadrons to dismount quickly & deploy to right & left in a fight. Urge commanders to *command their men in action* from a corpl up to Brigadier."[24]

Stuart was particularly concerned that Fitz provide enough provender to keep the mounts of his division in peak condition. To ease the strain on the army's commissary, at various points in the winter Fitz had furloughed whole regiments to their homes. Many benefited from the transfer, rejoining the army in better condition—and in greater strength—than they had left it, the result of local reprovisioning and recruiting programs. Once back in middle Virginia, however, they found forage so scarce that on April 13 Stuart ordered the entire division to move from its most recent bailiwick, Ashland Station and Hanover Junction, to Hamilton's Crossing, below Fredericksburg, "where the grass, by the time of arrival, will, with the corn furnished by rail, afford sufficient sustenance."[25]

At Hamilton's Crossing, Fitz reorganized his division in the wake of the loss of one of his brigades. Chambliss's men had been transferred to the new 3rd Cavalry Division of W. H. F. Lee. Late in March, Rooney had been welcomed back to the army following nine months' imprisonment in the North, one of his rewards being promotion to major general. In addition to Chambliss's brigade, Rooney's new command included the troopers of Brigadier General James B. Gordon, formerly of Hampton's division.

By the time Fitz relocated to Hamilton's Crossing, Stuart believed a return to combat imminent: "In the event of hostilities on your front (Fredericksburg) all the cavalry along the line of the R. P. & F R. R. [Richmond, Fredericksburg & Potomac Railroad] will be subject to your orders." It took two weeks, but Stuart's prediction finally appeared to come true when a brigade-size force of Yankee cavalry, trailed by supply wagons and ambulances, was seen heading toward Germanna Ford on the Rapidan, about eighteen miles upstream from

Fredericksburg. From his headquarters near Orange Court House, Robert E. Lee directed Fitz to "attend to" the oncomers.[26]

Fitz may have suspected that the movement was the maiden outing of Major General Philip H. ("Little Phil") Sheridan, the newly appointed successor to Pleasonton as commander of the cavalry of the Army of the Potomac. A transferee from the western theater where he mostly commanded infantry, the versatile Irishman was a protégé of another, higher-ranking, newcomer to the Virginia front, Ulysses S. Grant.

As the most successful of Lincoln's field leaders, Grant early in March had been assigned command, at the revived rank of lieutenant general, of all the Union armies. Aware that the war would be won or lost in the East, he had opted to make his field headquarters with the Army of the Potomac, which was still under the direct command of George Meade. Grant would proscribe strategy for the army while Meade handled the tactical details. For example, Grant would decide which location would be the army's next destination, and Meade would determine how the army got there—which roads it took, its marching order, the relative positions of infantry and cavalry—and how it fought if it found the Army of Northern Virginia waiting when it got there.[27]

The movement toward Germanna Ford proved to be a false alarm in the sense that it precipitated no fighting. The Yankee force maneuvered as if intending to cross the river but merely reconnoitered the north bank before withdrawing. Two weeks later, however, Fitz Lee and everyone else in the Army of Northern Virginia perceived the reason for the reconnaissance. On the morning of May 4, Meade's army pushed across the river at numerous points, including Germanna Ford, and drove south toward the Wilderness. Eventually it became evident that Grant intended to turn Lee's right flank, Meade's unsuccessful tactic of the previous November. Grant's strategy was predicated on Meade's ability to clear the forest before offering or accepting battle. That strategy was thrown out of kilter, however, when Lee rushed east along the Orange Pike and Orange Plank Roads and plowed into two of Meade's columns.[28]

Once south of the river, the Union cavalry covering those columns turned east and advanced toward Fitz's headquarters via the Plank Road. To arrest their progress he dispatched Colonel Munford, with a substantial force, toward Chancellorsville. Soon afterward he learned that Meade's main body had veered in the opposite direction, toward Orange Court House. Fitz began to suspect that a turning movement was under way; he decided to place himself in a better position to oppose it. Leaving a force to deal with the Yankees advancing toward him, early on May 5 he detoured southward with the major portion of his division. Following a brief stopover at Massaponax Church, he angled west, skirting the Wilderness so as not to become involved in the infantry's battle.

Reaching Spotsylvania Court House, Fitz turned in the direction of Todd's

Tavern. Two miles from that old hostelry on the southern edge of the forest, Lomax's brigade, leading the column, encountered the cavalry guarding Meade's left, part of the division of David Gregg. A sharp engagement ensued, ending with the Yankees driven off at a cost to Lomax of two dozen casualties. During the night that followed, which was given over to long-range skirmishing, Fitz established contact with Rosser's Laurel Brigade. The latter had just arrived from Orange Court House following a fatiguing march from the winter camp outside Charlottesville.

By the morning of May 6, Fitz was reporting to J. E. B. Stuart that a heavy force had gathered in his front and on his right flank. The enemy was "on the roads leading from Todd's Tavern to Spottsylvania C. H. & on the Catharpin Road; about 3/4 of a mile on each road from Todd's Tavern. His force is cavalry—a strong one—with a Battery of six guns in full view. He has the roads barricaded in my front." For hours Fitz's men had been engaged in heavy skirmishing; he doubted they were capable of more unless Rosser moved down the Brock Road and attacked Gregg from the rear. Instead, Fitz was concerned that Hampton was about to recall Rosser to Shady Grove Church, two and a half miles south of the tavern, in which event the 2nd Division might find itself in dire straits. As it was, "I am so close on the enemy that I can not withdraw without his perceiving it."[29]

But it was Gregg, responding to an order from army headquarters, who withdrew during the night. The order stemmed from an erroneous report that Confederates had interposed between Sheridan and Meade's infantry. Appreciating the value of the position Gregg relinquished, Fitz immediately occupied all sides of Todd's Tavern—only to be evicted after sunrise on the seventh by a large body of foot soldiers.

Retracing his steps to his original position, two miles south of Todd's, he had his men entrench and build log and rail breastworks. Behind the works he emplaced James Breathed's cannons and rank upon rank of dismounted men. The arrangement hinted that after years of fighting in the saddle, no matter what the tactical situation the troopers of the ANV had learned to emulate their opponents, who had shown power and tenacity fighting afoot at Bull Run, Kelly's Ford, Gettysburg, the Loudoun Valley, and many lesser-known fields.

Late in the morning, Fitz's position came under attack from two divisions of Sheridan's cavalry—Brigadier General Alfred Torbert's as well as Gregg's. Sheridan had been ordered to retake the ground given up as a result of Meade's erroneous report. Slowly but methodically, the Yankees drove south, gouging Fitz's men out of their works with massed firepower, much of it from repeating rifles and carbines. Just before being cut off, the Confederates would retreat to even more quickly erected defenses farther south. The fight-and-fall-back strategy endured through the day and into the early evening, by which time

Fitz's line had been shoved several miles down the road to Spotsylvania Court House.[30]

For his part, Fitz would never acknowledge relinquishing even a few yards: "My command fought most gallantly, and night found them holding every part of their hastily constructed rail breastworks—having effectively resisted the furious onsets of the enemy to dislodge them." He did admit to a heavy loss in men and especially in officers, including Colonel Charles R. Collins of the 15th Virginia, Lomax's brigade, whose death robbed the command of a man of "high scientific attainments, spotless integrity and great courage." Fitz also reported the severe wounding of the 3rd Virginia's Colonel Owen.[31]

Before sunrise on the eighth, Torbert's division, temporarily commanded by Brigadier General Wesley Merritt, resumed its attack on Fitz's position. Despite their heavier numbers, the Yankees made indifferent headway against the recently improved Rebel works. Fitz's defense compared favorably with the stubborn resistance his army's foot soldiers had demonstrated on May 5–6, which had brought Grant's grand offensive to a halt. His path to the Confederate right effectively blocked, the lieutenant general revamped his strategy. He now planned to head southwest out of the forest, forcing Lee to pursue him toward Richmond via Spotsylvania Court House.

But the road would not be an open one. About 3 A.M. on the eighth, Merritt's people, their progress slowed to a crawl, gave way to Major General G. K. Warren's V Army Corps. Like their mounted comrades, Warren's men did not advance far or fast, partly because of the continuing resistance of Fitz's troopers, partly because Merritt's artillery and wagons were blocking the road. The traffic snarl ensured that Meade would not reach Spotsylvania ahead of the First Corps of the Army of Northern Virginia, which was en route there from the west. Thus, Robert E. Lee would thwart Ulysses Grant's initial attempt to bypass the ANV on the way to the Confederate capital.[32]

Before the V Corps sorted itself out and advanced in proper alignment, Fitz hauled his regiments southward, fighting, as he had the previous day, from successive positions. By 8 A.M. his men were occupying heavy breastworks thrown up just north of Spotsylvania. Close by were the foot soldiers of the First Corps, now under Major General Richard H. Anderson, James Longstreet having been disabled by wounds in the Wilderness. Combined opposition from foot and horse soldiers, backed strongly by the artillery attached to both, ensured that the area around the courthouse would remain in Confederate hands until the balance of the Army of Northern Virginia arrived to secure the place.

Fitz Lee would always consider his division's role in seizing and holding Spotsylvania one of its most notable accomplishments. As he wrote two and a half years later, credit for the timely occupancy of Spotsylvania, "the strategic importance of [which] was well understood," was primarily "due to my command

. . . by reason of their stubborn fighting in resisting the enemy's advance to-
wards it upon the 7th and 8th."[33]

*   *   *

By May 9, Fitz's division was helping defend its army's right flank north of
Spotsylvania. There the troopers sparred with the advance of the IX Corps,
under the once-deposed commander of the Army of the Potomac, Ambrose
Burnside. About 1 P.M., the job abruptly ended as infantry came up to take the
cavalry's place inside the works. Fitz's men filed to the rear, wondering why they
had been relieved.

It had come about as the result of a message Fitz had received about five
hours earlier from General Wickham, whose brigade patrolled the extreme right
flank south of Fredericksburg. Wickham's vedettes had observed the advance
down the Telegraph Road of an extensive column of blue-clad horsemen. The
Yankees, who appeared to be on a raid, were heading in the general direction
of Beaver Dam Station, a Virginia Central depot some thirty miles north of
Richmond. It was also possible that they were aiming for Richmond itself—a
reprise, in greater strength, of Kilpatrick's expedition of two months earlier.[34]

Wickham's assessment of the movement had much to recommend it. The
Federals were in fact raiding—all ten thousand of them, accompanied by artillery, ammunition wagons, and pack mules. The geographical objective of
this, the first independent operation of the Cavalry Corps, Army of the Potomac, under Phil Sheridan, was indeed Richmond, but only in the sense that
an advance on that city would surely draw Stuart into a confrontation. That
was Sheridan's true objective—a showdown, a finish fight, with the Beau
Sabreur of the Confederacy. Little Phil had promised Grant and Meade that he
would defeat his opponent decisively, breaking up his formations, disabling
his leading officers, and proving the superiority of Union cavalry at the start of
this third year of the war.[35]

As soon as Stuart, at his headquarters outside Spotsylvania, received Wickham's report, he resolved to overtake Sheridan short of Richmond and the railroads that served it. He would have to do so, however, with only a portion of
his command. Hampton's division was locked in close combat southwest of the
courthouse, along the Po River, and could not easily disengage. That left only
Fitz Lee's brigades. Wickham would dog Sheridan's heels, and Lomax, with
whom both Stuart and Fitz would travel, would ride furiously until able to bar
the Yankees' path. At some point in the pursuit, Lomax would be augmented
by Gordon's brigade, recently transferred from Hampton's division to the new
command of Rooney Lee.

By midafternoon of the ninth, Stuart was hurrying southwestward with Fitz,
Lomax, and one and a half batteries of horse artillery under Breathed. Because
of Sheridan's head start, only Wickham's men, galloping south from Fredericks-

burg, made contact with the raiding column on the first day out. Wickham struck the Union rear time and again, inflicting so many casualties that Sheridan, late in the afternoon, ambushed him near Mitchell's Shop, thirty miles from the raiders' starting point. As Wickham's overanxious advance guard rounded a steep bend near the shop, troopers in roadside woods poured a blistering cross fire into it. Suffering heavy losses, their victims staggered backward out of harm's way. Thereafter only a small detachment kept up the pursuit. Wickham, with his main force, waited at Mitchell's for his superiors—now riding in two separate columns—to catch up with him.[36]

Fitz did not join Wickham until just before sundown, Stuart not until after dark. An hour later, the majority of Lomax's men arrived, followed at about midnight by Gordon's brigade, which had lost the most time withdrawing from Spotsylvania. After conferring with each of his lieutenants, Stuart dispatched Fitz, with both of his brigades, south to Beaver Dam where he would be in a position to defend the railroads that entered Richmond from the north. After his subordinate rode off, Stuart accompanied Gordon's men westward, where Sheridan might strike if he decided against a direct descent on Richmond.

Fitz's route, not Stuart's, was the right one. Early on the tenth, the division leader caught up to Sheridan, whose men were breaking camp on the South Anna River. Fitz shelled the enemy's rear, chasing the division of Brigadier General James H. Wilson over the stream to unite with the divisions of Torbert and Gregg, which were sacking Beaver Dam Station. After a brief duel, Sheridan, who disdained to fight only two of Stuart's brigades, resumed his trek to Richmond, twenty-seven miles away.[37]

A few hours after Sheridan departed, Stuart and Gordon joined Fitz amid the smoldering ruins of the rail depot. Taking careful note of his enemy's heading, Stuart again divided his command, sending Gordon to follow the Federals and directing Fitz, his brigades, and Breathed to hasten cross-country toward Hanover Junction, where the Virginia Central crossed the Richmond, Fredericksburg & Potomac Railroad—a logical objective of any raiding force. But when Fitz, again accompanied by Stuart, reached the junction late in the day, he found that Sheridan had bypassed the place, crossing the Little and South Anna Rivers and striking, instead, for Ashland Station.

Convinced that his opponent's true objective was the Confederate capital, at 3 A.M. on May 11 a concerned Stuart sent one of Fitz's regiments to Ashland, where it chased off Sheridan's rear guard. With Fitz, Lomax, Wickham, and Breathed, Stuart passed down the railroad for a few miles before cutting eastward to Yellow Tavern. They reached that dilapidated watering hole, near the intersection of the Mountain and Telegraph Roads six miles north of Richmond, in the early hours of the eleventh. There Stuart found to his satisfaction that he had gotten ahead of Sheridan, whose men were just then coming down the Mountain Road toward the tavern.[38]

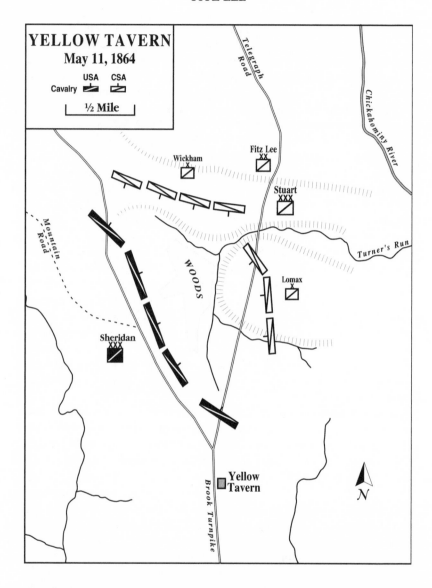

YELLOW TAVERN
May 11, 1864

USA   CSA
Cavalry

½ Mile

Telegraph Road

Chickahominy River

Wickham
X

Fitz Lee
XX

Stuart
XXX

Turner's Run

Mountain Road

WOODS

Lomax
X

Sheridan
XXX

Yellow
Tavern

Brook Turnpike

N

At Stuart's order, Fitz spread his troopers into long lines that covered every approach to the intersection—Lomax's brigade on the left, facing west, and Wickham's men farther to the north and west, in closer proximity to the new arrivals. Fitz had Breathed run his guns into battery at various points along his discontinuous line. They began to shell the Mountain Road as soon as the head of Sheridan's column came within range, at about 11 A.M.

Deploying hastily, the Union commander at once moved to the attack. He found himself fighting, however, in opposite directions at the same time—westward against Gordon's brigade, which thudded into the Union rear just after it reached Yellow Tavern, and eastward against Lomax and Wickham. Wilson's division, most of its men fighting afoot, challenged Wickham, while Torbert's command, still under Merritt, squared off against Lomax. Exploiting his advantages in manpower and weaponry, Sheridan made early and sustained progress against all sectors of Fitz's position. Despite heavy resistance from the Rebel troopers, many of whom emulated their opponents by fighting afoot, Sheridan, after about four hours of fighting, had driven Fitz's men from one line of works to another. Sheridan enjoyed his greatest success on the south end of the field where, in some of the fiercest close-in fighting of the war, Merritt's command captured the road fork and secured the upper reaches of the Brook Turnpike, which gave access to Richmond.

These were important gains, but the battle truly turned in late afternoon when a charge by two regiments of Custer's brigade, Merritt's division, overran a Maryland battery on Fitz's left, capturing two guns and hauling them off triumphantly. Sheridan, hoping to exploit the breakthrough, funneled his men toward the breach, widening it and chasing away the battery's supports. Soon Lomax's entire line was in danger of being overrun. The panic that broke out in that sector soon spread northward and begun to engulf Wickham's position as well.[39]

Stuart, who had spent the early phase of the battle at Fitz's side and later moved far afield of him, tried to stave off defeat, or at least prevent it from evolving into disaster. He rode forward to rally the troopers on Lomax's front. One of Fitz's enlisted men observed him in the saddle, firing "every load out of his revolver as coolly as I could fire at a squirrel, with his clarion voice all the time urging the men to stand steady, with 'Give it to them! Stand your ground!'"[40]

Nothing if not conspicuous in his scarlet sash, gilt-spangled uniform, and plumed hat, the general made a target that one Yankee could not miss. A .44-caliber pistol ball tore into Stuart's abdomen as he sat his horse, causing him to reel precariously in the saddle. Members of his staff reached up to keep him from toppling to the ground.[41]

Only minutes earlier, Stuart had ordered one of his most trusted staff officers, Major A. Reid Venable, to assist Lomax in rallying retreating troopers. Now he appointed Venable to personally inform Fitz Lee that the latter was in command of everyone battling Sheridan. The major started on his errand at once, although it took some time to locate Fitz on the field.[42]

Although hit hard by the news, Fitz was not stunned into irresolution or immobility. Even as he continued his efforts to stem the break in Lomax's line, he detailed a squad of the 1st Virginia to help Stuart, who, as Venable had told him, had refused to go to the rear. Several minutes later, the detail returned with a still-mounted Stuart hunched over his saddle, blood pooling under the waist of his jacket. A concerned but distracted Fitz rounded up a surgeon and an ambulance, had the general placed in the wagon, and, after exchanging a few words with him, sent the conveyance to the rear. "My own time was so much occupied," he later recalled, "I could not give more of it to his comfort . . . and did not well know the extent of his wound."[43]

He could not have known it then, but this was the last time he would ever see or speak to his superior, patron, and friend.

ELEVEN

Life after Stuart

Despite his most strenuous efforts, Fitz was unable to shore up the break on his left and, later, his right flank. Before sundown his troopers and horse artillerists were falling back across the Chickahominy River. Content to have battered Stuart into submission although unaware of his wounding, Sheridan elected to bivouack on the hard-won field. While he did, Fitz assembled his scattered regiments at Half-Sink Bridge and sent his scouts to monitor the enemy's movements.[1]

They had something to report by 3 A.M. on the twelfth, when Sheridan broke camp and started his men south under a persistent rain. Fitz's concern that the raiding leader intended to emulate Judson Kilpatrick increased when just after dawn, the advance element of Sheridan's column, Wilson's division, made contact with the defenders of Richmond. While Wilson sparred with the local forces, Sheridan suddenly pulled the rest of his force off the Brook Pike and pointed it toward the river. It became evident that Little Phil considered his mission already accomplished and thus had no inclination—or perhaps no stomach—for taking on the artillery-studded defenses of the capital. This realization relieved the minds not only of Fitz Lee but of numerous observers of Sheridan's movements. The latter included President Davis and his chief military advisor, Braxton Bragg, who had been relieved of command of the Army of Tennessee after being routed outside Chattanooga by Grant, with help from the XI and XII Corps.

Assured of Richmond's safety, Fitz led his division down the north side of the Chickahominy "to stop up the crossing at Meadow Bridge, the only exit of the enemy in that direction." Reaching the bridge in advance of Sheridan, Fitz's men tore up its wooden floor and then took up a position on riverside bluffs, from which they peppered the head of the just-arriving column. The several-hour battle that ensued was finally ended by the enemy's ability to cross an adjacent span under fire, drive off the nearest sharpshooters, and repair Meadow Bridge.[2]

After a brief stopover on the north bank, Sheridan recrossed the Chickahominy farther downstream at Bottom's Bridge and continued south toward the James River. He looked forward to resting and refurbishing his command at Haxall's Landing, the supply base of the army led by Major General Benjamin F. Butler that was operating against Richmond while Grant and Meade contended with Lee's army. The refit complete, Sheridan would make a quick return to the Army of the Potomac.[3]

Fitz was content to let him go. He had a myriad of other concerns just now, not the least being the burden of command that had only begun to weigh on him. The man who formerly carried that load would do so no more. Shortly after 7:30 P.M. that evening, the twelfth, J. E. B. Stuart succumbed to the effects of his wound, dying of internal injuries at the Richmond home of his brother-in-law. Quietly but deeply, Fitz mourned "my greatly beloved commander" while regretting his inability to be present either at Stuart's bedside or at his funeral in Richmond. He at least had the satisfaction of knowing that his father, now in charge of a Naval Department office in the capital, would stand in for him as one of Stuart's pallbearers.[4]

Later Fitz would reflect on Stuart's near-legendary contributions to his command as well as on the personal and professional qualities that had made him the quintessential cavalryman: "His rare genius, high toned spirit, indifference to danger, indefatigable energy, wonderful endurance in the saddle, supreme coolness in action, and enthusiastic devotion to the cause in which he offered up his life." As passing weeks would demonstrate, "the Cavalry of the Army of Northern Virginia only more keenly felt the irreparable loss the service had sustained" in the passing of James Ewell Brown Stuart.[5]

*   *   *

For a time after Sheridan reached the James, Fitz, from his new headquarters at Mechanicsville, continued to shadow him in the event he turned north for another go at Richmond. Although no such threat materialized, an even more serious danger reared its head only days later, when Ben Butler's thirty-five thousand-man Army of the James left its base of operations at Bermuda Hundred, a peninsula midway between Richmond and its support center to the south, Petersburg, and secured a foothold at Drewry's Bluff, on the southern doorstep of the capital. On May 16, however, that threat passed as quickly as it had emerged when Richmond's reinforced garrison attacked Butler's position under cover of a morning fog, collapsed it, and sent its displaced defenders scrambling back to their fortified peninsula.[6]

With Butler neutralized and Sheridan returning to his army by a route by-passing Richmond, Fitz was suddenly free to take on new projects. One came his way on the twenty-second when General Bragg, in response to a petition by disgruntled residents of Charles City County, ordered Fitz to attack an outpost on the lower James occupied by several hundred U.S. Colored Troops.

Fitz's troopers, and thousands of other Confederates, had a deep-rooted hatred of African-American enlisted men, their white officers, and the newly instituted policy of the U.S. government under which both had been recruited. This sentiment gave Fitz a basis for accepting the assignment with some enthusiasm. On the other hand, he was aware that his command was neither trained nor equipped to assault a heavily manned, artillery-protected fortification, regardless of the color of its garrison.

Despite his qualms, Fitz saluted and started on a long and tedious journey along the north bank of the James. Behind him came an eight hundred-man force composed of detachments from the brigades of Wickham, Lomax, and Gordon, the latter now led by Colonel Clinton M. Andrews, Gordon having been mortally wounded during the fighting at Meadow Bridge. On the morning of the twenty-fourth, Fitz's column pulled up at Wilson's Wharf and nearby Fort Pocahontas, a large, octagonal earthwork manned by several hundred black infantrymen and cannoneers. The fort mounted six guns, was shielded by a wide ditch and a heavy abatis as well as a steep scarp and counterscarp, and lay within supporting range of U.S. Navy gunboats in the James.[7]

Careful not to act intimidated by the unexpectedly formidable defenses, Fitz sent in a surrender demand that was harshly rejected by the local commander, Brigadier General Edward Wild, one of Ben Butler's most combative subordinates. Left with no other option, Fitz formed attack columns. As he later wrote, "though a very different state of things existed than was represented by citizens, upon whose accounts the expedition had been sent, I nevertheless resolved to make an attempt for the capture of the place, now that the march had been made."[8]

At about 3:30 P.M., bugles squalled and hundreds of Wickham's men rushed across a wide stretch of open ground toward the west face of the fort, while a second, smaller force assaulted the opposite flank. Under the shelling and rifle fire that poured out of the earthwork, augmented by salvos from the offshore gunboats, fallen cavalrymen began to litter the fields of approach. One eyewitness reported that "bravely, desperately, our boys pressed forward but getting into the abatis, they found it wholly impossible [to advance], whilst the fire was most galling."[9]

After losing ten men killed and fifty wounded, Fitz, who had gone forward with one of the columns, "exposing himself most heroically" to the fire, saw he could not capture the fort; he decided to abandon the effort before additional casualties accrued. By late afternoon he was leading his Virginians back to Richmond in preparation for a linkup with the balance of his uncle's army. He would have been forgiven had he hurled invective at Braxton Bragg and the good citizens of Charles City County whose outrage over the presence in their midst of "nigger troops" had triggered the useless sacrifice.

But even at this depressing juncture, Fitz maintained a sense of humor. On rejoining his command at Atlee's Station, he learned that in his absence the 1st Maryland Battalion of Lomax's brigade had gotten into a scrape with two of Custer's regiments, ending with the Marylanders in rapid retreat. Upon meeting one of the battalion's enlisted men, a trooper well known to him, Fitz exclaimed: "This is a pretty howdy-do for the Maryland cavalry—let the Yankees run you off the face of the earth." The trooper, who had taken a nasty wound in the fight, was not in the mood for such pointed jocularity, even when delivered by a division commander. "Well, General," he drawled, "one thing is certain, the people who have been after us were white men, we stayed long enough to find that out anyway."[10]

Another officer might have bristled at the retort and the tone in which delivered. Fitz Lee responded by throwing back his head and laughing at his own expense.

*   *   *

By May 27, the Army of the Potomac was swinging south from the line of the North Anna, where Robert E. Lee had again blocked its southward progress. This time Grant and Meade were heading for the Pamunkey River at Hanovertown, which Sheridan's horsemen, leading the way, were about to occupy. Thanks to its interior lines of maneuver, Lee's army made better time as it moved from Hanover Junction to the north bank of the Chickahominy near Mechanicsville. On the twenty-eighth, the ANV dropped down to Cold Harbor, a misnamed hamlet sweltering in near-summertime heat. To this same site, ten miles above Richmond, Grant intended to send Meade's army.

On the way south from Hanover Junction, the advance of Lee's main army reestablished contact with Fitz's troopers. For the first time in eighteen days, the cavalry corps was intact, Fitz welcoming Hampton and Rooney Lee to Atlee's Station. At this point a loaded question suddenly arose: who commanded the combined force? As Stuart's senior lieutenant, Hampton was the logical choice to assume the title, but Robert E. Lee—to his nephew's gratification—did not necessarily agree.[11]

The army commander professed not to know enough of Hampton's abilities to feel comfortable anointing him as Stuart's successor. Apparently, he was also concerned about the forty-six-year-old's energy and stamina quotient. Another possible reason for Lee's inaction related to personality: he may have regarded the South Carolinian as an indiscreet complainer. Over the past two years Hampton had accused J. E. B. Stuart, loudly and often, of favoritism toward the Virginia outfits in his command. Just as emphatically Hampton had decried his superior's alleged tendency to saddle his Deep South outfits with a heavier workload while attending less responsively to their wants and needs.[12]

Lee had looked into the matter and decided that Hampton's complaints were without basis. This greatly disturbed the army leader. He prized subordinates who comported themselves as gentlemen and cooperated wholeheartedly with their colleagues; by the same token, he looked askance at those who could not, or would not, get along with their peers and superiors. Although mindful of Hampton's abilities as a combat leader, Lee may have considered him a member of the latter class.

Until he could make an informed decision, Lee decreed that all three of the cavalry's division commanders, when operating apart from the others, would report directly to army headquarters. Only when Hampton's division served alongside Fitz's or Rooney's would he exercise overall command, and then strictly on the basis of seniority. It was an unusual and unwieldy arrangement, as well as connative of Lee's distrust, but if it bothered Hampton he did not let on. This was a point in his favor, suggesting discretion or unselfishness, or both, and assuredly Lee took note of it.[13]

For his part, Fitz kept just as quiet about the situation, which appeared to redound to his benefit. Others in the cavalry might view it as an example of preferential treatment toward a family member. Fitz saw it as a just rebuke to one who had overstepped himself by falsely claiming title to the cavalier tradition their lamented superior had embodied. As Fitz Lee knew, he alone was the rightful inheritor of Stuart's mantle, and only he could keep the great leader's memory burning bright. By refusing to name Hampton as Stuart's successor, Robert E. Lee appeared to endorse his nephew's view.

Yet Fitz's relief at not being overslaughed by one he considered his inferior appeared to be short-lived. Early on May 28, Robert E. Lee sent Hampton with his division, plus Wickham's brigade of Fitz's division and Chambliss's brigade of Rooney Lee's division, toward Hanovertown, about seven miles northeast of Atlee's Station. Two of Sheridan's divisions had crossed the river there, accompanied by infantry. Hampton's superior, however, was uncertain whether the rest of Meade's army intended to cross as well, or whether Sheridan's advance was a feint to draw attention from the real crossing site. Hampton's first job as presumptive successor to Stuart was to determine the facts and relay them to his commander as soon as possible.[14]

Either at his superior's order or for personal reasons, Fitz and Rooney accompanied their detachments on the eastward march to Hanovertown Ferry, where the Yankees had laid a pontoon bridge, perhaps to be used by a more substantial force. A few miles from the ferry, near Haw's Shop and Enon Church,

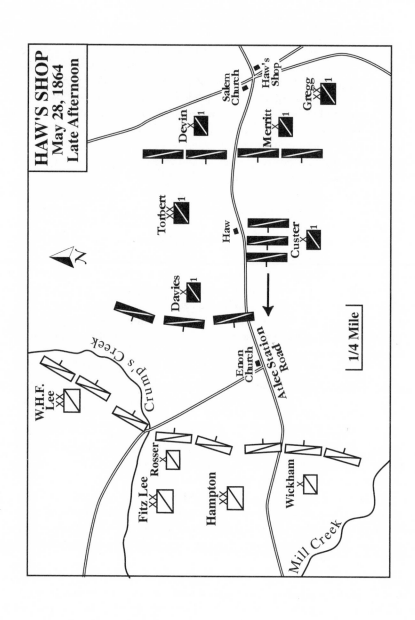

HAW'S SHOP
May 28, 1864
Late Afternoon

Salem
Church

Haw's
Shop

Gregg
XX

Devin
X
1

Merritt
X
1

Torbert
XX
1

Haw

Custer
X
1

Davies
X
1

N

Crump's Creek

Enon
Church

Atlee Station
Road

1/4 Mile

W.H.F.
Lee
XX

Fitz Lee
XX

Rosser
X

Hampton
XX

Wickham
X

Mill Creek

West Point, 1855 (USMA Archives)

Major General Lunsford L. Lomax, CSA
(Photographic History of the Civil War)

Brigadier General George D. Bayard, USA
(Library of Congress)

Brigadier General William W. Averell, USA
(Library of Congress)

Lieutenant Fitzhugh Lee, USA, ca. 1860 (Kansas State Historical Society)

General Robert E. Lee, CSA (Library of Congress)

General Joseph E. Johnston, CSA (Library of Congress)

Major General J. E. B. Stuart, CSA
(Library of Congress)

Brigadier General William E. ("Grumble")
Jones, CSA (Library of Congress)

Lieutenant Colonel John S. Mosby, CSA
(Library of Congress)

J. E. B. Stuart's Cavalry on the march (Author's collection)

Major General W. H. F. ("Rooney") Lee, CSA (Library of Congress)

Major General Wade Hampton, CSA (Library of Congress)

Major General Thomas J. Jackson, CSA
(Battles and Leaders of the Civil War)

Stuart's Raid on Catlett's Station, August 23, 1862 (Library of Congress)

Brigadier General Thomas T. Munford, CSA
(Library of Congress)

Brigadier General Williams C. Wickham,
CSA (Library of Congress)

Major General George Stoneman, USA (Library of Congress)

Major General Thomas L. Rosser, CSA
(Photographic History of the Civil War)

Battle of Kelly's Ford, March 17, 1863 (Library of Congress)

*Major General Alfred Pleasonton, USA
(Library of Congress)*

Brigadier General H. Judson Kilpatrick, USA
(Library of Congress)

Brigadier General John D. Imboden, CSA
(Library of Congress)

Major General Philip H. Sheridan, USA (Library of Congress)

Fitzhugh Lee, USA, ca. 1866 (Virginia Historical Society)

Fitzhugh Lee, USA, ca. 1885 (Virginia Historical Society)

Major General Fitzhugh Lee, USA, and staff, 1899 (Virginia Historical Society)

the head of the column encountered Sheridan's advance echelon, the division of David Gregg, that appeared to be on a reconnaissance of its own. East of the chapel and west of the blacksmith's shop, hundreds of troopers on both sides dismounted and scrambled to erect parallel breastworks astride the east-west–running road to Mechanicsville. Soon they were pounding each other with carbine and rifle fire. As soon as horse artillery units could gallop up and unlimber, they added heaping quantities of shell and canister to the deadly mix.

Fitz's horsemen held the right of Hampton's line, their left covered by the Laurel Brigade, while Rooney Lee's men staked out a position farther to the left and rear. For most of the day the combined force was opposed solely by Gregg's troopers, whose numerical inferiority was materially reduced by their quick-loading, rapid-fire carbines, a stark contrast to the muzzle-loaders that continued to predominate in the Rebel ranks.[15]

Relatively few antagonists changed position during the six-hour engagement, pinned as they were to their log-and-fence rail works by an impenetrable sheet of musketry and an almost incessant rain of case shot. The weather was exceedingly warm, but the concentration of firepower was so heavy and the field so compact that for these antagonists struggling to withstand the extraordinary pressure applied to them, the day was far hotter than any thermometer could measure.

The fight appeared to pivot on a couple of limited movements, including an abortive advance in midafternoon by Rosser's men, which for a time threatened to unhinge Gregg's center, and a promising but inadequate attempt by Rooney Lee to turn the Union right. For their part, Fitz's men simply held their ground, even though sticking one's head above the breastworks to squeeze off a shot too often meant quick death.

A few men remained mobile long enough to fall into enemy hands. From those he captured, Hampton learned, sometime before 4 P.M., that Meade's army was indeed crossing in full strength at Hanovertown. This being all he needed to know, he called for a general withdrawal—at the very moment that Torbert's recently arrived division spelled Gregg's fought-out troopers and made its presence felt through a mounted-dismounted attack by Custer's Michiganders. Hampton's simultaneous fallback and his subsequent withdrawal to Atlee's Station led Custer and his subordinates to declare their charge the key to victory. Hampton and his colleagues (or were they his subordinates?) knew better.[16]

*   *   *

In the aftermath of Haw's Shop, Fitz's command resumed its peripatetic existence, on May 30 moving to Mechanicsville and on the following day to Cold Harbor. At Cold Harbor, a place of no apparent strategic importance but toward which two armies were heading, Fitz's horsemen, backed by a brigade of

North Carolina infantry, repulsed a midafternoon attack by a sizable detachment of cavalry under Torbert and chased it away.

A few hours later, Torbert returned with supports of his own—the vanguard of Meade's army, the VI Corps in front. Even with Tarheel support, after three hours of stubborn resistance Fitz was driven out of the crossroads village and for about a half-mile beyond it. His tenacity had cost him numerous casualties, including the death of Major Thomas Flournoy, the talented commander of the 6th Virginia.[17]

Throughout June 1, Fitz, now augmented by the infantry division of Major General Robert F. Hoke, held his new position within cannon range of Cold Harbor while the better part of both armies closed in from opposite directions. That day and two days later, they engaged in one of the war's most horrid bloodbaths. The Federals, compelled to assume the offensive, suffered more heavily. Late on the afternoon of the third, Meade's army assaulted Lee's works west of Cold Harbor in double lines along a six-mile front, only to be blown apart by a deadly converging fire. Nearly seven thousand attackers fell dead or wounded, most during the first half-hour of fighting, as opposed to one-fifth as many defenders. Shocked by the losses, Grant ordered no more attacks.[18]

During the June 2 lull in the carnage, Fitz was ordered to Bottom's Bridge on the Chickahominy, where he took the time to rest his battle-scarred command. There, as at Cold Harbor, he was operating apart from Hampton. This, of course, is how he wanted it—free of subordination to a fellow commander whose sole claim to his obedience was seniority. Technically at least, he had served under Hampton at Haw's Shop, but during the fighting the two had been so widely separated that Fitz could believe (as he declared in an unpublished report of the battle) that Hampton "had supported me," not vice versa. The thought of relinquishing his autonomy began to throb painfully in his mind.[19]

The prospect became reality on the eighth, one day after Fitz relayed to army headquarters a report that Mede's engineers had begun to lay pontoons across the James. This was ominous news, but so was word out of cavalry headquarters that Sheridan had returned to the north bank of the Pamunkey with a substantial portion of his force, including several batteries. The same day, Fitz learned that the force was moving along the lower bank of the Mattapony, heading west toward—where? No one knew for certain, but the portents suggested a raid on the Virginia Central, the conduit by which Robert E. Lee tapped the lush bounty of the Shenandoah Valley.[20]

Hampton quickly concluded that Sheridan's objective was Gordonsville or Charlottesville. By midday of the eighth he was heading in that direction with his three brigades, including a new one commanded by the recently recuperated M. C. Butler. Hampton had sought permission to include Rooney Lee as well, but Robert E. Lee wanted his son by his side as he tried to determine why Meade was about to invade Southside Virginia.

For most of the eighth, Fitz Lee's status remained unresolved. Just when it seemed he would join his cousin in opposing Meade, late in the afternoon Rooney's troopers rode up with orders to relieve Fitz's. Finally, after dark, came a summons to join Hampton on the westward march.[21]

While the thought of serving under Hampton was depressing, Fitz was consoled by the realization that until the enemy was brought to bay he would operate apart from the man. Hampton's route of march, along the south side of the railroad, paralleled Sheridan's north of the tracks. Because he had the shorter distance to travel, Hampton would be the first to reach any section of the railroad that proved to be Sheridan's immediate target. Fitz, however, would not progress as far, as fast, as either of the ranking opponents. By the evening of June 10, Hampton had reached Green Spring Valley, three miles beyond Trevilian Station, while Sheridan had halted about five miles to the northeast at Ground Squirrel Bridge on the North Anna. Fitz, despite a "rapid march," had gotten only as far as Louisa Court House, five miles short of Trevilian.[22]

At Louisa, Fitz heard by courier from Hampton that the 1st Division would attack early the next morning before Sheridan, who had begun to descend on the railroad, could tear up track. Hampton would advance up the northeastward-leading Clayton's Store Road, which passed through the depot at Trevilian. He wished Fitz, as early in the day as possible, to join him via the northwestward-running road from Louisa Court House. That byway did not intersect the road to Clayton's Store but connected with a parallel road that would place Fitz in close contact with Hampton and facilitate coordination.

Considering the distance between Hampton's and Fitz's positions on the evening of the tenth and taking into account the usual vicissitudes of battle, it is not surprising that things did not work out the way Hampton planned. At about 5 A.M. on the eleventh, he charged up the Clayton's Store Road and into the head of Sheridan's column. Spirited, sometimes desperate, and occasionally confused fighting swirled along both sides of the thicket-lined road as the opposing horsemen clashed. Most of Sheridan's men dismounted to fight, as did a surprisingly large number of Confederates—testimony to Hampton's preference for dragoon-style warfare in contrast to Stuart's seemingly slavish devotion to mounted tactics.

The fighting raged for hours under a torrid sun with neither antagonist gaining a decisive advantage. One reason for this was that neither was at full strength. Sheridan lacked Custer's brigade, which had assumed a detached position off the Union left. Hampton was even more shorthanded, for at the hour he expected Fitz Lee to join him, Fitz was nowhere to be found.

Characteristically, Fitz never accounted for his late arrival. Perhaps he simply

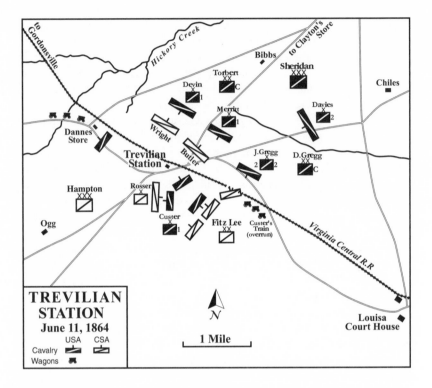

TREVILIAN
STATION
June 11, 1864

could not—if so, he was not alone. One of his regimental officers, looking back years later, recalled that "we deployed skirmishers, halted to reconnoitre, bought up & planted some 2 or 3 pieces of artillery—and somehow or other lost two or three hours."[23]

Afterward, all Fitz would say about his failure to appear on Hampton's flank in a timely manner was that after leaving Louisa Court House early that morning, he found "the converging point . . . too distant, and before I could reach its vicinity, the enemy had passed it, and was in Hampton's front." Thanks to another late arrival—Custer's—the Yankees were also in Hampton's rear. The Michigan Brigade had reached the field of battle via a diagonal track through the woods northeast of Trevilian that placed it—strictly by happenstance—behind Hampton's right flank. In that sector the newcomers seized hundreds of led horses whose riders were on the firing lines well to the north.[24]

Custer's path also enabled him to interpose between Hampton's and Fitz's divisions, but it exposed his lower flank and rear to Fitz's column, then nearing the field of battle. Yet instead of attacking immediately, Fitz lost time by countermarching until he gained what he considered a more advantageous position from which to strike. By then he found he did not have to attack alone. Thanks to reinforcements, Torbert's troopers had broken through Hampton's front, sending hundreds of Confederates racing toward the rear, and their mounts. On the way they encountered Custer's horse thieves, whom they attacked from two directions at once.[25]

Only then did Fitz commit his division against Custer's left and rear. The results were impressive. Later he claimed that his troopers alone recaptured every horse Custer had taken along with several supply wagons and caissons that had also fallen into the boy-general's hands. Fitz further declared that he captured Custer's own baggage wagons as well as at least one of his aides and some caissons belonging to the battery attached to his command. An especially hard-hitting charge led by Fitz's kinsman and staff officer, Major Robert F. Mason, was said to have done most of the damage. It forced Custer to defend so many sectors of his line at the same time that he fought in a complete circle—a formation that anticipated another battle he would wage twelve years hence, against opponents in war paint rather than Confederate gray.

Fitz claimed, too, that by late afternoon he was able to extend his left flank until connecting with Hampton's right. Thereafter, the two commands supposedly fought side by side until Torbert broke through to rescue Custer. Despite all the maneuvering that had taken place this day, Fitz contended that "night . . . found the relative positions of both sides about the same" as when the fight began.[26]

During the night, Fitz "shifted my position, and the next day reported to Genl Hampton, who had taken up a new line west of Trevillians, covering the Charlottesville and Gordonsville Roads." He failed to mention that to reach Hampton he was forced to make a long, circuitous march around Sheridan's lower flank. The detour suggests that the two divisions were not in such close proximity at day's end as Fitz would have one believe.[27]

No account has survived of what was said when Fitz reported to Hampton's headquarters, but it can be supposed that the South Carolinian was not in a jovial mood. Fitz's morning absence, which prevented him from supporting Hampton at a critical point, may have prevented a Confederate victory. In the interest of corporate harmony, however, Hampton withheld any criticism he might have intended to lodge against Fitz. Later, however, some of his officers accused Fitz of deliberate tardiness in the hope that their boss would be blamed for the failure of his battle plan. Late in life, Hampton appears to have come around to this way of thinking. In his report of the fight, he made no pejorative comments on Fitz's conduct and even praised his assistance. But in postwar correspondence with his former subordinates, Hampton indicted Fitz for unconscionable slowness, which he cited as the reason Sheridan was not routed on the eleventh.[28]

Throughout the morning and for half of the afternoon of June 12, Hampton waited for Sheridan, who had cast himself in the role of aggressor, to renew the fight. But Little Phil took his time. Not until 3:30 P.M., by which time his people had torn up a five-mile stretch of track, mostly east of the depot, did he treat Hampton to anything more threatening than long-range skirmishing. However, within minutes of Sheridan's advance against his opponent's new line, two and a half miles west of the depot, brisk skirmishing broke out, in which the cannons of both forces made their present felt. One of Fitz's officers found shells "flying right over where were lying at a height varying from 6 to 15 ft. above the ground."[29]

The fight heated up when one of Torbert's brigades assaulted the left flank of Hampton's eastward-facing and well-entrenched line. When a corresponding assault on the other flank failed to materialize, however, Hampton was able to concentrate against this single brigade, whose front he shredded with carbine and pistol fire. A dramatic charge by a regiment of Regulars temporarily drove back the brigade's assailants and stabilized Sheridan's position. Then, however, Fitz, whose division had been holding a reserve position, added his weight to the fight and it turned dramatically.

"Discovering an opportunity to turn the enemy's right flank," Fitz took the initiative. With Hampton's approval, he marched a large portion of Lomax's brigade, accompanied by several of Breathed's guns, through a woods, across the railroad, and into the enemy's right rear. Behind an extensive growth of underbrush he dismounted most of Lomax's men and formed them into a line of battle. After Breathed ran his guns to the front, Fitz had them open on the startled Yankees. Seconds later, his buglers sounded the charge. As Fitz wrote, "the enemy . . . offered but slight resistance—their right flank gave way, and they were driven back in confusion." Lomax attempted to pursue, but the brushy terrain, combined with an early end to daylight, scuttled his plans.[30]

At this point, Sheridan—who had suffered almost 1,000 casualties over the two days of fighting, some 150 more than his opponent—called it quits. During the night he broke contact with Hampton and countermarched on the same road he had taken to Trevilian. Little Phil appeared to have a strategic basis for withdrawing. He had already wrecked enough railroad track to satisfy that aspect of his mission; furthermore, a small army operating in the Valley under Major General David Hunter, whom the raiders were to have met and escorted eastward to augment Meade, had failed to establish contact with Sheridan. Then, too, Sheridan believed his decoy mission had been accomplished. By now Grant and Meade were surely well on their way to Petersburg, if they had not already captured the place.

These facts and probabilities furnished Sheridan with ample grounds for breaking off the fight. But they were also rationalizations. The true reason he turned about and went home was that despite outnumbering Hampton and enjoying a quantitative and qualitative advantage in material resources, Sheridan had been fought to a standstill on the first day of battle and badly beaten on the second.[31]

*   *   *

After burying the blue-clad corpses that lay piled outside their breastworks, the Confederates late on the twelfth began a two-column pursuit of their quickly retreating foe. While Hampton set out on the road by which he had come, Fitz followed directly behind Sheridan via Chilesburg, New Market, and Polecat Station on the Richmond, Fredericksburg & Potomac. At least partly due to the exhausted condition of his horses, Fitz failed to overtake his prey. Meanwhile, Hampton, thanks to those same interior lines he had enjoyed on the journey to Trevilian, forged ahead of Sheridan at several points but was unsuccessful in forcing him to stop and fight.

Unwilling to let the Yankees get off scot-free, Hampton on the nineteenth again surged ahead and made for White House on the Pamunkey. Hampton's scouts had informed him that the several hundred-wagon train of Sheridan's corps was parked at that supply base, which the Federals were in the process of abandoning for the second time in two years. Convinced that Sheridan would stop there to pick up his train, Hampton and his hard-riding troopers were waiting for him when, on the twentieth, the head of his column approached the base from the north. Hampton's horse artillery had already softened up the place with shot and shell, damaging warehouses, wharves, and railroad track and terrorizing its small caretaker force.[32]

Hampton was about to order an all-out assault on White House when Fitz, whose division had been a half-day's march behind his colleague's, reached the base. Disturbed by the exhausted condition of the would-be attackers as well as by their lack of scaling ladders and other resources, Fitz, who remembered all too vividly the assault on Fort Pocahontas, advised Hampton to call off the attack. Hampton's staff officers were astonished when, after some hesitation, their superior agreed. For all his personal and professional disagreements with Fitz, Hampton recognized good advice when he heard it.[33]

Hampton may have foregone this opportunity, but over the next five days he struck early and often at Sheridan's rear and flanks as he escorted his ponderous train from the Pamunkey to the Chickahominy. While Hampton harassed from the north, Fitz galloped to the lower river, which he prepared to hold from behind a formidable screen of earthworks. His position abutted that of Rooney Lee, who in Fitz's absence had occupied the area while battling Wilson's division, the only cavalry Meade had retained for his movement toward Petersburg.

Although Rooney refused to take any credit for it, his men had played a role in Meade's inability to take the "Cockade City" of Petersburg by storm. On June 15, Grant and Meade, having stolen a march on Robert E. Lee at Cold Harbor, combined with a large detachment of Ben Butler's army to attack the lightly defended support center. Almost incredibly, they had failed to gain entrance. Credit for this outcome was due to the stubborn resistance of the city's defenders, under the peripatetic P. G. T. Beauregard, as well as to an egregious lack of co-ordination and cooperation on the part of Meade's and Butler's subordinates. It took three days, but by the eighteenth Lee had finally come down from above the Chickahominy to secure Petersburg with the better part of the Army of Northern Virginia.[34]

Hampton and Fitz were still trying to catch Sheridan when word reached them from south of the James that Wilson's cavalry had begun a raid on the rail-roads north and west of Petersburg in cooperation with the small division of horsemen in Butler's army. Since the security of those lines was critical to Lee's ability to hold his present position, it was imperative that Wilson be stopped before he put them out of commission. Rooney Lee was ordered to pursue with half of his division. The other half, Chambliss's brigade, remained on the north side; by the twenty-fourth it had been temporarily added to Fitz's command, as had a recently organized brigade of Virginia and South Carolina cavalry under Brigadier General Martin W. Gary.[35]

The additions came in handy, for that day Hampton, having crossed the Chickahominy to unite with Fitz, determined to force a confrontation with Sheridan. By now Sheridan also had crossed, hauling his cumbersome train over Jones's Bridge. To cover the head and rear of his column, he had deployed his cavalry well out on the roads toward the James. Torbert's division held the for-wardmost position, near Charles City, with Gregg's several miles farther north, near Samaria Church and Nance's Shop.

Hampton saw how isolated Gregg was and determined to attack him with Fitz's division and his own minus Lomax's brigade, which Fitz had distributed along the main route to the James to keep an eye on Torbert. That morning the two generals put aside their personal differences long enough to cooperate in an all-out assault. Sometime after 3 P.M., their troopers charged the right flank of Gregg's line and then turned south to envelop the left. The Yankees reeled backward, nearly overthrown at first contact, before regaining equilibrium and battening down to defend their position.[36]

Although outnumbered, they held on for two hours, a tribute to their na-tive tenacity and to their supports, two of the finest horse artillery batteries in Union service. But by five o'clock, as their commander observed, "it became evident that the contest was too unequal to maintain it longer." At Gregg's word, large detachments withdrew by the right flank, falling back to their horses under a covering fire from comrades, then racing south to the safety of Torbert's perimeter. Gregg maintained that his regiments withdrew "without confusion or disorder," but Fitz claimed that under the incessant pounding of Wickham, Chambliss, Gary, and Breathed, the Yankees were "driven back in disorder" and barely escaped annihilation.[37]

Hundreds of Confederates took up a pursuit, which Fitz claimed went on for five hours until halted by darkness. Although most of Gregg's men escaped, a number of wounded troopers and captured wagons fell into Fitz's hands, as did 157 able-bodied prisoners, including 13 officers. All told, Gregg had lost upwards of 350 men, about 60 more than his enemy.[38]

Judging their assault a major success, Hampton and Fitz, preparing to resume the fight on the Richmond side of the James, spent the next three days monitoring Sheridan's preparations for crossing the river. But on the twenty-seventh, Hampton was called to Petersburg to help chase Wilson's raiders. That day he crossed the pontoon bridge near Chaffin's Bluff with his own brigades and that of Chambliss's. Fitz covered the crossing with Lomax's and Wickham's troopers before joining Hampton on the south bank the following day. He left Gary's little brigade on the Northside.[39]

For twenty-four hours or more, Fitz's men were at loose ends, expecting to be summoned to Petersburg but thus far without orders. Their commander chose to regard the period as party time. Accompanied by all of his staff officers, he repaired to the downtown home of one of them, where they made a "jolly night of it," singing, dancing, and laughing away the hours with the captain's family and other visitors as if the war were a distant memory. The highlight of the evening was a duet featuring Fitz and the comely sister of his host, followed by a rollicking rendition of J. E. B. Stuart's favorite ditty, "Jine the Cavalry." A guest observed that "Fitz and staff joined in the refrain with mighty zest, making the house ring with their hilarity."[40]

Toward the end of the festivities, some of the ladies filled the haversacks of Fitz and his aides with culinary delights, while other hostesses distributed home-made apparel to be worn in camp. At length it was time for farewells, a ritual that Fitz attended to with characteristic zeal. After his aide kissed his mother and sister goodbye, Fitz, "true to his cavalry instincts, began kissing also; this doubtless inspired his young captain to extend like courtesies to visitors as well as the family; and wherever he led, Fitz followed. By the time their plunder had been placed upon their steeds, and they, with jangling spurs, had scrambled to their saddles, Fitz Lee and staff had taken 'cavalry toll' from every pretty girl in sight. Finally, with many fond adieus and waving plumes, they rode away down Cary Street, their mounted banjoist playing the air, and they singing in chorus,— 'If you want to have a good time, jine the cavalry.'"[41]

The following day, Fitz added to his recent store of gifts. While he and his staff had partied, Hampton had caught up with the railroad raiders under Wilson and his cohort from the Army of the James, Brigadier General August V. Kautz. Returning eastward after laying waste to sixty miles of track on the Richmond & Danville and the Petersburg & Lynchburg, Wilson, Kautz, and their thirty-three hundred troopers had fallen into an ambush near Sappony Church and Stony Creek Station on the Petersburg & Weldon Railroad south of the Cockade City. On June 28 Hampton, supported by two brigades of infantry under Major General William Mahone, tore into the raiding column, inflicting dozens of casualties. The fighting went on for several hours until stopped by darkness.[42]

Hampton and Mahone expected to finish off the raiders come morning, but during the night Kautz, followed by Wilson, tried to slip away. Detecting their roundabout retreat, Hampton pursued in a straight line north and beat them to Reams's Station on the Weldon. There, six miles from Petersburg, the South Carolinian was joined on the morning of the twenty-ninth by Fitz and his two brigades. Soon afterward, the more fleet-footed of Mahone's men reached the scene as well. Outnumbered, outmaneuvered, and for a time nearly surrounded, the raiders fought gamely but eventually broke and fled, every man for himself. They left behind many evidences of their raiding mission, including hundreds of liberated slaves who were suddenly at the mercy of their assailants.[43]

One of Fitz's officers described the denouement: "The enemy retired rather sullenly until our sabres began to knock their caps off. They then fled precipitately[,] exposing to view about 1500 negroes scampering across the fields . . . with great bundles of plunder stolen from their masters' houses, upon their backs. Some fell over—bundles & all—others were knocked over—one or two were shot, whilst a few died of fright—such screaming & yelling as they sent up Pandemonium itself could scarcely beat."[44]

The African Americans were not alone in appropriating the property of slaveholders. The dozens of wagons Wilson and Kautz abandoned at Reams's Station contained a fantastic amount of plunder, looted from private homes and public and government storehouses all along their route—gold and silver, scrip and currency, choice victuals, items of clothing, home furnishings, even a communion service stolen from an Episcopal church. To these spoils were added the contents of the baggage, rations, and forage wagons belonging to Wilson, Kautz, and their men.

Hampton rounded up as many vehicles as he could find and divided their contents among Mahone's and Fitz's men and those of his own division. Fitz distributed his share to the officers and men of each of his regiments. His brigade commanders received the most valuable items, including gilt-encrusted sabers, ornate saddles, and dress uniforms. Regimental personnel fared slightly less well, although one captain observed that "every officer & nearly every man . . . got a nice trophy. I got a good overcoat, gun cloth & other small articles."[45]

Presumably, his commander could have reserved for himself anything he wanted. Yet, as the captain noted admiringly, Fitz appropriated only a few cans of fruit preserves.[46]

TWELVE

Corps Command

Following the escape of the Wilson-Kautz raiders, the cavalry of the Army of Northern Virginia went into camp along the Weldon Railroad, Fitz's division near Reams's Station, Hampton's command on its right near Sappony Church, and Rooney Lee's men on the left, connecting with the infantry's lines below Petersburg. Outside the Cockade City siege operations continued apace as Confederates huddling behind works and crouching in rifle pits exchanged sharpshooter and cannon fire on a daily basis with the combined armies of Meade and Butler, under Grant's overall command.

In a reversal of the normal state of affairs, while the infantry fought, the cavalry comrades remained in camp in the rear of the firing lines. The mounted arms of both sides had been so beaten down by near-constant campaigning—picketing, reconnoitering, raiding, skirmishing, and fighting a score or more of pitched battles—that required a break from the war. Men and mounts, benumbed by an ordeal never before experienced, finally enjoyed an interval of unbroken rest, regular rations, and stress relief.[1]

The respite lasted more than a month, broken by only a couple of combat missions. On July 12, Fitz, with detachments of both of his brigades, had a run-in with Gregg's cavalry while on a reconnaissance to Lee's Mill, cutting off and capturing thirty-two members of a Pennsylvania regiment. Two weeks later, after Grant dispatched Meade's II Corps as well as two of Sheridan's divisions to the north side of the James, Robert E. Lee countered by crossing several infantry brigades backed by the better part of Hampton's division.[2]

Over the next two days, the infantry mostly maneuvered while the cavalry fought several sharp engagements. Fitz's division did not join in the operation until the evening of the twenty-ninth. Passing through Petersburg and over the pontoons at Chaffin's Bluff, his troopers expected to see action as soon as they set foot on the Northside. Instead, they idled in the rear as the foot soldiers finally began to mix it up. Fitz moved up in the wee hours of the thirtieth, only to find that the enemy had returned to the south side of the James.

Shortly before 5 A.M., a massive explosion southeast of Petersburg divulged the reason for Grant's movement. It had been a feint to draw attention from the site of a gunpowder-filled tunnel that coal miners in Burnside's corps had dug under the enemy lines opposite them. The mine had worked perfectly, blasting an entranceway into downtown Petersburg, but an attack launched in its wake was horribly botched, and the siege went on.[3]

*   *   *

Since late June, ten thousand Confederates under Jubal Early had been operating far from the Army of Northern Virginia, first in the Shenandoah Valley, then north of the Potomac on a raid that carried them to the suburbs of Washington, D.C. Until heavy detachments from Meade's army came up to chase him away, Old Jube scared the wits out of the capital's residents. Having demonstrated Washington's vulnerability, he calmly returned to his multifaceted mission in the Valley, which he described as "to keep up a threatening attitude toward Maryland and Pennsylvania, and prevent the use of the Baltimore and Ohio Railroad and the Chesapeake and Ohio Canal, as well as to keep as large a force as possible from Grant's army to defend the Federal capital."[4]

Early could stir up politicians with impunity, but he made the mistake of provoking Ulysses S. Grant by his incessant attacks on Union outposts and supply depots. On August 1, Grant moved to end these depredations by sending to the Valley Sheridan, with the VI Army Corps and Torbert's cavalry division, later augmented by Wilson's. Upon reaching his new station, Little Phil added to his command—known as the Army of the Shenandoah—elements of two other infantry corps and a third mounted division, William Averell's.[5]

Within days of Sheridan's transfer, Robert E. Lee was gathering supports for Early's Army of the Valley: Brigadier General Joseph B. Kershaw's infantry division, Fitz Lee's horsemen, and an artillery battalion, the combined force being entrusted to now-Lieutenant General Richard Anderson. The additions would give Early almost twenty-five thousand troops, a few thousand more than Sheridan's initial complement. On August 5, Anderson and Kershaw began to head north and then west by rail. That same day Fitz's command was ordered to Richmond by overland march and in deep secrecy. Neither the troopers nor their commander knew they were bound for points west.

On the tenth, the 2nd Cavalry Division passed through the capital "in regular military array" and out the north end, heading for upstream fords on the

North Anna and the Rapidan. The next day, having reached Culpeper Court House, Fitz finally learned he was heading for the verdant pastures—and the killing fields—of the Shenandoah.

Debouching from Chester Gap in the Blue Ridge, his column reached Front Royal, just inside the Luray Valley, on the morning of the fourteenth. Anderson and Kershaw arrived later that day. Fitz saw at once that in their present location infantry and cavalry were perfectly situated to combine with Early, whose army lay across the mountains to the west, in crushing Sheridan's troops in bivouac along Cedar Creek. To sell his idea to his new superior, Fitz, accompanied by a single staff officer, made the hazardous crossing of Massanutten Mountain to Strasburg. So steep was the ascent and descent that both officers made the journey on muleback. The next day Fitz safely reached Early's headquarters, where he gained Old Jube's approval and cooperation. But on the sixteenth, as Early mobilized to strike him, Sheridan withdrew from his precarious position and headed north to Halltown, just across the Potomac from Union-held Harpers Ferry.[6]

Sheridan's retreat had been prompted by a communiqué from Grant, warning that Early had been reinforced and recommending that Little Phil act defensively until he, too, could be augmented, or until Anderson was recalled to Petersburg. There was an unspoken political dimension to Grant's warning. Abraham Lincoln, running for reelection on the Union Party ticket, would be harmed by a military setback in the Valley. The president's chances for a second term already had been damaged by the stalemate at Petersburg as well as by William T. Sherman's frustratingly slow advance on Atlanta, the great population and manufacturing center of the Deep South. Should Early overwhelm Sheridan, the November vote might sweep into office an antiwar Democrat. That Democrat would be chosen at the end of August: former General George B. McClellan, whose political platform would declare the war a failure while holding out hope of a negotiated peace with the Confederacy.[7]

On the sixteenth, as Sheridan continued his retrograde, Fitz's division, with support from one of Kershaw's brigades, attacked the enemy at Cedarville, along the banks of the Shenandoah River. Part of Wesley Merritt's command absorbed a blow that Merritt himself described as delivered with "great violence." In vigorous, close-up fighting, the attackers were beaten back, but then the Rebel infantry advanced and a new round of fighting began. Merritt would claim that he repulsed Kershaw with great loss, but Fitz always contended that the Yankees withdrew from the fight in unseemly haste. Whatever the truth, Sheridan did not so much as turn his head as he rushed to the lower Valley. His behavior gave Fitz, Early, and many other Confederates a poor opinion of his intestinal fortitude.[8]

Impressed by the power of the cavalry's assault at Cedarville, Early subsequently named Fitz chief of his army's horsemen. Fitz's command embraced, in addition to his own division, four brigades of so-called Valley Cavalry, mainly ill-disciplined and poorly armed and equipped western Virginians under John Imboden and Brigadier Generals William L. Jackson, John McCausland, and Bradley T. Johnson. The assignment made Fitz a corps commander, the highest position to which a cavalryman could rise. In addition to conferring on him expanded authority (but no increase in rank), the post virtually guaranteed that he would never again serve under Wade Hampton. This may have been Robert E. Lee's intent in sending his nephew to the Valley, for not until Fitz was on his way was Hampton announced as permanent successor to J. E. B. Stuart in command of the cavalry of the Army of Northern Virginia.

Fitz's elevation enabled him to promote deserving subordinates. To his friend Lomax, a future major general, he entrusted the Valley Cavalry, which was reorganized as a division. Command of Fitz's old division went to Williams Wickham—its brigades were assigned to Colonels William H. F. Payne of the 4th Virginia and Reuben B. Boston of the 5th. Excessive campaigning had worn down both divisions to skeletal size. Wickham's mounted fewer than two thousand able-bodied officers and men. On paper, Lomax's command was slightly larger, but its effectiveness was compromised by its lack of formal training and its inadequate weaponry—mostly single-shot, muzzle-loading rifles. Its new leader faced a Herculean task in attempting to raise its efficiency to the level of Wickham's division.[9]

Fitz and Lomax had little time to adjust to their enlarged responsibilities. Hoping to force Sheridan to accept battle before he could take up an impregnable position in the lower Valley, Early began to pursue in three columns via Bunker Hill, Berryville, and Charles Town. On August 21 near Smithfield, northeast of Winchester, one struck Sheridan's rear echelon. This time Fitz took on Wilson's newly arrived division as well as Merritt's, the entire force supervised by Torbert. As at Cedarville, the Federal cavalry—bound by the defensive strategy of their superior—quickly broke contact and retreated.

Although harassed at every step, the Army of the Shenandoah passed through Charles Town on the twenty-second and took refuge behind prepared works at Halltown. Over the next three days, Early demonstrated in front of these defenses, trying to draw Sheridan into the open. He succeeded only in skirmishing with the pickets of Sheridan's VIII and XIX Corps.[10]

In frustration, Early turned eastward on the twenty-fifth, hoping to lure his opponent after him by threatening strategic targets such as Harpers Ferry and the Baltimore & Ohio. Leaving Anderson, supported by Boston's and McCausland's troopers, to watch Sheridan, Early moved west and then north to Leetown with his four other infantry divisions: Robert Rodes's, Stephen Dodson Ramseur's, John Brown Gordon's, and Gabriel C. Wharton's—the last two part of a provisional corps under Early's senior subordinate, Major General John C. Breckinridge.

From Leetown Early sent Fitz, with the main portion of Wickham's division, toward a site familiar from the Gettysburg Campaign—Williamsport, Maryland. Meanwhile Early and the infantry headed for the B & O near Kearneysville, and from there to Shepherdstown on the Potomac. Opposite Williamsport, Fitz maneuvered in such a way as to give the impression that he was going to cross into Maryland, although he had no intention of doing so.

His gyrations produced minimal results. On the twenty-sixth Torbert came up to oppose Early at Shepherdstown, while a part of Averell's division sparred briefly with Fitz's troopers. In their first close encounter since Kelly's Ford, Fitz got the better of his old friend, chasing Averell's people over the river and holding them there. Fitz's success was gratifying, but Early's primary quarry, Sheridan's infantry, refused to confront him. The following day Fitz returned to Leetown and from there to Smithfield. On the twenty-eighth he ordered Lomax to retire toward Bunker Hill, some thirteen miles above Winchester.[11]

That day, the Yankees suddenly displayed some aggressiveness, Torbert attacking the Valley Cavalry and shoving it across Opequon Creek to Bunker Hill. At the same time, Sheridan's main body left its works and moved slowly toward Charles Town. Underlying the unexpected advance was Sheridan's receipt of a telegram from Grant, informing him that a pending offensive against both Richmond and Petersburg would undoubtedly draw Anderson, Kershaw, and Fitz Lee back to the ANV, thus giving Sheridan a manpower advantage against Early.

Although Early continued to consider his adversary fatally intimidated, Sheridan kept up his slow, deliberate advance. On September 3 a small body of his cavalry, followed by an equally compact force of infantry, marched via the Valley Turnpike from Charles Town toward Front Royal. At Front Royal, Fitz—back in the saddle after a bout with "intermittent fever"—hit Torbert head-on, pushing him backward for a considerable distance. Meanwhile, Anderson and Kershaw encountered near Berryville Torbert's infantry comrades, whom they drove from a line of breastworks. Fitz assumed that this string of recent setbacks would cause Sheridan to retreat, but he was mistaken. Soon, in fact, Little Phil would go over to the offensive, as if energized by the recently received news of Sherman's capture of Atlanta.[12]

Grant was proven prescient on September 14 when, at Robert E. Lee's behest, Anderson and Kershaw departed Early's new position between Bunker Hill and Winchester and headed back to Petersburg via Culpeper. Only one aspect of Grant's prediction failed to materialize: instead of accompanying the returnees, Fitz's horsemen remained in the Valley guarding the approaches to Winchester and vicinity.

Even in his weakened state, Early was confident of his continued ability to overawe Sheridan. He failed to take proper precautions against the possibility of an attack, a lapse that proved costly when, at 3 A.M. on the nineteenth,

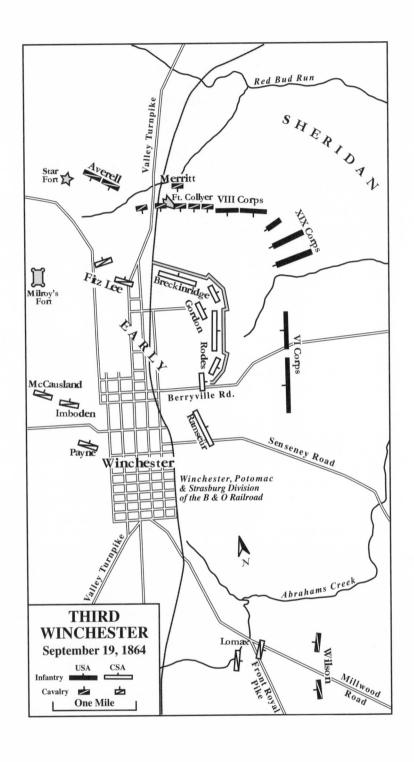

Red Bud Run

S H E R I D A N

Star Fort

Averell

Valley Turnpike

Merritt

Ft. Collyer

VIII Corps

XIX Corps

Milroy's Fort

Fitz Lee

Breckinridge

Gordon

Rodes

VI Corps

E A R L Y

McCausland

Imboden

Berryville Rd.

Ramseur

Payne

Winchester

Senseney Road

Winchester, Potomac & Strasburg Division of the B & O Railroad

N

Abrahams Creek

Lomax

Wilson

Valley Turnpike

Front Royal Pike

Millwood Road

THIRD WINCHESTER

September 19, 1864

Infantry

USA   CSA

Cavalry

One Mile

Sheridan attacked the Confederate lines at Winchester. Wilson's cavalry, followed closely by the VI Corps, with the XIX Corps in the latter's right rear, initiated the action by assailing Early's right flank, covered by Lomax's cavalry. First on the Berryville Pike, then farther south on the road from Millwood, Wilson's horsemen drove in the Rebel pickets and slammed into the infantry beyond—Ramseur's division, quickly reinforced by the troops of Gordon and Rodes. His right apparently stabilized, Early counterattacked about 11 A.M., aiming for a gap between the flanks of the VI and XIX Corps.[13]

The XIX Corps, despite being thrust backward by Early's counterstroke, extended its line to the north where it eventually linked with the troopers under Torbert. The combined force now drove forward against Early's left, held by Wharton's division, with Breckinridge in command. This was the sector where Early had stationed Fitz Lee, who for hours had been attempting to defend Breckinridge's left and rear with the understrength division that was once his and now Wickham's, backed by six cannons under James Breathed. Until now, Fitz had enjoyed more than a measure of success. Wickham's troopers had been contending manfully with their much more numerous adversaries, and Breathed had performed brilliantly in support not only of Wickham but also of Breckinridge and, farther south, Gordon. At one point the Yankees drove Gordon's division out of position. Their momentum carried them past the position occupied by Breathed, who wheeled his guns about and treated them to a devastating oblique fire that inflicted numerous casualties and made the rest of the attackers fall back.[14]

Despite these small triumphs, it was a matter of time before Sheridan's superior numbers would tell. By midafternoon, Little Phil had contained Early's counterattacks, driven Lomax's troopers virtually off the field, and hammered the enemy's main body into a compact defense perimeter due east of Winchester. While simultaneously pressing all parts of that line with the VI and XIX Corps, Sheridan committed two-thirds of the VIII Corps to a drive against the Rebel left and rear, spearheaded by Torbert's horsemen. Like a giant broom, the advancing troops combined to sweep everything from their path.

At this point, Fitz had given up hope of continued resistance. It seemed to him that Sheridan's late-day thrust had an inevitable, inexorable quality to it. He was not alone in this impression. Well before sundown, Early's men began to leave the field in numbers that increased geometrically with passing time. Most retreated southward along the Valley Turnpike in the direction of Strasburg and Fisher's Hill. One of Colonel Payne's officers, whose regiment had a commanding view of the turnpike, recalled that "we could see all below & sad it was to see. Our line, now attenuated by loss . . . seemed to be rapidly *melting* away—here and there were to be seen ambulances & batteries galloping off while two or three guns kept up a sullen fire. The Valley turnpike was filled with the retiring multitude of men, guns, wagons etc—and away off to the southeast Torbert from a high hill was 'pouring the hot shot' into them with his artillery."[15]

Eventually, Fitz was caught up in the surging retreat, although he did not leave the field under his own power. Sometime after 4 p.m. as he sat his war-horse, Nellie Gray, north of Winchester, he was struck in the thigh by a rifle ball. Unable to walk, even to hobble, he allowed himself to be carried from the field.[16]

The pain and debility stemming from the wound would bother him for a long time—in fact, for the rest of his life. Even more hurtful, however, was his superior's published imputation that Fitz's command was primarily responsible for the day's defeat. In his official report of the battle, Jubal Early would claim that even after the tide appeared to have turned against it, "our army could still have won the day if our cavalry would have stopped the enemy's; but . . . so demoralized was a larger part of ours, that no assistance was received from it. . . . I had already defeated the enemy's infantry, and could have continued to do so, but the enemy's very great superiority in cavalry and the comparative inefficiency of ours turned the scale against us."[17]

This falsehood was a low blow indeed. Fitz would need every ounce of his legendary amiability to maintain cordial relations with so caustic and unfair a critic as Jubal Early had shown himself to be.

*　　*　　*

Fitz's wound took more than three months to heal. From Winchester he was evacuated by train to the general hospital at Charlottesville, where he convalesced through late December. His recovery was slowed by a difficult-to-treat abscess that developed during his hospitalization, and possibly by infections.

Even as he suffered physically, his psychological health was compromised by the memory of the panicky retreat from Winchester. That memory was made even more painful by a letter Fitz's uncle wrote to him two days before the battle, which he received in the hospital. Robert E. Lee ended the letter with a direct order: "I want you to defeat Torbert when you get a chance."[18]

Fitz's mood further darkened upon receipt of news of the reverses his army and his cause experienced in the days and weeks following Winchester. Only three days after the battle, the Army of the Valley was thrashed anew by Sheridan at Fisher's Hill, forcing its survivors to seek refuge in the upper Valley. The outcome could not be blamed on the cavalry, for the majority of Early's horsemen, under Wickham, served apart from the main army throughout the fight. Only three weeks later, however, the mounted arm suffered a humiliating pounding that devastated its morale. On October 10 at Tom's Brook, near Woodstock, Torbert's Federals routed the divisions of Lomax and Rosser (the latter, with his Laurel Brigade, had just arrived from Petersburg to reinforce Early). Pursued at top speed, the Confederates retreated for no less than twenty-five miles. By the time they ceased running, they had suffered one hundred casualties and the loss of seventy horses, eleven artillery pieces, and almost fifty wagons and ambulances.[19]

The army's run of ill fortune was not over. On the nineteenth, Early launched a surprise attack on Sheridan's newly relocated camps on Cedar Creek, near Middletown. The unexpected blow staggered and dazed his powerful enemy, but then the offensive stalled and Sheridan turned near-disaster into victory with an overwhelming counterattack. Following this latest defeat, which added two thousand casualties to the twenty-three hundred his army had suffered at Winchester and Fisher's Hill, Early retreated south to New Market and then to Waynesboro. At the latter place, the remnants of his once-mighty command spent a winter made miserable by frigid weather, the lingering effects of repeated defeats, and the reelection of Abraham Lincoln—an event brought about, at least to some extent, by the dramatic beatings Early had suffered at the hands of a man he once considered "without enterprise" and "possessed [of] an excessive caution which amounted to timidity."[20]

*   *   *

Shortly before New Years 1865, Fitz Lee left the hospital on stiff and weakened legs. He reported to Early's headquarters, where, despite his continuing debility, he found himself in charge of what remained of the Army of the Valley while its leader traveled to Richmond and Petersburg on official business. Active operations were virtually suspended due to the raw weather, so Fitz had little to do during his only stint in army command. In a January 8 letter to Robert E. Lee's daughter, Agnes, he demonstrated that his recent ordeal had not cost him his sense of humor. While admitting that he could not "chronicle any great successes" in the role of commanding general, "if I could have got one of Sheridan's regiments off by itself and have received the cooperation of the *other* Gen. Lee's army, I would have attacked it, but the cooperation and the combination failed."[21]

Characteristically, when not on duty he devoted a certain amount of time to socializing. Although unable to waltz, he and his staff officers were fixtures at local balls, parties, and at least one wedding—that of Captain Hugh McGuire, one of Rosser's favorite subordinates.[22]

Early returned from Petersburg before January ended. He brought Fitz an order from Robert E. Lee: as soon as its men and horses could be outfitted for the march, he was to return with Wickham's division to the Army of Northern Virginia. Preparations attended to, on the morning of February 9 Fitz started eastward at the head of a noticeably thinner, somewhat more ragged incarnation of the column he had led from Culpeper to the Valley six months earlier. The journey, thankfully free of weather-related problems, ended on the morning of the eleventh at army headquarters at Petersburg. Here Fitz received a cordial welcome from his famous relation, who assigned him to the command "of all the cavalry now serving around Richmond and on the north side of the James river."[23]

After he and his uncle concluded a lengthy conversation touching on both army and family matters, Fitz returned to his column, which he led north along a trail parallel with the Richmond & Petersburg Railroad. As he rode, he could see just across the river evidence of the advances the enemy had made during his absence in the Valley: the fortified bridgehead at Deep Bottom, Yankee-occupied Fort Harrison, and other footholds on the doorstep to the Confederate capital, many of them gained during Grant's late-September offensive.

Crossing the James into Richmond, Fitz reported to the headquarters of his new superior, James Longstreet. Like Fitz, Longstreet had returned to duty relatively recently following a long convalescence from a wound. Back in his old position as commander of the First Corps, ANV, he had charge of all Confederate forces north of the James as well as George Pickett's infantry division, which for months had occupied a position opposite Butler's defenses at Bermuda Hundred.

For the next six weeks Fitz handled his assigned duties while he continued to regain the strength his wound had cost him. His primary mission was to keep tabs on those elements of Butler's army operating out of Deep Bottom and holding the extensive line of works that stretched north and west of the bridgehead. He managed to keep posted on events in other parts of the embattled Confederacy, as depressing as the news tended to be. By mid-March, Sherman's sixty thousand troops, having marched virtually unopposed from occupied Atlanta to evacuated Savannah, had turned northward. The invaders were now near Fayetteville, North Carolina, where they were opposed by the remnants of the Army of Tennessee under Joe Johnston, the cavalry portion of which had been entrusted to Wade Hampton.

In January Fitz's old rival had won Robert E. Lee's permission to return to South Carolina to help defend his state against a plague of blue-clad locusts. Johnston and Hampton were savvy fighters, especially on the defensive, but they had little or no hope of halting Sherman's advance. They made a valiant effort on the nineteenth and twentieth at Bentonville, but Sherman's numbers, despite being temporarily stymied, in the end proved overwhelming. A linkup with Grant and Meade now seemed a matter of time. That junction would surely break the stalemate at Petersburg and probably ensure the destruction of the Army of Northern Virginia.[24]

Another Yankee force en route to Petersburg in mid-March was a mounted column ten thousand strong under Phil Sheridan. Powerful, mobile, and self-confident, the troopers were fresh from a brief but bloody fight at Waynesboro. There, on the second of the month, they had fallen on what remained of Early's army and, after overcoming feeble resistance, had mashed it flat.

Left with no one to fight in the Valley, Sheridan was now determined to get in on the kill at Petersburg. Desperate to prevent that from happening, Longstreet, Pickett, and Fitz made plans to intercept the newcomers as they approached the north side of the James prior to crossing over to Grant's headquarters at City Point, northeast of Petersburg. Desperation, however, was no recipe for success. Hampered by manpower shortages, inadequate transportation facilities, and incomplete and misleading intelligence, the triumvirate of defenders proved unable to locate Sheridan, much less bar his path. Not until March 27, by which time the Federals had crossed the James at Deep Bottom, did Gary's cavalry brigade, a part of Fitz's command, get a fix on their location. By then it was too late to halt them short of City Point.[25]

Sheridan's return made Robert E. Lee suspect that Grant was planning a major offensive. If so, he had a good idea where it would be aimed. His right flank below Petersburg had been stretched perilously thin as a result of recent Union advances in that area. Those gains had moved the left flank of the Army of the Potomac to within a few miles of the Petersburg & Lynchburg (more commonly known as the South Side) Railroad, Petersburg's last open supply line. The South Side was one asset that the Army of Northern Virginia had to hold at all costs. Its capture would mean, in all likelihood, the evacuation not only of Petersburg but of Richmond as well.

The only troops available to shore up the embattled sector and protect the railroad were stationed at the opposite end of the Confederate line. Once Sheridan's arrival at City Point had been confirmed, Robert E. Lee let Longstreet know that he was going to detach heavily from his command, including all of Fitz's horsemen. Longstreet countered by advising that Lee move most, but not all, of his nephew's troopers, along with Pickett's infantry, which had been moved from opposite Bermuda Hundred to Swift Creek, just north of Petersburg. Foot and horse soldiers could follow Sheridan wherever he went—including to North Carolina, as rumors emanating from the Union lines had it.[26]

Longstreet's superior accepted his recommendation. Early on the twenty-eighth he formed an expeditionary force consisting of five brigades under Pickett (including three from his own division), six pieces of artillery under Colonel William J. Pegram, Fitz's command minus Gary's demibrigade, which would remain with Longstreet, and those horses and riders deemed unable to withstand the transfer. That afternoon orders reached Fitz at his headquarters at Hanover Court House, fourteen miles above Richmond, to group the scattered brigades he had brought from the Valley, now led by Payne and Munford (the latter having superseded Colonel Boston), and to prepare to march.

On the chilly morning of the twenty-ninth, Fitz started south with most of these troops—the more remotely located units would join him en route—heading for Sutherland's Station on the South Side. As per his orders, he stopped over in the Cockade City for another interview with his uncle. Robert E. Lee informed him that Sheridan had begun to concentrate between Dinwiddie Court House and Five Forks, about eighteen miles southwest of Petersburg. This area appeared to be a jumping-off point for a strike against the South Side, something Fitz and Pickett would have to resist with all their might.

Fitz would not have to picket, reconnoiter, and fight with only two brigades. With Hampton gone, he was the senior officer of cavalry in the ANV. On that basis, he was assigned command of every mounted unit in the army. These included Rooney Lee's division of two (later three) brigades, then breaking camp at Stony Creek Station on the Weldon Railroad south of Petersburg, and the division of Tom Rosser, which had arrived from the Valley two weeks earlier, following the debacle at Waynesboro. Rosser's division consisted of the Laurel Brigade, now led by Brigadier General James Dearing, and McCausland's brigade of western Virginians (the rest of the Valley Cavalry, under Lunsford Lomax, remained in and near the Shenandoah). The added cavalry would give the expeditionary force a total of twelve thousand troops of all arms—more than enough to defeat Sheridan, if manpower alone was the determinate factor in victory.[27]

*   *   *

On the rainy morning of the thirtieth, Fitz left Sutherland's Station, where he had conferred briefly with Pickett, and headed for the open country of Dinwiddie County. In his rear, Pickett's foot soldiers began their march to the same destination. Upon reaching Five Forks, Fitz placed pickets on every road that radiated from the strategically located crossroads. With Sheridan's brigades known to be concentrating only four miles or so to the south, he moved a large part of Payne's brigade in that direction.

Payne had barely started when he encountered, heading north from Dinwiddie Court House, the advance of Brigadier General Thomas C. Devin's division of what was still known as the Cavalry Corps, Army of the Shenandoah. Devin's command had a reputation for dispensing hard knocks; it added to the record on this occasion, shooting down several of Payne's men as well as the colonel himself.

When Payne's men appeared to recoil, Munford's brigade, which had followed closely from Sutherland's Station, advanced in force and assailed Devin from several directions simultaneously. After much maneuvering, Munford succeeded in virtually surrounding Brigadier General Alfred Gibbs's Reserve Brigade. He battled Gibbs for more than an hour in the continuing rain before allowing his battered and bruised opponent to retreat to Dinwiddie.[28]

Impressed by Munford's performance, as he had been on many former occasions, Fitz named him, despite his inferior rank, commander of the division that had once been Fitz's own and more recently Williams Wickham's (the latter had resigned his commission in December to take a seat in the Confederate

Congress). Yet Fitz considered this honor inadequate recompense for Munford's consistent good leadership and stoical bearing in the face of adversity. Since June 1863, the colonel had been passed over for promotion time and again for no apparent reason other than the black mark he had acquired at Brandy Station. While hurt and disappointed by the string of rejections, Munford had not allowed it to embitter him or color his relations with superiors and subordinates.

Fitz, who knew what it felt like to be stigmatized for a single lapse in judgment, appreciated his subordinate's perseverance. Although he was not certain he had the authority to do so, on April 6 he would appoint Munford a brigadier general. The Confederate Congress, having adjourned, could not confirm the appointment, but Munford would be touched as well as gratified by Fitz's gesture. For the rest of his life, he would insist on being addressed—justifiably, it would seem—as a former general officer.[29]

About 6 P.M. on the thirtieth, just as Merritt and Devin were withdrawing from Five Forks, Pickett's infantry and Pegram's artillery reached the area. About two hours later Rosser's division arrived, and Rooney Lee's rode in shortly after midnight. The commanders hashed out the offensive that Pickett, as senior major general and expeditionary leader, intended to launch the following morning. He planned to bar the Federals' advance toward the South Side by striking frontally with his foot soldiers and turning their left flank with Fitz's horsemen.

When put into execution at 10 A.M. on the rainy last day of March, Pickett's blueprint held up fairly well, although in the end he gained little from it. Even as Sheridan advanced from Dinwiddie, this time accompanied by the divisions of Devin and Major General George Crook, Pickett headed south from the crossroads before veering eastward across a marshy creek bottom, Chamberlain's Bed. While Pickett's infantry plowed into one of Crook's brigades and forced it backward, Fitz, with Rooney Lee's horsemen in front, followed by Rosser's, drove in another component of Crook's division. Meanwhile, back at Five Forks, Munford repulsed an advance by two of Devin's brigades. By early afternoon, more than half of Sheridan's force was in full retreat to Dinwiddie Court House.[30]

The retrograde did not cease until around 5 P.M., when Custer's division relinquished a wagon-guarding mission in the Union rear to assist its comrades. Sheridan had most of his men dismount and build an entrenched line a half-mile or so above the courthouse. They held this position against repeated attacks not only by Pickett's foot soldiers but by Rooney Lee and Rosser, who several times attempted to collapse Sheridan's left. The well-constructed works and the firepower of Spencer repeaters and Sharps breechloaders in the Yankees' hands were keys to Sheridan's ability to hold his position until night ended the fighting.[31]

By day's end, Pickett had gained some slight tactical success—and a precarious position. Not far to the north and east of Dinwiddie Court House, thousands of Meade's infantrymen were advancing toward the Petersburg lines, many within supporting distance of Sheridan. Already, in fact, Little Phil had petitioned Grant for reinforcements, and Grant had agreed to send Warren's V Corps to Dinwiddie. Although Grant supposed Warren would reach Sheridan by midnight, the recent rains had washed out bridges and turned roads into lagoons, preventing the infantry from making much progress toward the courthouse until late in the morning of April 1. Long before that time, Pickett, fearful of being cut off from his comrades at Petersburg, had ordered his command to return to Five Forks. The head of the gray column reached the crossroads as early as 11 P.M., but Fitz and his troopers, who covered the retreat, did not get back until 9 A.M. on April 1.[32]

Sometime before Fitz's return, Pickett reportedly received a message from Robert E. Lee enjoining him to hold Five Forks at all hazards. For about three hours early on the first, Pickett's men, including Fitz's troopers, strengthened and extended a line of breastworks that had been erected on the thirtieth along the White Oak Road, the main fork of the crossroads. These works, which included a shallow ditch in front, ran for almost two miles, with the crossroads in their center. The greater part of the line was occupied by Pickett's infantry, with Pegram's cannons spaced at strategic intervals. Munford's cavalry protected the left, or east, flank, while to the west Rooney Lee guarded the far right. Fitz had placed Rosser, whose horses were reported to be played out, in reserve above Hatcher's Run, a stream that flowed about a mile north of the Forks.

Though strongly occupied, the works, even after their improvement, appeared to some observers to be poorly laid out and constructed. Pickett seemed not to notice or, if he did, not to care, perhaps because he had come to believe that troops from Petersburg would soon reinforce him.[33]

None did, but the V Corps finally came in from the east to assist Sheridan. By that time—the middle of the afternoon of the first—Sheridan had moved north from Dinwiddie on his own and was in close contact with Pickett. He had formulated a plan that called for a feint against the Rebel left and center by Custer's division, while Devin's troopers, in close cooperation with Warren's foot soldiers, attacked the enemy right. Warren's initial objective was the point at which Pickett's left was "refused" at a forty-degree angle to the north.

Execution of the plan was held up by Warren's apparent tardiness in getting into his assigned position. He was not ready to attack in cooperation with the cavalry until about an hour before sunset. Although angered by his colleague's dilatory habits, Sheridan needed the offensive punch that only infantry could deliver. Thus, he held his temper in check—but only for a time. Before day's end, he would use authority given him by Grant to relieve his colleague from command and send him to the rear in disgrace.[34]

Despite being in contact with Sheridan's skirmishers, neither Pickett nor his ranking subordinates displayed concern or, for that matter, close attention to their duties. As Fitz later explained, they all believed that by driving Sheridan back to Dinwiddie Court House, they had preempted his advance against the railroad, the resumption of which would take some time.

In the interim, they felt secure enough to indulge in some fine dining in the field. In his brigade's recent position along the Nottoway River, Tom Rosser had caught a mess of shad, which he had packed in a tub of ice carried in one of his ambulances, waiting for the proper occasion to serve them. April 1 was the day, and to enhance the feast he invited Pickett and Fitz to join him. Both assented, and by about 2 P.M., as the skirmishing outside their works continued, Rosser's guests joined him north of Hatcher's Run. Choosing a peaceful glade for their picnic, the trio spent the next couple of hours sharing the fish as well as other delicacies, perhaps including alcoholic beverages.[35]

Pickett and his cavalry leader had chosen a poor time to desert their posts. Even before Sheridan and Warren attacked, a cooperating division of cavalry from the Army of the James had burst through the thin cavalry screen that connected the left flank at Five Forks with the Petersburg defenses, thereby isolating Pickett's force from its main army. Then, at about 4:15 P.M., the V Corps, finally in position, assaulted the same flank, supported by Devin's horsemen. The first wave of attackers missed the target, passing too far to the east, but the troops behind corrected the heading and struck the angle squarely.

Munford's men put up a determined defense in this sector but were eventually overwhelmed and pushed aside. Warren's troops then turned west and began to roll up the enemy line. Well before 5 P.M., Pickett's entire position was collapsing. On the right, Rooney Lee's dismounted troopers held their position to the bitter last, but they too were forced to saddle up and race to the rear. As senior officer on the field, Rooney commanded the Confederate defense throughout the attack, but he never knew it. When Pickett, Fitz, and Rosser went to lunch, none thought to inform him that they were leaving him in charge.[36]

Due to an acoustical quirk, the sounds of battle did not penetrate to the glade where the ruling triumvirate of the expeditionary force was eating and drinking. Not until a panic-stricken courier splashed over the run with dire news did the generals depart their luncheon nook in hot haste. Pickett immediately rode to the scene of the debacle, where he attempted in vain to engineer an orderly retreat. Rosser remained with his command north of the run, where Fitz returned to join him after failing to find an unblocked ford across Hatcher's.

Protected by the stream bed, Rosser's men held their position until early evening, repulsing a Union attempt to cross in their front, an effort in which Fitz presumably took part. This cannot be established, because we know little of Fitz's actions, or even his whereabouts, during the hours immediately following the breakup of his picnic lunch. Nor do we know what he thought or felt at this time, although it can be assumed that he had at least some sense of the magnitude of the disaster that had overtaken not only his army and his cause but perhaps his reputation as well.[37]

*　　*　　*

Years later, Fitz would correctly describe Five Forks as "the beginning of the end." The end took another week to arrive, but that week moved swiftly to an inevitable conclusion. The position at Five Forks gone, Robert E. Lee's right flank also went under as the enemy took possession of a long section of the South Side Railroad. The night after Pickett's defeat, the commander of the ANV evacuated both Petersburg and Richmond, Confederate officials including Jefferson Davis fleeing the capital by special train toward Danville. As the defenders of both cities fled their posts, they formed two massive columns retreating westward into the Virginia countryside. To some observers, the retreating men resembled not soldiers but refugees, and the ANV not an army but a mob of stragglers. "I have never seen an Army so demoralized," wrote a diarist in Fitz's command. "Our men are scattered to the four winds."[38]

In actuality, the cavalry maintained better cohesion than the majority of the retreating troops. The day after Five Forks, it joined the pitifully small column of infantry that had escaped death, disabling, or capture at Sheridan's hands. Thanks to their mobility, Munford's, Rosser's, and Rooney Lee's men had fled the battlefield relatively intact, organizationally. They formed one of the more coherent components of an otherwise heterogeneous column that also consisted of the remnants of Richard H. Anderson's corps.

The column Fitz accompanied eventually joined the main wave of Petersburg evacuees. This wave seeped along a road that paralleled on the south the one taken by the fugitives from Richmond. On April 4, both bodies converged at Amelia Court House on the Richmond & Danville Railroad, about thirty miles west of Petersburg.[39]

Despite its relative cohesiveness, Fitz's troopers were only occasionally a match for the horsemen under Sheridan who dogged their heels throughout the week-long retreat. They were routed at Namozine Church on April 3 as well as along Sailor's Creek three days later, and in several smaller actions in between. When they mustered the strength to turn on their pursuers, however, they enjoyed some heartening success. On April 5, near Paineville and Amelia Springs, Rosser's and Munford's commands, under Fitz's leadership, scattered a portion of Crook's division that had captured and burned a wagon train out of Richmond. The following day, the same units, Fitz's finest horsemen, attacked a detachment of infantry from the Army of the James, preventing it from burning strategic High Bridge over the Appomattox River. In both cases, success came at an almost prohibitive price—stalwarts of Fitz's command who lost their lives included James Dearing; Reuben Boston; Captain James Thomson, one of the army's finest horse artillerymen; and Hugh McGuire, whose wedding Fitz had attended in Waynesboro four months before.[40]

These short-lived triumphs did not alter the outcome of the flight from Richmond and Petersburg, which came to a bitter close on the morning of the ninth outside the village of Appomattox Court House, more than seventy miles from the starting points of the retreat. By now Sheridan's hard-riding troopers had gotten around the fugitives' lower flank and were positioned on and adjacent to the road to Lynchburg, the next objective of a weary but not dispirited Robert E. Lee. Infantry had not gotten as far as Sheridan, but troops of the Armies of the Potomac and the James were not far behind, and they were coming fast, propelled by a sense that a final, lasting victory lay just a few miles ahead.

At a war council held at army headquarters on the evening of the eighth, Robert E. Lee had briefed his remaining senior subordinates—Longstreet, John Brown Gordon, and Fitz—on his plan to surge west of the courthouse and punch through the as-yet-thin line of enemy troops in their front. The elder Lee was certain that only cavalry barred the way, but Fitz believed that large numbers of infantry were close by. If this was true, his uncle admitted, he would be forced to accept the surrender demands that General Grant had been sending through the lines over the past two days. Fitz voiced no objection to his uncle's proposal, but he did made known his intention to "try to extricate the cavalry" if a surrender was forced on the army, "provided it could be done without compromising the action of the commanding general."[41]

On the morning of the ninth, Fitz's pessimistic view of things proved all too accurate. Attacking at 7 A.M. in conjunction with their infantry comrades in line of battle farther to the south and east, Fitz's horsemen surged forward on the Lynchburg State Road. At first they made significant headway against the enemy's cavalry, including both mounted and dismounted defenders under Generals Crook and Custer, routing a few units and capturing three pieces of horse artillery. But at about nine o'clock, with the Lynchburg Road open at last and infantry and cavalry poised to move out on it, the advance echelon of the Army of the James flooded onto the battlefield, followed closely by Meade's V Corps. The new arrivals slammed shut the door that had been briefly opened by Fitz Lee's few but plucky and determined troopers. In the cavalry's rear, truce flags suddenly went up, and the racket of battle began to taper off all across the field. Fitz saw at once that his uncle, his path to Lynchburg securely blocked, was activating his contingency plan of surrender.[42]

Prior to forming their commands for the morning's battle, several of Fitz's subordinates had vowed that they would not surrender unless completely and hopelessly surrounded—and then only to avoid a further, unnecessary bloodletting. That situation, however, had not materialized. By the time the fighting

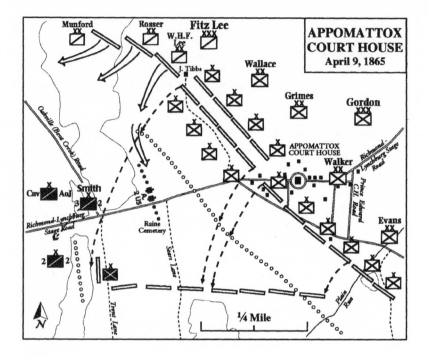

ceased west of Appomattox, two of Fitz's three divisions had already passed the flanks of the blue infantry blocking the road to Lynchburg, in whose rear they now were. Only Rooney Lee, the left flank of whose division abutted the right of the infantry near the courthouse, was in a position from which he could not escape.

Fitz, Munford, and Rosser were home free if they chose to be. Would they surrender in place, or would they avail themselves of the opportunity to avoid handing over their arms and flags to a victorious foe? Consulting briefly with his division leaders, Fitz found them adamant in their determination to ride on rather than bow to an enemy they continued to regard as their social and professional inferiors.

"You can imagine my feelings," Fitz would remark to John Esten Cooke of Stuart's staff, "as I sat on my horse . . . watching the long lines of Federal *Infantry* closing in on our devoted little band.—Orders had already been sent for the Cavalry to 'get out' and they were disappearing, but I still remained with those of my staff gazing at the blue masses, rapidly approaching."[43]

Finally, he gave his permission to proceed westward, leading his once-formidable command, now only a few hundred strong, to Lynchburg and, possibly, beyond. As the thin gray line shuddered into motion, he must have realized that his was a futile gesture, one that flew in the face of reality. The war was winding down, if it was not already over. Still, he could not drive from his mind and heart "the fond, though forlorn, hope that future operations were still in store" for the Cavalry Corps, Army of Northern Virginia.[44]

THIRTEEN

From Model Farmer
to Second Redeemer

On April 12, 1865, Major General John Gibbon, commanding the XXIV Corps, Army of the James, whose troops had ended Robert E. Lee's hope of escaping a surrender at Appomattox Court House, was told by a sentry that General Lee was outside and wished to see him. Gibbon supposed the commander of the Army of Northern Virginia had a question about the cavalry unit that had been detailed to escort him to his home in Richmond. The corps commander left the room he had appropriated for an office in the house of Wilmer McLean, in whose parlor, three days earlier, Lee had tendered his sword to Ulysses S. Grant, and went to the front door. As he later recalled, "I found General *Fitz* Lee seated on his horse, and looking, I thought, somewhat uneasy. He had been a cadet under me at West Point, and I had not seen him for years. As I looked at him a vision of the past came up before me, and I could only think of a little rollicking fellow dressed in *cadet* gray, whose jolly songs and gay spirits were the life of his class. My salutation of 'Hello, Fitz! Get off and come in,' seemed to put him at his ease at once."[1]

Accompanying his former instructor to his office, Fitz took a chair and told the story of how he and his officers had avoided surrender on the ninth. They had reached Lynchburg safely, but after a few days of uneasy freedom Fitz and many others convinced themselves that the war was over and that they had to deal with their army's defeat. Leaving Lynchburg with five members of his staff, Fitz slipped through Union lines to Farmville, twenty-three miles east of Appomattox, the home of one of his aides, Captain Charles Minnigerode, who had been severely wounded during an exchange of gunfire minutes before the cessation of hostilities on the ninth. After visiting the young officer, who later recovered his health, Fitz and his staff reported to the local provost marshal and gave themselves up. They were advised to return to Appomattox to be paroled.[2]

Having relinquished his "fond, though forlorn, hope" of further cavalry service, Fitz did as suggested, signing the papers that made him a paroled prisoner of the U.S. government. Under the terms of the agreement, he was free to return to his home, bound only by the pledge he had made never again to bear arms against the Union. But he spent the night of the twelfth not at home but as Gibbon's guest, sharing the rude accommodations available to them both. "Lying on the floor," wrote Gibbon, Fitz "slept as soundly as a child, after, as he said, having had no sleep for a week. Nothing could dampen his high spirits, and with us he seemed to rejoice that the war was over." Fitz proved as much the next morning when, "with a grim humor, he took from his pocket a five-dollar Confederate note, and writing across its face, 'For Mrs. Gibbon, with the compliments of Fitz Lee,' he said: 'Send that to your wife, and tell her it's the last cent I have in the world.'"[3]

* * *

While Fitz may have thought of himself as staring poverty in its ugly face, he was more fortunate than many other Confederates who had lost everything in the war—their homes, their fortunes, their livelihoods. After a second and longer visit to Farmville to be with his convalescing aide, he returned to his family in Richmond, where he discovered that his fortunes were not as bleak as they might otherwise have been. The family's home, Clermont, had suffered greatly from enemy occupation and was no longer habitable, but Fitz's godmother, "Aunt Maria" Fitzhugh, retained not only most of her prewar fortune (thanks to property holdings that had not been confiscated by the U.S. government and notes and bonds safely stored in Northern banks) but also her generosity to Fitz's family. She allowed Smith Lee and his brood to reside, rent free, at one of her several estates, Richland, in the Stafford County countryside four miles north of Aquia Creek and forty miles south of Washington, D.C.[4]

Soon after Fitz's family settled into their new home, his Uncle Robert wrote to say he was "glad to hear that you are about establishing yourself in Stafford. . . . I have always heard that Richland was a beautiful & prosperous farm & I hope will make you a pleasant home." But Robert E. Lee was living in the past, for although spacious, the manor house, the only dwelling on the property, was in need of rehabilitation, and the fields around lay untilled and overgrown with brush and weeds. In the words of one postwar visitor, "decay and desolation greeted the eye, while the entire premises were sadly out of repair." These drawbacks aside, the acquisition of Richland was a boon to the Lee family, as it offered a base from which they might rebuild even as their state and region struggled to rise from the ashes of defeat.[5]

Neither Fitz nor any of his five brothers, all recently returned from the war, had experience as farmers. Still, their family's financial condition, complicated by their father's failing health—a war-related condition that precluded him from finding employment and that would contribute to his death, at sixty-seven, in the summer of 1869—forced them to make a living from the soil. It was hard, often backbreaking work, founded on trial and error and the raising of subsistence crops, especially corn and wheat, and a few fruits and vegetables. In time, however, Richland turned a modest profit that saved the family from absolute ruin. Demonstrating that he had lost none of his trademark sense of humor, or his talent for self-deprecation, Fitz wrote his friend Manning Kimmel, then living in exile in Mexico, that "I am busy ploughing, reaping and sowing. . . . I just wish you could see Squire Lee of Stafford as he rides through the growing corn, his broad brim hat and long coat tails oscillating against the golden grain. . . . I raise more corn that I ever got from the Quartermaster."[6]

At the start, the Richland workforce consisted of Fitz and his brothers, but in time it came to include nine farmhands of all ages and both races, described by Fitz as "4 negro men, 1 half negro and half white, 1 Dutchman [i.e., a German immigrant], 1 woman and 2 boys (black)." Originally, the family's livestock numbered one horse—Fitz's cherished steed, Nellie. Over the months he managed to add some animals of dubious quality: "4 horses, 1 lame, 1 blind, 1 thickminded and one with only one eye." Later additions, however, proved more serviceable and productive, and they helped put Fitz on the road to becoming what he professed to aspire to, a "model farmer." Even so, he harbored reservations about his new lifestyle, so different from the only other career he had known. Almost a year into his husbandry, he informed Thomas Munford that "I am down here on the Potomac, having like Cincinatus turned 'my sword into a ploughshare,' but find it dull work after the recent exciting events."[7]

Those events sometimes intruded harshly in Fitz's new life. He retained an allegiance to the principles that underlay the cause for which he had fought so long and hard. In fact, he seemed to glory in his identity as "an unrepentant rebel," proclaiming that "[I] am glad I have sinned beyond forgiveness." As for the U.S. government, "in the language of the 'old rebel,' am glad I fit agin it, only wish I'd won; and ain't gwine to ax no pard[on]ing for anything I've done."[8]

But he could not sustain this attitude, especially in the wake of Lincoln's assassination, the imprisonment of Jefferson Davis and many other Confederate officials, and the election of so-called Radical Republicans on the state and national levels. In such a highly charged political atmosphere, he found that his Appomattox parole did not protect him against acts of retaliation by the government he had "fit agin." In early June 1865, a federal grand jury sitting in

Norfolk indicted Fitz for treason, along with his uncle, his cousins Rooney and Custis, fourteen other Confederate generals, and nineteen other persons.

Since the court action violated the terms of the defendants' paroles, its legality was dubious at best. But the fact that the case went forward at all told Fitz that he must seek some guarantees against prosecution and persecution. Just as he had in the days after the Fort Sumter crisis, he followed his uncle's example, this time by applying on July 7 to Lincoln's successor, Andrew Johnson, for a pardon. In his letter, Fitz offered no justification for resigning his U.S. army commission in 1861, admitted to no wrongdoing by entering the Confederate ranks, and made no plea for official forgiveness. Five days later, he appeared before federal officials in Alexandria and took the oath of amnesty required under a proclamation issued by Johnson on May 29.[9]

He later claimed that his request for pardon amounted to "nothing except an increase in humiliation." It did, however, remove certain disagreeable restrictions—the necessity, for instance, of gaining War Department permission to travel beyond the borders of his state. Therefore, Fitz urged expatriates such as Kimmel to return home and avail themselves of the pardon process if only for the security it afforded: "You can go anywhere and not be molested in any way—no questions asked."[10]

It cannot be determined when or if Fitz was officially pardoned, but he would have been included among those covered by Johnson's later, more general amnesty proclamations. His legal difficulties, however, did not cease until February 1869, when the treason indictment against him and his relatives was nolle prossed. At that point, finally, he could dismiss his fear of government reprisal for his past actions and look to a brighter future for his family, his state, and his reunited nation.[11]

*   *   *

Financial security came slowly to Fitz's family, and prosperity took more than a decade and was achieved only through inheritance. Slowly but surely, the profits returned by the farmlands of Richland produced a growing inventory of material possessions. By the late 1860s, Fitz had built or purchased a grist mill that quickly became a paying enterprise. He also constructed a fishing pier while acquiring a small fleet of river craft, including schooners and tugboats. Over time, the fishing operation grew to such dimensions that he had to hire a man to manage it. He also turned his lifelong passion for horses into a thriving stud farm.[12]

Through his varied commercial interests, he was able to hold onto Richland even as relatives and neighbors, beset by prewar debts and postwar failures, lost the homes and farms that had been in their families for generations. Not only did he withstand the regional financial pressures common to Reconstruction, he survived the cyclical depressions that struck nationwide, including the ruinous Panic of 1873. Although he divested himself of parcels of his estate from time to time, he was able to retain title to it until selling it at a considerable profit in 1893. He did not legally own Richland, however, until April 1875, when it passed into his hands under terms of his godmother's will. In addition to Richland, Aunt Maria bequeathed to her namesake many thousands of dollars' worth of stocks and bonds. Moreover, she left Fitz's brothers a neighboring estate, Arkindale, profits from the sale of which were divided among the five of them. Through her will, Fitz and his brothers were also granted fishing rights to other Potomac River properties she had owned.[13]

By the early 1870s, the squire of Richland was secure enough financially to give serious consideration to marrying and raising a family. The charm, wit, courtliness, and pleasing appearance that had been salient features of Fitzhugh Lee since youth had spawned a series of romantic attachments, from innocent flirtations to serious affairs of the heart that, had circumstances been slightly different, might have led him to the altar. On one occasion, speaking of a young woman from St. Louis whom he met on a vacation trip, Fitz confided to a friend that "had she remained three days longer—only three—she would have been Mrs. Lee."[14]

During his first five or six years as an ex-soldier, he adopted, or at least professed, a view of romance both dismal and lighthearted. He would describe the several eligible young women he knew as "troublesome," adding that "with the flies mosquitoes & this hot weather [they] form a combination of torments that hastens materially my decline." In a letter to Stuart's staff officer John Esten Cooke, he observed, perhaps only half in jest, that marriage did not appear to be "as profitable as wheat or corn, hence I stick & shall continue to stick . . . to the latter and let the former alone."[15]

Both during and after the war, he maintained a lengthy but curiously tepid relationship with Nannie Enders, a young Richmond socialite whom one admirer described as "pretty, jolly and bright, as natural as a fawn, though not so shy," capable of speaking "piquant things with a *naivete* that tickled as it touched." Much of the courtship—if such it was—was carried on through correspondence that showcased Fitz's wit, humor, and fondness for nonsense prose and poetry, but in which he failed unambiguously to state his feelings toward the young woman. Yet despite his flirtatious evasions, which may have been a means of cushioning his ego against the possibility of rejection, and although the two eventually parted and she married another, it seems clear that Fitz was smitten by this leading light of young Richmond society.[16]

By the end of the 1860s, Fitz was approaching his late thirties and, despite a series of liaisons and dalliances, seemed content with bachelorhood. His attitude appears to have distressed his uncle, who on several occasions advised Fitz to add "such comforts to [your] house" as a wife and daughter. As late as February 1869, Robert E. Lee was writing his brother Smith that "Fitz will never settle down till he is married—of course will not prosper till then. Tell him he must ask his sweethearts to let him marry one at a time. In that way he may accommodate them all. He cannot marry them all at once."[17]

As always, Fitz took his famous relative's advice. Within six months of Uncle Robert's latest expression of dismay over his nephew's love life, Fitz met another Virginia belle to whom he gave his heart—this time without insulating it in layers of flirtatious badinage. During the autumn of 1869, the model farmer was forced temporarily to cease plowing in order to recuperate from an acute eye infection. Apparently while seeking treatment in Alexandria, he met seventeen-year-old Ellen Bernard "Nellie" Fowle, daughter of George D. Fowle of that city. Probably to his astonishment, Fitz quickly formed an attachment to Nellie deeper and more meaningful than any he had ever experienced.

Fitz's feelings for the pretty teenager may have owed in part to the pangs of loneliness that had gnawed at him since the passing of his father, pangs that increased after the death of his beloved Uncle Robert in October of 1870. Another event that may have steered him toward a serious relationship was a growing sense of isolation from his family as his brothers, one after another, left Richland for nonfarming employment elsewhere. Whatever influences might have been at work, following a year's courtship Fitz and Nellie were married at her Alexandria home on April 19, 1871.[18]

Despite the difference in their ages and family backgrounds, from the first theirs was a happy and mutually satisfying union. It produced seven children, five of whom reached maturity: Ellen, Fitzhugh Jr., George, Nannie, and Virginia. The firstborn, a daughter named after Fitz's godmother, and the last child, a son who bore the name of Fitz's father, died in infancy.[19]

Fitz proved to be a generous husband and a doting father. Although in later life he traveled extensively, he enjoyed nothing more than to be at home with his family, especially because they were an appreciative audience for his inveterate storytelling. One of his biographers notes that he "spent countless hours telling his wife and children the stirring and entertaining experiences of his frontier and war years with the cavalry of two nations."[20]

His passionate devotion to his particular branch of service struck a chord with his children. Both of his surviving sons would earn commissions in the 7th U.S. Cavalry, the regiment George Armstrong Custer had led to tragic glory two decades earlier at the Little Bighorn. Black-eyed, black-haired Fitzhugh Jr. would also have a career in the infantry and the engineers, while red-haired George would emulate his father by attending West Point, although without graduating. To complete the family cavalry tradition, each of Fitz's daughters would marry officers in their brothers' regiment.[21]

*   *   *

Made wealthy by his godmother's bequest (he was one of her executors as well as the principal beneficiary of her will), Fitz by the 1870s could afford to devote less time to farming and more to his interests and hobbies, including writing and lecturing about his military experiences. He was drawn to these endeavors by a growing nationwide interest in the Civil War, which produced a voluminous literature of postwar writings by high-ranking Union and Confederate participants. This trend would peak in the early 1880s with the publication in *Century Magazine* of numerous first-person accounts of war service, most of which were later included in the monumental four-volume collection, *Battles and Leaders of the Civil War.*

Fitz's earliest literary efforts contributed to a long-lasting and often bitter controversy over Confederate failures in the campaign and battle of Gettysburg. By the early 1870s, proponents of the "lost cause" theory—which included Fitz, who never doubted the validity of secession or the rightness of Confederate ideals—were seeking to determine just when and where that cause was lost. Gettysburg, which had come to be seen as the pivotal military event of the conflict, was the center of the literary attention. The strategic and tactical decisions that affected the battle's outcome became the grist of dozens of articles and printed speeches over the last quarter of the nineteenth century—mostly, of course, in Southern circles.

At first Fitz was reluctant to enter the debate for fear of stirring up intrasectional animosities at a time when the South should devote all her energy to securing economic prosperity and political and social harmony. But in 1872–73, a series of speeches and articles by high-ranking Confederates, including Fitz's 1864 Valley Campaign superior, Jubal Early, cast James Longstreet as the chief villain of the Gettysburg tragedy. Early and others accused Longstreet of being criminally slow in attacking the Union left flank on Cemetery Ridge on the second day of the battle and of failing enthusiastically to carry out Robert E. Lee's orders to strike the enemy's center the following day. Longstreet's postwar conversion to the Republican Party made him something of an apostate to his home region and thus a convenient culprit for the failure to win a critical battle.[22]

The often vituperative attacks on his war record prompted Longstreet to fire back with equal, if not greater, heat. In an article published in a Republican newspaper in New Orleans in January 1876, he effectively defended himself against many of the charges lodged against him, but he made the mistake of blaming Robert E. Lee for tactical decisions at Gettysburg that were rash and ill-considered. Moreover, he claimed that Lee later acknowledged as much to him and regretted his refusal to follow Longstreet's advice and scrap Pickett's Charge. In effect, "Lee's Old Warhorse" made his much-loved superior the scapegoat for the defeat that sank the Confederacy.

At this point, Fitz felt compelled to enter the lists and defend his family's honor. He began modestly enough by asking Longstreet to produce evidence to back up his contentions, including a wartime letter the corps commander alleged his superior had written him that would corroborate his assertions about

Gettysburg. When Longstreet not only refused Fitz's petition but publicly impugned his motives, Fitz sent a letter to the editor of the *Southern Historical Society Papers,* later published in that journal, that countered, rather politely, the most inflammatory of Longstreet's statements. Not surprisingly, Longstreet took issue with Fitz's comments as well as with his subsequent critiques of the corps commander's version of the Gettysburg story. In his counterattacks, Longstreet was not averse to using immoderate and even insulting language.[23]

The controversy over who lost the great battle would rage for almost twenty years without producing definitive conclusions or satisfying all concerned. To some extent, however, the reputations of both Lee and Longstreet suffered as a result of the tortuously extended argument, along with those of Early and other agenda-driven, politically motivated participants. Yet, as one historian asserts, "in general, the Gettysburg controversy was beneficial to the public image of Fitzhugh Lee," for he alone among the major participants spoke and acted with moderation and decorum.[24]

Unlike others involved in the controversy, Fitz neither asserted nor implied that he possessed all the facts of the case, and he refused to return the verbal barbs that Longstreet and some of his defenders threw his way, even the gratuitous, ad hominem criticisms of Fitz's generalship that appeared in Longstreet's memoirs, published in 1896. Tangible evidence of the stature Fitz retained was his popularity thereafter as a speaker on war events in both the North and the South. To audiences in New York and Philadelphia as well as in Richmond and Norfolk, he sounded an increasingly popular theme of reunion and reconciliation. For this reason he became almost as much a fixture at the banquets of Union veterans as at the gatherings of the Association of the Army of Northern Virginia.

Fitz's writings on the Gettysburg debate were the first of his numerous contributions to the history of the war. Over time his literary output included magazine and newspaper pieces as well as several articles for the *Southern Historical Society Papers,* published by the Richmond-based Southern Historical Society (SHS), in which he became a leading light. Many of these publications were reprints of lectures he delivered before veterans' associations or to audiences throughout the South as a paid employee of the SHS. They included his most famous war-related oration, "Chancellorsville," delivered before the Virginia Division of the Association of the Army of Northern Virginia in October 1879.

Fitz's most ambitious war-related work was a single-volume biography of his famous uncle, which he compiled late in life. Published in 1894 by D. Appleton and Company of New York as part of its Great Commanders series, *General Lee* was a straightforward and unpretentious but not inelegant tribute to the great Confederate. Perhaps its primary strength was its inclusion of excerpts from many unpublished letters written by the general, in the possession of the Lee family. A more egocentric author intimately involved in many of the events recorded in his book would have seized the opportunity to showcase his personal experiences, but Fitz modestly subordinated himself to the story of his famous relative. His boundless respect and affection for his subject shows in every page without descent into hagiography. Happily, the book was an immediate favorite with the reading public, especially the Southern portion thereof, and was generally well received by the critics.[25]

*   *   *

By the mid-1870s, Fitz was finding himself drawn not only into literary circles but into the political arena as well. As a notable Confederate general from a distinguished family, he seemed a natural to succeed in the world of local and state politics—perhaps even on the national level. Due to his personal interests and attitudes, however, his political opportunities were circumscribed. He would not allow himself to become a politician in the professional sense. He never developed a mind for the esoteric details of party politics, the patience to endure the mundane but critical allocation of patronage, or the ability to forge personal relationships strictly for their political benefits. And yet in terms of popularity among the electorate, few politicos of the latter nineteenth-century South could approach the standing of the man Virginians referred to, fondly, as "Our Fitz."

His entrance into politics began with his involvement in civic associations dedicated to promoting public reverence for Virginia's Confederate past. In 1873 he became actively involved in committees to erect memorials honoring both his wartime superior and his revered uncle. In April of that year, in an address before the Richmond city council, he started a movement to replace J. E. B. Stuart's simple grave in Hollywood Cemetery with something "more expressive" of Stuart's contributions to the Confederacy. The following month he helped expand the base of a small local organization that hoped to erect a monument to Robert E. Lee.[26]

Later he became a consultant to the committee that financed a recumbent statue of the army leader to adorn his burial vault in the campus chapel at Washington College in Lexington, the institution whose president he had been for the last five years of his life. And in March 1884, the Virginia General Assembly appointed Fitz *ex officio* president of the Lee Monument Association. In this role he successfully melded the staffs and the functions of two organizations dedicated to this same task. Through his efforts as much as anyone's, the sixty-one-foot-high equestrian statue—the work of French sculptor Jean Antoine Mercie—was finally unveiled on May 29, 1890. Fitz was on hand as grand marshal of the ceremonies, which were attended by thousands of Richmonders and scores of invited guests including ex-Generals Joseph Johnston, Jubal Early, John Brown Gordon, Wade Hampton (with whom Fitz had buried the hatchet years before), and, in a masterstroke of irony, James Longstreet.[27]

Fitz's became increasingly comfortable in the public realm as a result of his association with these high-visibility committees; the well-received lectures he gave before civic, fraternal, and economic societies from Boston to New Orleans; and the popularity accorded him as the first president of the Virginia Division of the Association of the Army of Northern Virginia. Those who helped shape popular opinion began to take note of his increasing stature as a public figure. Reporting on a speech Fitz gave in the late 1870s before a Confederate veterans' association, a reporter for a Lynchburg newspaper lauded Fitz's "ready wit and festive grace which showed that he might have won an enviable reputation in some profession requiring a readier use of the tongue than of the sword."[28]

Gradually, tentatively, he became involved at the grassroots level in the workings of the Conservative Party, as the fusion of old-line Democrats and moderate Whigs was known throughout Virginia. In 1872, for the first time in his life, he campaigned actively for a presidential candidate. This came about as the result of being chosen as a delegate to the Liberal Republican Convention in Cincinnati. The third-party organization had nominated Horace Greeley in opposition to the regular Republican candidate, Ulysses S. Grant, then seeking a second term in the White House. Greeley won Fitz's support because he ran on a platform that called for an end to Radical Reconstruction and espoused other political and social issues many an old-line Southern Democrat could support. After the May convention, Fitz stumped for Greeley throughout his home district, although suspecting, correctly, that the celebrated editor of the *New York Tribune* had little chance of unseating Grant.[29]

Prior to 1872, Fitz probably never considered aspiring to a political post, for as a Confederate officer above the rank of colonel he was barred not only from voting but from holding public office. In May of that year, however, the U.S. Congress, having reached the same conclusion as the majority of the American public—that as a mechanism for social change, Military Reconstruction was a practical failure—removed those political disabilities.

Even though Virginia had been readmitted to the Union early in 1870 and had been spared the horrors of military rule from which almost every other Southern state had suffered, Congress's action constituted a milestone in state political history. That fall, Fitz's friend, General James Lawson Kemper, a wounded veteran of Pickett's Charge, redeemed Virginia from years of Republican and carpetbagger rule. Fitz, whose war record was at least as impressive as Kemper's, began to see opportunities in a world he had thought forever closed to him.

He wasted no time making use of his restored rights. In the summer of 1874 he announced his candidacy as Stafford County representative to the General Assembly. Perhaps to his surprise, the local Conservatives nominated him. He lost the election, but he may have been ambivalent about the outcome, for his opponent had been one of his old subordinates, Major Beverly B. Douglas of the 9th Virginia Cavalry.[30]

Two years later, Fitz again tested the political waters, though without enthusiasm. In June of that year he attended his second Democratic National Convention, this time as a delegate-at-large. The St. Louis gathering nominated for president Samuel J. Tilden of New York, who during that fall's election won a clear majority of the popular vote against Republican Rutherford B. Hayes but failed to gain the White House due to voter irregularities, canvassing board manipulation, and a bargain between the contending parties that brought an end to Military Reconstruction. The removal of occupation troops from South Carolina in April 1877 enabled Governor Wade Hampton to redeem his state just as Kemper had relieved the Old Dominion from the Republican yoke. Manfully, Fitz congratulated his old rival on his victory, even though the local carpetbagger regime's refusal to accept the result prevented Hampton from exercising the power of his office for almost a year after his election.[31]

In 1877, Fitz was persuaded by the Stafford County Conservatives to run for governor, which he agreed to do despite some misgivings. His candidacy received lukewarm support from party members outside Stafford, a typical reaction being that of the *Richmond Dispatch,* which preferred Lieutenant Governor John L. Marye but "would settle for Fitz, that gallant soldier and honest farmer of Stafford."[32]

For a time early in the canvass, Fitz was judged a viable candidate, but in the last weeks before the party convention he began to lose ground to other contenders such as disabled war veteran John Warwick Daniel, Lynchburg-based scion of the powerful publishing family that ran the *Richmond Examiner.* One reason for Fitz's slippage was his support of free schools. The issue was wrapped up in the so-called Readjuster Movement that was, in turn, an outgrowth of Virginia's postwar and Confederate debt, which by the time of the state's readmission to the Union approached fifty million dollars.[33]

Numerous factors had combined to place Virginia in this predicament, including state resources ravaged by the war, uncollectible loans, a paucity of returns on infrastructure improvements, monies owed bondholders and other creditors that included many foreign investors, and a dearth of revenues, a situation aggravated by the coupons issued to many bondholders, permitting them to pay their taxes at discount. In 1871 Conservative members of the General Assembly had enacted a full funding bill that, they contended, would protect the state's honor by ensuring she met her lawful obligations—but at the risk, opponents claimed, of plunging the state into financial ruin.

As the Conservatives failed to foresee, even with the issuance of new bonds and the inducements offered to creditors to retire earlier, higher-interest securities, state revenues proved insufficient to pay interest on the debt and also cover normal operating expenses. One popular resort was to draw on funds earmarked for the state's public school system to meet other expenses and make interest payments. This expedient could, and did, lead to teacher layoffs and even the closing of schools. Given the racial climate of the times, black teachers and schools were favorite targets of officials seeking to free up state funds.[34]

Although a staunch proponent of full funding of the state debt, Fitz vocally opposed making the schools bear the brunt of the state's financial woes. On August 11, 1877, his name was placed in nomination for governor by one of his former subordinates, General William H. F. Payne, who in a long, flowery speech of endorsement noted that "in Virginia's history . . . whenever she is assailed with danger or stricken with suffering, she has ever beckoned these Lees to her side, and been happier when her hand was in theirs." Fitz Lee would carry on this hallowed tradition by assuming the role of Virginia's advisor, defender, and "physician to heal her wounds."[35]

Flights of oratorical flattery notwithstanding, Fitz's stance on the free school issue cost him the gubernatorial nomination, which went instead to Frederick W. M. Holliday of Winchester, who that November became governor. Apparently as something of a consolation prize, the Conservatives made Fitz the First Congressional District's nominee for the U.S. House of Representatives, a prize he had little hope of securing. His principal opponent, Charles Herndon, took the nomination but failed to win the congressional seat.

In 1879, Fitz was prevailed upon once again to run for office. This time he lowered his sights and vied for a seat in the Virginia House of Delegates. Reportedly, he entered the race without enthusiasm and merely to keep the local party in the hands of friends. His lack of commitment may have shielded him from the disappointment of losing yet another election, this time to an experienced old poll, Duff Green. The latter had run on the ticket of a third party that had sprung up in response to the state's debt crisis and that would make inroads in state politics over the next several years.[36]

That February had seen the formation of the Readjuster Party, whose supporters were committed to a reduction of the debt as well as to the enactment of various economic and political reforms affecting many branches of state government. Membership in the new party, whose standard-bearer was Confederate general and railroad executive William Mahone of Petersburg, cut across party, racial, and social lines; it allied lower- and middle-class whites of all political persuasions, mostly farmers and small businessmen, with African Americans, who, while not tendered political power, were promised benefits including the reopening of closed schools, the discontinuance of the obnoxious poll tax, and the abolition of the whipping post as a state-sanctioned means of punishment. By aligning along class lines, the Readjusters cast themselves in direct opposition to the Bourbons—old-money conservatives with glittering pedigrees, many of them high-ranking Confederate veterans—who had controlled the state since the end of Republican dominance. In other words, men such as Fitzhugh Lee.[37]

Fitz's defeat in his halfhearted bid for a General Assembly seat demonstrated the power that the Readjusters wielded only months after their organization. Over the next four years, they succeeded in scaling back the debt without noticeable effect on state pride, enacting modest reforms that benefited white men as well as black, and electing to the U.S. Senate not only Mahone but another party stalwart, Harrison H. Riddleberger.

Still, the Readjusters' hold on power was relatively short-lived. By 1883 the party's perceived support of African-American legislation hurt it in the eyes of the state's racist majority. In November, just before Election Day, a race riot in the outstate community of Danville, apparently orchestrated by white Conservatives who had falsely but loudly claimed that the city's government was controlled by its black minority, drastically lowered the Readjusters' standing statewide. The party continued in existence for some years more, mainly as a faction within the Republican Party. It effectively died in the fall of 1887, when Riddleberger lost his Senate seat.[38]

By 1883, Virginia Conservatives saw such an opportunity for major political gains that they reverted to their prewar title of Democrats. Recent successes had encouraged them to hope for more. In November 1881, they had placed one of their own, William E. Cameron, in the governor's office (Cameron had beaten a field of fellow Conservatives that once again included Fitz Lee). Now, by making race the dominant issue of the 1883 campaign, the renamed party gained a two-thirds majority in both houses of the legislature.[39]

The Democrats did not call on Fitz to run in 1883, but two years later he was again a contender for the governor's chair that had eluded him in 1877 and 1881. This time he was much better positioned to make a run: his name, family credentials, and military record were better known throughout his state and the South. His popularity had been established through the lectures he delivered throughout Virginia and other states in behalf of the SHS as well as through the speeches he made on public occasions, including the September 1881 dedication of the Yorktown Memorial. His public visibility had further been magnified by his recent appointment as a brigadier general in the state militia.[40]

Outside Virginia, he had made several well-publicized appearances that elevated his national stature. He was an invited guest at the February 1883 banquet of Brooklyn's 13th Regiment, National Guard—the first time an ex-Confederate had been so honored by a New York military organization. In February 1885, he received national exposure in the role of parade marshal during ceremonies preceding the dedication of the Washington Monument. An even more dramatic appearance on horseback occurred less than two weeks later, during ceremonies celebrating the inauguration of Grover Cleveland, the first Democrat to occupy the White House since the Civil War. Fitz had stumped all across his state on Cleveland's behalf; one of his rewards was a prominent role in the inaugural parade. Leading a body of Virginia militia up Pennsylvania

Avenue toward Cleveland's new residence, Fitz, an inspiring sight astride his black stallion, received the loudest ovation of anyone in the procession, including, apparently, the president-elect.[41]

Fitz's enhanced standing as a war hero revered by veterans North and South, and the attractiveness of his image as a nonprofessional politician, helped him win his party's nod for governor in 1885. Although not a favorite of many Democratic insiders, he was promoted by other party leaders purely out of self-interest. In the end, a bargain with John Daniel, who gained Fitz's support in a run for Mahone's Senate seat, helped secure his nomination. At his party's convention, he won a majority of votes on the first ballot; his nomination was then made unanimous.

As the Democratic candidate, he was aided by the controversial affiliation of the Readjusters with the minority Republicans. Fitz was also assisted by the strategy of the Democratic leadership, which kept him from debating his much more experienced opponent, John Sargent Wise, son of a former governor and Confederate general. While Fitz was a polished orator, Wise was, in the words of one historian, "an adept debater famed for his slashing attacks and ravaging repartees." On those occasions when it became impossible to avoid joint appearances by the candidates, more experienced Democrats would stand in for Fitz on the speakers' platform.[42]

The strategy of keeping Fitz above the political fray, while emphasizing his war record and especially his family connections, paid dividends. Wise became so frustrated at having to aim at a moving (or absent) target that when stumping Fitz's home area of Alexandria he viciously ridiculed his opponent, thereby creating a statewide backlash against his own candidacy. In the wake of the "Alexandria Affair," Democratic spokesmen began to retaliate in kind, not only demonizing Wise but branding his organization "the black party," an always effective appeal to race antagonisms.

Despite Fitz's built-in advantages and Wise's self-invited tribulations, the gubernatorial vote in November was quite close. Fitz won by 16,000 votes out of 290,000 cast. Perhaps, however, he had coattails: Democratic gains extended to the General Assembly, where the party won seventeen of twenty-one contested seats in the Senate and a two-thirds majority in the House of Delegates. Given the several years in which the Readjuster Republicans had dominated state politics, Fitz's victory was hailed by many of his supporters as a "second redemption" of his state. To Fitz, however, it meant something else—that he had achieved a victory on a par with any he had experienced in Confederate gray.[43]

FOURTEEN

"Our Peerless 'Old Fitz'"

On New Year's Day 1886, Fitzhugh Lee was sworn in as Virginia's tenth elected governor (prior to 1852, governors had been chosen by the legislature). The inaugural ceremony began shortly before noon with a procession into the hall of the House of Delegates where, before a joint session of the legislature, Fitz and his lieutenant governor, John Massey, took the oath of office from Judge L. L. Lewis of the state supreme court. A reporter noted that as the oath was read, Fitz "listened with marked attention. His eyes sparkled, and a ray of happiness seemed to illuminate his countenance. Without moving a muscle, he stood there amid the gaze of six or eight hundred people and pledged himself to support the Constitution and uphold the laws of the State."[1]

The new chief executive did not mark the occasion with any speech, but as soon as he stepped down from the speaker's stand he was congratulated lovingly by Nellie and the children and then with more decorum by outgoing Governor Cameron and leading members of the Senate and House. Then Fitz pumped the hands of numerous relatives, professional acquaintances, friends, neighbors, and cherished comrades from two armies, including Jack Hayes, late bugler, 2nd U.S. Cavalry, now a captain in Fitz's old regiment.

The inaugural festivities included an evening ball at the armory of the city's 1st Regiment of militia, an affair arranged and funded by "the leading people of the city, anxious to give some expression to their affection for the name of Lee and their gratification at being duly installed as Governor . . . a nephew of the great General Robert E. Lee." All who attended agreed that the ball, which began promptly at 8:45, followed by an elegant banquet served next door on the upper floors of Sanger Hall, fulfilled its "much talked about . . . promise of being an outstanding event in the city's social history."[2]

To this elegant accompaniment, the governorship of Fitzhugh Lee got under way. Unfortunately, Fitz's administration would not be recalled as long or as fondly as the gala events that ushered it in. The view of some historians that more could have, or should have, been accomplished during Fitz's tenure is largely based on the fact that unlike his recent predecessors, Fitz did not have to contend with a legislature controlled by political opponents who would obstruct him or resist his legislative agenda. One of Fitz's biographers, Harry W. Readnor, has suggested ironically that this situation contributed to a lack of accomplishment: "The shortage of meaningful precedents and the changes in circumstances from previous administrations—plus his natural temperament—contributed to Lee's reluctance to attempt dynamic innovation during his gubernatorial term."[3]

One reason for the dearth of change, reform, and innovation was Fitz's natural inclination to manage the state without ruling it. His view of his office was that of a conduit between the legislature and the citizenry—a manager of government rather than an arbiter of how it should function. Added to the general atmosphere of social stability and political peace, and his lack of interest in and attention to the minute details of the executive process, this view virtually guaranteed that his administration would not be known for great things achieved or attempted.

The only truly vexing issue Fitz had to deal with in his four years in office was the seemingly age-old bugaboo of the state debt. His handling of the issue was aided by his acceptance of the impracticality of full funding. Early in his tenure he sought to mediate a standoff between the legislature, most of whose members also appreciated the need to reduce the debt, and a council representing those British investors who held about 80 percent of the old, higher-interest state bonds. Fitz believed that the council's oft-repeated proposals, which called for a principal due of almost twenty-five million dollars and an annual interest payment of nearly one million, were too much for Virginia to bear. Most other state officials agreed.

As a means of getting the debt down to manageable proportions, the General Assembly had agreed to abide by the terms of the Riddleberger (or Readjuster) Act of February 1882, which Governor Cameron had signed into law. This measure reduced the total debt to just over twenty-one million and saddled the state of West Virginia—whose breaking off from the Commonwealth in 1863 was responsible for a portion of the debt—with paying one-third of the principal and interest. Further, the Riddleberger Act lowered the interest on state bonds to 3 percent and required the exchange of old bonds for new. An accompanying measure was known by the self-explanatory nickname "Coupon Killer Act."[4]

Despite the urgency of the problem and the logic of his arguments, Governor Lee could not persuade the General Assembly to work out an amicable agreement with the overseas bondholders. The lack of legislative action forced him, despite his inexperience in financial matters and accounting procedures, to enter personally into negotiations with the creditors. At times he was reduced to pleading for a lowering of demands and for an end to the use of tax coupons in defiance of state statutes. The latter practice, encouraged by a U.S. Supreme Court ruling invalidating the Coupon Killer legislation, increased fivefold during Fitz's administration, even as state revenues remained distressingly static.

Late in the first year of his term, Fitz's efforts appeared to bear fruit when the council representing the foreign creditors hinted that it might agree to a compromise along the lines of the Riddleberger Act. But a settlement was not reached until after Fitz, increasingly concerned about the effect of court rulings on the state's finances, called a special session of the General Assembly. Finally attentive to his dire warnings, the legislature established a Joint Committee on the Debt and gave it the power to negotiate a final settlement. The committee eventually produced a compromise agreeable to all parties, but it was not implemented until two years after the governor left office. Long before that time, as Readnor notes, Fitz's "vision of the governor's office being a pleasant and enjoyable position [had] evaporated."[5]

*   *   *

If finding a viable solution to the debt question was the first item on Governor Lee's agenda, state funding and promotion of education was a close second. Given his own notorious academic record, his championing of this issue might seem ironic. Yet he firmly and consistently believed that a strong state-supported public school system was a linchpin of economic prosperity and social advancement. Throughout his tenure he strove to instill this belief in his Democratic colleagues, many of whom continued to regard state support of free schools as a Readjuster program to be opposed on principle.

Fitz was particularly concerned that Virginia's school system should maintain a firm economic footing. He believed that whenever possible, educational appropriations should be increased. The efficacy of his efforts is difficult to gauge, since appropriations increased only slightly during his term. But that they grew at all during a period of statewide financial uncertainty is testimony to his unflagging support of the issue.[6]

He put almost as much energy into promoting federal programs in support of state education, strongly backing the Blair Bill, a congressional proposal to allocate part of the federal surplus to the states based on illiteracy rates. In this effort, Fitz showed his ability to move beyond traditional Southern opposition to federal involvement in state matters. He also demonstrated the courage to withstand criticism from within his own party that the Blair Bill would benefit

African-American students as much as Caucasian children. State-level opposition eventually sent the bill to defeat, forcing the governor to work even harder to identify and earmark state funds for educational purposes.

Fitz also espoused legislation to increase appropriations to institutions of higher learning. In one of his most eloquent statements on any social issue, he declared that the prosperity of a state depended on "liberal culture in the various professions. . . . [A]n enlightened policy demands the protection and promotion of literature, science, and art, as . . . constituting of themselves, apart from their practical utility, prominent features in an advanced civilization, and hence the value of institutions especially adapted to higher literary, scientific, and technical training."[7]

Other items on Governor Lee's agenda attracted less attention than his stands on the debt question and the free school issue. Even more ironic, perhaps, than his promotion of educational programs was his signing of the General Local Option Act, a temperance measure passed by the General Assembly in 1886. Fitz's action was a concession to the nationwide popularity of the Temperance Movement. Yet it militated against his personal belief that moderation in the consumption of alcoholic beverages "is not produced by law makers but by the influence of education, morality and religion."[8]

Fitz also devoted much attention to the promotion of matters of civil order. Although in early 1885 he had resigned his position as general officer in the militia, he maintained an abiding interest in state military affairs. He pored over reports of militia activities and regularly reviewed the various companies, regiments, and brigades of state troops. He encouraged these units to participate in outstate drill and readiness competitions and stood ready to use the state's military forces when any locality was threatened with civil disturbances or beset by natural disasters. On other issues of civil order, he wielded his pardoning powers carefully and conscientiously, especially in capital cases, and he sought to reform the state penal system, especially in the area of prison-labor contracts. He worked hard, but with indifferent success, to impress on lawmakers the justice of segregating youthful offenders from hardened criminals in the state's penitentiary.[9]

Governor Lee strove to advance both the agricultural and industrial interests of his state. Influenced by his own experiences as the squire of Richland, he sought to expand state services to farmers, who made up the great majority of Virginia's workforce, and to increase the power of the commissioner of agriculture to collect and disseminate the statistics and information farmers needed to stay profitable. He also sought, but generally failed to secure, direct relief to farmers beset by market woes, drought, and other adverse circumstances beyond their control.

Thanks largely to legislative apathy, he failed to relieve the increasing pressures being applied to small farmers. He was more successful in promoting industrial interests, especially the railroads whose ever-expanding profitability brought badly needed funds into state coffers. While he still thought of himself as a gentleman farmer, he was increasingly driven by a vision of a new, industrialized South with railroads at the heart of the transformation. On every trip he made into the North, he tried to line up investments in the state industries, and he vigorously advocated the emigration to Virginia of highly skilled Northern craftsmen. He was a major force behind the Richmond Exposition of 1888, which showcased the state's economic progress and promoted its narrow but expanding industrial base. As Readnor notes, to Governor Lee "industrial development was the key to Virginia's prosperous future."[10]

When Fitzhugh Lee's administration ended on January 1, 1890, his state was enjoying a period of prosperity and slow but encouraging economic growth. His term had produced no accomplishments dramatic or influential enough to make his administration truly memorable. Still, historians point out that his record compares favorably with that of his immediate predecessors as well as that of the executives who followed him through century's end. Compared with his counterparts elsewhere in the South, he stands as progressive and reformist.

Because he served during a period free of social unrest and political turmoil, Fitzhugh Lee's popularity among his constituents remained at least as high—and conceivably higher—when he left office as when he entered it. As the *Richmond Dispatch* wrote of him on the day he delivered the keys of government to his handpicked successor, Philip W. McKinney, "'Our Fitz' retires to private life with the assurance that Virginia never had a governor who was more beloved or who tried more conscientiously to do his duty."[11]

*   *   *

At the time ex-Governor Lee returned to civil pursuits, he truly looked like the man he had become—a generally healthy fifty-two-year-old who had enjoyed decades of hearty eating and, with the exception of almost daily outings on horseback, had gone for years without regular exercise or physical conditioning. The stoutness that had characterized him since early manhood had taken a turn toward corpulence. Midway through his gubernatorial term he had shaved off the chest-length beard he had grown during the war and trimmed considerably in after years. The mustache that remained was graying, as was the full head of hair he retained. He still carried himself erect in the manner of a proud cavalryman, although his girth could not be hidden by the most well-tailored coat, and his family often complained that he did not enjoy enough leisure time or outdoor activity.

His well-fed appearance gave him the image of a successful businessman, which he was, and of a veteran politician, which he never considered himself to be. That image, coupled with the popularity he retained upon leaving office, brought him a number of professional opportunities. He was still prominent in the ranks of the Democratic Party on both state and national levels. In fact, in mid-1888 he had been considered for second place on his party's presidential ticket. Fitz, however, preferred to continue as governor, and the movement quickly died.[12]

In retrospect, the outcome would appear fortunate, since Cleveland was defeated for reelection that fall, although he would rebound in 1892 to regain the presidency. Determined to keep his political options open, even though he did not hold the post of honor as he had four years before, Fitz rode in the inaugural parade of Cleveland's victorious opponent, Benjamin Harrison, who although a Midwesterner hailed from a family with deep Virginia roots. Sensing that the defeated candidate had not passed from the national stage, Fitz maintained close ties with Cleveland and while still governor accompanied the ex-president on a tour of Cuba. Both men shared a vision of that Spanish colony as a major trading partner with her neighbor to the north.[13]

The ex-governor could afford to sift carefully through the professional opportunities that came his way. He rejected several, including an invitation to become superintendent of the Virginia Military Institute. Instead, he moved his family to Lexington, where he assumed management of a speculative enterprise known as the Rockbridge Company, which promoted the industrial potential of the county of that name and surrounding communities. The region abounded in mineral deposits that promised to make it a center of iron and steel production.[14]

The local backers of the company had high hopes of attracting wealthy investors, especially given the stature of its president. During the first eighteen months of Fitz's term, the concern either bought or acquired options to purchase several thousand acres. Its most visible asset was the factory town of Glasgow on the James River, which it established in the hope of reaping profits from land sales, and to which Fitz moved his family from Lexington. Yet although many well-heeled investors, including members of England's royal family, put small amounts of money into the venture, long-term investments were too few to provide the needed capital. When a number of outstate firms that had received loans from the company to establish themselves in the area defaulted on their obligations, the enterprise faltered. A railroad of which Fitz was to be president, grandly styled the Pittsburgh & Virginia, failed to lay any track. The Panic of 1893 finished off what remained of the company, and the following year Fitz resigned his position. By then he had lost several thousand dollars of his own, but he consoled himself that other investors had fared much worse.[15]

While the Rockbridge Company, as well as a second failed venture in industrial speculation known as the Chicago Town Company, hurt Fitz financially, he suffered a psychological and emotional blow even as these ventures were collapsing. The death in 1892 of John S. Barbour, who had taken Harrison Riddleberger's seat in the U.S. Senate, required Fitz's successor, Philip McKinney, to select someone to complete the unexpired term. Fitz was considered for the appointment, but in the end it went to a seventy-year-old retired congressman who had no desire to seek the full term that would commence in March 1895. Fitz did so desire, however, and although he did not campaign openly for the seat he made known his availability as a candidate.

Thanks to his well-regarded administration as governor and the immense popularity he enjoyed among the voting public, Fitz came to believe that he had the appointment sewed up months before it was formally made. The trouble was that the seat would be filled by vote of the Virginia Senate. Fitz spent much of his time leading to the selection caucus burnishing his already gleaming image before the public. Meanwhile, his chief rival for the seat, Thomas Staples Martin, a soft-spoken lawyer and railroad lobbyist virtually unknown to the electorate but who knew how to play the political game in ways alien to Fitz, was quietly engineering an effective campaign to secure the support of key senators. His effort was funded by monies provided by the railroad industry, whose interests he had energetically promoted on the state level.[16]

When the legislative caucus met in early December 1893 to select Virginia's next U.S. senator—who would not begin serving his term for another fifteen months—Martin led every ballot and in the end defeated Fitz by a vote of sixty-six to fifty-five. It was one of the greatest upsets in state political history. Even the senators who had given Martin his margin of victory were not certain how he had managed it. Newspapers that had predicted a triumph for Fitz Lee indignantly asked, "Who is Tom Martin?"

Fitz was understandably shocked and upset by his defeat, so much so that he did not dissuade his legislative friends from seeking a formal investigation into the affair. His friends prevailed, but the result gave them little comfort. The senate investigative panel made brief inquiries into the voting process before concluding that although "certain practices and acts" had taken place that the committee members "do not commend . . . such practices and acts were without the assent or approbation of any candidate."[17]

In so ruling, the committee deftly sidestepped the question of where Martin had gotten the money to finance his behind-the-scenes campaign. Fitz believed he knew, but as a party loyalist he was reluctant to make a public airing of his suspicions. He could not afford to disrupt the mutually beneficial relationship between the Democrats and the railroad interests. In the end he repressed his disappointment and forever relinquished his dream of holding high public office.

*   *   *

With the second Cleveland administration in full swing, Fitz had reason to hope he would be tendered a patronage job, one that would tide him over until another major professional opportunity came his way. His faith was rewarded when, early in 1895, he was offered the post of collector of internal revenue for the western district of Virginia. It was a local position without high visibility and paid only forty-five hundred dollars a year. On the other hand, the collector's authority was wide-ranging—it extended to fifty-two counties and more than one hundred inspectors—and after his recent financial reverses Fitz needed the money. The *Richmond Times* felt compelled to assure its readers that his acceptance of the post did not lower his standing as "the most popular man in the State."[18]

The position saddled Fitz with duties he would have preferred to avoid, including an immense amount of paperwork, most of it relating to balancing the reports of tobacconists and distillers. He seems to have spent much of his time trying to persuade the commissioner of the Internal Revenue Service in Washington to appoint friends and relatives to positions within the department. He also sought to supplement his salary with royalties from magazine articles he prepared on various subjects, mainly his wartime experiences and famous soldiers he had served with, including Stuart and Jackson.[19]

One literary offer that came his way he had to decline. In April 1896, the publishers of *Confederate Military History,* a proposed state-oriented study of the war from a Southern perspective, asked him to contribute a volume on Virginia's role in the conflict. The project appealed to him, but he was forced to devote his full attention to another opportunity that came his way as a result of his close relations with the Cleveland administration.[20]

On the tenth of the month he wrote his superior in Washington that "I have decided to accept the President's offer, with the hope that possibly I can tender some service to the country as well as respond to the wishes of Mr. Cleveland, to whom I have ever been loyal." The proffered position was that of U.S. consul general in Havana, Cuba, a city Fitz had visited seven years before in company with the president and with whose political and commercial situation he was deeply familiar.[21]

Since its first settlement, Cuba had been a subordinate crown colony of the Spanish Empire. The mother country's authority over the island was exercised through a governor general, who, as Fitz would later observe, "has generally wielded the arbitrary power of a czar." The colony had long labored under the stick of military despotism, Spain's carrot being her repeated promises of greater political privileges and, eventually, the grant of self-rule. As Fitz noted, however, all such pledges, "down to the latest and present autonomy scheme, have been the merest subterfuges, void of the true essence of local self-government."[22]

Military oppression had been coupled with "a system of exorbitant taxation, such as has never been known elsewhere in the world." To Fitz and many other Americans—especially those "jingoists" who favored an aggressive policy toward

Cuba's oppressor—the island's plight was all too reminiscent of what the American colonies had endured before forcing a break from their parent across the Atlantic.[23]

Several attempts had been made by the Cuban people to throw off the Spanish yoke—the most recent being the so-called Ten Years' War, which had ended in 1878—but each had been either ruthlessly suppressed or halted by false promises of political and social reforms. The most recent concession to those agitating for independence was a policy of limited autonomy, or home rule—a policy, however, that the current governor general, Valeriano Weyler, proceeded to table indefinitely. Known as "the Butcher," Weyler had made himself hated and feared through a *Reconcentrado* program that many Cubans believed was designed to wipe out the native population. Fitz Lee believed so as well: "How successful Weyler's policy has been, partially carried out, can be answered by the graves of a fourth of the population" of the island.[24]

In February 1895 a new uprising broke out when a small but dedicated band of revolutionaries under the command of Jose Marti, a Cuban-born fifteen-year resident of New York City, invaded the island and proclaimed a new Cuban Republic. Marti was later killed in action against the Spanish, but his followers carried on the revolutionary movement he had fomented, attacking Spanish outposts, supply columns, and arms depots with enough success to establish the credibility of their insurgency. The War of Independence was ongoing when on June 3, 1896, Fitzhugh Lee arrived on the island to take up the duties of his office.[25]

Fitz understood that one of his most important responsibilities was to keep the Cleveland administration posted on all facets of the political and military situation in Cuba. The president was being buffeted by congressional demands that the United States recognize the belligerency status of the rebels. Thus, almost as soon as arriving Fitz informed himself, through extensive interviews with occupation officials and representatives of the insurgents, about the aims, intentions, and political and military tactics of both forces.

From the intelligence thus gathered, he developed a view of the war that over time would change in degree but not in substance. He had concluded that neither the corruption-riddled colonial forces nor the determined but disorganized and outmanned rebels had the wherewithal to achieve a lasting victory. Yet the Spanish were too xenophobic and imperialistic to give back the island and the rebels too committed to their cause to surrender. The standoff was productive only of tremendous losses in human life and material resources—resources that in a climate of peace would make Cuba a major trading partner with the United States and other lands.

During his first weeks on the island, Consul General Lee developed a three-option plan by which the United States might end the internecine warfare. The plan called for a willingness to mediate between the belligerents; a proposal to

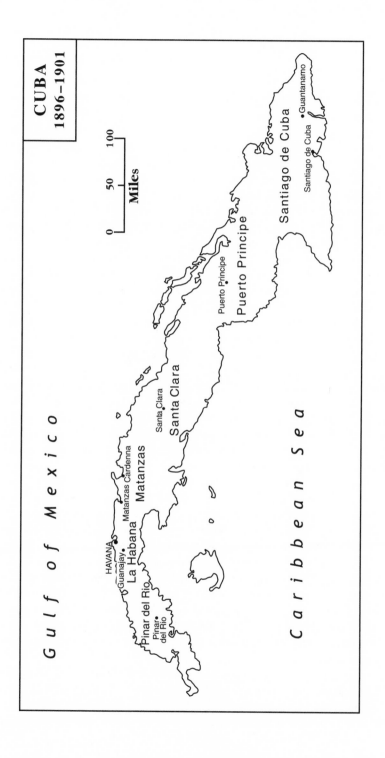

CUBA
1896–1901

Miles
0   50   100

Gulf of Mexico

HAVANA
Guanajay
La Habana
Matanzas Cardenna
Matanzas
Pinar del Rio
Pinar del Rio
Santa Clara
Santa Clara
Puerto Principe
Puerto Principe
Santiago de Cuba
Santiago de Cuba
Guantanamo

Caribbean Sea

monitor sweeping social, political, and economic reforms; and an offer to purchase the island from Spain. Fitz believed that the first two options were unrealistic—he favored the third, believing that in U.S. hands the country could be organized into a republic "under our government's direction and guidance." Such a policy would not only free the people of military oppression but would protect the interests of American investors and industrialists, especially the large exporters of sugar, bananas, and tobacco products.[26]

If the Spanish rejected the offer to buy, Fitz recommended that the United States simply declare the island's independence, "after the order of President [Andrew] Jackson's treatment of the Texas question in 1836." He did not, either then or later, advocate war between America and the Spanish Empire, but if one occurred, it would be "short and decisive" to American arms. The cost of the conflict could be rolled into the America's purchase offer, which the defeated occupiers would surely accept. Fitz went so far as to suggest—purely for contingency purposes—that a warship be placed on station off Key West, "under a discreet officer, with a full complement of marines."[27]

His recommendations were not well received in the White House. Cleveland had hoped that by playing the part of the quiet, discreet diplomat whose personal popularity gave weight to his moderate proposals, Fitz would protect the administration against the strident demands of jingoists and their supporters in the press who considered American intervention—by force, if necessary—the only acceptable alternative to Spanish recalcitrance. Cleveland thought the idea of buying the island absurd, especially if the United States was not to govern it. Concerned that the consul general had "fallen into the style of rolling intervention like a sweet morsel under his tongue," he began to repent of having made Fitz America's man in Havana.[28]

Another regret of the president was that the consul general's popularity was growing to unassailable proportions. Through his well-publicized actions and utterances, Fitz had served notice to the world that he intended to defend the rights of American citizens and business interests in Cuba, Spanish objections notwithstanding. Time and again he bruised Spanish sensibilities while making headlines with his forceful protests against the treatment accorded Cuban Americans by Spanish magistrates, police officials, and military officers. He also defended American journalists and adventurers against illegal detainment and prosecution on charges of aiding and abetting the rebels. Lurid news stories of Cuban officials strip-searching Cuban women and murdering imprisoned Americans got Fitz's angry attention and involved him in numerous, sometimes polite but occasionally acrimonious, confrontations with General Weyler and later with his successor, the more polished and affable but equally intransigent Ramon Blanco.

The American popular press hailed Fitz for his willingness to stand up to a decadent, repressive regime and champion American rights in the face of repeated threats and reprisals. They cheered the news that the Spanish foreign office had pressed, unsuccessfully, for his recall, a sure sign that the nephew of Robert E. Lee (now a hero revered by the entire nation) was "the right man in the right place at the right time" for his country.[29]

In contrast to the unalloyed approval of his contemporaries, historians have given Consul General Lee's tenure mixed reviews. Some have praised his activist zeal, his accurate assessment of the views and objectives of the belligerents, and his prophetic comments about the inevitability of America intervention. Other chroniclers have faulted him for being too quick to brand the various concessions made by Spain as devious stratagems aimed at dividing the opposition. They have also accused Fitz of hoping to profit from personal investments in Cuban "business propositions," once peace and economic prosperity settled upon the island.[30]

Still other historians have accused Fitz of turning the Cuban crisis to partisan political advantage. This charge, at least, is backed up by hard evidence. During the 1896 Democratic National Convention, when the party's western and southern blocs combined to nominate the populist editor and orator William Jennings Bryan for president, business-oriented conservatives such as Fitz and Cleveland were shocked and distressed. In letters to his superiors in the State Department, Fitz suggested the convening of a second convention, one that would reflect the policies of the Cleveland administration. Fitz believed that those policies should include a strong endorsement of U.S. mediation of the war in Cuba or, failing that, American intervention. Such a stance would receive so much popular support that the party would be saved from defeat by Bryan's Republican opponent, William McKinley. But Fitz's advice went unheeded, and in November McKinley won the White House.[31]

Republican insiders expected that Fitz would be relieved of his duties as soon as the new administration took over. The outgoing president, still simmering over Fitz's apparent defection to the jingoists, recommended that course to his successor. To the surprise of many observers, McKinley elected to keep Fitz on, partly the result of his stature back home and partly because any change in personnel might be construed by the Spanish as a change in policy.[32]

Like Cleveland, McKinley hoped to avoid intervention, especially the military kind. Yet even more so than his predecessor, he was pushed toward a military solution by those legislators, newspapermen, and private citizens who saw armed force as the only way America could fulfill her responsibilities as a defender of democracy throughout the Western world. Events conspired against the president in January 1898 when rioting broke out in the streets of Havana and the American consulate became a potential target of Spanish retaliation.

Remaining calm throughout the crisis, Fitz argued against sending to Cuba the battleship that had been stationed off the Florida coast, for fear it would arouse Spanish passions and endanger American lives. Against his wishes, late in January Washington ordered the second-class battleship *Maine* to Havana harbor. By the time of her arrival, on the twenty-fifth, Fitz had changed his mind about the need for a war vessel, calling her arrival "a beautiful sight." In later weeks he made numerous visits to the ship; invited its captain, Charles Sigsbee, to his office and hotel for dinner (the two would develop a close friendship); and accompanied the crew to bullfights and various functions thrown by the occupation forces in an apparent effort to promote international goodwill.[33]

Fitz was in his hotel room when, on the evening of February 15, the *Maine* exploded with a force that shook windows for miles around. He repaired at once to the site of the blast to find the ship a mass of burning, twisted, half-submerged metal. That night and in later days he went to great lengths to care for the wounded, prepare the bodies of the dead for shipment to the States (the death toll eventually reached 266), and furnish shelter to Sigsbee and the rest of the survivors. When time permitted, he received the condolences of Spanish officials at all levels. All expressed their horror over the tragedy, their desire to assist the victims, and their absolute conviction that no Spaniard had a hand in the disaster.

Fitz's reaction to the sinking was commendably restrained. His initial impression was that the explosion was an accident—neither then nor afterward did he suspect that Governor General Blanco or any other high Spanish official was responsible for its occurrence. But in the supercharged diplomatic atmosphere that accompanied the sinking, his call for calmness and clear thinking went unheard. International tensions rose to crisis level in the weeks that followed, and by the close of March the harried McKinley reluctantly prepared a war message to Congress. At Fitz's request, the president withheld its issuance for five days to allow diplomatic personnel, their dependents, and other Americans to evacuate the island. On April 9, Fitz locked his office and repaired to a ship that awaited him in the harbor. He was the last American to leave Cuba before war was declared.[34]

*   *   *

Fitz came home to a hero's welcome, one that followed his special train from Key West to Washington. Newspapers chronicled his return with banner headlines such as "Lee's Triumphal Progress North," "Fitz Lee the Hero," and "Honor to Fitz Lee." At every water stop, crowds gathered to shower him with cheers, cannon salutes, martial music, even fireworks. In Richmond, he was greeted not only by Nellie and the children but by ten thousand other well-wishers, including Governor James H. Tyler, his staff, and militia units in full panoply. Those who turned out to welcome "Our Fitz" could not cheer loudly enough or shake his hand often enough. Words and gestures seemed insufficient to convey the pride and affection Virginians felt for the portly, gray-haired warrior who had stirred the nation's pride through his unwavering defense of American honor and his promotion of American ideals.[35]

Reaching the capital on the eleventh, he conferred at length with the president as well as with officials of the State, War, and Navy Departments. In the wake of the president's message, which would be followed before month's end by a congressional declaration of war, many government observers supposed that Fitz would be tendered high rank and authority to be wielded during the fighting that lay ahead. These honors were duly conferred upon him, but they proved to be hollow gestures, devoid of substance. Fitz Lee's role in the momentous events that had brought war to America, Spain, and Cuba was virtually at an end. Everything that followed his departure from Cuba smacked of anticlimax.

From Washington he returned to Richmond, where he and his family now occupied an elegant home on Park Avenue. There, for weeks afterward as the nation mobilized for her first conflict since the Civil War, he greeted well-wishers from every social class and walk of life. He was feted at banquets, was an honored guest at dozens of civic functions, and became a popular sight at parades and rallies designed to foster support for the war effort. On May 4 the War Department informed him of his appointment as a major general of volunteers. Three weeks later, he was named commander of the VII Army Corps, which was to be organized at Jacksonville and Tampa.[36]

Fitz's appointment was hailed nationwide as a masterpiece of public relations. It resonated with an increasingly popular North-South reunion theme, one further strengthened by the general officer appointments that went to three other ex-Confederate commanders, all of them cavalrymen, two of them old colleagues of Fitz's—Tom Rosser, Matthew Calbraith Butler, and Congressman Joseph Wheeler of Alabama, erstwhile commander of the mounted forces of the Army of Tennessee. At a typical reception in Fitz's honor, thrown by the Richmond-based Lee Camp of the United Confederate Veterans, he was saluted by dozens of veterans of the Army of Northern Virginia who remarked proudly about his new blue uniform even as they saluted him as "the beau saber of the Army of Northern Virginia . . . so brave and debonair . . . our peerless 'Old Fitz'!"[37]

On May 24, Fitz left Richmond for Jacksonville, but that was as close to the war as he got. His command was still forming and logistical support for it remained lacking when, in mid-July, major operations ceased on Cuba. The armistice that followed on August 12 led to Spain's surrender and the removal of her troops from Cuba. Though disappointed that he had not seen action as Joe Wheeler had during the battles of Las Guasimas and San Juan Hill, Fitz took satisfaction from the well-publicized fact that his Florida camps were among the cleanest and most sanitary in the volunteer army and his command's sick list one of the lowest. He also took pride in the fact that the staff he had formed consisted not only of one of his sons, the grandnephew of Robert E. Lee, but also Captain Algernon Sartoris, grandson of Ulysses S. Grant.[38]

Even after he finally reached Cuba, his service had an anticlimactic quality to it. Following numerous consultations with Washington officials, he returned to the island that September at the head of a large detachment of occupation troops. For a time he appeared to be in line for the chief post on the island, that of military governor, but it went to Major General John Rutter Brooke, a Union Army veteran who had remained in the service since the war. Instead, Fitz returned to his old bailiwick as the commander of the military district headquartered at Havana. When the Spanish left the island on January 1, 1899, under terms of the surrender agreement, Fitz formally assumed command of the Department of the Province of Havana. Three and a half months later, the department of the neighboring province of Pinar del Rio was added to his jurisdiction.[39]

Fitz's military service in Cuba lasted a little more than two years. It was a frustrating, sometimes exasperating, experience, mainly due to the wretched condition in which he found his domain and the ambivalence of its people toward substituting one foreign occupier for another. His immediate concern was the "deplorable condition of the Island after it was evacuated by the Spanish. . . . Business of all sorts was suspended. Agricultural operations had ceased; large sugar estates with their enormous and expensive machinery were destroyed; houses burned; stock driven off for consumption by the Spanish troops, or killed. There was scarcely an ox left to pull a plow, had there been a plow left." The forlorn vistas that met his eye at every turn must have reminded him of the dead fields of Richland when he first occupied his Stafford County estate. As for the people of his realm, "chaos, confusion, doubt, and uncertainty filled with apprehension the minds of the Cubans, who, for the first time had been relieved of the cruel care of those who, for centuries, controlled their country and their destiny."[40]

Fitz took such steps, both immediate and long-term, as he could to ease the suffering of the populace and restore to it some semblance of social and economic order. His basic objective—and that of the other departmental leaders, Major Generals Leonard Wood (who would replace Brooke as military governor), James Harrison Wilson (another Civil War cavalryman, a frequent opponent of Fitz's in 1864), and William Ludlow—was to pacify Cuba and make her ready to govern herself, at which time the American troops would emulate their Spanish predecessors and go home.

General Lee found the job as burdensome and vexatious as his first stint in Havana, though in different ways. The primary problem was a general and consistent lack of guidance from Washington as to the army's immediate and long-term objectives. Fitz discovered that the government itself had no clear-cut plan for Cuba beyond its immediate pacification. Thus he spent the majority of his time tending to immediate, local concerns—restoring public order, fighting disease, warding off starvation and pestilence. These basic efforts would continue to occupy him throughout his time on the island.

Occupation policy, such as it was, came gradually in the form of measures passed by the U.S. Congress. By mid-1899, Fitz was advising the new secretary of war, Elihu Root, that the United States should begin implementing the Teller Amendment, enacted in April 1898, that prohibited annexation of Cuba and outlined steps to prepare the country for self-government. He urged the calling of a constitutional convention and the election of local officials so that "the pledged faith of the Government of the United States to Cuba can be kept."[41]

In a subsequent report to the War Department, Fitz opined that Cubans were "as capable of organizing a form of government today as they will ever be." In actuality, he doubted that self-government would succeed. He suspected that at some future date the Teller Amendment would be repealed and America would annex the island, if only because of the countries' mutual economic interests. Even so, he believed that America was honor bound to give the Cubans, as soon as possible, the opportunity to succeed or fail on their own terms.[42]

Some of Fitz's proposals appeared to receive official acceptance. In his final weeks on the island, he witnessed the convening of a constitutional convention, which would give rise to a new Republic of Cuba. But in February 1901, the U.S. Congress passed the Platt Amendment, providing for American intervention in Cuban affairs and according the island a protectorate status rather than an established mechanism for achieving self-rule. Many Cubans felt betrayed by the measure, but Fitz considered it the best that could be done for the island under the circumstances then obtaining.[43]

With no real sense of having accomplished more than basic relief for a suffering population, Fitz left Cuba for good on November 15, 1900. By then military occupation was winding down, with only one military district remaining in operation. In Washington he met with President McKinley, who thanked him warmly for his services, received his final report of occupation duty, then offered his visitor a command in the States that would round out his military service. Fitz accepted, and in early December he reported at Omaha, Nebraska, headquarters of the Department of the Missouri. His tenure there was brief, and his duties were perfunctory; he resigned the post and retired from the U.S. Army on March 2, 1901, at the permanent grade of brigadier general in the regular service.[44]

Although he could have remained longer in uniform, he was now sixty-five and in declining health (as early as several years before, family members had expressed concern that when they walked with him, he would have to stop every few minutes to catch his breath). He nevertheless kept busy during the remainder of his life—perhaps too much so. Following his retirement ceremony in Omaha and a subsequent vacation trip to the West Coast, he and Nellie moved from Richmond to Charlottesville. Fitz left the comfortable house they occupied in the college town only to visit relatives, including their sons in the service and their daughters, wives of army officers; to lecture; to attend veterans' reunions; and to serve on committees in support of funding for the university.[45]

In September 1902, Fitz abruptly returned to a peripatetic life when induced to accept the presidency of the Jamestown Exposition Company. The venture, the brainchild of Virginia businessmen and civic leaders, had been set up to fund, organize, and stage a great public exhibition to be held in Hampton Roads five years hence in commemoration of the three hundredth anniversary of the settlement of the country's first permanent English-speaking community.[46]

The work Fitz thereby took on carried him, at frequent intervals and for long periods, far from home. His duties, mainly of a fund-raising nature, required him to seek out investors from each of the states to be represented at the exposition. In conjunction with the job, he delivered speeches before civic and business organizations, chambers of commerce, and state legislatures. His was a demanding schedule, and he worked himself to death trying to meet it. In the early hours of April 28, 1905, he was returning by train from an appearance before the legislatures of Massachusetts and Connecticut when he was struck down en route to Washington, D.C. Although partially paralyzed, he remained on board until he could be hospitalized in the capital. At 11:30 P.M., he succumbed to the effects of a stroke at Providence Hospital, twenty-four hours before Nellie and the children could reach his side.[47]

Throughout April 30, Fitz Lee's body lay in state at Washington's Episcopal Church of the Epiphany, where, the following day, a brief service was conducted by the rector, Dr. Randolph H. McKim, former chaplain of the 2nd Virginia Cavalry. Shortly after noon, his remains, escorted by a military funeral detail, were conveyed to the Pennsylvania Railroad depot. At Richmond, the coffin, draped with the flags of both the United States and the Confederate States of America, lay in state at City Hall. There hundreds of Richmonders of all ages, races, and walks of life turned out to pay farewell to "Our Fitz." Burial took place the following day, May 2, at Hollywood Cemetery, where a simple granite shaft was later erected on the grave site.[48]

Of the many eulogies read over his grave and at the several memorial services held for him, perhaps the simplest and yet most expressive was offered by a member of one of those veterans' organizations at which Fitz had so often spoken and where he had been very much at home in the company of the old soldiers who had fought under or alongside him. In the words of Companion C. H. Stewart of Portsmouth's Stonewall Jackson Camp, United Confederate Veterans: "He nobly fought the battles of life. Trouble stood in his way like milestones on a turnpike, but he reached the goal with greater achievements than he reckoned, and his name is burned into our hearts as a hero whom we love."[49]

Notes

Abbreviations Used in Notes

B&L	*Battles and Leaders of the Civil War*
CV	*Confederate Veteran*
CW&M	College of William and Mary
FL	Fitzhugh Lee
LC	Library of Congress
LV	Library of Virginia
MB	*Maine Bugle*
MC	Museum of the Confederacy
MSS	Correspondence, Manuscripts
OR	*The War of the Rebellion: A Compilation of the Official Records of the Union and Confederate Armies*
REL	Robert E. Lee
SHSP	*Southern Historical Society Papers*

UNC   University of North Carolina

USMA   United States Military Academy

UV   University of Virginia

VHS   Virginia Historical Society

VMH&B   *Virginia Magazine of History and Biography*

CHAPTER ONE

1. The sources for the expedition on which Lieutenant Lee was wounded are several: James R. Arnold, *Jeff Davis's Own: Cavalry, Comanches, and the Battle for the Texas Frontier* (New York, 2000), 231–46; Martin L. Crimmins, "'Fitz' Lee Kills an Indian," *Bulletin of the New York Public Library* 41 (1937): 385; Robert G. Hartje, *Van Dorn: The Life and Times of a Confederate General* (Nashville, Tenn., 1967), 70–74; E. M. Hayes, "Fitzhugh Lee as an Indian Fighter," *The Monthly Chronicle: Episcopal High School . . . Alexandria, Va.* 7 (Feb. 1895), 3–5; James L. Nichols, *General Fitzhugh Lee: A Biography* (Lynchburg, Va., 1989), 10–11; Harry W. Readnor, "General Fitzhugh Lee, 1835–1905: A Biographical Study" (M.A. thesis, University of Virginia, 1971), 17–24; Theophilus F. Rodenbough and William L. Haskin, eds., *The Army of the United States: Historical Sketches of Staff and Line . . .* (New York, 1896), 223; Joseph B. Thoburn, "Indian Fight in Ford County in 1859," *Collections of the Kansas State Historical Society* 12 (1912): 316–23; Robert M. Utley, *Frontiersmen in Blue: The United States Army and the Indian, 1848–1865* (New York, 1967), 133–35. The quotation is from Hayes, "Fitzhugh Lee as an Indian Fighter," 3.
2. Hayes, "Fitzhugh Lee as an Indian Fighter," 4.
3. Ibid.
4. Ibid., 5.
5. Ibid.
6. Ibid.
7. Ibid.
8. Ibid.; Thoburn, "Indian Fight in Ford County," 324–25.
9. FL to his parents, June 3, 1859, FL MSS (formerly known as the Fitzhugh Lee Opie Papers), UV.
10. Edmund Jennings Lee, *Lee of Virginia, 1642–1892: Biographical and Genealogical Sketches of the Descendants of Colonel Richard Lee . . .* (Philadelphia, 1895), 49–64, 408–13, 489; T. C. DeLeon, *Belles, Beaux and Brains of the 60's* (New York, 1907), 430–37; Readnor, "General Fitzhugh Lee," 1–2; Ardyce Kinsley, comp., *The Fitzhugh Lee Sampler* (Lively, Va., 1992), 163.

11. Ibid., 164; Readnor, "General Fitzhugh Lee," 2–3.

12. "Mother of Gen. Fitzhugh Lee," *CV* 6 (1898): 501–02; Nichols, *General Fitzhugh Lee,* 4.

13. Nichols, *General Fitzhugh Lee,* 5.

14. DeLeon, *Belles, Beaux and Brains of the 60's,* 437–40; Kinsley, *Fitzhugh Lee Sampler,* 163.

15. "Fitzhugh Lee, Governor-Elect of Virginia," *The Welcome Friend* (Dec. 1887), 92.

16. Lee, *Lee of Virginia,* 489; Nichols, *General Fitzhugh Lee,* 5.

17. FL to Anna Maria Fitzhugh, May 8, 1850, FL MSS, UV.

18. Lee, *Lee of Virginia,* 408–10; Robert E. Lee Jr., *Recollections and Letters of Gen. Robert E. Lee, by His Son* (Garden City, N.Y., 1926), 362; Kinsley, *Fitzhugh Lee Sampler,* 160–62; Isaac Toucey to Sidney S. Lee, July 10, 1860, FL MSS, UV.

19. Douglas Southall Freeman, *R. E. Lee: A Biography,* 4 vols. (New York, 1934–35), 1:218–300, 316–18.

20. Readnor, "General Fitzhugh Lee," 5; Nichols, *General Fitzhugh Lee,* 5–6.

21. *Official Register of the Officers and Cadets of the U.S. Military Academy, West Point, N.Y.* . . . (West Point, N.Y.: Privately published, 1853 (p. 13), 1854 (p. 12), 1855 (p. 9), 1856 (p. 8)); "Fitzhugh Lee's Academic Record while a Cadet at the United States Military Academy, 1 July 1852–1 July 1856," USMA; Samuel J. Bayard, *The Life of George Dashiell Bayard* . . . (New York, 1874), 42; Nichols, *General Fitzhugh Lee,* 179.

22. Ibid.; Freeman, *R. E. Lee,* 1:72–73.

23. "Fitzhugh Lee, Governor-Elect of Virginia," 92; "Fitzhugh Lee's Academic Record while a Cadet," USMA; Readnor, "General Fitzhugh Lee," 6–8; Nichols, *General Fitzhugh Lee,* 6–8; Kinsley, *Fitzhugh Lee Sampler,* 12.

24. Nichols, *General Fitzhugh Lee,* 6–7; Freeman, *R. E. Lee,* 1:82.

25. "Fitzhugh Lee, Governor-Elect of Virginia," 92.

26. "Orders Relating to Fitzhugh Lee while a Cadet at the USMA, 1 July 1852 to 1 July 1856," USMA; David Knapp Jr., *The Confederate Horsemen* (New York, 1966), 98–99; Nichols, *General Fitzhugh Lee,* 7.

27. "Orders Relating to Fitzhugh Lee while a Cadet," USMA; Deborah McKeon-Pogue, USMA Library, to the author, Jan. 16, 2003.

28. Knapp, *Confederate Horsemen,* 99; FL to Anna Maria Fitzhugh, Apr. 1, 1855, FL MSS, UV.

29. FL, "Speech of General Fitz Lee at A.N.V. Banquet, October 28th, 1875," *SHSP* 1 (1876): 99–100.

30. Nichols, *General Fitzhugh Lee,* 8; Daniel M. Lee to Beverly D. Munford, May 28, 1908, Beverly Bland Munford MSS, VHS.

CHAPTER TWO

1. "Fitzhugh Lee's Academic Record while a Cadet," USMA; George Washington Cullum, comp., *Biographical Register of the Officers and Graduates of the United States Military Academy at West Point, N.Y.,* 2 vols. (Boston, 1891), 2:672; Nichols, *General Fitzhugh Lee,* 8.

2. Rodenbough and Haskin, *Army of the United States,* 221; Thoburn, "Indian Fight in Ford County," 312–13.

3. Ibid.; *Thirty-sixth Annual Reunion of the Association of the Graduates of the United States Military Academy, at West Point, New York, June 13th, 1905* (Saginaw, Mich., 1905), 101; Freeman, *R. E. Lee,* 1:360–61.

4. Utley, *Frontiersmen in Blue,* 126.

5. Bayard, *Life of George Dashiell Bayard,* 94; Elizabeth Lindsay Lomax, *Leaves from an Old Washington Diary, 1854–1863,* ed. Lindsay Lomax Wood (New York, 1943), 54–57.

6. William W. Averell, *Ten Years in the Saddle: The Memoir of William Woods Averell, 1851–1862,* ed. Edward K. Eckert and Nicholas J. Amato (San Rafael, Calif., 1978), 54.

7. Thomas G. Tousey, *Military History of Carlisle and Carlisle Barracks* (Richmond, Va., 1939), 212.

8. Ibid., 210–14.

9. Readnor, "General Fitzhugh Lee," 9–10; Lomax, *Old Washington Diary,* 64.

10. Averell, *Ten Years in the Saddle,* 76.

11. Ibid., 75.

12. Ibid.

13. Ibid.

14. Readnor, "General Fitzhugh Lee," 9–10; Bayard, *Life of George Dashiell Bayard,* 94–95; George B. Price, *Across the Continent with the Fifth [U.S.] Cavalry* (New York, 1883), 483, 600.

15. Robert W. Frazer, *Forts of the West: Military Forts . . . West of the Mississippi River to 1898* (Norman, Okla., 1965), 152–53, 155.

16. FL to Anna Maria Fitzhugh, Sept. 15, 1858, FL MSS, UV.

17. FL to Maria Wheaton, Sept.—, 1858, FL MSS, UV.

18. FL to Anna Maria Fitzhugh, Sept. 1, 1859, FL MSS, UV.

19. FL to Anna Maria Fitzhugh, Sept. 15, 1858, FL MSS, UV.

20. Ibid.

21. Frazer, *Forts of the West,* 122–23; Arnold, *Jeff Davis's Own,* 70, 79–80; "Cavalry Fights with the Comanches," *Magazine of American History* 11 (1884): 172–73; Utley, *Frontiersmen in Blue,* 130–32.

22. Arnold, *Jeff Davis's Own,* 224–25, 231.

23. Thoburn, "Indian Fight in Ford County," 325.

24. FL to his parents, June 3, 1859, FL MSS, UV; FL to Anna Maria Fitzhugh, Sept. 1, 1859, FL MSS, UV.

25. Edmund Kirby Smith to Sidney S. Lee, May 14, 1859, FL MSS, UV; Bayard, *Life of George Dashiell Bayard,* 142–43.

26. Kinsley, *Fitzhugh Lee Sampler,* 33; Arnold, *Jeff Davis's Own,* 280.

27. Frazer, *Forts of the West,* 147; Nichols, *General Fitzhugh Lee,* 12; FL to Anna Maria Fitzhugh, Sept. 1, 1859, FL MSS, UV.

28. Francis MacDonnell, "The Confederate Spin on Winfield Scott and George Thomas," *Civil War History* 44 (1998): 260–61; J. William Jones, "Thomas and Lee—Historical Facts," *CV* 11 (1903): 559.

29. Frazer, *Forts of the West,* 146; Nichols, *General Fitzhugh Lee,* 12; Hayes, "Fitzhugh Lee as an Indian Fighter," 6.

30. FL to Edmund Kirby Smith, Jan. 20, 1860, FL MSS, UV; Nichols, *General Fitzhugh Lee,* 12–13; Hayes, "Fitzhugh Lee as an Indian Fighter," 6–8; Crimmins, "'Fitz' Lee Kills an Indian," 385–88; *San Antonio Ledger,* Jan. 27, 1860; Arnold, *Jeff Davis's Own,* 282–84.

31. FL to Edmund Kirby Smith, Jan. 20, 1860, FL MSS, UV; Crimmins, "'Fitz' Lee Kills an Indian," 388.

32. FL to "Cousin Anna," June 6, 1860, FL MSS, UV.

33. Lomax, *Old Washington Diary,* 131, 133.

34. James M. McPherson, *Ordeal by Fire: The Civil War and Reconstruction* (New York, 1982), 117–26.

35. Lomax, *Old Washington Diary,* 133.

36. Readnor, "General Fitzhugh Lee," 32, 34.

37. Tully McCrea, *Dear Belle: Letters from a Cadet & Officer to His Sweetheart, 1858–1865,* ed. Catherine S. Crary (Middletown, Conn., 1965), 88; James L. Morrison Jr., *"The Best School in the World": West Point, the Pre–Civil War Years, 1833–1866* (Kent, Ohio, 1986), 127–28.

38. McPherson, *Ordeal by Fire,* 127–37.

39. Cullum, *Biographical Register of Officers and Graduates,* 1:672; FL to his mother, Apr. 8, 1861, FL MSS, UV.

40. FL to his mother, Apr. 8, 1861, FL MSS, UV; Readnor, "General Fitzhugh Lee," 34; FL, Appointment as First Lieutenant, Confederate States Artillery, Apr. 3, 1861, FL MSS, UV.

41. *Thirty-sixth Annual Reunion . . . United States Military Academ,* 102; Lee, *Lee of Virginia,* 495.

42. McPherson, *Ordeal by Fire,* 140–45.

43. McCrea, *Dear Belle,* 88–89.

44. Ibid.; Joseph Pearson Farley, *West Point in the Early Sixties, with Incidents of the War* (Troy, N.Y., 1902), 71–72.

45. Mary A. R. C. Lee to REL, May 9, 1861, REL MSS, VHS; Nichols, *General Fitzhugh Lee,* 15; Freeman, *R. E. Lee,* 1:436–37, 636–37.

46. Lee Jr., *Recollections and Letters of Robert E. Lee,* 26–27; Freeman, *R. E. Lee,* 1:444.

CHAPTER THREE

1. Dale E. Floyd, ed., "I Have Severed My Connections with the North . . . ," *Manuscripts* 26 (1974): 140.

2. Ibid., 140–41.

3. *OR,* I, 2:37–44.

4. Nichols, *General Fitzhugh Lee,* 16. For information on the Confederacy's abortive Regular Army, see Richard P. Weinert, *The Confederate Regular Army* (Shippensburg, Pa., 1991).

5. Freeman, *R. E. Lee,* 1:462–63, 637–38; William C. Davis, *Battle at Bull Run: A History of the First Major Campaign of the Civil War* (Garden City, N.Y., 1977), 15–34.

6. Ezra J. Warner, *Generals in Gray: Lives of the Confederate Commanders* (Baton Rouge, 1959), 84–85; Campbell Brown, "General Ewell at Bull Run," *B&L* 1:260; *OR,* I, 2:536.

7. *OR,* I, 2:537; Davis, *Battle at Bull Run,* 90–95, 154–58.

8. Davis, *Battle at Bull Run,* 132–43; Joseph E. Johnston, *Narrative of Military Operations during the Civil War* (New York, 1874), 32–34.

9. *OR,* I, 2:479, 486, 491; Brown, "General Ewell at Bull Run," 260; Sidney S. Lee to "My Dear Carter," Sept. 30, 1864, FL MSS, UV.

10. *OR,* I, 2:536–37.

11. John J. Hennessy, *The First Battle of Manassas: An End to Innocence, July 18–21, 1861* (Lynchburg, Va., 1989), 68–121.

12. Davis, *Battle at Bull Run,* 243–44; Nichols, *General Fitzhugh Lee,* 17.

13. Nichols, *General Fitzhugh Lee,* 16; Mary Boykin Chesnut, *A Diary from Dixie,* ed. Ben Ames Williams (Boston, 1961), 107.

14. *OR,* I, 51, pt. 1:316; Special Order #289, CSA Adjutant and Inspector General's Office, Sept. 27, 1861, FL MSS, UV; Joseph E. Johnston to FL, Sept. 30, 1861, FL MSS, UV; FL to "Cary Invincibles," Nov. 4, 1861, FL MSS, VHS; *OR,* I, 5:181.

15. Hennessy, *First Battle of Manassas,* 80–82; Davis, *Battle at Bull Run,* 184, 205–08; William W. Blackford, *War Years with Jeb Stuart* (New York, 1945), 24–31.

16. *OR,* I, 51, pt. 1:320; Warner, *Generals in Gray,* 166–17; Emory M. Thomas, *Bold Dragoon: The Life of J. E. B. Stuart* (New York, 1986), 69, 83–84.

17. "'Grumble' Jones: A Personality Profile," *Civil War Times Illustrated* 7 (June 1968): 35–41; Thomas, *Bold Dragoon,* 68–76; Warner, *Generals in Gray,* 296–97; Edward G. Longacre, *Lee's Cavalrymen: A History of the Mounted Forces of the Army of Northern Virginia, 1861–1865* (Mechanicsburg, Pa., 2002), 1–7; Robert J. Driver Jr., *1st Virginia Cavalry* (Lynchburg, Va., 1991), 29; FL, "Speech of General Fitz Lee at A. N. V. Banquet," 99–100.

18. Thomas, *Bold Dragoon,* 91, 108; Longacre, *Lee's Cavalrymen,* 34, 73; Blackford, *War Years with Jeb Stuart,* 50–51.

19. John Singleton Mosby, *The Memoirs of Colonel John S. Mosby,* ed. Charles Wells Russell (Boston, 1917), 48–49; Robet L. Krick, *Lee's Colonels: A Biographical Register of the Field Officers of the Army of Northern Virginia* (Dayton, Ohio, 1979), 338.

20. Frank A. Bond, "Fitz Lee in [the] Army of Northern Virginia," *CV* 6 (1898): 421.

21. Ibid.; John Singleton Mosby, *The Letters of John S. Mosby,* ed. Adele H. Mitchell (n.p., 1986), 71.

22. Mosby, *Letters of John S. Mosby,* 71, 127. In his *Stuart's Cavalry in the Gettysburg Campaign* (New York, 1908), Mosby variously underrates and ignores Fitz Lee's contributions to Stuart's operations before and at Gettysburg.

23. Longacre, *Lee's Cavalrymen,* 56–60.

24. Blackford, *War Years with Jeb Stuart,* 50.

25. Ibid., 443.

26. Ibid., 51–54.

27. *OR,* I, 5:441–43.

28. Ibid., 5:443.

29. Ibid., 5:442; James Parker, "Mounted and Dismounted Action of Cavalry," *Journal of the Military Service Institution of the United States* 39 (1906): 381–82; William Y. Chalfant, *Cheyennes and Horse Soldiers: The 1857 Expedition and Battle of Solomon's Fork* (Norman, Okla., 1989), 192.

30. Mosby, *Letters of John S. Mosby,* 18; Bond, "Fitz Lee in Army of Northern Virginia," 421.

31. Bond, "Fitz Lee in Army of Northern Virginia," 421.

32. Ibid.

33. *OR,* I, 5:442–43.

34. Ibid., 5:439, 443.

CHAPTER FOUR

1. Longacre, *Lee's Cavalrymen,* 55, 63–64.

2. *OR,* I, 5:490–94; Henry B. McClellan, *Life and Campaigns of Maj. Gen. J. E. B. Stuart, Commander of the Cavalry of the Army of Northern Virginia* (Boston, 1885), 43–45.

3. C. S. Navy Dept. to Sidney S. Lee, Feb. 8, 1862, FL MSS, UV; *Official Records of the Union and Confederate Navies in the War of the Rebellion,* 2 series, 30 vols. (Washington, D.C., 1894–1922), I, 6:758; 7:749; 8:634–35.

4. Johnston, *Narrative of Military Operations,* 102–03; Blackford, *War Years with Jeb Stuart,* 59–60; Driver, *1st Virginia Cavalry,* 30.

5. Driver, *1st Virginia Cavalry,* 31.

6. Ibid., 30–31; *OR,* I, 11, pt. 3:406–07, 415–17.

7. *OR,* I, 11, pt. 3:415–16; Stephen W. Sears, *To the Gates of Richmond: The Peninsula Campaign* (New York, 1992), 34–36.

8. Sears, *To the Gates of Richmond,* 28–32; *Official Records of the Union and Confederate Navies,* I, 7:3–73.

9. Longacre, *Lee's Cavalrymen,* 71; Thomas, *Bold Dragoon,* 103–04.

10. Sears, *To the Gates of Richmond,* 37–45.

11. Douglas Southall Freman, *Lee's Lieutenants: A Study in Command,* 3 vols. (New York, 1942–44), 1:278n; Driver, *1st Virginia Cavalry,* 32.

12. Mosby, *Memoirs,* 109; Freeman, *Lee's Lieutenants,* 1:279–80.

13. Sears, *To the Gates of Richmond,* 61–66; Driver, *1st Virginia Cavalry,* 33.

14. *OR,* I, 11, pt. 1:423–46; Sears, *To the Gates of Richmond,* 68–84.

15. Sears, *To the Gates of Richmond,* 84–86; *OR,* I, 11, pt. 1:613–33.

16. William Clark Corson, *My Dear Jennie: A Collection of Love Letters from a Confederate Soldier to His Fiancée during the Period 1863–1865,* ed. Blake W. Corson Jr. (Richmond, Va., 1982), 77–78; John T. Thornton to his wife, May 10, 1862, Thornton MSS, UV; Henry W. Coons to his sister, May 18, 1862, Coons MSS, VHS.

17. *OR,* I, 11, pt. 1:637–50; Edward G. Longacre, *Lincoln's Cavalrymen: A History of the Mounted Forces of the Army of the Potomac, 1861–1865* (Mechanicsburg, Pa., 2000), 82–85.

18. Blackford, *War Years with Jeb Stuart,* 69–70; Ella Lonn, *Foreigners in the Confederacy* (Chapel Hill, N.C., 1940), 171–75.

19. Heros von Borcke, *Memoirs of the Confederate War for Independence,* 2 vols. (New York, 1938), 1:19–20.

20. Ibid.

21. Ibid.

22. *OR,* I, 11, pt. 1:933.

23. Ibid., 934–35, 939–41, 943–46; Sears, *To the Gates of Richmond,* 117–38.

24. Sears, *To the Gates of Richmond,* 142–44; *OR,* I, 11, pt. 1:940, 992–94.

25. *OR,* I, 11, pt. 3:569; Freeman, *R. E. Lee,* 2:72–79.

26. Freeman, *R. E. Lee,* 1:554–600, 607–31.

27. J. E. B. Stuart to Samuel Cooper, June 7, 1862, FL MSS, UV.

28. Freeman, *R. E. Lee,* 1:346, 352, 393–401; Thomas, *Bold Dragoon,* 28–29, 54–59.

29. J. E. B. Stuart to Robert E. Lee, June 4, 1862, Stuart MSS, Henry E. Huntington Library.

30. *OR,* I, 11, pt. 1:1036.

31. Freeman, *R. E. Lee,* 2:97; *OR,* I, 11, pt. 3:590–91.

32. *OR,* pt. 1:1036, 1042–44; McClellan, *Life and Campaigns of Stuart,* 53–54.

33. Edwin C. Bearss, "'. . . Into the very jaws of the enemy . . .': Jeb Stuart's Ride around McClellan," in *The Peninsula Campaign of 1862: Yorktown to the Seven Days,* ed. William J. Miller, 3 vols. (Campbell, Calif., 1997), 1:81–85.

34. *OR,* I, 11, pt. 1:1036; McClellan, *Life and Campaigns of Stuart,* 54; Freeman, *Lee's Lieutenants,* 1:294.

35. Bearss, "Into the very jaws of the enemy," 84–89; John Esten Cooke, *Wearing of the Gray: Being Personal Portraits, Scenes and Adventures of the War* (Baton Rouge, 1997), 168.

36. *OR,* I, 11, pt. 1:1037, 1043–44; McClellan, *Life and Campaigns of Stuart,* 55–57.

37. *OR,* I, 11, pt. 1:1037; W. T. Robins, "Stuart's Ride around McClellan," *B&L* 2:272.

38. Robins, "Stuart's Ride around McClellan," 2:272; *OR,* I, 11, pt. 1:1037.

39. *OR,* I, 11, pt. 1:1037–38; McClellan, *Life and Campaigns of Stuart,* 57–58; Mosby, *Letters of John S. Mosby,* 221–22.

40. Robins, "Stuart's Ride around McClellan," 272–73; McClellan, *Life and Campaigns of Stuart,* 60–61; Bearss, "Into the very jaws of the enemy," 99–107.

41. Bearss, "Into the very jaws of the enemy," 117–19; Cooke, *Wearing of the Gray,* 174–75.

42. Cooke, *Wearing of the Gray,* 175–77; *OR,* I, 11, pt. 1:1039; McClellan, *Life and Campaigns of Stuart,* 63–64; Robins, "Stuart's Ride around McClellan," 273–74.

43. *OR,* I, 11, pt. 1:1039; Bearss, "Into the very jaws of the enemy," 120–24; Cooke, *Wearing of the Gray,* 178–79.

44. *OR,* I, 11, pt. 1:1039–40, 1043; McClellan, *Life and Campaigns of Stuart,* 65–66; 136–37; Robins, "Stuart's Ride around McClellan," 275.

45. *OR,* I, 11, pt. 1:1043.

CHAPTER FIVE

1. *OR,* I, 11, pt. 1:1041.

2. Freeman, *Lee's Lieutenants,* 1:395–410; Sears, *To the Gates of Richmond,* 97–103, 110, 112, 157–58.

3. Freeman, *R. E. Lee,* 2:102–12.

4. Sears, *To the Gates of Richmond,* 183–89; *OR,* I, 11, pt. 2:513, 525, 528; McClellan, *Life and Campaigns of Stuart,* 72–73; George W. Beale, *A Lieutenant of Cavalry in Lee's Army* (Boston, 1918), 33–34.

5. *OR,* I, 11, pt. 2:513, 526; Robert S. Hudgins II, *Recollections of an Old Dominion Dragoon: The Civil War Experiences of Sgt. Robert S. Hudgins, II, Company B, 3rd Virginia Cavalry,* ed. Garland C. Hudgins and Richard B. Kleese (Orange, Va., 1993), 60; Edward G. Longacre, *Gentleman and Soldier: A Biography of Wade Hampton III* (Nashville, Tenn., 2003), 36–48.

6. *OR,* I, 11, pt. 1:1041; pt. 2:513–14, 552; Blackford, *War Years with Jeb Stuart,* 71.

7. *OR,* I, 11, pt. 2:514.

8. Ibid.; McClellan, *Life and Campaigns of Stuart,* 73–74.

9. *OR,* I, 11, pt. 2:490, 514.

10. Ibid., 514–15; Blackford, *War Years with Jeb Stuart,* 72–73.

11. *OR,* I, 11, pt. 2:515; Thomas, *Bold Dragoon,* 133–34.

12. Longacre, *Lincoln's Cavalrymen,* 91–92.

13. Freeman, *R. E. Lee,* 2:159–61.

14. *OR,* I, 11, pt. 2:515–16, 524, 528; McClellan, *Life and Campaigns of Stuart,* 76–77.

15. *OR,* I, 11, pt. 2:516; Sears, *To the Gates of Richmond,* 104; Mary Bandy Daughtry, *Gray Cavalier: The Life and Wars of General W. H. F. "Rooney" Lee* (New York, 2002), 79–81.

16. *OR,* I, 11, pt. 2:516–17; McClellan, *Life and Campaigns of Stuart,* 78.

17. *OR,* I, 11, pt. 2:517–18; Charles R. Chewning diary, June 30, 1862, Handley Regional Library.

18. Freeman, *Lee's Lieutenants,* 1:635–37; Sears, *To the Gates of Richmond,* 308–36.

19. *OR,* I, 11, pt. 2:519–20, 530–31; Freeman, *Lee's Lieutenants,* 1:641–43; McClellan, *Life and Campaigns of Stuart,* 82–85; FL, *General Lee* (New York, 1894), 165–66; Edward Porter Alexander, *Fighting for the Confederacy: The Personal Recollections of General Edward Porter Alexander,* ed. Gary A. Gallagher (Chapel Hill, N.C., 1989), 114–15.

20. *OR,* I, 11, pt. 2:521; Nichols, *General Fitzhugh Lee,* 31.

21. FL, *General Lee,* 172; Francis B. Heitman, comp., *Historical Register and Dictionary of the United States Army . . . ,* 2 vols. (Washington, D.C., 1903), 1:311.

22. J. E. B. Stuart to FL, July 28, 1862, FL MSS, UV.

23. *OR,* I, 11, pt. 3:657; 12, pt. 3:920; Manly Wade Wellman, *Giant in Gray: A Biography of Wade Hampton of South Carolina* (New York, 1949), 84.

24. Wellman, *Giant in Gray,* 81–85; Longacre, *Gentleman and Soldier,* 80–83.

25. Longacre, *Gentleman and Soldier,* 83–84; Cooke, *Wearing of the Gray,* 47–52.

26. *OR,* I, 11, pt. 3:657; McClellan, *Life and Campaigns of Stuart,* 86.

27. John J. Hennessy, *Return to Bull Run: The Campaign and Battle of Second Manassas* (New York, 1993), 21–22.

28. *OR,* I, 11, pt. 3:652, 657; Robert E. L. Krick, *Staff Officers in Gray: A Biographical Register of the Staff Officers in the Army of Northern Virginia* (Chapel Hill, N.C.,

2003), 199, 388–89; Daughtry, *Gray Cavalier,* 44–47; Freeman, *R. E. Lee,* 2:258–67; Hennessy, *Return to Bull Run,* 5–22.

29. Hennessy, *Return to Bull Run,* 23–26; Nichols, *General Fitzhugh Lee,* 33.

30. Hennessy, *Return to Bull Run,* 28–30.

31. *OR,* I, 12, pt. 2:119; 51, pt. 2:611; Longacre, *Gentleman and Soldier,* 88–91; Wade Hampton to Lafayette McLaws, Aug. 18, 1862, Rives Family MSS, VHS.

32. *OR,* I, 12, pt. 2:120.

33. Ibid., 119–21.

CHAPTER SIX

1. Blackford, *War Years with Jeb Stuart,* 97; *OR,* I, 12, pt. 2:550n, 725; REL, *The Wartime Papers of Robert E. Lee,* ed. Clifford Dowdey and Louis H. Manarin (Boston, 1961), 255.

2. *OR,* I, 12, pt. 2:726; Lee, *General Lee,* 183.

3. *OR,* I, 12, pt. 2:725–26; Cooke, *Wearing of the Gray,* 196–99; McClellan, *Life and Campaigns of Stuart,* 89–90; Mosby, *Memoirs,* 136–37; Hennessy, *Return to Bull Run,* 42–49.

4. *OR,* I, 12, pt. 2:726.

5. Ibid., 2:726–29; McClellan, *Life and Campaigns of Stuart,* 92; Daniel A. Grimsley, *Battles in Culpeper County, Virginia, 1861–1865* (Culpeper, Va., 1900), 3; George M. Neese, *Three Years in the Confederate Horse Artillery* (New York, 1911), 96; John T. Thornton to his wife, Aug. 25, 1862, Thornton MSS.

6. REL, *Lee's Dispatches: Unpublished Letters of General Robert E. Lee, C. S. A., to Jefferson Davis and the War Department of the Confederate States of America,* ed. Douglas Southall Freeman and Grady McWhiney (New York, 1957), 42–43.

7. Warner, *Generals in Gray,* 259–60; J. E. B. Stuart to Flora Cooke Stuart, Oct. 21, 1861, Stuart MSS, Robert W. Woodruff Library, Emory University; *OR,* I, 12, pt. 2:726.

8. *OR,* I, 12, pt. 2:727.

9. Ibid., 726–28, 745–46; McClellan, *Life and Campaigns of Stuart,* 92–93.

10. Ibid., 93; *OR,* I, 12, pt. 2:730; Hennessy, *Return to Bull Run,* 62–67; Charles M. Blackford and Susan Leigh Blackford, *Letters from Lee's Army . . . ,* ed. Charles Minor Blackford III (New York, 1947), 119.

11. *OR,* I, 12, pt. 2:730–31; Blackford, *War Years with Jeb Stuart,* 99–100; Freeman, *R. E. Lee,* 2:292–93.

12. *OR,* I, 12, pt. 2:731; Blackford, *War Years with Jeb Stuart,* 100–108; B. J. Haden, *Reminiscences of J. E. B. Stuart's Cavalry . . .* (Charlottesville, Va., ca. 1890), 15; Neese, *Confederate Horse Artillery,* 101; McClellan, *Life and Campaigns of Stuart,* 94–95; Hennessy, *Return to Bull Run,* 77–78; REL, *Wartime Papers,* 262.

13. W. Roy Mason, "Marching on Manassas," *B&L* 2:528.

14. *OR*, I, 12, pt. 2:732; pt. 3:942; Freeman, *R. E. Lee*, 2:297n; Freeman, *Lee's Lieutenants*, 2:71; Hennessy, *Return to Bull Run*, 80–81.

15. *OR*, I, 12, pt. 2:732–34, 747–48; McClellan, *Life and Campaigns of Stuart*, 95–96; Blackford, *War Years with Jeb Stuart*, 108–15; Hennessy, *Return to Bull Run*, 92–94; Charles Marshall, *An Aide-de-Camp of Lee: Being the Papers of Colonel Charles Marshall . . .* , ed. Sir Frederick Maurice (Boston, 1927), 129; James Hardeman Stuart diary, Aug. 24, 1862, Mississippi Deptartment of Archives and History; W. B. Taliaferro, "Jackson's Raid Around Pope," *B&L* 2:502.

16. Taliaferro, "Jackson's Raid Around Pope," 503; *OR*, I, 12, pt. 2:643–44, 720–25, 734, 739, 741–43; McClellan, *Life and Campaigns of Stuart*, 96–102; Hennessy, *Return to Bull Run*, 113–15.

17. *OR*, I, 12, pt. 2:554–55, 734–35, 748–50; McClellan, *Life and Campaigns of Stuart*, 103; Janet Hewett et al., comps., *Supplement to the Official Records of the Union and Confederate Armies*, 3 series, 99 vols. (Wilmington, N.C., 1994–2001), I, 2:597; Taliaferro, "Jackson's Raid Around Pope," 504.

18. *OR*, I, 12, pt. 2:739; Nichols, *General Fitzhugh Lee*, 37; Kenneth L. Stiles, *4th Virginia Cavalry* (Lynchburg, Va., 1985), 18–19; Daughtry, *Gray Cavalier*, 90.

19. Hewett et al., *Supplement to Official Records*, I, 2:597; Taliaferro, "Jackson's Raid Around Pope," 504.

20. Hennessy, *Return to Bull Run*, 143–52, 168–90.

21. Ibid., 429–34.

22. Ibid., 362–80, 448–51; *OR*, I, 12, pt. 2:737–38, 743–44, 751; Blackford, *War Years with Jeb Stuart*, 134; Longacre, *Gentleman and Soldier*, 92–93.

23. *FL, General Lee*, 193–94; *OR*, I, 12, pt. 3:809–10; *Thirty-sixth Annual Reunion . . . United States Military Academy*, 103–04; Heitman, *Historical Register and Dictionary*, 529.

24. *OR*, I, 19, pt. 1:144; Freeman, *R. E. Lee*, 2:350–53.

25. *OR*, I, 19, pt. 1:814, 822; pt. 2:595; James Ewell Brown Stuart, *The Letters of Major General James E. B. Stuart*, ed. Adele H. Mitchell (n.p., 1990), 266; R. Channing Price to his mother, Sept. 5 and 10, 1862, Price MSS, UNC; McClellan, *Life and Campaigns of Stuart*, 109–10; Stephen W. Sears, *Landscape Turned Red: The Battle of Antietam* (New Haven, Conn., 1983), 2–15.

26. *OR*, I, 19, pt. 1:814–15.

27. Ibid., 815; Blackford, *War Years with Jeb Stuart*, 140–42; Thomas, *Bold Dragoon*, 164–65.

28. *OR*, I, 19, pt. 1:815–19.

29. Ibid., 608, 817, 1052; McClellan, *Life and Campaigns of Stuart*, 117–19; Daniel H. Hill, "The Battle of South Mountain, or Boonsboro'," *B&L* 2:561–81; *FL, General Lee*, 205; Daughtry, *Gray Cavalier*, 92–94.

30. Freeman, *R. E. Lee,* 2:378–83; *OR,* I, 19, pt. 1:819–20; McClellan, *Life and Campaigns of Stuart,* 123; Blackford, *War Years with Jeb Stuart,* 148; R. Channing Price to his mother, Sept. 18, 1862, Price MSS, UNC.

31. *OR,* I, 19, pt. 1:819–20, 874, 971, 1010; McClellan, *Life and Campaigns of Stuart,* 127–30; Robert E. L. Krick, "Defending Lee's Flank: J. E. B. Stuart, John Pelham, and Confederate Artillery on Nicodemus Hights," in *The Antietam Campaign,* ed. Gary A. Gallagher, 192–222 (Chapel Hill, N.C., 1999); John G. Walker, "Sharpsburg," *B&L* 2:679–80; Robert T. Hubard memoirs, 57, William R. Perkins Library, Duke University; R. Channing Price to his mother, Sept. 18, 1862, Price MSS, UNC; Sears, *Landscape Turned Red,* 190–91, 274–76, 291; William R. Carter diary, Sept. 17, 1862, LV; Beale, *Lieutenant of Cavalry,* 48–50.

32. *OR,* I, 19, pt. 1:820.

CHAPTER SEVEN

1. McClellan, *Life and Campaigns of Stuart,* 132.

2. Ibid., 133; *OR,* I, 19, pt. 1:151, 820.

3. Blackford, *War Years with Jeb Stuart,* 154–55; von Borcke, *Memoirs,* 1:289–92.

4. REL to Charlotte Wickham Lee, Oct. 19, 1862, and John Bolling to "Dear Sir," Sept. 24, 1862, Bolling MSS, VHS; William R. Carter diary, Sept. 25, 1862; Robert T. Hubard memoirs, 60.

5. *OR,* I, 19, pt. 2:13–14, 145; 21:1014–15, 1019–21; 51, pt. 2:647; von Borcke, *Memoirs,* 1:273–76; Blackford, *War Years with Jeb Stuart,* 162; Freeman, *Lee's Lieutenants,* 2:284–309; Longacre, *Lee's Cavalrymen,* 141–50; R. L. T. Beale, *History of the Ninth Virginia Cavalry in the War between the States* (Richmond, Va., 1899), 54; Charles R. Chewning diary, Nov. 19, 1862.

6. *OR,* I, 21:544; Daughtry, *Gray Cavalier,* 103.

7. *OR,* I, 21:84–95, 550–55; Freeman, *R. E. Lee,* 2:443–66.

8. *OR,* I, 21:112, 142 and n, 144, 547, 553, 631; R. Channing Pice to his mother, Dec. 17, 1862, Price MSS, UNC; McClellan, *Life and Campaigns of Stuart,* 195; Blackford, *War Years with Jeb Stuart,* 102–93; Beale, *Ninth Virginia Cavalry,* 56–57; Jennings Cropper Wise, *The Long Arm of Lee; or, The History of the Artillery of the Army of Northern Virginia . . . ,* 2 vols. (Lynchburg, Va., 1915), 1:382–85; A. Wilson Greene, "Opportunity to the South: Meade versus Jackson at Fredericksburg," *Civil War History* 33 (1987): 303.

9. *OR,* I, 21:13–16, 689–97; 51, pt. 2:653; McClellan, *Life and Campaigns of Stuart,* 187–88; Wade Hampton III et al., *Family Letters of Three Wade Hamptons, 1782–1901,* ed. Charles E. Cauthen (Columbia, S.C., 1953), 89–90; Longacre, *Gentleman and Soldier,* 114–18.

10. *OR,* I, 21:731, 735, 737, 741, 1075–76; McClellan, *Life and Campaigns of Stuart,* 197; Freeman, *Lee's Lieutenants,* 2:399 and n, 400 and n; Edward G. Longacre, "Stuart's Dumfries Raid," *Civil War Times Illustrated* 15 (July 1976): 18–22.

11. *OR,* I, 21:731–32, 738–39; McClellan, *Life and Campaigns of Stuart,* 198; Robert T. Hubard memoirs, 63–64.

12. *OR,* I, 21:732–33, 736–37.

13. Ibid., 733, 736–37, 739–41; McClellan, *Life and Campaigns of Stuart,* 199–201; Freeman, *Lee's Lieutenants,* 2:402–03; U. R. Brooks, *Butler and His Cavalry in the War of Secession, 1861–1865* (Columbia, S.C., 1909), 88; R. Channing Price to his sister, Jan. 20, 1863, Price MSS, UNC.

14. *OR,* I, 21:733–34, 737.

15. Ibid., 21:734, 739; McClellan, *Life and Campaigns of Stuart,* 201–02; R. Channing Price to his sister, Jan. 20, 1863, Price MSS, UNC; Krick, *Staff Officers in Gray,* 199.

16. *OR,* I, 21:734; Freeman, *Lee's Lieutenants,* 2:405–06.

17. Freeman, *Lee's Lieutenants,* 406; McClellan, *Life and Campaigns of Stuart,* 202.

18. Thomas Lawrence Connelly, *Army of the Heartland: The Army of Tennessee, 1861–1862* (Baton Rouge, 1967), 205–42, 256–67; Thomas Lawrence Connelly, *Autumn of Glory: The Army of Tennessee, 1862–1865* (Baton Rouge, 1971), 44–68.

19. Edwin Cole Bearss, *The Campaign for Vicksburg,* 3 vols. (Dayton, Ohio, 1985–86), 1:155–229, 307–47.

20. "The Second Virginia Regiment of Cavalry, C. S. A.," *SHSP* 16 (1888): 354–56; Driver, *1st Virginia Cavalry,* 54; Stephen W. Sears, *Chancellorsville* (Boston, 1996), 40.

21. Mrs. Burton Harrison, *Recollections Grave and Gay* (New York, 1912), 97–99, 101, 114–15.

22. REL, *Wartime Papers,* 409.

23. *OR,* I, 25, pt. 1:25; McClellan, *Life and Campaigns of Stuart,* 204.

24. *OR,* I, 25, pt. 1:25–26; J. E. B. Stuart to John R. Cooke, Feb. 28, 1863, Cooke MSS, VHS; Robert T. Hubard memoirs, 65–66; William R. Carter diary, Feb. 25, 1863.

25. *OR,* I, 25, pt. 1:21–25; Longacre, *Lincoln's Cavalrymen,* 130–32.

26. Longacre, *Lincoln's Cavalrymen,* 133; Walter H. Hebert, *Fighting Joe Hooker* (Indianapolis, 1944), 186.

27. REL, *Wartime Papers,* 402–03; *OR,* III, 3:10–11; Sears, *Chancellorsville,* 111.

28. *OR,* I, 25, pt. 2:654.

29. Ibid., pt. 1:44; John Singleton Mosby, "A Bit of Partisan Service," *B&L* 3:149–51.

30. John Singleton Mosby to Joseph Bryan, Jan. 30, 1904, Bryan MSS, VHS.

31. Ibid.

32. *OR,* I, 25, pt. 1:60–61.

33. Ibid., 61.

34. Ibid., 48–49, 61; McClellan, *Life and Campaigns of Stuart,* 209; W. H. Ware, *Battle of Kelly's Ford, Fought March 17, 1863* (Newport News, Va., 1922), 6; Freeman, *Lee's Lieutenants,* 2:457–60.

35. William R. Carter diary, Mar. 17, 1863.

36. Ibid.; *OR,* I, 25, pt. 1:59; McClellan, *Life and Campaigns of Stuart,* 210–11; Hudgins, *Old Dominion Dragoon,* 65; Thaddeus Fitzhugh memoirs, 19–20, MC.

37. *OR,* I, 25, pt. 1:50, 56–57; Blackford, *War Years with Jeb Stuart,* 201–02; Cooke, *Wearing of the Gray,* 116–19; Ware, *Battle of Kelly's Ford,* 7; R. Channing Price to his mother, Mar. 21, 1863, Price MSS, UNC.

38. *OR,* I, 25, pt. 1:50, 54–55; McClellan, *Life and Campaigns of Stuart,* 212–13.

39. McClellan, *Life and Campaigns of Stuart,* 213–14; Robert T. Hubard memoirs, 66–67.

40. *OR,* I, 25, pt. 1:61.

41. Ibid.; Longacre, *Lincoln's Cavalrymen,* 137–38.

42. *OR,* I, 25, pt. 1:59–60; pt. 2:148; John Bigelow Jr., *The Campaign of Chancellorsville: A Strategic and Tactical Study* (New Haven, Conn., 1910), 101–03.

CHAPTER EIGHT

1. *OR,* I, 25, pt. 1:58–59.

2. Ibid., 64.

3. Ibid., pt. 2:622, 652–53, 685–86, 721; III, 3:10–11; Sears, *Chancellorsville,* 111, 125.

4. Sears, *Chancellorsville,* 118–21.

5. *OR,* I, 25, pt. 1:85, 87–89; pt. 2:725, 730; REL, *Wartime Papers,* 434–36; McClellan, *Life and Campaigns of Stuart,* 219–20.

6. *OR,* I, 25, pt. 1:1045, 1057–58, 1065; Sears, *Chancellorsville,* 131–32, 154–76; Lee, *Wartime Papers,* 444–45; McClellan, *Life and Campaigns of Stuart,* 226.

7. *OR,* I, 25, pt. 1:796–97, 1045–46; Freeman, *R. E. Lee,* 2:509–16.

8. *OR,* I, 25, pt. 1:1045–47, 1098; Sears, *Chancellorsville,* 162, 166–67, 172–73, 182, 254, 367–70, 392, 438–40; Daughtry, *Gray Cavalier,* 116–20.

9. *OR,* I, 25, pt. 1:1046–47; McClellan, *Life and Campaigns of Stuart,* 227–30; Sears, *Chancellorsville,* 175–76; Haden, *Reminiscences of J. E. B. Stuart's Cavalry,* 18–19.

10. *OR,* I, 25, pt. 1:669, 728, 774, 778–79, 1047; McClellan, *Life and Campaigns of Stuart,* 227–30; Sears, *Chancellorsville,* 175–76; Alfred Pleasonton, "The Successes and Failures of Chancellorsville," *B&L* 3:175; Hewett et al., *Supplement to Official Records,* I, 4:678–79.

11. *OR,* I, 25, pt. 1:796–97; Freeman, *R. E. Lee,* 2:508–19.

12. FL, "Chancellorsville—Address of General Fitzhugh Lee before the Virginia Division, A. N. V. Association, October 29th, 1879," *SHSP* 7 (1879): 563.

13. Ibid., 569–71; Sears, *Chancellorsville,* 238–43.

14. FL, "Chancellorsville," 572.

15. Ibid.

16. Ibid.

17. Ibid., 573.

18. Ibid.; McClellan, *Life and Campaigns of Stuart,* 233.

19. *Thirty-sixth Annual Reunion . . . United States Military Academy,* 105.

20. Sears, *Chancellorsville,* 275–366; *OR,* I, 25, pt. 1:798–99.

21. Freeman, *Lee's Lieutenants,* 2:563–69, 635–43, 667–82.

22. Sears, *Chancellorsville,* 308–39.

23. Ibid., 298–99, 314–16, 324–25, 330; *OR,* I, 25, pt. 1:887–88; Thomas, *Bold Dragoon,* 210–13.

24. *OR,* I, 25, pt. 1:800–803; Sears, *Chancellorsville,* 378–86.

25. FL, "Chancellorsville," 580; *OR,* I, 25, pt. 1:889; FL to "General," May 3, 1863, Compiled Service Records of Confederate General and Staff Officers, Record Group 109, National Archives.

26. Sears, *Chancellorsville,* 420–22.

27. Edwin B. Coddington, *The Gettysburg Campaign: A Study in Command* (New York, 1968), 5–7.

28. *OR,* I, 25, pt. 2:789.

29. Ibid., 2:788–89; Longacre, *Lincoln's Cavalrymen,* 149–51.

30. Robert B. Jones to his wife, June 2, 1863, Jones MSS, VHS.

31. *OR,* I, 25, 789–90, 819–21, 825–26, 836, 848.

32. McClellan, *Life and Campaigns of Stuart,* 261–62; Freeman, *Lee's Lieutenants,* 3:2; Blackford, *War Years with Jeb Stuart,* 211–12; Hudgins, *Old Dominion Dragoon,* 75–76; Neese, *Confederate Horse Artillery,* 166–70; G. Moxley Sorrel, *Recollections of a Confederate Staff Officer* (New York, 1905), 161; John N. Opie, *A Rebel Cavalryman with Lee, Stuart, and Jackson* (Chicago, 1899), 145–46.

33. Millard K. and Dean M. Bushong, *Fightin' Tom Rosser, C. S. A.* (Shippensburg, Pa., 1983), 42–43; Thomas L. Rosser Jr. to Douglas Southall Freeman, May 17, 1938, Freeman MSS, Library of Congress; Halsey Wigfall to anon., June 4, 1863, Wigfall MSS.

34. FL to Thomas L. Rosser, Jan. 10, 1889, FL MSS, UV; *OR,* I, 27, pt. 2:680, 687.

35. *OR,* I, 27, pt. 2:679–83, 737–39.

36. Ibid., 682–83; Daughtry, *Gray Cavalier,* 131–36, 141–46.

37. *OR,* I, 27, pt. 2:683, 737–38; McClellan, *Life and Campaigns of Stuart,* 283; Jeffry D. Wert, "His Unhonored Service," *Civil War Times Illustrated* 24 (June 1985): 32.

38. *OR,* I, 27, pt. 2:293, 295, 305–06, 313, 340; Freeman, *Lee's Lieutenants,* 3:20; Mosby, *Stuart's Cavalry in the Gettysburg Campaign,* 59; Franklin M. Myers, *The Comanches: A History of White's Battalion, Virginia Cavalry, Laurel Brig., Hampton['s] Div., A. N. V., C. S. A.* (Baltimore, 1871), 103–04, 188; Wilbur S. Nye, *Here Come the Rebels!* (Baton Rouge, 1965), 165.

39. *OR,* I, 27, pt. 3:81–82, 87–89; Hebert, *Fighting Joe Hooker,* 237.

40. *OR,* I, 27, pt. 2:687–91, 739–48, 758–59; Longacre, *Lee's Cavalrymen,* 197–202.

41. *OR,* I, 27, pt. 1:171–72, 193; pt. 2:692, 915; pt. 3:913, 915, 923; Marshall, *Aide-de-Camp of Lee,* 202–02, 205–06, 208; Freeman, *Lee's Lieutenants,* 3:41 and n, 47–48, 550; Coddington, *Gettysburg Campaign,* 107–08; Randolph H. McKim, "The Confederate Cavalry in the Gettysburg Campaign," *Journal of the Military Service Institution of the United States* 46 (1910): 418; J. E. B. Stuart to Beverly H. Robertson, June 24, 1863, Stuart MSS, Gilder Lehrman Collection; John Singleton Mosby, "Confederate Cavalry in the Gettysburg Campaign," *B&L* 3:251–52; John Singleton Mosby, *Mosby's War Reminiscences and Stuart's Cavalry Campaigns* (Boston, 1887), 178–82.

42. *OR,* I, 27, pt. 2:692–94; pt. 3:309, 318, 376–77; McClellan, *Life and Campaigns of Stuart,* 318–24, 336; Blackford, *War Years with Jeb Stuart,* 223–25; Cooke, *Wearing of the Gray,* 226–36; Freeman, *Lee's Lieutenants,* 3:58–66; McKim, "Confederate Cavalry in the Gettysburg Campaign," 420; Beale, *Ninth Virginia Cavalry,* 78–80; William R. Carter diary, June 25–28, 1863; Beale, *Lieutenant of Cavalry,* 112–13.

43. *OR,* I, 27, pt. 2:694–95.

44. Ibid., 202, 694–95; pt. 3:396, 403–04; Cooke, *Wearing of the Gray,* 239; Nye, *Here Come the Rebels,* 319–20.

45. *OR,* I, 27, pt. 2:695–96; McClellan, *Life and Campaigns of Stuart,* 328; Blackford, *War Years with Jeb Stuart,* 225–26; *Encounter at Hanover: Prelude to Gettysburg* (Hanover, Pa., 1963), 22, 24, 61, 66, 93.

46. *OR,* I, 27, pt. 1:992, 1008–09, 1011–12, 1018; pt. 2:696; McClellan, *Life and Campaigns of Stuart,* 328–29; Blackford, *War Years with Jeb Stuart,* 226–27; Cooke, *Wearing of the Gray,* 241–42; William R. Carter diary, June 30, 1863.

47. *OR,* I, 27, pt. 2:220, 467–68, 696; McClellan, *Life and Campaigns of Stuart,* 330; Freeman, *Lee's Lieutenants,* 3:71, 136–37; Mosby, *Stuart's Cavalry in the Gettysburg Campaign,* 183 and n, 184n; Beale, *Lieutenant of Cavalry,* 114; William R. Carter diary, July 1, 1863.

48. *OR,* I, 27, pt. 2:224, 696–97; FL to his mother, July 26, 1863, FL MSS, UV; McClellan, *Life and Campaigns of Stuart,* 331; Nye, *Here Come the Rebels,* 325; Readnor, "General Fitzhugh Lee," 54–55.

49. *OR,* I, 27, pt. 2:221, 697; Cooke, *Wearing of the Gray,* 245; Freeman, *Lee's Lieutenants,* 3:137–38.

CHAPTER NINE

1. Hudgins, *Old Dominion Dragoon,* 82.

2. Edward G. Longacre, *The Cavalry at Gettysburg: A Tactical Study of Mounted Operations during the Civil War's Pivotal Campaign, 9 June–14 July 1863* (Rutherford, N.J., 1986), 180–92.

3. Ibid., 198–201; *OR,* I, 27, pt. 1:992, 999; pt. 2:221, 224, 497, 504, 697, 724; McClellan, *Life and Campaigns of Stuart,* 330–31; William R. Carter diary, July 2, 1863; Wellman, *Giant in Gray,* 115–16.

4. *OR,* I, 27, pt. 2:307, 321, 697, 699; Coddington, *Gettysburg Campaign,* 207, 520; William L. Royall, *Some Reminiscences* (New York, 1909), 25; J. G. Harbord, "The History of the Cavalry of the Army of Northern Virginia," *Journal of the United States Cavalry Association* 14 (1904): 456–57.

5. *OR,* I, 27, pt. 2:697; McClellan, *Life and Campaigns of Stuart,* 338–39.

6. *OR,* I, 27, pt. 1:956, 1050; pt. 2:697–98; McClellan, *Life and Campaigns of Stuart,* 339–40; William E. Miller, "The Cavalry Battle Near Gettysburg," *B&L* 3:400–403.

7. *OR,* I, 27, pt. 1:956–57; pt. 2:697–98; McClellan, *Life and Campaigns of Stuart,* 339–40; Miller, "Cavalry Battle Near Gettysburg," 400–404; Hudgins, *Old Dominion Dragoon,* 82, 84.

8. *OR,* I, 27, pt. 2:697, 724.

9. Ibid., pt. 1:1051; pt. 2:322, 698, 724–25; McClellan, *Life and Campaigns of Stuart,* 338–39; Miller, "Cavalry Battle Near Gettysburg," 404; Longacre, *Cavalry at Gettysburg,* 230–31, 237–39; Cooke, *Wearing of the Gray,* 247; Wellman, *Giant in Gray,* 118–20; Hampton et al., *Letters of Three Wade Hamptons,* 94.

10. *OR,* I, 27, pt. 2:322, 699; John D. Imboden, "Confederate Retreat from Gettysburg," *B&L* 3:420–21.

11. Imboden, "Confederate Retreat from Gettysburg," 422–24; Longacre, *Cavalry at Gettysburg,* 245–46.

12. Imboden, "Confederate Retreat from Gettysburg," 425; John A. Dahlgren, *Memoir of Ulric Dahlgren* (Philadelphia, 1872), 166.

13. *OR,* I, 27, pt. 2:214, 280, 437, 703; pt. 3:547–49; Coddington, *Gettysburg Campaign,* 552; Robert J. Driver and H. E. Howard, *2nd Virginia Cavalry* (Lynchburg, Va., 1995), 93.

14. *OR,* I, 27, pt. 1:917, 977–78, 1059; pt. 3:582, 584, 593, 602, 621; Coddington, *Gettysburg Campaign,* 813n–14n.

15. Imboden, "Confederate Retreat from Gettysburg," 425–27; *OR,* I, 27, pt. 2:214, 280, 437, 703; pt. 3:347–49; Coddington, *Gettysburg Campaign,* 552, 554.

16. Robert T. Hubard memoirs, 78–79.

17. *OR,* I, 27, pt. 1:929, 935, 940–41, 958, 1007; pt. 2:703–04.

18. Ibid., pt. 1:146, 663–64, 925–26, 929, 936, 941–42, 1033; pt. 2:398–99, 704; pt. 3:621.

19. Ibid., pt. 1:118, 664, 988–89, 929, 971, 996, 999–1000, 1016–17; pt. 2:226, 246, 704–05, 753, 762, 1008; pt. 3:649, 657–58, 664–65, 669, 675, 851, 657–58, 660, 664, 987–88, 994–95, 998; REL to J. E. B. Stuart, July 11, 1863, Stuart MSS, Henry E. Huntington Library; REL to John D. Imboden, July 13, 1863, Lee MSS, Gilder Lehrman Collection; Robert T. Hubard memoirs, 78; Coddington, *Gettysburg Campaign,* 566–67.

20. *OR,* I, 27, pt. 2:327, 705; pt. 3:1001; REL to J. E. B. Stuart, July 13, 1863, Stuart MSS, Henry E. Huntington Library; Robert T. Hubard memoirs, 79; Neese, *Confederate Horse Artillery,* 199; Blackford, *War Years with Jeb Stuart,* 234–35.

21. *OR,* I, 27, pt. 1:929, 936–37, 942, 990, 998–1000; pt. 2:640–42, 705; pt. 3:685.

22. *OR,* I, 27, pt. 2:713–19.

23. FL, "Letter from General Fitz. Lee," *SHSP* 4 (1877): 73–75; FL, "A Review of the First Two Days' Operations at Gettysburg and a Reply to General Longstreet by General Fitz. Lee," *SHSP* 5 (1878): 164–67.

24. FL to his mother, July 26, 1863, FL MSS, UV.

25. *OR,* I, 27, pt. 2:706; Driver, *1st Virginia Cavalry,* 69–70; Driver and Howard, *2nd Virginia Cavalry,* 94–95; Andrew A. Humphreys, *Gettysburg to the Rapidan: The Army of the Potomac, July, 1863, to April, 1864* (New York, 1883), 8; Robert T. Hubard memoirs, 79.

26. Grimsley, *Battles in Culpeper County, Virginia,* 14–15; Halsey Wigfall to his mother, Aug. 13, 1863, Wigfall MSS; Charles McVicar memoirs, 21–22, Library of Congress.

27. REL, *Wartime Papers,* 594; Corson, *My Dear Jennie,* 109.

28. *OR,* I, 27, pt. 3:1068–69.

29. Warner, *Generals in Gray,* 190–91.

30. *OR,* I, 29, pt. 2:707–08.

31. FL, [Farewell Address to the 2nd Cavalry Brigade, Army of Northern Virginia], Sept. 12, 1863, FL MSS, MC; J. E. B. Stuart to FL, Sept. 4, 1863, FL MSS, UV.

32. *OR,* I, 29, pt. 1:195–96, 200–202, 207–08, 215, 730–31, 742–43; pt. 2:167, 169, 172, 706, 720–21, 743; Hewett et al., *Supplement to Official Records,* I, 5:585–89; McClellan, *Life and Campaigns of Stuart,* 372–76 and n; Thomas L. Rosser to his wife, Sept. 15, 1863, Rosser MSS, UV; Opie, *Rebel Cavalryman,* 195; Grimsley, *Battles in Culpeper County,* 15–17; Neese, *Confederate Horse Artillery,* 208–11.

33. *OR,* I, 29, pt. 1:410, 439–45, 455, 458, 460, 463, 465, 474; pt. 2:220, 227; 51, pt. 2:772–73, 775; McClellan, *Life and Campaigns of Stuart,* 377–83; Driver, *1st Virginia Cavalry,* 72; Neese, *Confederate Horse Artillery,* 217–18; Driver and Howard, *2nd Virginia Cavalry,* 97–100; Stiles, *4th Virginia Cavalry,* 36–37; Robert T. Hubard memoirs, 82; Beale, *Lieutenant of Cavalry,* 129; Corson, *My Dear Jennie,* 111–12.

34. *OR,* I, 29, pt. 1:447–49, 456, 461; 51, pt. 2:776–77; McClellan, *Life and Campaigns of Stuart,* 385–92; Robert T. Hubard memoirs, 82.

35. *OR,* I, 29, pt. 1:426–27, 430–32, 448–49, 459, 466.

36. Ibid., 449–51, 464, 466; McClellan, *Life and Campaigns of Stuart,* 393–94; Hasley Wigfall to his father, Oct. 23, 1863, Wigfall MSS; Robert T. Hubard memoirs, 83.

37. *OR,* I, 29, pt. 1:411, 451–52, 461; 51, pt. 2:778; McClellan, *Life and Campaigns of Stuart,* 394–95; Cooke, *Wearing of the Gray,* 265–66; Driver, *1st Virginia Cavalry,* 73–74; Thomas L. Rosser, *Fighting with Rosser,* ed. S. Roger Keller (Shippensburg, Pa., 1997), 4–5; Halsey Wigfall to his father, Oct. 19, 23, 1863, Wigfall MSS; Robert T. Hubard memoirs, 82–84; William R. Carter diary, Oct. 19, 1863.

CHAPTER TEN

1. Robert E. Lee Jr., *Recollections and Letters of Gen. Robert E. Lee,* 113.

2. Chesnut, *Diary from Dixie,* 333.

3. *OR,* I, 29, pt. 1:555–58, 561–62, 574–77, 609–29; Grimsley, *Battles in Culpeper County,* 23.

4. *OR,* I, 29, pt. 1:806–07, 825–30, 898–907; REL, *Wartime Papers,* 630; Hampton et al., *Letters of Three Wade Hamptons,* 97.

5. *OR,* I, 29, pt. 1:970–71; REL, *Wartime Papers,* 643; Rawleigh W. Downman to his wife, Dec. 16, 1863, Downman MSS, VHS; Halsey Wigfall to his father, Dec. 15, 1863, Wigfall MSS; Jubal A. Early, *War Memoirs: Autobiographical Sketch and Narrative of the War between the States,* ed. Frank E. Vandiver (Bloomington, Ind., 1960), 326–28; Thomas L. Rosser to his wife, Dec. 27, 1863, Rosser MSS, UV.

6. *OR,* I, 29, pt. 1:971.

7. Ibid., 924–25; Averell, *Ten Years in the Saddle,* 391–92.

8. *OR,* I, 29, pt. 1:972.

9. Ibid., 971–72.

10. Ibid., I, 33:7; Thomas L. Rosser to his wife, Dec. 24, 27, 1863, Jan. 8, 1864, Rosser MSS, UV; Rosser, *Riding with Rosser,* 15–18.

11. *OR,* I, 33:7–8.

12. Ibid., 8.

13. Ibid.; REL, *Wartime Papers,* 656; Richard H. Dulany et al., *The Dulanys of Welbourne: A Family in Mosby's Confederacy,* ed. Margaret Ann Vogtsberger (Berryville, Va., 1995), 125.

14. Lee Jr., *Recollections and Letters of Gen. Robert E. Lee,* 120–21.

15. Harrison, *Recollections Grave and Gray,* 172.

16. Ibid., 172–75.

17. *OR,* I, 33:169–70.

18. Ibid., 167–68; 51, pt. 2:823; Hewett et al., *Supplement to Official Records,* I, 6:284–85; Nichols, *General Fitzhugh Lee,* 63.

19. *OR,* I, 33:170–77, 181–87, 199–204; McClellan, *Life and Campaigns of Stuart,* 403–04; Longacre, *Gentleman and Soldier,* 172–74.

20. J. William Jones, "Kilpatrick-Dahlgren Raid Against Richmond," *SHSP* 13 (1885): 515–51; FL, "The Death of Colonel Dahlgren," *SHSP* 13 (1885): 552–54; G. Watson James, "Dahlgren's Raid," *SHSP* 39 (1914): 63–72; Chesnut, *Diary from Dixie,* 388; *OR,* I, 33:171, 178–79, 207–10.

21. *OR,* I, 33:217, 224; FL, "Death of Colonel Dahlgren," 555.

22. *OR,* I, 33:180, 218–24; Bruce Catton, *A Stillness at Appomattox* (Garden City, N.Y., 1953), 9–10, 18.

23. Chesnut, *Diary from Dixie,* 396.

24. J. E. B. Stuart to FL, Mar. 24, 1864, FL MSS, UV.

25. Ibid.

26. J. E. B. Stuart to FL, Apr. 13, 1864, FL MSS, UV; REL, *Wartime Papers,* 706; REL, *Lee's Dispatches,* 166.

27. Ulysses S. Grant, *Personal Memoirs of U. S. Grant,* ed. E. B. Long (New York, 2001), 359–60.

28. Ibid., 391–405; Freeman, *R. E. Lee,* 3:269–80.

29. FL, [Report of Operations of Lee's Division, Cavalry Corps, Army of Northern Virginia, May 1–Sept. 19, 1864], Dec. 20, 1866, 1–4, MC; FL to J. E. B. Stuart, May 6, 1864, FL MSS, UV.

30. FL, [Report of Lee's Division], 4–6; *OR,* I, 36, pt. 1:774–76, 778–89; 51, pt. 1:248–49; pt. 2:897–98.

31. FL, [Report of Lee's Division], 5–6; McClellan, *Life and Campaigns of Stuart,* 408.

32. FL, [Report of Lee's Division], 6–10; *OR,* I, 36, pt. 1:540–41; McClellan, *Life and Campaigns of Stuart,* 408–09; Wise, *Long Arm of Lee,* 2:794–96; Robert T. Hubard memoirs, 89.

33. FL, [Report of Lee's Division], 10.

34. Ibid., 10–11; Gordon C. Rhea, *The Battles for Spotsylvania Court House and the Road to Yellow Tavern, May 7–12, 1864* (Baton Rouge, 1997), 114.

35. Grant, *Memoirs,* 378; Philip H. Sheridan, *Personal Memoirs of P. H. Sheridan,* 2 vols. (New York, 1888), 1:366–67; *OR,* I, 36, pt. 1:788–89; pt. 2:553.

36. *OR,* I, 36, pt. 2:853, 857, 861; Thomas P. Nanzig, *3rd Virginia Cavalry* (Lynchburg, Va., 1989), 49; Stiles, *4th Virginia Cavalry,* 47; Rhea, *Battles for Spotsylvania,* 114–15.

37. FL, [Report of Lee's Division], 11–12; *OR,* I, 36, pt. 1:790; 51, pt. 2:911–14; McClellan, *Life and Campaigns of Stuart,* 410.

38. FL, [Report of Lee's Division], 12–13; McClellan, *Life and Campaigns of Stuart,* 411–12; Burke Davis, *Jeb Stuart, the Last Cavalier* (New York, 1957), 400–401.

39. FL, [Report of Lee's Division], 13–15; *OR,* I, 36, pt. 1:818; McClellan, *Life and Campaigns of Stuart,* 412; Freeman, *Lee's Lieutenants,* 3:421; Thaddeus Fitzhugh memoirs, 39–40.

40. Cyrus McCormick, "How Gallant Stuart Met His Death," *CV* 39 (1931): 99.

41. Ibid.; FL, "Speech of General Fitz Lee at A. N. V. Banquet," 102; "The Death of General J. E. B. Stuart, by a Private of the Sixth Virginia Cavalry, C. S. A.," *B&L* 4 (1887–88): 194.

42. Andrew Reid Venable to FL, June 7, 1888, Venable MSS, VHS.

43. FL, [Report of Lee's Division], 15.

CHAPTER ELEVEN

1. FL, [Report of Lee's Division], 15–16.

2. Ibid., 18.

3. Ibid., 18–19; *OR,* I, 36, pt. 1:777–79, 781, 792, 814; pt. 2:683, 765–66, 797–98, 858, 931–32; pt. 3:199–200; 51, pt. 1:250; Sheridan, *Personal Memoirs,* 1:383–90; Robert T. Hubard memoirs, 94–95.

4. FL, [Report of Lee's Division], 17; Thomas, *Bold Dragoon,* 293–95; William Parker Snow, *Southern Generals: Who They Are, and What They Have Done* (New York, 1865), 373.

5. FL, [Report of Lee's Division], 17.

6. FL to "General," May 15, 1864, FL MSS, MC; *OR,* I, 36, pt. 2:11–12, 37–40, 116–18, 196–97, 201–04.

7. FL, [Report of Lee's Division], 21–22.

8. Ibid., 22.

9. Ibid., 22–24; *OR,* I, 36, pt. 2:269–72; "Brook Church Fight and Something About the Fifth North Carolina Cavalry . . . ," *SHSP* 29 (1901): 139–41; Robert T. Hubard memoirs, 95.

10. Ibid., 95–96; Robert J. Driver Jr., *First & Second Maryland Cavalry, C. S. A.* (Charlottesville, Va., 1999), 80.

11. FL, [Report of Lee's Division], 25.

12. Hampton et al., *Letters of Three Wade Hamptons,* 91–92, 99–102; Longacre, *Lee's Cavalrymen,* 168, 267–70.

13. Edward L. Wells, *Hampton and His Cavalry in '64* (Richmond, Va., 1899), 263–65; Longacre, *Gentleman and Soldier,* 182–83.

14. FL, [Report of Lee's Division], 25; Freeman, *R. E. Lee,* 3:362–65.

15. Gordon C. Rhea, "'The Hottest Place I Ever Was In': The Battle of Haw's Shop, May 28, 1864," *North & South* 4 (Apr. 2001): 42–47.

16. Ibid., 47–57; FL, [Report of Lee's Division], 25–26; Robert T. Hubard memoirs, 96–97.

17. FL, [Report of Lee's Division], 26–27; *OR*, I, 51, pt. 2:967–68.

18. FL, [Report of Lee's Division], 27; Grant, *Memoirs*, 438–42.

19. FL, [Report of Lee's Division], 27–28.

20. Ibid., 28; *OR*, I, 36, pt. 1:1095; 51, pt. 2:986–87.

21. FL, [Report of Lee's Division], 28–29.

22. Ibid., 29; Wells, *Hampton and His Cavalry*, 193–97; Hewett et al., *Supplement to Official Records*, I, 6:815.

23. Myers, *The Comanches*, 291; Robert T. Hubard memoirs, 96–97.

24. FL, [Report of Lee's Division], 29.

25. Ibid.; *OR*, I, 36, pt. 1:784–85, 800–801, 823–24, 841, 850, 855, 858; Wade Hampton to Edward L. Wells, Jan. 18, 1900, Wells MSS, Charleston Library Society; Sheridan, *Personal Memoirs*, 1:420–22; Wells, *Hampton and His Cavalry*, 198–99; Rosser, *Riding with Rosser*, 38; Charles McVicar memoirs, 40; Robert T. Hubard memoirs, 99.

26. FL, [Report of Lee's Division], 30–31.

27. Ibid.; Jay Monaghan, "Custer's 'Last Stand'—Trevilian Station, 1864," *Civil War History* 8 (1962): 249–55; Theophilus F. Rodenbough, "Sheridan's Trevilian Raid," *B&L* 4:233–34; M. C. Butler, "The Cavalry Fight at Trevilian Station," *B&L* 4:237–38; Rosser, *Riding with Rosser*, 37–38.

28. Wade Hampton to Edward L. Wells, Feb. 22, 1900, Wells MSS; Longacre, *Gentleman and Soldier*, 198; Eric J. Wittenberg, *Glory Enough for All: Sheridan's Second Raid and the Battle of Trevilian Station* (Washington, D.C., 2001), 315–17.

29. Rodenbough, "Sheridan's Trevilian Raid," 234; Robert T. Hubard memoirs, 100.

30. Robert T. Hubard memoirs, 100–101; *OR*, I, 36, pt. 1:784–85, 808–09, 824, 845–46, 850–51, 1096; 51, pt. 2:1009; Sheridan, *Personal Memoirs*, 1:425; FL, [Report of Lee's Division], 31–32; Butler, "Cavalry Fight at Trevilian Station," 238–39; Brooks, *Butler and His Cavalry*, 247–54.

31. Sheridan, *Personal Memoirs*, 1:422–25; Wittenberg, *Glory Enough for All*, 337–45.

32. FL, [Report of Lee's Division], 32; *OR*, I, 40, pt. 1:747; pt. 2:669–70; 51, pt. 2:1081; Hewett et al., *Supplement to Official Records*, I, 7:264, 337–38; Charles McVicar memoirs, 48–50; Wise, *Long Arm of Lee*, 2:843–44.

33. FL, [Report of Lee's Division], 32; Robert T. Hubard memoirs, 102.

34. FL, [Report of Lee's Division], 33; Grant, *Memoirs*, 454–57; P. G. T. Beauregard, "Four Days of Battle at Petersburg," *B&L* 4:540–44.

35. FL, [Report of Lee's Division], 33; *OR*, I, 40, pt. 1:620–21.

36. FL, [Report of Lee's Division], 33; *OR*, I, 36, pt. 1:1096–97; Wittenberg, *Glory Enough for All*, 263–69.

37. Wittenberg, *Glory Enough for All,* 269–76; *OR,* I, 36, pt. 1:855–56, 1097; FL, [Report of Lee's Division], 33–34.

38. FL, [Report of Lee's Division], 34; Wittenberg, *Glory Enough for All,* 276–79; *OR,* I, 36, pt. 1:856.

39. FL, [Report of Lee's Division], 34.

40. John S. Wise, *The End of an Era* (Boston, 1899), 336.

41. Ibid., 336–37.

42. *OR,* I, 40, pt. 1:622–23, 808; James Harrison Wilson, *Under the Old Flag: Recollections of Military Operations in the War for the Union, the Spanish War, the Boxer Rebellion, etc.,* 2 vols. (New York, 1912), 1:465–66.

43. Wilson, *Under the Old Flag,* 466–70; *OR,* I, 40, pt. 1:629–30, 732, 808; FL, [Report of Lee's Division], 35.

44. Robert T. Hubard memoirs, 104.

45. Ibid., 105.

46. Ibid.

CHAPTER TWELVE

1. Longacre, *Lee's Cavalrymen,* 307–08; Longacre, *Lincoln's Cavalrymen,* 294–95.

2. FL, [Report of Lee's Division], 37; Hewett et al., *Supplement to Official Records,* I, 7:343; REL, *Wartime Papers,* 821.

3. FL, [Report of Lee's Division], 37; Wade Hampton to FL, July 13, 1864, FL MSS, MC; Myers, *The Comanches,* 318.

4. Jubal A. Early, "Early's March to Washington in 1864," *B&L* 4:492–99; Jubal A. Early, "Winchester, Fisher's Hill, and Cedar Creek," *B&L* 4:522.

5. Sheridan, *Personal Memoirs,* 1:461–63, 472, 474; *OR,* I, 40, pt. 3:640–41, 669; 42, pt. 2:46; 43, pt. 1:501, 516, 681, 719, 744.

6. *OR,* I, 43, pt. 1:799, 822, 990; FL, [Report of Lee's Division], 37–39; Wesley Merritt, "Sheridan in the Shenandoah Valley," *B&L* 4:500–501.

7. Merritt, "Sheridan in the Shenandoah Valley," 501; Sheridan, *Personal Memoirs,* 1:500; Jeffry D. Wert, *From Winchester to Cedar Creek: The Shenandoah Campaign of 1864* (Carlisle, Pa., 1987), 36–37.

8. Merritt, "Sheridan in the Shenandoah," 502–03; FL, [Report of Lee's Division], 39–40.

9. FL, [Report of Lee's Division], 40; *OR,* I, 42, pt. 2:1173; 43, pt. 1:993, 1003–04; REL, *Lee's Dispatches,* 268–69.

10. FL, [Report of Lee's Division], 40–41; Merritt, "Sheridan in the Shenandoah," 504.

11. FL, [Report of Lee's Division], 41–42; Sheridan, *Personal Memoirs,* 1:494–95; Merritt, "Sheridan in the Shenandoah," 504–05; *OR,* I, 42, pt. 1:1025; 43, pt. 1:45, 424–25, 440, 473, 517; Wilson, *Under the Old Flag,* 1:540–42.

12. FL, [Report of Lee's Division], 42–43; Merritt, "Sheridan in the Shenandoah," 505–06; Sidney S. Lee to "My Dear Carter," Sept. 30, 1864, FL MSS, UV; Wert, *From Winchester to Cedar Creek,* 38–39.

13. FL, [Report of Lee's Division], 44–45; Merritt, "Sheridan in the Shenandoah," 506–07; *OR,* I, 43, pt. 1:46–47, 427, 443, 454, 481–82, 498, 518; Sheridan, *Personal Memoirs,* 2:11–12.

14. FL, [Report of Lee's Division], 46–48.

15. Merritt, "Sheridan in the Shenandoah," 507, 509–10; Early, "Winchester, Fisher's Hill, and Cedar Creek," 523–24; Robert T. Hubard memoirs, 107–08.

16. FL, [Report of Lee's Division], 49–50; Hewett et al., *Supplement to Official Records,* I, 7:513; Sidney S. Lee to "My Dear Carter," Sept. 30, 1864, FL MSS, UV.

17. *OR,* I, 43, pt. 1:555.

18. Readnor, "General Fitzhugh Lee," 59; REL to FL, Sept. 17, 1864, FL MSS, UV.

19. Early, "Winchester, Fisher's Hill, and Cedar Creek," 524–25; *OR,* I, 43, pt. 1:28–29, 554–55, 559, 612–13, 1028–30; Rosser, *Riding with Rosser,* 47–49; Corson, *My Dear Jennie,* 130; Robert T. Hubard memoirs, 107–14.

20. Early, *War Memoirs,* 414–15; Wert, *From Winchester to Cedar Creek,* 37–38.

21. *OR,* I, 46, pt. 1:511; FL to Agnes Lee, Jan. 8, 1865, FL MSS, VHS.

22. Henry Kyd Douglas, *I Rode with Stonewall: Being Chiefly the Experiences of the Youngest Member of Jackson's Staff* . . . (Chapel Hill, N.C., 1940), 323–24.

23. *OR,* I, 46, pt. 1:514; Hewett et al., *Supplement to Official Records,* I, 7:734; REL, *Wartime Papers,* 893; Special Order No. 45, HQ, Dept. of Northern Virginia, Feb. 11, 1865, REL MSS, VHS.

24. Jeffry D. Wert, *General James Longstreet, the Confederacy's Most Controversial Soldier: A Biography* (New York, 1993), 394–98; REL, *Lee's Dispatches,* 315; REL to Wade Hampton, Aug. 1, 1865, Edward L. Wells MSS; Longacre, *Gentleman and Soldier,* 222–37.

25. *OR,* I, 46, pt. 1:480, 503; pt. 2:994, 1281–82, 1289–91, 1294, 1301–04, 1306–15, 1317; pt. 3:14–15, 38, 41, 43, 1317–18, 1324, 1357–58; James Longstreet, *From Manassas to Appomattox: Memoirs of the Civil War in America* (Philadelphia, 1896), 591; Rawleigh W. Downman to his wife, Mar. 18, 1865, Downman MSS; Mottrom D. Ball to Thomas L. Rosser, Mar. 19, 1865, Rosser MSS, UV; Martin W. Gary to FL, Mar. 18, REL MSS, VHS; FL to James Longstreet, Mar. 18, 19, 20, 21, 24, 25, REL MSS, VHS.

26. *OR,* I, 46, pt. 1:388; pt. 3:1357, 1360; Edwin C. Bearss and Chris M. Calkins, *The Battle of Five Forks* (Lynchburg, Va., 1985), 10.

27. *OR,* I, 46, pt. 3:1358–59, 1362, 1371; Walter Harrison, *Pickett's Men: A Fragment of War History* (New York, 1870), 142–43; Wert, *James Longstreet,* 394–95; Freeman, *Lee's Lieutenants,* 3:656–57.

28. *OR,* I, 46, pt. 1:390, 1116, 1122, 1128, 1141, 1144, 1299; Hewett et al., *Supplement to Official Records,* I, 7:779; 8:440, 467, 474, 530–32, 620–21; Thomas T. Munford, "Last Days of Fitz Lee's Cavalry Division," 9, VHS; Sheridan, *Personal Memoirs,* 2:141–42.

29. FL to Marcus J. Wright, n.d. [copy by Thomas T. Munford], Munford MSS, VHS; Munford, "Last Days of Fitz Lee's Cavalry," 77–78, 83–84.

30. *OR,* I, 46, pt. 1:1102, 1110, 1116–17, 1122–23, 1128–30, 1141, 1144, 1148, 1154–57, 1299; pt. 2:1122–23, 1144, 1148–49, 1157; pt. 3:339, 381–82; Hewett et al., *Supplement to Official Records,* I, 7:780–81, 829–30; 8:440–41, 467, 474–75, 533, 614, 620–21; Sheridan, *Personal Memoirs,* 2:149–52; Munford, "Last Days of Fitz Lee's Cavalry," 14–17; Rosser, *Riding with Rosser,* 63–64; Henry E. Tremain, *Last Hours of Sheridan's Cavalry: A Reprint of War Memoranda* (New York, 1904), 43–49; Bearss and Calkins, *Battle of Five Forks,* 32–47.

31. *OR,* I, 46, pt. 1:1102–03, 1117, 1130, 1134–35, 1144; Robert T. Hubard memoirs, 118; Sheridan, *Personal Memoirs,* 2:151–53; Tremain, *Last Hours of Sheridan's Cavalry,* 50.

32. *OR,* I, 46, pt. 1:1299; pt. 3:324–25, 380, 1371; Hewett et al., *Supplement to Official Records,* I, 8:469–70; Munford, "Last Days of Fitz Lee's Cavalry," 23–27.

33. *OR,* I, 46, pt. 3:1371; Harrison, *Pickett's Men,* 138; Freeman, *Lee's Lieutenants,* 3:661 and n; Hewett et al., *Supplement to Official Records,* I, 7:781; Bearss and Calkins, *Battle of Five Forks,* 77–78.

34. *OR,* I, 46, pt. 1:819–26, 1103–04, 1117, 1123, 1130; pt. 3:435–37; Sheridan, *Personal Memoirs,* 2:155–60; Horace Porter, "Five Forks and the Pursuit of Lee," *B&L* 4:711–12; "Battle of Mamazine [Namozine] Creek," [2]–[8], Freeman MSS, Library of Congress.

35. Rosser, *Riding with Rosser,* 64; Munford, "Last Days of Fitz Lee's Cavalry," 34, 53–56; Hewett et al., *Supplement to Official Records,* I, 8:467, 481; Thomas T. Munford to Charles R. Irving, July 20, 1905, Munford MSS, LV.

36. *OR,* I, 46, pt. 1:831–35, 838–39, 869–70, 879–80, 1244–45, 1248, 1251, 1255; Hewett et al., *Supplement to Official Records,* I, 7:781–83; 8:441–44, 535, 537; Munford, "Last Days of Fitz Lee's Cavalry," 34–41; Daughtry, *Gray Cavalier,* 257–59.

37. *OR,* I, 46, pt. 1:1299–1300; Hewett et al., *Supplement to Official Records,* I, 8:471–72; Rosser, *Riding with Rosser,* 64–65.

38. FL, *General Lee,* 376; *OR,* I, 46, pt. 1:1263, 1300; Hewett et al., *Supplement to Official Records,* I, 7:746, 783; Munford, "Last Days of Fitz Lee's Cavalry," 65; Chris M. Calkins, *The Appomattox Campaign, March 29–April 9, 1865* (Conshohocken, Pa., 1997), 53–55; John B. Moseley diary, Apr. 2, 1865, VHS.

39. Calkins, *Appomattox Campaign,* 67–76.

40. *OR,* I, 46, pt. 1:682, 905–06, 913–15, 979, 1107–08, 1115, 1119–20, 1124–25, 1129, 1131–32, 1136, 1138–40, 1142–43, 1145–46, 1150–51, 1155, 1158,

1258, 1265–66, 1283–84, 1289–90, 1294–95, 1297, 1301–03; Hewett et al., *Supplement to Official Records,* I, 7:747, 776, 797–98; Tremain, *Last Hours of Sheridan's Cavalry,* 125–75; Sheridan, *Personal Memoirs,* 2:179–83; Munford, "Last Days of Fitz Lee's Cavalry," 72–78; Rosser, *Riding with Rosser,* 69–70; Rawleigh W. Downman to his wife, Apr. 6, 1865, Downman MSS; Longstreet, *From Manassas to Appomattox,* 612; Burleigh Cushing Rodick, *Appomattox: The Last Campaign* (New York, 1865), 72–73; Henry C. Lee diary, Apr. 6, 1865, MC.

41. *OR,* I, 46, pt. 1:1303–04; Hewett et al., *Supplement to Official Records,* I, 7:793, 800; Munford, "Last Days of Fitz Lee's Cavalry," 83–84.

42. *OR,* I, 46, pt. 1:1126–29, 1138, 1140–43, 1155–56, 1159, 1152–63, 1175, 1181, 1187, 1196, 1203–04, 1215, 1236, 1239, 1243, 1245–46, 1266, 1303; Hewett et al., *Supplement to Official Records,* I, 7:777, 793, 798–801; Calkins, *Appomattox Campaign,* 144–45.

43. FL to John Esten Cooke, Mar. 21, 1868, Cooke MSS, William R. Perkins Library, Duke University; Alexander, *Fighting for the Confederacy,* 535–36.

44. *OR,* I, 46, pt. 1:1304.

CHAPTER THIRTEEN

1. John Gibbon, "Personal Recollections of Appomattox," *Century Illustrated Monthly Magazine* 63 (1902): 942.

2. Ibid.; Nichols, *General Fitzhugh Lee,* 87–88.

3. Gibbon, "Personal Recollections of Appomattox," 943; John Gibbon to his wife, Apr. 14, 1865, USMA.

4. Nichols, *General Fitzhugh Lee,* 90; Readnor, "General Fitzhugh Lee," 70–71.

5. REL to FL, Sept. 1, 1865, REL MSS, VHS; *Alexandria Gazette,* June 3, 1875.

6. FL to Manning M. Kimmel, Oct. 1, 1867, FL MSS, CW&M.

7. Ibid.; FL to Thomas T. Munford, Feb. 25, 1866, Munford MSS, VHS.

8. FL to Manning M. Kimmel, Oct. 1, 1867, FL MSS, CW&M.

9. FL to Andrew Johnson, July 7, 1866, FL MSS, UV; Readnor, "General Fitzhugh Lee," 68; Kinsley, *Fitzhugh Lee Sampler,* 92.

10. FL to Manning M. Kimmel, Aug. 12, 1866, FL MSS, CW&M.

11. Freeman, *R. E. Lee,* 4:381.

12. Nichols, *General Fitzhugh Lee,* 92.

13. Ibid.; Readnor, "General Fitzhugh Lee," 76–77, FL MSS, UV; FL to Manning M. Kimmel, Aug. 12, 1866, Oct. 1, 1867, FL MSS, UV; FL to Nannie Enders, Apr. 8, 1866, FL MSS, UV; REL to Sidney S. Lee, Apr. 16, June 26, 1867, FL MSS, UV.

14. FL to Manning M. Kimmel, Oct. 1, 1867, FL MSS, CW&M.

15. FL to REL, Sept. 7, 1865, FL MSS, UV; FL to John Esten Cooke, Mar. 21, 1866, Cooke MSS.

16. DeLeon, *Belles, Beaux and Brains of the 60's,* 148–50; FL to Nannie Enders, Apr. 8, Sept. 23, 1866, Mar. 22, Oct. 25, 1867, Jan. 3, Feb. 18, Mar. 7, 1869, Mar. 29, 1870, FL MSS, UV.

17. REL to FL, Feb. 18, 1867, FL MSS, UV; REL to Sidney S. Lee, Feb. 20, 1869, FL MSS, UV.

18. Nichols, *General Fitzhugh Lee,* 97–99, 181; Readnor, "General Fitzhugh Lee," 74–75, 171; *Thirty-sixth Annual Reunion . . . United States Military Academy,* 108–09; Kinsley, *Fitzhugh Lee Sampler,* 103, 177; "Mrs. Fitzhugh Lee," *CV* 5 (1897): 125; *Alexandria Gazette,* Apr. 19, 1871; FL to Jefferson Davis, Mar. 1, 1871, Davis MSS, MC.

19. Frederick Warren Alexander, comp., *Stratford Hall and the Lees Connected with Its History . . .* (Oak Grove, Va., 1912), 309–10.

20. Readnor, "General Fitzhugh Lee," 76.

21. Ibid.; Heitman, *Historical Register and Dictionary,* 1:623–24.

22. Nichols, *General Fitzhugh Lee,* 107–14; Readnor, "General Fitzhugh Lee," 88–94; Samuel Richards Johnston to FL, Feb. 11, 1878, Johnston MSS, VHS; FL to Samuel Richards Johnston, Feb. 14, 1878, Johnston MSS, VHS; FL to Henry B. McClellan, July 31, 1878, McClellan MSS, VHS; Wert, *General James Longstreet,* 422–23.

23. FL, "Letter from General Fitz. Lee," *SHSP* 4 (1877): 69–76; FL, "A Review of the First Two Days' Operations at Gettysburg and a Reply to General Longstreet by General Fitz. Lee," *SHSP* 5 (1878): 162–68; Readnor, "General Fitzhugh Lee," 91–92.

24. Readnor, "General Fitzhugh Lee," 93–94.

25. Nichols, *General Fitzhugh Lee,* 112–13; FL to Robert M. Hughes, Feb. 22, 1894, Hughes MSS, CW&M.

26. Nichols, *General Fitzhugh Lee,* 116.

27. "The Monument to General Robert E. Lee," *SHSP* 17 (1889): 198–99; Readnor, "General Fitzhugh Lee," 173; Robert Beverly Munford Jr., *Richmond Homes and Memories* (Richmond, Va., 1936), 46–47; John A. Cutchins, *A Famous Command: The Richmond Light Infantry Blues* (Richmond, Va., 1934), 194–95.

28. Kinsley, *Fitzhugh Lee Sampler,* 108.

29. Nichols, *General Fitzhugh Lee,* 115; Robert C. Glass and Carter Glass Jr., *Virginia Democracy: A History of the Achievements of the Party and Its Leaders in the Mother of Commonwealths, the Old Dominion,* 3 vols. (n.p., 1937), 1:205–06.

30. Charles E. Wynes, *Race Relations in Virginia, 1870–1902* (Charlottesville, Va., 1951), 1–12; Readnor, "General Fitzhugh Lee," 99; Kinsley, *Fitzhugh Lee Sampler,* 108.

31. Nichols, *General Fitzhugh Lee,* 120; Longacre, *Gentleman and Soldier,* 261–67.

32. Kinsley, *Fitzhugh Lee Sampler,* 110; Nichols, *General Fitzhugh Lee,* 121.

33. Nichols, *General Fitzhugh Lee,* 122; Charles Chilton Pearson, *The Readjuster Movement in Virginia* (New Haven, Conn., 1917), 8; Glass and Glass, *Virginia Democracy,* 1:213–14.

34. Wynes, *Race Relations in Virginia,* 15–20.

35. Readnor, "General Fitzhugh Lee," 100–101; "Remarks of Gen. W. H. Payne, of Fauquier [County], Nominating General Fitz. Lee for Governor," FL MSS, CW&M.

36. Kinsley, *Fitzhugh Lee Sampler,* 110.

37. John W. Johnston, "Repudiation in Virginia," *North American Review* 134 (1882): 149–60; Charles T. O'Ferrall, *Forty Years of Active Service: Being Some History of the War between the Confederacy and the Union* . . . (New York, 1904), 211–27; Pearson, *Readjuster Movement in Virginia,* 1–16; William DuBose Shelton, *Populism in the Old Dominion: Virginia Farm Politics, 1885–1900* (Princeton, N.J., 1935), 51–62; Nelson Morehouse Blake, *William Mahone of Virginia, Soldier and Political Insurgent* (Richmond, Va., 1935), 164–82; Stanley P. Hirshon, *Farewell to the Bloody Shirt: Northern Republicans & the Southern Negro, 1877–1893* (Bloomington, Ind., 1962), 94–98, 105–22; Wynes, *Race Relations in Virginia,* 16–38; Richard L. Morton, *The Negro in Virginia Politics, 1865–1902* (Spartanburg, S.C., 1973), 98–131.

38. Wynes, *Race Relations in Virginia,* 21–38.

39. Kinsley, *Fitzhugh Lee Sampler,* 111; Readnor, "General Fitzhugh Lee," 109–10; Wynes, *Race Relations in Virginia,* 28–29.

40. *Thirty-sixth Annual Reunion* . . . *United States Military Academy,* 107; Readnor, "General Fitzhugh Lee," 94; Nichols, *General Fitzhugh Lee,* 122–23; "Dedication of the Tomb of the Army of Northern Virginia Association and Unveiling of the Statue of Stonewall Jackson at New Orleans," *SHSP* 9 (1881): 212–16; "General Fitzhugh Lee's Tour," *SHSP* 10 (1882): 569–75; "General Fitz. Lee's Southern Tour," *SHSP* 11 (1883): 44–48; "General Fitzhugh Lee Invited to Lecture in New England," *SHSP* 11 (1883): 43–44; "General Fitzhugh Lee . . . Second Lecturing Tour," *SHSP* 11 (1883): 142; "General Fitzhugh Lee's Second Tour in Behalf of the Southern Historical Society," *SHSP* 11 (1883): 228–38; Kinsley, *Fitzhugh Lee Sampler,* 111, 167; Cutchins, *A Famous Command,* 181–82; J. William Jones, *Virginia's Next Governor: Gen'l Fitzhugh Lee* (New York, 1885), 20–21.

41. Kinsley, *Fitzhugh Lee Sampler,* 111; Nichols, *General Fitzhugh Lee,* 124; Readnor, "General Fitzhugh Lee," 111; Allan Nevins, *Grover Cleveland: A Study in Courage* (New York, 1933) 1–3; Jones, *Virginia's Next Governor,* 21.

42. Nichols, *General Fitzhugh Lee,* 124; Readnor, "General Fitzhugh Lee," 115–22; Curtis Carroll Davis, "Very Well-Rounded Republican: The Several Lives of John S. Wise," *VMH&B* 71 (1963): 476–77; Kinsley, *Fitzhugh Lee Sampler,* 166–69; O'Ferrall, *Forty Years of Active Service,* 224–25; Allen W. Moger, *Virginia: Bourbonism to Byrd, 1870–1925* (Charlottesville, Va., 1968), 57–61.

43. Davis, "Very Well Rounded Republican," 478; O'Ferrall, *Forty Years of Active Service,* 225; Moger, *Virginia: Bourbonism to Byrd,* 60–61; Pearson, *Readjuster*

Movement in Virginia, 169–70; Readnor, "General Fitzhugh Lee," 134–35; Nichols, *General Fitzhugh Lee,* 125–26.

CHAPTER FOURTEEN

1. *Fredericksburg Star,* Jan. 6, 1886.
2. Ibid.; Munford, *Richmond Homes and Memories,* 110–12.
3. Readnor, "General Fitzhugh Lee," 137–39. Readnor's work is the main source of information for the following summary of Governor Lee's administration.
4. Ibid., 109, 144–45; Glass and Glass, *Virginia Democracy,* 1:233–34; Blake, *William Mahone of Virginia,* 175.
5. Readnor, "General Fitzhugh Lee," 143–54.
6. Ibid., 156–60.
7. Ibid., 160–62; *Journal of the Senate of the Commonwealth of Virginia . . .* (Richmond, Va., 1889–90), 23.
8. Nichols, *General Fitzhugh Lee,* 129; Moger, *Virginia: Bourbonism to Byrd,* 297.
9. Readnor, "General Fitzhugh Lee," 162–66; Nichols, *General Fitzhugh Lee,* 130–31.
10. Readnor, "General Fitzhugh Lee," 176–84.
11. Ibid., 174–75; *Richmond Dispatch,* Dec. 31, 1889.
12. Nichols, *General Fitzhugh Lee,* 128, 134.
13. Ibid., 134–35, 149.
14. *Richmond Dispatch,* July 5, 6, 9, 14, 18, 1889; Nichols, *General Fitzhugh Lee,* 138–40.
15. C. Vann Woodward, *Origins of the New South, 1877–1913* (Baton Rouge, 1951), 137–39; Readnor, "General Fitzhugh Lee," 185–92; Allen W. Moger, "Railroad Practices and Policies in Virginia after the Civil War," *VMH&B* 59 (1951): 451; Raymond Pulley, *Old Virginia Restored: An Interpretation of the Progressive Impulse, 1870–1930* (Charlottesville, Va., 1968), 26.
16. Nichols, *General Fitzhugh Lee,* 139–40; Readnor, "General Fitzhugh Lee," 199–210; Eppa Hunton, *Autobiography of Eppa Hunton* (Richmond, Va., 1933), 216–18; Paschal Reeves, "Thomas S. Martin, Committee Statesman," *VMH&B* 68 (1960): 344–52; Pulley, *Old Virginia Restored,* 53–54; Moger, *Virginia: Bourbonism to Byrd,* 111–14; Marshall W. Fishwick, *Gentlemen of Virginia* (New York, 1961), 204–09.
17. Readnor, "General Fitzhugh Lee," 210–15; Nichols, *General Fitzhugh Lee,* 142–43; Reeves, "Thomas S. Martin," 352–53; Moger, *Virginia: Bourbonism to Byrd,* 114–21; Glass and Glass, *Virginia Democracy,* 1:262–65.
18. Nichols, *General Fitzhugh Lee,* 145–46; *Richmond Times,* Apr. 20, 1895; FL to Joseph S. Miller, Apr. 10, 1896, FL MSS, LV.
19. Nichols, *General Fitzhugh Lee,* 146; FL to Joseph S. Miller, Apr. 10, 11, 28, May 6, 1896, FL MSS, LV; Mary Anna Jackson, *Memoirs of Stonewall Jackson by His Widow . . .* (Louisville, Ky., 1895), 607–12.

20. C. C. Penick to FL, Apr. 24, 1896, FL MSS, UV.

21. FL to Joseph S. Miller, Apr. 10, 1896, FL MSS, LV.

22. FL and Joseph Wheeler, *Cuba's Struggle against Spain, with the Causes for American Intervention and a Full Account of the Spanish American War, Including Final Peace Negotiations* (New York, 1899), 78–79.

23. Ibid.

24. Ibid., 81–83.

25. Ibid., 83–84; Allan R. Millett, *The Politics of Intervention: The Military Occupation of Cuba, 1906–1909* (Columbus, Ohio, 1968), 19–29; David F. Trask, *The War with Spain in 1898* (New York, 1981), 1–6; FL to his wife, June 3, 1896, FL MSS, UV.

26. Nichols, *General Fitzhugh Lee,* 149.

27. Ibid., 149–50; FL to his wife, June 17, 1896, FL MSS, UV; Readnor, "General Fitzhugh Lee," 224–26; Gerald C. Eggert, "Our Man in Havana: Fitzhugh Lee," *Hispanic American Historical Review* 47 (1967): 466–69.

28. Grover Cleveland, *Letters of Grover Cleveland, 1850–1908,* ed. Allan Nevins (Boston, 1933), 448; Walter Millis, *The Martial Spirit: A Study of Our War with Spain* (Boston, 1931), 72; Eggert, "Our Man in Havana," 469.

29. Nichols, *General Fitzhugh Lee,* 152–54; Readnor, "General Fitzhugh Lee," 237–42; French Ensor Chadwick, *The Relations of the United States and Spain: Diplomacy* (New York, 1909), 489–90; "Gen. Fitzhugh Lee in Havana," *CV* 16 (1908): 188–89; Finley Peter Dunne, *Mr. Dooley in Peace and War* (Boston, 1899), 10–13; Michael Blow, *A Ship to Remember: The* Maine *and the Spanish-American War* (New York, 1992), 62–65; Eggert, "Our Man in Havana," 463, 472–75.

30. Eggert, "Our Man in Havana," 470–71, 479, 483–85; Peggy Samuels and Harold Samuels, *Remembering the* Maine (Washington, D.C., 1995), 10–11.

31. FL to Richard Olney, June 22, 1896, FL MSS, UV; Eggert, "Our Man in Havana," 469–70; Readnor, "General Fitzhugh Lee," 230–31.

32. Nichols, *General Fitzhugh Lee,* 153; Robert L. Scribner, "Ex-Confederate in Blue," *Virginia Cavalcade* 5 (Spring 1956): 17; Readnor, "General Fitzhugh Lee," 234–36; Cleveland, *Letters of Grover Cleveland,* 488; Margaret Leech, *In the Days of McKinley* (New York, 1959), 162–63; Eggert, "Our Man in Havana," 476–77; H. Wayne Morgan, *America's Road to Empire: The War with Spain and Overseas Expansion* (New York, 1965), 23.

33. Eggert, "Our Man in Havana," 480–81; Leech, *In the Days of McKinley,* 163–64; Chadwick, *Relations of United States and Spain,* 531–38; Trask, *War with Spain,* 24–25; Blow, *A Ship to Remember,* 81–86.

34. Nichols, *General Fitzhugh Lee,* 156–60; Millis, *Martial Spirit,* 102–04; Leech, *In the Days of McKinley,* 166–83; Blow, *A Ship to Remember,* 187–88.

35. Nichols, *General Fitzhugh Lee,* 160–61; Eggert, "Our Man in Havana," 463; Ella L. McCrary, "Life and Public Services of Fitzhugh Lee," *Midland Monthly* 10 (1898): 46; Scribner, "Ex-Confederate in Blue," 18.

36. Nichols, *General Fitzhugh Lee,* 161; Readnor, "General Fitzhugh Lee," 252–55.

37. Leech, *In the Days of McKinley,* 229; Millis, *Martial Spirit,* 162; Nichols, *General Fitzhugh Lee,* 164.

38. Nichols, *General Fitzhugh Lee,* 163–65; Readnor, "General Fitzhugh Lee," 255–57; Scribner, "Ex-Confederate in Blue," 19–20.

39. Nichols, *General Fitzhugh Lee,* 165; Readnor, "General Fitzhugh Lee," 257–58; *Roster of Troops of the Department of the Province of Havana and Pinar del Rio, Brigadier General Fitzhugh Lee, Commanding . . . May 5, 1899* (Havana, 1899), 1–11; *Roster of Troops of the Department of the Province of Havana and Pinar del Rio, Brigadier General Fitzhugh Lee Commanding . . . May 1900* (Havana, 1900), 1–31; Scribner, "Ex-Confederate in Blue," 20–21; David F. Healy, *The United States in Cuba, 1898–1902: Generals, Politicians, and the Search for Policy* (Madison, Wis., 1963), 53–60.

40. FL, *Report of Commanding General Fitzhugh Lee Outlining Governmental, Economic, and Social Conditions in the Department of Havana and Pinar del Rio at the Beginning of the U.S. Occupation, and Resulting Changes* (Havana, 1899), 1–2.

41. Readnor, "General Fitzhugh Lee," 260.

42. Nichols, *General Fitzhugh Lee,* 166–69; Readnor, "General Fitzhugh Lee," 260–61; Healy, *United States in Cuba,* 93–97, 111–12; Millett, *Politics of Intervention,* 29–30; Wilson, *Under the Old Flag,* 2:479–80.

43. Readnor, "General Fitzhugh Lee," 263–64; Millett, *Politics of Intervention,* 39–42.

44. Nichols, *General Fitzhugh Lee,* 170–73; Readnor, "General Fitzhugh Lee," 264–65.

45. Readnor, "General Fitzhugh Lee," 265; Nichols, *General Fitzhugh Lee,* 173–75; FL to "My Dear Mrs. New," Apr. 22, 1902, USMA.

46. Nichols, *General Fitzhugh Lee,* 174–75; Readnor, "General Fitzhugh Lee," 266; Robert T. Taylor, "The Jamestown Tricentennial Exposition of 1907," *VMH&B* 65 (1957): 169–78.

47. Nichols, *General Fitzhugh Lee,* 175–77; Readnor, "General Fitzhugh Lee," 266–67; Taylor, "Jamestown Tricentennial Exposition," 179–85; "Gen. Fitzhugh Lee," *CV* 13 (1905): 280–81.

48. Nichols, *General Fitzhugh Lee,* 177–78; *Thirty-sixth Annual Reunion . . . United States Military Academy,* 113; Readnor, "General Fitzhugh Lee," 268; "Gen. Fitzhugh Lee," 281; "Fitzhugh Lee's Burial in Hollywood [Cemetery]," *CV* 14 (1906): 175.

49. "Gen. Fitzhugh Lee," 281.

Bibliography

UNPUBLISHED SOURCES

Bolling, John. Correspondence. Virginia Historical Society, Richmond.

Carter, William R. Correspondence and Diaries, 1862–64. Library of Virginia, Richmond.

Chewning, Charles R. Diaries, 1862–65. Handley Regional Library, Winchester, Va.

Compiled Service Records of Confederate General and Staff Officers. Record Group 109, National Archives, Washington, D.C.

Cooke, John Esten. Correspondence. William R. Perkins Library, Duke University, Durham, N.C.

Cooke, John R. Correspondence. Virginia Historical Society, Richmond.

Coons, Henry W. Correspondence. Virginia Historical Society, Richmond.

Downman, Rawleigh W. Correspondence. Virginia Historical Society, Richmond.

Fitzhugh, Thaddeus. Memoirs. Elenor S. Brockenbrough Library, Museum of the Confederacy, Richmond, Va.

Freeman, Douglas Southall. Papers. Library of Congress, Washington, D.C.

Gibbon, John. Letter of April 14, 1865. U.S. Military Academy Library, West Point, N.Y.

Hampton, Wade III. Correspondence. Rives Family Papers, Virginia Historical Society, Richmond.

———. Correspondence and Memoirs. Hampton Family Papers, South Caroliniana Library, University of South Carolina, Columbia.

Hubard, Robert T. Memoirs. Wilson Library, University of North Carolina, Chapel Hill.

Jones, Robert B. Correspondence. Virginia Historical Society, Richmond.

Lee, Daniel M. Letter of May 28, 1908. Beverly Bland Munford Papers, Virginia Historical Society, Richmond.

Lee, Fitzhugh. Correspondence. Bolling Family Papers, Virginia Historical Society, Richmond.

———. Correspondence. Eleanor S. Brockenbrough Library, Museum of the Confederacy, Richmond, Va.

———. Correspondence. Henry B. McClellan Papers, Virginia Historical Society, Richmond.

———. Correspondence. J. E. B. Stuart Papers, Virginia Historical Society, Richmond.

———. Correspondence. Mrs. Burton Harrison Papers, Virginia Historical Society, Richmond.

———. Correspondence. Robert E. Lee Papers. Virginia Historical Society, Richmond.

———. Correspondence. Samuel Richards Johnston Papers, Virginia Historical Society, Richmond.

———. "Fitzhugh Lee's Academic Record while a Cadet at the United States Military Academy, 1 July 1852–1 July 1856." United States Military Academy Archives, West Point, N.Y.

———. Letter of April 22, 1902. United States. Military Academy Library, West Point, N.Y.

———. Letter of December 5, 1885. Powell Family Papers. Earl Gregg Swem Library, College of William and Mary, Williamsburg, Va.

———. Letter of February 22, 1894. Robert M. Hughes Papers, Earl Gregg Swem Library, College of William and Mary, Williamsburg, Va.

———. Letter of September 10, 1866. Cooke Family Papers, Virginia Historical Society, Richmond.

———. "Orders Relating to Fitzhugh Lee while a Cadet at the USMA, 1 July 1852 to 1 July 1856." United States Military Academy Archives, West Point, N.Y.

———. Papers. Alderman Library, University of Virginia, Charlottesville.

———. Papers. Earl Gregg Swem Library, College of William and Mary, Williamsburg, Va.

———. Papers. Henry E. Huntington Library, San Marino, Calif.

———. Papers. Library of Virginia, Richmond.

———. [Report of Operations of Lee's Division, Cavalry Corps, Army of Northern Virginia, May 1–September 19, 1864], December 20, 1866. Eleanor S. Brockenbrough Library, Museum of the Confederacy, Richmond, Va.

Lee, Henry C. Diary, 1865. Eleanor S. Brockenbrough Library, Museum of the Confederacy, Richmond, Va.

Lee, Robert E. Papers. Gilder Lehrman Collection, New York, N.Y.

———. Papers. Virginia Historical Society, Richmond.

Lee, W. H. F. Correspondence. Alderman Library, University of Virginia, Charlottesville.

———. Correspondence. Library of Congress, Washington, D.C.

———. Correspondence. Library of Virginia, Richmond.

———. Correspondence. Virginia Historical Society, Richmond.

Lomax, Lunsford L. Correspondence. Maryland Historical Society, Baltimore.

———. Correspondence. Virginia Historical Society, Richmond.

———. Correspondence. Wilson Library, University of North Carolina, Chapel Hill.

McVicar, Charles W. Memoirs. Library of Congress, Washington, D.C.

Mosby, John Singleton. Letter of January 30, 1904. Joseph Bryan Papers, Virginia Historical Society, Richmond.

Moseley, John B. Diary, 1865. Virginia Historical Society, Richmond.

Munford, Thomas T. Correspondence. Library of Congress, Washington, D.C.

———. Correspondence. Library of Virginia, Richmond.

———. Correspondence. Virginia Historical Society, Richmond.

———. Correspondence. William R. Perkins Library, Duke University, Durham, N.C.

———. "Last Days of Fitz Lee's Cavalry Division." Virginia Historical Society, Richmond.

———. Correspondence. Library of Virginia, Richmond.

Payne, William H. F. Correspondence. Virginia Historical Society, Richmond.

———. Memoirs. Eleanor S. Brockenbrough Library, Museum of the Confederacy, Richmond, Va.

Price, R. Channing. Correspondence. Virginia Historical Society, Richmond.

———. Correspondence. Wilson Library, University of North Carolina, Chapel Hill.

Quinn, James T. "John S. Barbour and the Restoration of the Virginia Democracy, 1880–1892." M.A. thesis, University of Virginia, 1966.

Readnor, Harry W. "General Fitzhugh Lee, 1835–1905: A Biographical Study." M.A. thesis, University of Virginia, 1971.

Rosser, Thomas L. Correspondence. Alderman Library, University of Virginia, Charlottesville.

———. Correspondence. Virginia Historical Society, Richmond.

Smith, James D. "Virginia during Reconstruction, 1865–1870: A Political, Economic, and Social Study." Ph.D. dissertation, University of Virginia, 1960.

Stuart, J. E. B. Correspondence. Alderman Library, University of Virginia, Charlottesville.

———. Correspondence. Henry E. Huntington Library, San Marino, Calif.

———. Correspondence. Robert W. Woodruff Library, Emory University, Atlanta, Ga.

———. Correspondence. Virginia Historical Society, Richmond.

Stuart, James Hardeman. Correspondence and Diary, 1862. Mississippi Department of Archives and History, Jackson.

Thornton, John T. Correspondence. Alderman Library, University of Virginia, Charlottesville.

Venable, Andrew Reid. Papers. Virginia Historical Society, Richmond.

Wells, Edward L. Correspondence. Charleston Library Society, Charleston, S.C.

Wickham, Williams C. Correspondence. Eleanor S. Brockenbrough Library, Museum of the Confederacy, Richmond, Va.

―――. Letter of December 6, 1862. Virginia Historical Society, Richmond.

Wigfall, Halsey. Correspondence. Library of Congress, Washington, D.C.

NEWSPAPERS

Alexandria Gazette

Daily Richmond Examiner

Fredericksburg Star

National Intelligencer (Washington, D.C.)

New York Times

Richmond Dispatch

Richmond Enquirer

Richmond Times

Richmond Whig

San Antonio Ledger

ARTICLES AND ESSAYS

Agnew, N. J. "With the Virginia Cavalry." *Confederate Veteran* 32 (1924): 344–45.

Bates, Alfred E., and Edward J. McClernand. "The Second Regiment of Cavalry." In *The Army of the United States: Historical Sketches of Staff and Line . . .* , ed. Theophilus F. Rodenbough and William L. Haskin, 73–92. New York: Merrill & Co., 1906.

Beale, R. L. T. "Part Taken by the Ninth Virginia Cavalry in Repelling the Dahlgren Raid." *Southern Historical Society Papers* 3 (1877): 219–21.

Bearss, Edwin C. "' . . . Into the very jaws of the enemy . . . ': Jeb Stuart's Ride around McClellan." In *The Peninsula Campaign of 1862: Yorktown to the Seven Days,* 3 vols., ed. William J. Miller, 1:71–172. Campbell, Calif.: Savas Publishing Co., 1997.

Beauregard, P. G. T. "The First Battle of Bull Run." *Battles and Leaders of the Civil War* 1 (1887–88): 196–227.

―――. "Four Days of Battle at Petersburg." *Battles and Leaders of the Civil War* 4 (1887–88): 540–44.

Bond, Frank A. "Fitz Lee in [the] Army of Northern Virginia." *Confederate Veteran* 6 (1898): 420–21.

Bouldin, Edwin E. "The Last Charge at Appomattox: The Fourteenth Virginia Cavalry." *Southern Historical Society Papers* 28 (1900): 78–81.

"Brook Church Fight and Something About the Fifth North Carolina Cavalry . . . " *Southern Historical Society Papers* 29 (1901): 139–44.

Brown, Campbell. "General Ewell at Bull Run." *Battles and Leaders of the Civil War* 1 (1887–88): 259–61.

Butler, M. C. "The Cavalry Fight at Trevilian Station." *Battles and Leaders of the Civil War* 4 (1887–88): 237–39.

Campbell, William. "Stuart's Ride and Death of Latane . . . " *Southern Historical Society Papers* 39 (1914): 86–90.

Carpenter, Louis H. "Sheridan's Expedition around Richmond, May 9–25, 1864." *Journal of the United States Cavalry Association* 1 (1888): 300–324.

"Cavalry Fights with the Comanches." *Magazine of American History* 11 (1884): 170–73.

"Company A, First Maryland Cavalry." *Confederate Veteran* 6 (1898): 78–80.

Conrad, Holmes. "The Cavalry Corps of the Army of Northern Virginia." *The Photographic History of the Civil War* 4 (1911): 76–114.

Cooke, John Esten. "General Stuart in Camp and Field." In *Annals of the War, Written by Leading Participants, North and South,* 665–76. Philadelphia: Times Publishing Co., 1879.

Couch, Darius N. "The Chancellorsville Campaign." *Battles and Leaders of the Civil War* 3 (1887–88): 154–71.

Crimmins, Martin L. "'Fitz' Lee Kills an Indian." *Bulletin of the New York Public Library* 41 (1937): 385–88.

———. "'Jack' Hayes Story of Fitzhugh Lee's Indian Fight." *West Texas Historical Association Yearbook* 13 (1937): 40–49.

Davis, Curtis Carroll. "Very Well-Rounded Republican: The Several Lives of John S. Wise." *Virginia Magazine of History and Biography* 71 (1963): 461–87.

Davis, George B. "The Cavalry Combat at Brandy Station, Va., on June 9, 1863." *Journal of the United States Cavalry Association* 25 (1914): 190–98.

———. "The Cavalry Combat at Kelly's Ford in 1863." *Journal of the United States Cavalry Association* 25 (1915): 390–402.

———. "The Operations of the Cavalry in the Gettysburg Campaign." *Journal of the United States Cavalry Association* 1 (1888): 325–48.

———. "The Richmond Raid of 1864." *Journal of the United States Cavalry Association* 24 (1914): 707–22.

———. "The Stoneman Raid." *Journal of the United States Cavalry Association* 24 (1914): 533–52.

"The Death of General J. E. B. Stuart, by a Private of the Sixth Virginia Cavalry, C.S.A." *Battles and Leaders of the Civil War* 4 (1887–88): 194.

"Dedication of the Tomb of the Army of Northern Virginia Association and Unveiling of the Statue of Stonewall Jackson at New Orleans." *Southern Historical Society Papers* 9 (1881): 212–19.

Early, Jubal A. "Early's March to Washington in 1864." *Battles and Leaders of the Civil War* 4 (1887–88): 492–99.

———. "Winchester, Fisher's Hill, and Cedar Creek." *Battles and Leaders of the Civil War* 4 (1887–88) 522–30.

Eggert, Gerald G. "Our Man in Havana: Fitzhugh Lee." *Hispanic American Historical Review* 47 (1967): 463–85.

"Fitzhugh Lee, Governor-Elect of Virginia." *The Welcome Friend* (December 1887): 92.

"Fitzhugh Lee's Burial in Hollywood [Cemetery]." *Confederate Veteran* 14 (1906): 175.

Floyd, Dale E., ed. "I Have Severed My Connections with the North . . . " *Manuscripts* 26 (1974): 140–41.

"General Fitzhugh Lee Invited to Lecture in New England." *Southern Historical Society Papers* 11 (1883): 43–44.

"General Fitzhugh Lee . . . Second Lecturing Tour." *Southern Historical Society Papers* 11 (1883): 142.

"General Fitzhugh Lee's Second Tour in Behalf of the Southern Historical Society." *Southern Historical Society Papers* 11 (1883): 228–38.

"General Fitzhugh Lee's Tour." *Southern Historical Society Papers* 10 (1882): 569–75.

"General Fitz. Lee's Southern Tour." *Southern Historical Society Papers* 11 (1883): 44–48.

"Gen. Fitzhugh Lee." *Confederate Veteran* 13 (1905): 280–81.

"Gen. Fitzhugh Lee in Havana." *Confederate Veteran* 16 (1908): 188–89.

"Gens. Fitzhugh Lee and Wade Hampton." *Confederate Veteran* 6 (1898): 156.

Gibbon, John. "Personal Recollections of Appomattox." *Century Illustrated Monthly Magazine* 63 (1902): 936–43.

Greene, A. Wilson. "Opportunity to the South: Meade versus Jackson at Fredericksburg." *Civil War History* 33 (1987): 295–314.

Gregg, David McMurtrie. "The Union Cavalry at Gettysburg." In *Annals of the War, Written by Leading Participants, North and South,* 372–79. Philadelphia: Times Publishing Co., 1879.

"'Grumble Jones': A Personality Profile." *Civil War Times Illustrated* 7 (June 1968): 35–41.

Harbord, J. G. "The History of the Cavalry of the Army of Northern Virginia." *Journal of the United States Cavalry Association* 14 (1904): 423–503.

Harrison, George F. "Ewell at First Manassas." *Southern Historical Society Papers* 14 (1886): 356–59.

Hassler, William W. "The Battle of Yellow Tavern." *Civil War Times Illustrated* 5 (November 1966): 5–11, 46–48.

Haw, John R. "The Battle of Haw's Shop, Va." *Confederate Veteran* 3 (1925): 373–76.

Hayes, E. M. "Fitzhugh Lee as an Indian Fighter." *The Monthly Chronicle: Episcopal High School . . . Alexandria, Va.* 7 (February 1895): 3–8.

Hill, Daniel H. "The Battle of South Mountain, or Boonsboro'." *Battles and Leaders of the Civil War* 2 (1887–88): 559–81.

Hunter, Robert W. "Fitzhugh Lee: An Address Delivered on Fitzhugh Lee Day at the Jamestown Exposition." *Southern Historical Society Papers* 35 (1907): 132–45.

Imboden, John D. "The Confederate Retreat from Gettysburg." *Battles and Leaders of the Civil War* 3 (1887–88): 420–29.

Jackson, Huntington W. "Sedgwick at Fredericksburg and Salem Heights." *Battles and Leaders of the Civil War* 3 (1887–88): 224–32.

James, G. Watson. "Dahlgren's Raid." *Southern Historical Society Papers* 39 (1914): 63–72.

Johnston, John W. "Repudiation in Virginia." *North American Review* 134 (1882): 149–60.

———. "Thomas and Lee—Historical Facts." *Confederate Veteran* 11 (1903): 559–60.

Jones, J. William, comp. "Kilpatrick-Dahlgren Raid against Richmond." *Southern Historical Society Papers* 13 (1885): 515–51.

"Kilpatrick's and Dahlgren's Raid to Richmond." *Battles and Leaders of the Civil War* 4 (1887–88): 95–96.

Krick, Robert E. L. "Defending Lee's Flank: J. E. B. Stuart, John Pelham, and Confederate Artillery on Nicodemus Heights." In *The Antietam Campaign,* ed. Gary A. Gallagher, 192–222. Chapel Hill: University of North Carolina Press, 1999.

Lee, Fitzhugh. "Chancellorsville—Address of General Fitzhugh Lee before the Virginia Division, A.N.V. Association, October 29th, 1879." *Southern Historical Society Papers* 7 (1879): 545–85.

———. "Cuba and Her Struggle for Freedom, from Personal Observations and Experiences." *Fortnightly Review* 63 (1898): 855–66.

———. "The Death of Colonel Dahlgren." *Southern Historical Society Papers* 13 (1885): 552–55.

———. "Letter from General Fitz. Lee." *Southern Historical Society Papers* 4 (1877): 69–76.

———. "A Review of the First Two Days' Operations at Gettysburg and a Reply to General Longstreet by General Fitz. Lee." *Southern Historical Society Papers* 5 (1878): 162–68.

———. "Sketch of the Late General S. Cooper." *Southern Historical Society Papers* 3 (1877): 269–74.

———. "Speech Made in New York by Gen. Fitzhugh Lee on Immigration." *Southern Planter and Farmer* 27 (1876): 13–15.

———. "Speech of General Fitz Lee at A.N.V. Banquet, October 28th, 1875." *Southern Historical Society Papers* 1 (1876): 99–103.

———. "Synopsis of Gen. Fitzhugh Lee's Address Exhibiting His Plan to Secure Immigration to Virginia." *Southern Planter and Farmer* 27 (1876): 118–22.

Longacre, Edward G. "Cavalry Clash at Todd's Tavern." *Civil War Times Illustrated* 16 (October 1977): 12–21.

————. "The Long Run for Trevilian Station." *Civil War Times Illustrated* 18 (November 1979): 28–39.

————. "Stuart's Dumfries Raid." *Civil War Times Illustrated* 15 (July 1976): 18–26.

MacDonnell, Francis. "The Confederate Spin on Winfield Scott and George Thomas." *Civil War History* 44 (1998): 255–66.

Mason, W. Roy. "Marching on Manassas." *Battles and Leaders of the Civil War* 2 (1887–88): 528–29.

McClellan, Henry B. " . . . Address of Major H. B. McClellan on the Life, Campaigns, and Character of Gen'l J. E. B. Stuart." *Southern Historical Society Papers* 8 (1880): 433–56.

McClernand, Edward J. "Cavalry Operations: The Wilderness to the James River." *Journal of the Military Service Institution of the United States* 30 (1902): 321–43.

McCormick, Cyrus. "How Gallant Stuart Met His Death." *Confederate Veteran* 39 (1931): 98–100.

McCrary, Ella L. "Life and Public Services of Fitzhugh Lee." *Midland Monthly* 10 (1898): 42–47.

McKim, Randolph H. "The Confederate Cavalry in the Gettysburg Campaign." *Journal of the Military Service Institution of the United States* 46 (1910): 414–27.

Merritt, Wesley. "Sheridan in the Shenandoah Valley." *Battles and Leaders of the Civil War* 4 (1887–88): 500–521.

Miller, Samuel H. "Yellow Tavern." *Civil War History* 2 (1956): 57–81.

Miller, William E. "The Cavalry Battle Near Gettysburg." *Battles and Leaders of the Civil War* 3 (1887–88): 397–406.

Monaghan, Jay. "Custer's 'Last Stand'—Trevilian Station, 1864." *Civil War History* 8 (1962): 245–58.

Moger, Allen W. "Railroad Practices and Policies in Virginia after the Civil War." *Virginia Magazine of History and Biography* 59 (1951): 423–57.

"The Monument to General Robert E. Lee." *Southern Historical Society Papers* 17 (1889): 187–335.

Morrison, James L. "The Struggle between Sectionalism and Nationalism at Antebellum West Point, 1830–1861." *Civil War History* 19 (1973): 138–48.

Mosby, John Singleton "A Bit of Partisan Service." *Battles and Leaders of the Civil War* 3 (1887–88): 148–51.

————. "The Confederate Cavalry in the Gettysburg Campaign." *Battles and Leaders of the Civil War* 3 (1887–88): 251–52.

"Mother of Gen. Fitzhugh Lee." *Confederate Veteran* 6 (1898): 501–02.

"Mrs. Fitzhugh Lee." *Confederate Veteran* 5 (1897): 125.

Munford, Thomas T. "Reminiscences of Cavalry Operations: Paper No. 1." *Southern Historical Society Papers* 12 (1884): 342–50.

———. "Reminiscences of Cavalry Operations, Paper Number 2: Battle of Winchester, 19th September '64." *Southern Historical Society Papers* 12 (1884): 447–59.

Parker, James. "Mounted and Dismounted Action of Cavalry." *Journal of the Military Service Institution of the United States* 39 (1906): 381–87.

Pleasonton, Alfred. "The Campaign of Gettysburg." In *Annals of the War, Written by Leading Participants, North and South*, 447–59. Philadelphia: Times Publishing Co., 1879.

———. "The Successes and Failures of Chancellorsville." *Battles and Leaders of the Civil War* 3 (1887–88): 172–82.

Porter, Horace. "Five Forks and the Pursuit of Lee." *Battles and Leaders of the Civil War* 4 (1887–88): 708–22.

Purifoy, John. "Stuart's Cavalry Battle at Gettysburg, July 3, 1863." *Confederate Veteran* 32 (1924): 260–63.

Rawle, William Brooke. "Further Remarks on the Cavalry Fight on the Right Flank at Gettysburg." *Journal of the United States Cavalry Association* 4 (1891): 157–60.

———. "Gregg's Cavalry Fight at Gettysburg, July 3, 1863." *Journal of the United States Cavalry Association* 4 (1891): 257–75.

Redwood, Allen C. "Following Stuart's Feather." *Journal of the Military Service Institution of the United States* 49 (1911): 111–21.

Reeves, Paschal. "Thomas S. Martin, Committee Statesman." *Virginia Magazine of History and Biography* 68 (1960): 344–64.

Rhea, Gordon C. "'The Hottest Place I Ever Was In': The Battle of Haw's Shop, May 28, 1864." *North & South* 4 (April 2001): 42–57.

Robins, W. T. "Stuart's Ride around McClellan." *Battles and Leaders of the Civil War* 2 (1887–88): 271–75.

Rodenbough, Theophilus F. "Sheridan's Richmond Raid." *Battles and Leaders of the Civil War* 4 (1887–88): 188–93.

———. "Sheridan's Trevilian Raid." *Battles and Leaders of the Civil War* 4 (1887–88): 233–36.

Rowland, Thomas. "Letters of Thomas Rowland at West Point, 1859–1861." *South Atlantic Quarterly* 14 (1915): 330–47.

Ryckman, W. G. "Clash of Cavalry at Trevilians." *Virginia Magazine of History and Biography* 75 (1967): 443–58.

Scribner, Robert L. "Ex-Confederate in Blue." *Virginia Cavalcade* 5 (Spring 1956): 16–21.

"The Second Virginia Regiment of Cavalry, C.S.A." *Southern Historical Society Papers* 16 (1888): 354–56.

Starr, Stephen Z., ed. "Dinwiddie Court House and Five Forks: Reminiscences of Roger Hannaford, Second Ohio Volunteer Cavalry." *Virginia Magazine of History and Biography* 87 (1978): 417–37.

"Stuart's Ride around McClellan." *Confederate Veteran* 5 (1897): 53–54.

Sword, Wiley. "Cavalry on Trial at Kelly's Ford." *Civil War Times Illustrated* 13 (April 1974): 32–40.

Taliaferro, W. B. "Jackson's Raid Around Pope." *Battles and Leaders of the Civil War* 2 (1887–88): 501–22.

Taylor, Robert T. "The Jamestown Tricentennial Exposition of 1907." *Virginia Magazine of History and Biography* 65 (1957): 169–208.

Thoburn, Joseph B. "Indian Fight in Ford County in 1859." *Collections of the Kansas State Historical Society* 12 (1912): 312–29.

"Two Cavalry Chieftains." *Southern Historical Society Papers* 16 (1888): 451–54.

Walker, John G. "Sharpsburg." *Battles and Leaders of the Civil War* 2 (1887–88): 675–82.

Watson, Thomas Jackson. "Was with 'Jeb' Stuart When He Was Shot." *Confederate Veteran* 11 (1903): 553.

Weakley, T. P. "'Jack' and 'Fitz.'" *Confederate Veteran* 11 (1903): 272–73.

Wert, Jeffry. "His Unhonored Service." *Civil War Times Illustrated* 24 (June 1985): 29–34.

BOOKS AND PAMPHLETS

Alexander, Edward Porter. *Fighting for the Confederacy: The Personal Recollections of General Edward Porter Alexander,* ed. Gary A. Gallagher. Chapel Hill: University of North Carolina Press, 1989.

———. *Military Memoirs of a Confederate: A Critical Narrative.* New York: Charles Scribner's Sons, 1907.

Alexander, Frederick Warren, comp. *Stratford Hall and the Lees Connected with Its History . . .* Oak Grove, Va.: Privately published, 1912.

Arnold, James R. *Jeff Davis's Own: Cavalry, Comanches, and the Battle for the Texas Frontier.* New York: John Wiley & Sons, 2000.

Averell, William W. *Ten Years in the Saddle: The Memoir of William Woods Averell, 1851–1862,* ed. Edward K. Eckert and Nicholas J. Amato. San Rafael, Calif.: Presidio Press, 1978.

Bayard, Samuel J. *The Life of George Dashiell Bayard . . .* New York: G. P. Putnam's Sons, 1874.

Baylor, George. *Bull Run to Bull Run; or, Four Years in the Army of Northern Virginia . . .* Richmond, Va.: B. F. Johnson Co., 1900.

Beale, George W. *A Lieutenant of Cavalry in Lee's Army.* Boston: Gorham Press, 1918.

Beale, R. L. T. *History of the Ninth Virginia Cavalry in the War between the States.* Richmond, Va.: B. F. Johnson Co., 1899.

Bearss, Edwin C. *The Campaign for Vicksburg.* 3 vols. Dayton, Ohio: Morningside, 1985–86.

Bearss, Edwin C., and Chris M. Calkins. *The Battle of Five Forks.* Lynchburg, Va.: H. E. Howard, Inc., 1985.

Bigelow, John, Jr. *The Campaign of Chancellorsville: A Strategic and Tactical Study.* New Haven, Conn.: Yale University Press, 1910.

Blackford, Charles M., and Susan Leigh Blackford. *Letters from Lee's Army* . . . Ed. Charles Minor Blackford III. New York: Charles Scribner's Sons, 1947.

Blackford, William W. *War Years with Jeb Stuart.* New York: Charles Scribner's Sons, 1945.

Blake, Nelson Morehouse. *William Mahone of Virginia, Soldier and Political Insurgent.* Richmond, Va.: Garrett & Massie, 1935.

Blow, Michael. *A Ship to Remember: The* Maine *and the Spanish-American War.* New York: William Morrow & Co., Inc., 1992.

Brackett, Albert G. *History of the United States Cavalry . . . to the 1st of June, 1863.* New York: Harper & Brothers, 1865.

Brooks, U. R. *Butler and His Cavalry in the War of Secession, 1861–1865.* Columbia, S.C.: State Co., 1909.

Brooksher, William R., and David K. Snider. *Glory at a Gallop: Tales of the Confederate Cavalry.* Washington, D.C.: Brassey's, 1995.

Bushong, Millard K., and Dean M. Bushong. *Fightin' Tom Rosser, C.S.A.* Shippensburg, Pa.: Beidel Printing House, 1983.

Calkins, Chris M. *The Appomattox Campaign, March 29–April 9, 1865.* Conshohocken, Pa.: Combined Books, 1997.

Carter, Samuel, III. *The Last Cavaliers: Confederate and Union Cavalry in the Civil War.* New York: St. Martin's Press, 1979.

Carter, William R. *Sabres, Saddles, and Spurs: The Diary of Lt. Col. William R. Carter, 3rd Virginia Cavalry.* Ed. Walbrook D. Swank. Shippensburg, Pa.: Burd Street Press, 1998.

Catton, Bruce. *A Stillness at Appomattox.* Garden City, N.Y.: Doubleday & Co., Inc., 1953.

Chadwick, French Ensor. *The Relations of the United States and Spain: Diplomacy.* New York: Charles Scribner's Sons, 1909.

Chalfant, William Y. *Cheyennes and Horse Soldiers: The 1857 Expedition and Battle of Solomon's Fork.* Norman: University of Oklahoma Press, 1989.

Chesnut, Mary Boykin. *A Diary from Dixie.* Ed. Ben Ames Williams. Boston: Houghton Mifflin Co., 1961.

Cleveland, Grover. *Letters of Grover Cleveland, 1850–1908.* Ed. Allan Nevins. Boston: Houghton Mifflin Co., 1933.

Coddington, Edwin B. *The Gettysburg Campaign: A Study in Command.* New York: Charles Scribner's Sons, 1968.

Connelly, Thomas Lawrence. *Army of the Heartland: The Army of Tennessee, 1861–1862.* Baton Rouge: Louisiana State University Press, 1967.

———. *Autumn of Glory: The Army of Tennessee, 1862–1865.* Baton Rouge: Louisiana State University Press, 1971.

Cooke, Jacob B. *The Battle of Kelly's Ford, March 17, 1863.* Providence, R.I.: Privately published, 1887.

Cooke, John Esten. *Wearing of the Gray: Being Personal Portraits, Scenes and Adventures of the War.* Baton Rouge: Louisiana State University Press, 1997.

Corson, William Clark. *My Dear Jennie: A Collection of Love Letters from a Confederate Soldier to His Fiancée during the Period 1861–1865.* Ed. Blake W. Corson Jr. Richmond, Va.: Dietz Press, 1982.

Cullum, George Washington, comp. *Biographical Register of the Officers and Graduates of the United States Military Academy at West Point, New York.* 2 vols. Boston: Houghton, Mifflin Co., 1891.

Current, Richard N., ed. *Encyclopedia of the Confederacy.* 4 vols. New York: Simon & Schuster, 1993.

Cutchins, John A. *A Famous Command: The Richmond Light Infantry Blues.* Richmond, Va.: Garrett & Massie, 1934.

Dahlgren, John A. *Memoir of Ulric Dahlgren.* Philadelphia: Privately published, 1872.

Daughtry, Mary Bandy. *Gray Cavalier: The Life and Wars of General W. H. F. "Rooney" Lee.* New York: Da Capo Press, 2002.

Davis, Burke. *Jeb Stuart, the Last Cavalier.* New York: Rinehart & Co., 1957.

Davis, Richard Harding. *The Cuban and Porto Rican Campaigns.* New York: Charles Scribner's Sons, 1904.

Davis, William C. *Battle at Bull Run: A History of the First Major Campaign of the Civil War.* Garden City, N.Y.: Doubleday & Co., Inc., 1977.

DeLeon, T. C. *Belles, Beaux and Brains of the 60's.* New York: G. W. Dillingham Co., 1907.

Doubleday, Abner. *Chancellorsville and Gettysburg.* New York: Charles Scribner's Sons, 1882.

Douglas, Henry Kyd. *I Rode with Stonewall: Being Chiefly the War Experiences of the Youngest Member of Jackson's Staff . . .* Chapel Hill: University of North Carolina Press, 1940.

Driver, Robert J., Jr. *First & Second Maryland Cavalry, C.S.A.* Charlottesville, Va.: Rockbridge Publishing Co., 1999.

————. *1st Virginia Cavalry.* Lynchburg, Va.: H. E. Howard, 1991.

Driver, Robert J., Jr., and H. E. Howard. *2nd Virginia Cavalry.* Lynchburg, Va.: H. E. Howard, 1995.

Dulany, Richard H., et al. *The Dulanys of Welbourne: A Family in Mosby's Confederacy.* Ed. Margaret Ann Vogtsberger. Berryville, Va.: Rockbridge Publishing Co., 1995.

Dunne, Finley Peter. *Mr. Dooley in Peace and in War.* Boston: Small, Maynard & Co., 1899.

Early, Jubal A. *War Memoirs: Autobiographical Sketch and Narrative of the War between the States.* Ed. Frank E. Vandiver. Bloomington: Indiana University Press, 1960.

Eliot, Ellsworth, Jr. *West Point in the Confederacy.* New York: G. A. Baker & Co., Inc., 1941.

Encounter at Hanover: Prelude to Gettysburg. Hanover, Pa.: Hanover Chamber of Commerce, 1963.

Farley, Joseph Pearson. *West Point in the Early Sixties, with Incidents of the War.* Troy, N.Y.: Pafraets Book Co., 1902.

Fishwick, Marshall W. *Gentlemen of Virginia.* New York: Dodd, Mead & Co., 1961.

———. *Virginia: A New Look at the Old Dominion.* New York: Harper & Brothers, 1959.

Frazer, Robert W. *Forts of the West: Military Forts . . . West of the Mississippi River to 1898.* Norman: University of Oklahoma Press, 1965.

Freeman, Douglas Southall. *Lee's Lieutenants: A Study in Command.* 3 vols. New York: Charles Scribner's Sons, 1942–44.

———. *R. E. Lee: A Biography.* 4 vols. New York: Charles Scribner's Sons, 1934–35.

Furgurson, Ernest B. *Chancellorsville: The Souls of the Brave.* New York: Alfred A. Knopf, 1992.

Garraty, John A., and Mark C. Carnes, eds. *American National Biography.* 24 vols. New York: Oxford University Press, 1999.

Glass, Robert C., and Carter Glass, Jr. *Virginia Democracy: A History of the Achievements of the Party and Its Leaders in the Mother of Commonwealths, the Old Dominion.* 3 vols. N.p.: Democratic Historical Association, Inc., 1937.

Godson, William F. H., Jr. *The History of West Point, 1852–1902.* Philadelphia: Privately published, 1934.

Grant, Ulysses S. *Personal Memoirs of U. S. Grant.* Ed. E. B. Long. New York: Da Capo Press, 2001.

Grimsley, Daniel A. *Battles in Culpeper County, Virginia, 1861–1865.* Culpeper, Va.: Raleigh-Travers-Green Co., 1900.

Haden, B. J. *Reminiscences of J. E. B. Stuart's Cavalry . . .* Charlottesville, Va.: Progress Publishing Co., ca. 1890.

Hampton, Wade, III, et al. *Family Letters of Three Wade Hamptons, 1782–1901.* Ed. Charles E. Cauthen. Columbia: University of South Carolina Press, 1953.

Harrison, Mrs. Burton. *Recollections Grave and Gay.* New York: Charles Scribner's Sons, 1912.

Harrison, Walter. *Pickett's Men: A Fragment of War History.* New York: D. Van Nostrand, 1870.

Hartje, Robert G. *Van Dorn: The Life and Times of a Confederate General.* Nashville, Tenn.: Vanderbilt University Press, 1967.

Healy, David F. *The United States in Cuba, 1898–1902: Generals, Politicians, and the Search for Policy.* Madison: University of Wisconsin Press, 1963.

Hebert, Walter H. *Fighting Joe Hooker.* Indianapolis: Bobbs-Merrill Co., 1944.

Heitman, Francis B., comp. *Historical Register and Dictionary of the United States Army* . . . 2 vols. Washington, D.C.: Government Printing Office, 1903.

Hennessy, John J. *The First Battle of Manassas: An End to Innocence, July 18–21, 1861.* Lynchburg, Va.: H. E. Howard, 1989.

———. *Return to Bull Run: The Campaign and Battle of Second Manassas.* New York: Simon & Schuster, 1993.

Hewett, Janet, et al., comps. *Supplement to the Official Records of the Union and Confederate Armies.* 3 series, 99 vols. Wilmington, N.C.: Broadfoot Publishing Co., 1994–2001.

Hirshon, Stanley P. *Farewell to the Bloody Shirt: Northern Republicans & the Southern Negro, 1877–1893.* Bloomington: Indiana University Press, 1962.

House Document No. 406 (55th Congress, 2nd Session): Consular Correspondence Respecting the Condition of the Reconcentrados in Cuba, the State of the War in That Island, and the Prospects of the Projected Autonomy. Washington, D.C.: Government Printing Office, 1898.

Hudgins, Robert S., II. *Recollections of an Old Dominion Dragoon: The Civil War Experiences of Sgt. Robert S. Hudgins, II, Company B, 3rd Virginia Cavalry.* Ed. Garland C. Hudgins and Richard B. Kleese. Orange, Va.: Publisher's Press, 1993.

Humphreys, Andrew A. *Gettysburg to the Rapidan: The Army of the Potomac, July, 1863, to April, 1864.* New York: Charles Scribner's Sons, 1883.

Hunton, Eppa. *Autobiography of Eppa Hunton.* Richmond, Va.: William Byrd Press, 1933.

Jackson, Mary Anna. *Memoirs of Stonewall Jackson by His Widow* . . Louisville, Ky.: Prentice Press, 1895.

Johnston, Joseph E. *Narrative of Military Operations during the Civil War.* New York: D. Appleton & Co., 1874.

Jones, J. William. *Life and Letters of Robert Edward Lee, Soldier and Man.* New York: Neale Publishing Co., 1906.

———. *Virginia's Next Governor: Gen'l Fitzhugh Lee.* New York: N.Y. Cheap Publishing Co., 1885.

Jones, Virgil Carrington. *Eight Hours before Richmond.* New York: Henry Holt & Co., 1957.

Journal of the House of Delegates of the State of Virginia . . . Richmond, Va.: Various publishers, 1885–89.

Journal of the Senate of the Commonwealth of Virginia . . . Richmond, Va.: Various publishers, 1885–89.

Kinsley, Ardyce, comp. *The Fitzhugh Lee Sampler.* Lively, Va.: Brandylane Publishers, 1992.

Knapp, David, Jr. *The Confederate Horsemen.* New York: Vantage Press, 1966.

Krick, Robert E. L. *Staff Officers in Gray: A Biographical Register of the Staff Officers in the Army of Northern Virginia.* Chapel Hill: University of North Carolina Press, 2003.

Krick, Robert L. *Lee's Colonels: A Biographical Register of the Field Officers of the Army of Northern Virginia.* Dayton, Ohio: Morningside Bookshop, 1979.

Lee, Edmund Jennings. *Lee of Virginia, 1642–1892: Biographical and Genealogical Sketches of the Descendants of Colonel Richard Lee . . .* Philadelphia: Privately published, 1895.

Lee, Fitzhugh. *General Lee.* New York: D. Appleton & Co., 1894.

———. *Report of Commanding General Fitzhugh Lee Outlining Governmental, Economic, and Social Conditions in the Department of Havana and Pinar del Rio at the Beginning of the U.S. Occupation, and Resulting Changes.* Havana: Adjutant General's Office, Headquarters Department of the Province of Havana & Pinar del Rio, 1899.

Lee, Fitzhugh, and Joseph Wheeler. *Cuba's Struggle against Spain, with the Causes for American Intervention and a Full Account of the Spanish American War, Including Final Peace Negotiations.* New York: American Historical Press, 1899.

Lee, Robert E. *Lee's Dispatches: Unpublished Letters of General Robert E. Lee, C.S.A., to Jefferson Davis and the War Department of the Confederate States of America.* Ed. Douglas Southall Freeman and Grady McWhiney. New York: G. P. Putnam's Sons, 1957.

———. *The Wartime Papers of R. E. Lee.* Ed. Clifford Dowdey and Louis H. Manarin. Boston: Little, Brown & Co., 1961.

Lee, Robert E., Jr. *Recollections and Letters of Gen. Robert E. Lee, by His Son.* Garden City, N.Y.: Garden City Publishing Co., 1926.

Leech, Margaret. *In the Days of McKinley.* New York: Harper & Brothers, 1959.

Lomax, Elizabeth Lindsay. *Leaves from an Old Washington Diary, 1854–1863.* Ed. Lindsay Lomax Wood. New York: Books, Inc., 1943.

Long, A. L. *Memoirs of Robert E. Lee: His Military and Personal History . . .* New York: J. M. Stoddart & Co., 1886.

Longacre, Edward G. *The Cavalry at Gettysburg: A Tactical Study of Mounted Operations during the Civil War's Pivotal Campaign, 9 June–14 July 1863.* Rutherford, N. J.: Fairleigh-Dickinson University Press, 1986.

———. *Gentleman and Soldier: A Biography of Wade Hampton III.* Nashville, Tenn.: Rutledge Hill Press, 2003.

———. *Lee's Cavalrymen: A History of the Mounted Forces of the Army of Northern Virginia, 1861–1865.* Mechanicsburg, Pa.: Stackpole Books, 2002.

———. *Lincoln's Cavalrymen: A History of the Mounted Forces of the Army of the Potomac, 1861–1865.* Harrisburg, Pa.: Stackpole Books, 2000.

Longstreet, James. *From Manassas to Appomattox: Memories of the Civil War in America.* Philadelphia: J. B. Lippincott Co., 1896.

Lonn, Ella. *Foreigners in the Confederacy.* Chapel Hill: University of North Carolina Press, 1940.

Maddex, Jack P., Jr. *The Virginia Conservatives, 1867–1879.* Chapel Hill: University of North Carolina Press, 1970.

Marshall, Charles. *An Aide-de-Camp of Lee: Being the Papers of Colonel Charles Marshall* . . . Ed. Sir Frederick Maurice. Boston: Little, Brown & Co., 1927.

McClellan, Henry B. *Life and Campaigns of Maj. Gen. J. E. B. Stuart, Commander of the Cavalry of the Army of Northern Virginia.* Boston: Houghton, Mifflin & Co., 1885.

McCrea, Tully. *Dear Belle: Letters from a Cadet & Officer to His Sweetheart, 1858–1865.* Ed. Catherine S. Crary. Middletown, Conn.: Wesleyan University Press, 1965.

McKim, Randolph H. *A Soldier's Recollections: Leaves from the Diary of a Young Confederate* . . . New York: Longmans, Green, & Co., 1910.

McPherson, James M. *Ordeal by Fire: The Civil War and Reconstruction.* New York: Alfred A. Knopf, 1982.

Millett, Allan R. *The Politics of Intervention: The Military Occupation of Cuba, 1906–1909.* Columbus: Ohio State University Press, 1968.

Millis, Walter. *The Martial Spirit: A Study of Our War with Spain.* Boston: Houghton, Mifflin Co., 1931.

Moger, Allen W. *Virginia: Bourbonism to Byrd, 1870–1925.* Charlottesville: University Press of Virginia, 1968.

Morgan, H. Wayne. *America's Road to Empire: The War with Spain and Overseas Expansion.* New York: John Wiley & Sons, Inc., 1965.

Morrison, James L., Jr. *"The Best School in the World": West Point, the Pre-Civil War Years, 1833–1866.* Kent, Ohio: Kent State University Press, 1986.

Morton, Richard L. *The Negro in Virginia Politics, 1865–1902.* Spartanburg, S.C.: Reprint Co., 1973.

Mosby, John Singleton. *The Letters of John S. Mosby.* Ed. Adele H. Mitchell. N.p.: Stuart-Mosby Historical Society, 1986.

———. *The Memoirs of Colonel John S. Mosby.* Ed. Charles Wells Russell. Boston: Little, Brown & Co., 1917.

———. *Mosby's War Reminiscences and Stuart's Cavalry Campaigns.* Boston: G. A. Jones & Co., 1887.

———. *Stuart's Cavalry in the Gettysburg Campaign.* New York: Moffat, Yard & Co., 1908.

Munford, Robert Beverly, Jr. *Richmond Homes and Memories.* Richmond, Va.: Garrett & Massie, 1936.

Myers, Franklin M. *The Comanches: A History of White's Battalion Virginia Cavalry. Laurel Brig., Hampton['s] Div., A.N.V., C.S.A.* Baltimore: Kelly, Piet & Co., 1871.

Nanzig, Thomas P. *3rd Virginia Cavalry.* Lynchburg, Va.: H. E. Howard, 1989.

Neese, George M. *Three Years in the Confederate Horse Artillery.* New York: Neale Publishing Co., 1911.

Nesbitt, Mark. *Saber and Scapegoat: J. E. B. Stuart and the Gettysburg Campaign.* Mechanicsburg, Pa.: Stackpole Books, 1994.

Nevins, Allan. *Grover Cleveland: A Study in Courage.* New York: Dodd, Mead & Co., 1933.

Newhall, F. C. *How Lee Lost the Use of His Cavalry before the Battle of Gettysburg.* Philadelphia: Privately published, 1878.

Nichols, James L. *General Fitzhugh Lee: A Biography.* Lynchburg, Va.: H. E. Howard Co., 1989.

Nye, Wilbur S. *Here Come the Rebels!* Baton Rouge: Louisiana State University Press, 1965.

O'Ferrall, Charles T. *Forty Years of Active Service: Being Some History of the War between the Confederacy and the Union . . .* New York: Neale Publishing Co., 1904.

Official Records of the Union and Confederate Navies in the War of the Rebellion. 2 series, 30 vols. Washington, D.C.: Government Printing Office, 1894–1922.

Official Register of the Officers and Cadets of the U.S. Military Academy, West Point, N.Y. . . . West Point, N.Y.: Privately published, 1853–57.

O'Neill, Robert F., Jr. *The Cavalry Battles of Aldie, Middleburg and Upperville: "Small But Important Riots," June 10–27, 1863.* Lynchburg, Va.: H. E. Howard, Inc., 1993.

Opie, John N. *A Rebel Cavalryman with Lee, Stuart, and Jackson.* Chicago: W. B. Conkey Co., 1899.

Pearson, Charles Chilton. *The Readjuster Movement in Virginia.* New Haven, Conn.: Yale University Press, 1917.

Pratt, Julius W. *Expansionists of 1898: The Acquisition of Hawaii and the Spanish Islands.* New York: Peter Smith, 1951.

Price, George D., comp. *Across the Continent with the Fifth [United States] Cavalry.* New York: D. Van Nostrand, 1883.

Pulley, Raymond. *Old Virginia Restored: An Interpretation of the Progressive Impulse, 1870–1930.* Charlottesville: University Press of Virginia, 1968.

Ramage, James A. *Gray Ghost: The Life of Col. John Singleton Mosby.* Lexington: University Press of Kentucky, 1999.

Rawle, William Brooke. *The Right Flank at Gettysburg: An Account of the Operations of General Gregg's Cavalry Command. . . .* Philadelphia: Allen, Lane & Scott, 1878.

———. *With Gregg in the Gettysburg Campaign.* Philadelphia: McLaughlin Brothers, 1884.

Rhea, Gordon C. *The Battles for Spotsylvania Court House and the Road to Yellow Tavern, May 7–12, 1864.* Baton Rouge: Louisiana State University Press, 1997.

Rodenbough, Theophilus F., and William L. Haskin, eds. *The Army of The United States: Historical Sketches of Staff and Line . . .* New York: Merrill & Co., 1896.

Rodick, Burleigh Cushing. *Appomattox: The Last Campaign.* New York: Philosophical Library, 1965.

Rosser, Thomas L. *Riding with Rosser.* Ed. S. Roger Keller. Shippensburg, Pa.: White Mane Publishing Co., 1997.

Roster of Troops of the Department of Havana and Pinar del Rio, Brigadier General Fitzhugh Lee, Commanding . . . May 1900. Havana: Adjutant General's Office, Headquarters Department of Havana & Pinar del Rio, 1900.

Roster of Troops of the Department of the Province of Havana and Pinar del Rio, Brigadier General Fitzhugh Lee, Commanding . . . May 5,1899. Havana: Adjutant General's Office, Headquarters Department Province of Havana & Pinar del Rio, 1899.

Royall, William L. *Some Reminiscences.* New York: Neale Publishing Co., 1909.

Samuels, Peggy, and Harold Samuels. *Remembering the* Maine. Washington, D.C.: Smithsonian Institution Press, 1995.

Sears, Stephen W. *Chancellorsville.* Boston: Houghton Mifflin Co., 1996.

———. *Landscape Turned Red: The Battle of Antietam.* New Haven, Conn.: Ticknor & Fields, 1983.

———. *To the Gates of Richmond: The Peninsula Campaign.* New York: Ticknor & Fields, 1992.

Shelton, William DuBose. *Populism in the Old Dominion: Virginia Farm Politics, 1885–1900.* Princeton, N.J: Princeton University Press, 1935.

Sheridan, Philip H. *Personal Memoirs of P. H. Sheridan.* 2 vols. New York: Charles L. Webster & Co., 1888.

Snow, William Parker. *Southern Generals: Who They Are, and What They Have Done.* New York: Charles B. Richardson, 1865.

Sorrel, G. Moxley. *Recollections of a Confederate Staff Officer.* New York: Neale Publishing Co., 1905.

Stiles, Kenneth L. *4th Virginia Cavalry.* Lynchburg, Va.: H. E. Howard, 1985.

Stribling, Robert M. *Gettysburg Campaign and Campaigns of 1864 and 1865 in Virginia.* Petersburg, Va.: Franklin Press Co., 1905.

Stuart, James Ewell Brown. *Letters of General J. E. B. Stuart to His Wife, 1861.* Ed. Bingham Duncan. Atlanta: Emory University Publications, 1943.

———. *The Letters of General James E. B. Stuart.* Ed. Adele H. Mitchell. N.p.: Stuart-Mosby Historical Society, 1990.

Thirty-sixth Annual Reunion of the Association of the Graduates of the United States Military Academy, at West Point, New York, June 13th, 1905. Saginaw, Mich.: Seemann & Peters, 1905.

Thomas, Emory M. *Bold Dragoon: The Life of J. E. B. Stuart.* New York: Harper & Row, 1986.

Thomas, Hugh. *Cuba: The Pursuit of Freedom.* New York: Harper & Row, 1971.

Thomason, John W., Jr. *Jeb Stuart.* New York: Charles Scribner's Sons, 1930.

Tousey, Thomas G. *Military History of Carlisle and Carlisle Barracks.* Richmond, Va.: Dietz Press, 1939.

Trask, David. *The War with Spain in 1898.* New York: Macmillan Co., 1981.

Tremain, Henry E. *Last Hours of Sheridan's Cavalry: A Reprint of War Memoranda.* New York: Bonnell, Silver & Bowers, 1904.

Tyler, Lyon Gardiner, ed. *Encyclopedia of Virginia Biography.* 5 vols. New York: Lewis Historical Publishing Co., 1915.

Utley, Robert M. *Frontiersmen in Blue: The United States Army and the Indian, 1848–1865.* New York: Macmillan Co., 1967.

von Borcke, Heros. *Memoirs of the Confederate War for Independence.* 2 vols. New York: Peter Smith, 1938.

Ware, W. H. *The Battle of Kelly's Ford, Fought March 17, 1863.* Newport News, Va.: Warwick Printing Co., 1922.

Warner, Ezra J. *Generals in Blue: Lives of the Union Commanders.* Baton Rouge: Louisiana State University Press, 1964.

———. *Generals in Gray: Lives of the Confederate Commanders.* Baton Rouge: Louisiana State University Press, 1959.

War of the Rebellion: A Compilation of the Official Records of the Union and Confederate Armies. 4 series, 70 vols. in 128. Washington, D.C., 1880–1901.

Weinert, Richard P., Jr. *The Confederate Regular Army.* Shippensburg, Pa.: White Mane Publishing Co., Inc., 1991.

Wellman, Manly Wade. *Giant in Gray: A Biography of Wade Hampton of South Carolina.* New York: Charles Scribner's Sons, 1949.

Wells, Edward L. *Hampton and His Cavalry.* Richmond, Va.: B. F. Johnson Publishing Co., 1899.

Wert, Jeffry D. *From Winchester to Cedar Creek: The Shenandoah Campaign of 1864.* Carlisle, Pa.: South Mountain Press, Inc., 1987.

———. *General James Longstreet, the Confederacy's Most Controversial Soldier: A Biography.* New York: Simon & Schuster, 1993.

Wilson, James Harrison. *Under the Old Flag: Recollections of Military Operations in the War for the Union, the Spanish War, the Boxer Rebellion, etc.* 2 vols. New York: D. Appleton & Co., 1912.

Wise, Jennings Cropper. *The Long Arm of Lee; or, The History of the Artillery of the Army of Northern Virginia . . .* 2 vols. Lynchburg, Va.: J. P. Bell, 1915.

Wise, John S. *The End of an Era.* Boston: Houghton, Mifflin Co., 1899.

Wittenberg, Eric J. *Glory Enough for All: Sheridan's Second Raid and the Battle of Trevilian Station.* Washington, D.C.: Brassey's, Inc., 2001.

Woodward, C. Vann. *Origins of the New South, 1877–1913.* Baton Rouge: Louisiana State University Press, 1951.

Wynes, Charles E. *Race Relations in Virginia, 1870–1902.* Charlottesville: University of Virginia Press, 1961.

Index

Breckenridge, John C. (major general), 25, 172, 175

Brien, L. Tiernan (colonel), 47, 54, 70

Brooke, John Rutter (major general), 216

Brown, John, 52

Bryan, William Jennings, 213

Buford, John, 75, 120, 127, 132

Bullock, J. N. (captain), 92

Bull Run, xi, 31, 32–33, 82

Burke's Station, 94, 116

Burnside, Ambrose E. (major general), 90–91, 97, 148

Butler, Benjamin F. (major general), 154–55

Butler, Matthew Calbraith (brigadier general), 62, 93, 131, 160, 215

Cameron, William E., 200, 203

Camp Cooper, 23

Camp Radziminski, 20

Carlisle Barracks, 16–17; Fitz Lee's burning of, 119

Carter, Richard Welby (captain), 38

Cary, Constance, 95–96, 141

Catlett's Station, 79–80, 133

cavalry warfare, 41, 105, 118; Confederate initial superiority in, 40; Confederate reliance on, 105

Cedar Creek, 177

Cedar Mountain, 72

Cedarville, 171

Centreville, 133

Century Magazine, 194

Chambersburg, 90

Chambliss, John R., Jr. (colonel), 115, 137, 166

Chancellorsville, xi, 106–7, 108, 110–11

"Chancellorsville" (F. Lee Sr.), 195

Charles City County, 67–68, 72

Charlottesville, 71, 141

Chattanooga, 132–33

Chesnut, James, Jr., 35

Chesnut, Mary Boykin, 35–36, 136, 144

Chew, R. Preston (major), 78, 142

Chicago Town Company, 207

Chickahominy River, xi, 49, 51

Chickamauga Creek, 132

Chief Buffalo Hunt, 20

Civil War, postwar interest in, 194

Clermont, 5, 189

Cleveland, Grover, 200, 207, 212, 213

Clitz, Henry B. (major), 68

Cobb, Thomas R. R. (colonel), 62

Cobb Legion, 62

Cold Harbor, 156, 159–60

Collins, Charles R. (colonel), 147

Comanches, 1–4, 19, 20, 24

Confederate Military History, 209

Conservative Party, 197

Cooke, Philip St. George (brigadier general), 57–58, 65

Cosby, George B. (brigadier general), 4, 56

Cress's Ridge, 122

Crooked Creek, 2–4

Cuba, 209–10, 211 (map), 212–14

Culpeper Court House, 76, 95, 112, 113, 132

Custer, George Armstrong (brigadier general), 28, 118, 122, 125, 142, 159, 162–63

Dahlgren, Ulric (colonel), 126, 142–43; death, 143

Dahlgren Papers, 143–44

Daniel, John Warwick, 198, 201

Danville race riot, 200

Davies, Henry E. (brigadier general), 134

Davis, Jefferson F., 11, 27, 35, 44, 69, 98, 112, 131, 143, 153; imprisonment, 190; retreat from Richmond, 184

Davis, Varina Howell, 136

Dearing, James (brigadier general), 180; death, 184

Deep Bottom, 178

Democratic Party, 200

Devin, Thomas C. (brigadier general), 180

Dinwiddie Court House, 180, 181, 183

Dispatch Station, 65

Dorsey, Gustavus W. (lieutenant), 38

Douglas, Beverly B. (major), 197

Douglas, Stephen A., 25

Drake, James H. (lieutenant colonel), 38, 70, 93, 224; death, 130

Dumfries, 91, 92

Early, Jubal A. ("Old Jubal") (major general), 108, 137, 138, 170, 171, 172, 173, 175, 176–77, 194, 196

Emory, William H. (captain), 15

Enders, Nannie, 192

Esten Cooke, John (lieutenant), 56, 69

Evelington Heights, 67

Ewell, Richard Stoddert (brigadier general), 32–34, 114, 129